This is the most important map in American history. Drawn by Virginia-born John Mitchell in 1755 and titled *A Map of the British and French Dominions in North America*, it was originally intended to emphasize Britain's territorial claims on North America. But the map's fame comes from its being put to another purpose. Refined and updated after Mitchell's death in 1768, it was used by British and American negotiators to formulate the 1783 Treaty of Paris, bringing an end to the Revolutionary War and defining the borders of the newly established United States of America. Impressive in its detail, Mitchell's map, commented Thomas Jefferson, "was made with great care," particularly "in those western parts with which we have lately become acquainted." It helped to settle border disputes between eastern states as late as 1932.

(opposite page)

Kevin Antoine (right) was on his way to a basketball tournament when he heard a radio report of a rally on the boardwalk in nearby Biloxi, Mississippi, to show support for flying the Confederate battle flag at a public memorial. Antoine immediately fetched an American flag from his mother's home, the one that had draped his father's coffin, and drove to the site of the rally, where he marched alone for thirty minutes carrying the Stars and Stripes. "I wanted to show respect for the country that my father, my brothers, and I served," says Antoine, a forty-two-year-old African-American lawyer and Air Force veteran who claims he also has Jewish, Native-American, Creole, and white ancestry. "If there is to be any flag to rally around, it should be the American flag." Many of those in attendance had another opinion.

(overleaf)

The "state fair" is an American tradition dating to 1807, when Massachusetts farmer Elkanah Watson, trying to compete with imported British wool, tethered his flock of sheep for inspection under an elm tree. "Many farmers," he wrote, "even women, were excited by curiosity to attend." Today every state has a fair, and most counties do, too. The State Fair of Texas, held nearly every September and October since 1886 in Dallas, is the country's largest. More than three million people attended in 2001, drawn by the livestock exhibitions, corn dogs, pig races, tractor-pulls, and "Big Tex," the fair's four-story mechanical cowboy. Among those there on this day were Lee and Sandra Alaniz of Dallas and their daughter, Crystal. Only weeks after September 11, the fair briefly halted business to honor the dead, and "Big Tex" led the crowd in the Pledge of Allegiance.

In Search of America

2001

In Search of America

by Peter Jennings and Todd Brewster

Photographs edited by Vivette Porges

HYPERION

NEW YORK

Additional Staff for This Book

Historian Adviser: Fred Siegel
Professor of History, The Cooper Union for the Advancement of Science and Art

Design: Elton Robinson

Associate Editors: Elisabeth King, Peter Meyer

Research: Anne Hollister

Photography: Vivette Porges *(editor)*, Lisa Patrick *(assistant)*

Contributors: Russell Shorto, Mark Frankel, George Howe Colt

Administration: Gretchen Babarovic, Josephine Heck

 For information address Hyperion, 77 West 66th Street, New York, New York 10023-6298.

ISBN 0-7868-6708-6

Hyperion books are available for special promotions and premiums. For details, contact Hyperion Special Markets, 77 West 66th Street, 11th floor, New York, New York 10023-6298, or call 212-456-0100.

A list of credits, constituting a continuation of the copyright page, begins on page 292.

First Edition
10 9 8 7 6 5 4 3 2 1

*In memory of those who conceived the American experiment,
those who improved upon it, those who defended it,
and those who died because they were a symbol of it.*

Contents

For most of American history, children acquired what learning they got in between the farm chores, at home. Patrick Henry was homeschooled; so were President John Quincy Adams and, famously, Thomas Edison. After a couple of years commuting by boat from remote Green's Island, Maine, to attend school at slightly less remote Vinalhaven, Tristan Jackson (left) and his brother, Dylan, petitioned their parents to do their studies at home, joining, in the process, almost two million modern-day homeschoolers (up from 50,000 in 1985). Like the homeschoolers of old, Jackson, eighteen, learns a lot "by doing." But when he's not hiking a mountain range or working on an organic farm, he's here, on Penobscot Bay, deep in a book.

Introduction

> *"Our peculiar claim to greatness as a nation rests on the fact that we have done without many elements that might be thought of as the marks of a great people, among them a myth of origin. Americans have been suckled by no wolf, sired by no Trojan fleeing Troy; they are not descended from the sun or from the dragon's teeth sown in the earth . . . Indeed . . . our greatness consists precisely in the fact that we are making it up as we go along — that we are perpetually in the process of devising ourselves as a people."*
>
> —Robert Pinsky
> *Poet*

So here was our experiment: become reacquainted with the principles of the American founding and the men who first presented them back in the turbulent days of the eighteenth century; then go out and look about us for evidence in this America of the country they so long ago established. If we tell you now that we discovered it — indeed, that the foundations laid back then and built upon in the 225 or so years since, still form the essence of the American identity — it should not spoil the experience of this book. In fact, that is the message we hope you will see in every page: that the America of Jefferson and Madison, Hamilton and Franklin, Washington and Adams is as alive now as ever before.

You can hear it in the arguments before a South Carolina school board considering the line between church and state as the community it serves initiates a campaign to build a more "moral" society (Chapter 1), and in the hallways of a multinational corporation as it conceives a marketing plan to sell the potato chip — and with it, the gospel of the free market — to the underdeveloped world (Chapter 3). You can detect it in the chatter of Washington political activists using the debate over a president's plan for tax relief to make their case for the appropriate balance of power between the federal government and the states, between *any* government and the "sacred" individual (Chapter 2), and you can watch it in the staging of an American musical — that quintessentially American art form — as presented by Colorado high school students who find in its lyrics and melodies the expression of a still idealistic people, embracing freedom, equality, and the spirit of rebellion (Chapter 5).

To become reacquainted with the founders was, for us, its own reward. Like so many others, we had come to regard them in the form of

Though the ship he was on was headed to New York City, Alexis de Tocqueville's 1831 American journey began here, in Newport, Rhode Island, when heavy winds forced an unscheduled landing. The passengers disembarked at a time when the coastline, left, was pitch black, and not, as it is today, also dotted with the lights of commerce. Tocqueville wrote his mother that the residents of Newport differed only "superficially from the French." But by the end of his visit, he had grown to see Americans as the embodiment of a new civilization.

"**Students know that Thomas Jefferson had slaves. They don't know that he had ideas.**"

SHEILA MANN
American Political Science Association

caricature, on the one hand raised up by the myths of the uncritical biography (one thinks of Parson Weems's myth-ridden biography of Washington) and, on the other, just as ceremoniously torn down by the debunking screed. The trend of the past few years has been a somewhat cynical one, dismissive of the glorification of the founders as if the recognition of their achievement was little more than an exercise in American self-congratulation. But we discovered that, as with most subjects, the truth lies somewhere between competing extremes, and it is this: America was founded by a collection of astonishingly brave, talented, brilliant, creative, and committed men who, despite their exemplary qualities, were also very human and, therefore, flawed. They are not to be seen as a collection of gods, looked upon with reverence and fear (nor would they have wanted us to see them that way), but as the initiators of a governmental framework remarkable in its fairness and adaptability, in its respect for life and human dignity, and in the value it puts on the fulfillment of the human spirit.

The founders meant that framework to be handed down like a precious family heirloom, to be reinterpreted when needed from one era to the next, while always holding on to its essential qualities. And our discovery is that, to a degree that surprised us, it has. Americans do not form a race, in the way that the Germans or the Japanese do, but they do form a people, united around a set of ideas that the founders made concrete in the form of America's defining institutions and documents. Those ideas are only most directly confronted in political argument. Indeed, they reach deep into the fabric of the American life, informing the way that Americans raise their children, speak their language, pursue their professions, pray to their God (or choose not to pray to any God), conduct their leisure, play their games, even the way they make each other laugh.

Americans are unique in their vision of a dynamic, idea-driven identity, a fact that is demonstrated in one method of national self-criticism. In what other nation has a constitution — a document laying out the machinery of government — taken on the quality of a sacred text? Where else but in America does the claim, "that's *un*-Constitutional" ring with the quality of accusation, as if it were calling attention to the "immoral," the "unnatural," or even the "impossible"? Indeed, where else can the *un* prefix be applied to a people, the way that we say something is "un-American"? The French cannot be "un-French," the German "un-German." The twentieth-century German political theorist Carl Friedrich took note of that when he declared "to be an American is an ideal, while to be a Frenchman is a fact."

We conceived our book as a journey, and you will note that it is laid out that way. We did this in part as a method of organizing the material

In "vacant" North Dakota: Watching the return of the frontier

The declining population of the Great Plains has prompted many to recall the once-sturdy image of frontier America, as depicted by painter Albert Bierstadt, right, 1890. Trains still run through Marmarth, but none stop there. The 1908 station, below, is now abandoned.

When Merle Clark drives into Marmarth, an old frontier cattle station in the southwest corner of North Dakota, he sees a dying town. The railroad depot where, as a boy, he eagerly awaited mail-order packages from Montgomery Ward in faraway Minneapolis, is boarded up and beset by weeds. The brick opera house, where traveling vaudeville acts and minor divas once performed, has been empty for three decades. Main Street, once-bustling with thirty businesses, is a toothless row of vacant lots and abandoned buildings. A mini-mart and a bar are the sole survivors. *The Marmarth Mail* published its last issue in 1933, the hospital closed several years after that, and when the high school burned to the ground in 1965, they didn't bother building a new one. A century ago, Marmarth boasted two thousand-some citizens; there are now 140. "It looks like a ghost town," admits Clark, sixty-four, a third-generation rancher whose cowboy grandfather was among those who settled the prairie in the decades after Custer was defeated at Little Big Horn.

All across the Great Plains, the old frontier towns are emptying out. The exodus started in the Great Depression, when drought turned the grasslands into the "dust bowl," and has continued steadily, if less dramatically, ever since. During the 1990s, while America's population grew by 13 percent, nearly two thirds of the counties in the Great Plains showed a decline. Almost 900,000 square miles of the Plains is now so sparsely populated that it meets the nineteenth-century Census Bureau definition of *frontier*. Indeed, the "frontier" — officially, two to six people per square mile — is now larger than it has been in a hundred years. With less than one person per square mile, Slope County, in which Marmarth sits, now meets the definition of *vacant*.

As towns like Marmarth fade away, many of the frontier's original inhabitants are returning. Over the last few decades, American Indians have moved back, comprising the only significant population increase in wide areas of the Plains. (North Dakota's Indian population has grown by 20 percent.) Threatened species like prairie dogs, black-footed ferrets, and bighorn sheep have made comebacks. A century ago, fewer than three hundred buffalo roamed the Plains; there are now more than 300,000. Abandoned farmland once again blooms with sagebrush, coneflower, and wood lilies. Quite possibly, the landscape looks the way it did when Clark's grandfather arrived here in the 1800s. The American frontier, it seems, is being reborn.

Such an irony would have startled the thirty-one-year-old historian who, on a hot, humid July evening in 1893, stood before the podium at the Chicago Art Institute and announced that the American frontier was dead. The speaker was Frederick Jackson Turner, a reporter-turned-history-professor from the University of Wisconsin. The setting was the World's Columbian Exposition, a six-month celebration commemorating the four hundredth anniversary of Columbus's arrival. The audience was small. Many of the country's most distinguished scholars, feeling that the Exposition's hurly-burly setting wasn't sufficiently dignified, had stayed home. As for fairgoers, given the choice of a map of the United States made entirely of pickles, the glow of Thomas Edison's 18,000-bulb Tower of Light, or the belly-dancing girls of the Egyptian Village, few opted to hear an all-but-unknown professor lecture on "The Significance of the Frontier in American History." Yet with the possible exception of George Washington Ferris's new 264-foot wheel, Turner's speech would prove to be the fair's most enduring legacy: a simple, eloquent statement that changed the way Americans looked at themselves.

Before that evening, America and its institutions had been interpreted primarily through the prism of Europe, "the study of European germs developing in an American environment," as Turner put it. But Turner, who grew up in a small Wisconsin town, now countered that Americans were Americans. The wilderness was the crucible in

Turner, above second from right, with students, 1893.

which the national identity was forged, imprinting Americans with what Turner called "frontier characteristics": self-reliance, individualism, inventiveness, pragmatism, mobility, restlessness. Even democracy was a product of frontier individualism; thrown onto their own resources, pioneer Americans were simply too scornful of hierarchy to kowtow to a central political authority.

But now, noted Turner, quoting a passage from the 1890 Census, the West was so broken by isolated settlements that there could no longer be said to be a frontier line. The buffalo had been nearly wiped out, the few remaining Indian tribes had been relegated to reservations, and the Wild West was well on its way to confinement in museums, history books, and memory's amber. The closing of the frontier, said Turner, brought to an end the first great era of this country's history: "The American energy will continually demand a wider field for its exercise. But never again will such gifts of free land offer themselves." Without that land, where would that energy turn? Would Americans, like Europeans, seek other lands to conquer? Or would they, asked Turner, look for more metaphoric frontiers in the form of spiritual and social challenges?

Turner's lecture provoked little immediate reaction. But over the following decades, the "frontier thesis" resonated in an American population longing for the gritty simplicity of pioneer life. Courses on the American West proliferated on college campuses; frontier archetypes dominated novels, movies, and, eventually, television shows. Turner's theory would dictate the way Americans interpreted themselves and their history for the next half-century. Indeed, when John Kennedy assumed the presidency in 1961, he christened his new administration, with its emphasis upon space and technology, "the *New* Frontier."

Turner found his own inner wilderness within the cosmopolitan confines of Harvard University, where in the early twentieth century he taught a course on the American West and became the pre-eminent historian of his time. A handsome man with bright blue eyes, a quiet sense of humor, and a Midwestern openness, he was beloved by his students. Although remaining, he insisted, "a Western man in all but my residence," Turner found sufficient excitement in the tamer frontiers of the East: perfecting his fly-fishing technique in mountain streams, hiking near his cottage in Maine, pitching a tent on the front porch of his Brattle Street home on balmy summer evenings.

After Turner's death in 1932, his work came under increasing attack for ignoring the contributions of racial and ethnic minorities to the history of the West and for describing a frontier without women. Others suggested that Turner developed the frontier thesis primarily because he was himself a product of that frontier — as a boy, he had watched army officers march Indians through the streets of his town on their way to reservations — and therefore saw the West through the rose-colored glasses of nostalgia. Yet the paper Turner presented that midsummer evening in Chicago more than a century ago remains, according to one contemporary scholar, "the single most influential piece of writing in the history of American history."

One wonders how the man who composed the frontier's obituary might explain its reappearance. Like many Plains towns, Marmarth is looking for its future in its pioneer past, as a new wave of tourists arrives from the East to see the ghost towns and the abandoned homesteads decaying in the prairie. Responding to this new interest, the Marmarth Historical Society has restored the Mystic Theatre and there's talk of trying to turn the old opera house into a museum. Although Clark's cattle ranch is surviving, some ranchers say the money's not in cattle, it's in raising buffalo — and bringing in tourists to see them.

Those who are left in Marmarth — and other dying Plains towns on what might be called the "neo-frontier" — face a struggle no less difficult, if less dramatic, than that faced by their pioneer ancestors. Without a high school — or the prospect of work after graduation — there's little to keep young people here. Without a hospital there's little to keep older folks around, either. Locals must drive twenty miles to shop at a supermarket, a hundred miles to eat a Big Mac. Yet, while the frontier itself may wax and wane, the individualism and resilience described by Turner have never departed. "It's still a wide-open place where you can look for miles and see no sign of habitation," says Merle Clark. "It's still a harsh environment, where people look out for each other, and a rugged place where only the hardy survive."

and demonstrating its scope, but also because of the resonance we felt it provided with our topic. One of the beauties of the American story is that it is itself a journey, that the founders conceived it to be one, and that the ideals they set forth were just that — ideals — perhaps unattainable, but worthy goals for a nation of strivers. America, as the founders imagined it, was to be a nation in perpetual process, always in the act of becoming, often falling short of its own ambitions for itself, yet always ready to resume them. Americans set out to be just, but do not always achieve justice; they pride themselves on living in a free society, yet they do not always respect freedoms; they revere democracy, but they are sometimes undemocratic. The nation's avowed principles are distorted to serve evil purposes, as in the bombing of the Murrah Federal Building in Oklahoma City, and they are sometimes used against us: only in a free society could men with sinister aims, like those responsible for the terrorist attacks on the World Trade Center and the Pentagon, move about at will, preparing their assault. Over the years, America's principles have been shaken, molded, adapted, assaulted, but, remarkably, they endure.

Perhaps the first person to take stock of America in a way that measured the nation against the founders' intentions was the Frenchman, Alexis Charles Henri Clerel de Tocqueville. It was Tocqueville, who, in 1831, came to these shores and, in a period of just nine months, identified with remarkable prescience the political convictions and national preoccupations that set Americans apart from the rest of the world. Tocqueville found Americans different in that they were more socially egalitarian, more interested in a society built around merit, more individualistic, more concerned with rights, and more devout than Europeans. They represented, he felt, the "New Man," and their country was destined to rise to a position of leadership among nations, destined to command the world. Tocqueville saw Americans as essentially unchanged from the time of the Pilgrims, which is interesting because reading his *Democracy in America* we can only conclude that they have not changed since the time of Tocqueville, even though the nation he saw was, in geography, about one third the size of the America of today; even though the Western frontier ended, for him, at Memphis; even though the America he saw contained only around 13 million people, most of them white, and a plurality of those whites Anglo-American. We remember well the reaction of one editor when we referred to this French aristocrat's work in the proposal for this book. "Tocqueville's a cliché," he said, somewhat dismissively. And then we remember our own musing on the nature of clichés in our last book, *The Century*: "Clichés are clichés," we wrote, "because they encapsulate something so unalterably true, one cannot resist repeating them over and over again." And so, in the way a traveler

"Go back, look at the baby in its mother's arms. The whole man is there, if one may put it so, in the cradle. Something analogous takes place in nations. If it were possible to examine the first monuments of their history, I do not doubt that we could discover in them the first causes of prejudices, habits, dominant passions, of all that finally composes the national character."

—Alexis de Tocqueville
Democracy in America, 1835

pockets his passport, we carried our well-worn copy of Tocqueville as we went out "in search of America."

Tocqueville's *Democracy in America* was the first contribution to what became a genre of American literature: the "journey book." In fact, when we set out to do this project, we were astonished by how many attempts preceded ours. Then we realized that it only made sense. If a nation is always in the act of becoming, it stands to reason that it would change from generation to generation and that sociologists, historians, literati, and, dare we say, even journalists would heed the call to take stock of that change. Sometimes the "journey" is more like a detailed observation. We think of the academic Frederick Jackson Turner's "frontier thesis" put forward in the 1890s, defining Americans as a people of pioneer impulses; of Robert and Helen Lynd's *Middletown*, a sociological study which became a best-selling book in the 1920s when it demonstrated the arrival of the consumer society; and of Luigi Barzini's 1977 *O America*, detailing an immigrant's appreciation for his adopted land.

"This is what America has been since the very beginning: the sum of the imaginary landscapes of each individual American."

— Luigi Barzini
O America

Other times the "journey book" really does document an old-fashioned road trip. In John Steinbeck's 1962 *Travels with Charley*, the celebrated author of *The Grapes of Wrath* describes how he loaded his dog Charley into the back of a pickup truck and went out to rediscover "this monster land," the color and quality of its light, the pulse of its people, and of how he met many along the way who shared his "virus" of restlessness. "Nearly every American hungers to move," Steinbeck concluded after witnessing the same aching look in people of every state he visited. "[It's] the dream I've had all my life, and there is no cure." In 1978, William Least Heat-Moon borrowed from the same impulse to create *Blue Highways*, his homage to the country he found on America's back roads. Heat-Moon, who claims a distinctive American identity in his combination of European and Native-American ancestry, set out on his mission when, after losing both his job and his wife in one day, he concluded that "a man who couldn't make things go right could at least go." And in 1979, former *New York Times* newsman Richard Reeves went out to actually re-create Tocqueville's path for *American Journey* and in so doing measure the distance from 1831. Indicative of the dark mood that characterized the seventies, Reeves discovered an excessively litigious country with people looking to sue at every opportunity. Each of these works attempted to come to grips with the ever-changing American character, evaluating it against the past and projecting outward from it to the future. With this volume, we hope that we have added some small something of the same order for these times.

Like the trips of many before us, ours was a figurative one. We did not, like the hippies of the sixties, load up a Volkswagen bus and start driving. We "traveled" through the research and reporting of dozens of people committed to this project, some of whom worked directly on this book (you can read their names in the staff list at the front), others who, while producing television episodes for the companion ABC series, "In Search of America," shared their materials with us. Our journey was also one of the mind. A project like this one is not created out of a single inspiration, fully shaped and ready for execution. It evolves over time and with careful consideration. Like the journalists that we are, we examined the material over and over again, questioning our assumptions, reevaluating our strategies, and we relied upon the canon of wisdom created by historians of the American story, most notably, Fred Siegel, our consultant on this project, but also the works of dozens of others whom we credit in the notes section in the back.

In the end, as you will see when you read this book, we have taken an unusual perspective on the present. Each chapter of *In Search of America* uses a contemporary story as a metaphor for an arena of American life: race, government, business, immigration, religion, culture. We then seek through that metaphor to discover its historical connections, first at the founding, but also at some later moment of historical importance. Thus, we consider the challenge to the teaching of evolution in the schools of Aiken, South Carolina, both within the context of the original arguments about church and state and in a reevaluation of the *Scopes* "Monkey Trial" of 1925. We examine the clash of a large and largely illegal Latino population in Salt Lake City with the dictates of American immigration policy by reestablishing the founders' generally welcoming attitude toward newcomers, but also by reminding the reader of the "nativist" movement of the early twentieth century which, by establishing immigrant quotas by nationality, attempted to preserve America's Anglo-Saxon complexion. Each chapter also contains several sidebars (or "side-*trips*" as we called them around the office). Do not think of these as the dutiful delivery of "essential" information, as in, say, a textbook, but, in the spirit of a journey, as a kind of reflection, odd musing, or rediscovery related to the larger subject. Thus, while we are considering the founders' attitudes toward religious faith, we visit the New York home of Thomas Paine, the fiery transatlantic rebel whose pamphlet, *Common Sense*, helped inspire the Revolution. Paine was one of America's earliest champions of the secular state. While watching a group of American businessmen market potato chips to the third world, we take a moment to look in on a Monopoly tournament in Michigan and note how a game that was originally conceived to display the evils of capitalism became transformed by the American thirst for wealth and enterprise.

Finally, a picture essay running throughout the book finds the same kind of distinctively American qualities in a collection of images from ordinary life: a child expresses the free American spirit as he jumps from the back of a pickup and soars into a mud puddle in rural West Texas; a Wisconsin lawyer clutches the nape of a murder defendant's neck in camaraderie as a verdict of "not guilty" is read out by the foreman of a jury of his peers; a Korean-American girl tries on a blond wig at her family's store in Tucson, Arizona, while her immigrant aunt looks on, nervously anticipating the inevitable exchange of Old World values for those of the New. These appear here as a collection of "frozen moments," as historians of photography sometimes describe them, pictures as symbolic as they are ordinary. We hope they inspire you to look around your world and see America looking back at you the way that we saw it looking back at us, and that they will remind you that we do not live on an island, separated from time, but as part of a long continuum that, in the establishment of the American identity, begins in 1776.

Tocqueville didn't just look about; he engaged the people of America, too. When he wasn't ruminating about the American character or complaining about the quality of his transport (*Democracy in America* is filled with descriptions of the inferior nature of American carriages), the French aristocrat was often relating stories of his encounters with the American people — a businessman and a politician, a priest and a slave owner. We sought to personalize our journey, too. Our last book looked at the history of the twentieth century from the vantage point of the common man, and in this volume we decided to carry that idea forward to the twenty-first. If we were in search of America, we felt certain we were more apt to find it not in the halls of power, but on the streets and in the churches, in the lives of emerging businesspeople and new immigrant workers, in the relationship between teenage children, beginning to spread their wings, and their proud parents.

We write at a very different time from Tocqueville's. We also write at a very different time from that of the Lynds or of Luigi Barzini, of John Steinbeck or Richard Reeves. Indeed, we write at a different time than that we wrote of only a few years ago in *The Century*. With the collapse of the Soviet Union and its alliance of Communist states, the cold war no longer defines America the way that it had for a generation. The rise of new communications technologies has altered the sense, if not the fact, of a world divided by national borders, leading to new electronic communities that have no political or ethnic basis. The advent of globalization has made American business part of a vast network of interwoven markets, making some nationalists uneasy. ("Are you sovereign or are you global?" demanded a man from Michigan who approached our Ford Explorer as we exited a parking lot at the Gettysburg National Historic

In central Indiana: Coping with a reputation as "Middletown"

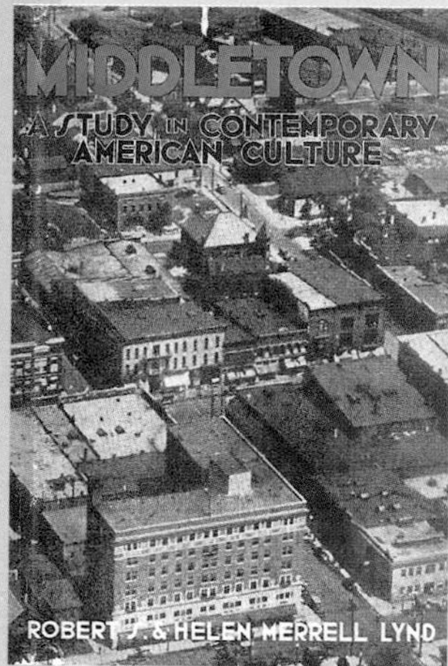

The Lynds' 1929 publication of Middletown, *left, caused a sensation, in part because it documented the increasingly materialist American culture. Right, today Muncie's McGalliard Road is, like similar streets in a lot of midsized American towns, overrun with commercial enterprises.*

Muncie, Indiana, is a town of wide streets flanked by stolid brick houses, a place compact enough that you can drive from one end of town to the other in under twenty minutes and where people embrace their typical "Americanness." Indeed, ever since a landmark sociological study was undertaken here in the 1920s, identifying Muncie as the kind of representative American community worthy of the title "Middletown," the city has served as a kind of barometer of the average American life. Here locals like to joke: "We're so ordinary, we're unique."

Robert and Helen Lynd arrived in Muncie eight decades ago with the mission of studying its inhabitants as dispassionately as anthropologists studying an unknown Amazon tribe. Later, when the Lynds published their work, *Middletown, A Study in Modern American Culture,* it gave an image of American small-town life just as it was shedding its rural, agrarian traditions and embracing the urban, industrial twentieth century. Long before there was polling, even before there was anything known as "mass media," *Middletown* gave Americans the first substantive, and scientific, study of the American people. The book, one of the first sociological studies of any kind, went on to be a best seller. Excited by the future, sad about the departure of the solid past, people simply wanted to know more about the changes that their world was undergoing.

The Lynds' road to Muncie was a roundabout one. A Hoosier himself, born in 1892, Robert Lynd was a young seminary student when he accepted an assignment from the Presbyterian Board of Home Missions to go to a Wyoming oil-drilling camp operated by a subsidiary of Standard Oil Company of Indiana and, in his words, "kill or cure my question of what a personal ministry could do." The camp was a dismal collection of tents and tar-paper shacks inhabited by five hundred discouraged workers and their families. But through force of personality, Lynd forged them into a community. Then, in 1921 he wrote an article for an obscure journal, detailing the appalling conditions he had witnessed and attacking Standard Oil's owner, John D. Rockefeller, Jr., as the one responsible.

Ironically, Lynd's criticism of the corporate titan impressed his target. A devout Baptist with surprisingly liberal ideas, Rockefeller had recently established a committee to study Americans' religious practices in an effort to reconcile the elbows-out, hard-charging capitalism of the early twentieth century with his own deeply held Protestant beliefs. Rockefeller was also eager to prove that the organization would be independent and beyond his control. He did so in 1923 by naming Lynd, his avowed critic, as head of the agency's Small City Study, charged with "ascertaining the religious and ethical attitudes and capacities of the people" in a single industrial city.

After briefly considering Decatur, Illinois, and Kokomo, Indiana, Lynd chose Muncie to be his subject. It fit his needs: small (thirty-eight thousand people), relatively self-contained, Midwestern, and economically diverse. Equally important, Muncie was almost devoid of racial or religious minorities. At the close of one of America's greatest periods of Immigration, 92 percent of the city's inhabitants were "native white of native parentage." Lynd claimed that he had chosen homogeneous Muncie because it permitted him to study cultural changes unimpeded by racial or religious differences, but it also reflected his deep belief that native-born, white Protestants represented the bedrock of American society and bore the country's hope. Like many Americans, Lynd had grown concerned that America was losing touch with the original national ethos, the adventurous and morally uplifting spirit that had shaped the country at its beginnings. In looking at a traditional American society, one protected from modern trends, he hoped to capture an image of a community at the center of old-fashioned American virtue and help identify those trends working to undermine its character. In this, Lynd shared some of the ideas of the rural populist William Jennings Bryan: a devotion to improving social conditions and restraining the growing power of the corporation.

Lynd arrived in Muncie in 1924, with his wife, Helen, who would help him write up his findings for Rockefeller's committee. But the couple soon concluded they could not study religion in a vacuum and decided to expand their work to cover all aspects of Muncie life. They investigated conditions in Muncie's factories, as well as the manner in which the wives of the city's small elite entertained guests. They attended meetings of the Kiwanis Club and Rotary, and asked people what they read.

What they uncovered was a community rushing headlong into the twentieth century. Rapid industrialization had transformed people's lives. In 1890, most residents of Muncie lived on isolated farms, drew their water from wells, performed chores by kerosene light, and were lucky to attend school through the eighth grade. By 1920, most residents lived inside town limits, labored at the Ball Brothers glass plant (Muncie's largest employer) or one of the city's many other factories, and high school attendance was nearly universal. "In the quiet county seat of the middle eighties," the Lynds wrote, "men lived relatively close to the earth and its products. In less than four decades, business class and working class, bosses and bossed, have been caught up by Industry."

The "Muncie Boys Band," above in 1922, was one pillar of old America that was still in operation when the Lynds studied the town.

The daily rhythms of life had been made vastly easier by modern conveniences such as central heating, hot and cold running water, electric lighting, and the telephone. Thanks to such labor-saving devices, some women were beginning to work outside the home. One of the greatest changes was the automobile: nearly two thirds of Muncie families owned one by 1923. For many families, the traditional Sunday dinner with family was being supplanted by an afternoon drive in the country.

The Lynds published their findings in 1929. Encompassing more than five hundred pages, packed with footnotes and tables, *Middletown* was an unlikely popular hit. Yet the study also perturbed many with its portrait of American life. "Those who cling to their childhood illusions about their native land will wish that the Lynds had scrutinized the Patagonians instead. For the portrait of Middletown is not flattering," opined the *New York Times*. *Middletown* showed that despite Americans' egalitarian ideals, the city was divided by an entrenched class system. Residents belonged to either the small "business" class or far larger "working" class. The two camps had their own values and expectations and rarely mingled. Most disturbing to Lynd himself was the discovery that Muncie, too, demonstrated the erosion of old virtues. Even here, the old Puritan spirit had been replaced by consumerism, the cutthroat ethics of the modern corporation, and materialism. Lynd noted as well the replacement of men with machines and the failure of the church to hold back the onslaught.

Lynd returned to Muncie a few years later (by which time it was well-known as Middletown) to report on the impact of the Great Depression. But, by that time, he had become completely disillusioned with America. He had come to see aspects of American capitalism as a perverse antagonist of the social gospel and looked with favor on the Marxist experiment being established in the Soviet Union. Waves of subsequent sociologists have made their own journeys to Muncie to study the changes wrought by the passage of time upon the community, but the trends have not been consistent. One momentous reversal, noted Theodore Caplow, author of 1982's *Middletown Families*, was the erosion of class differences. He found that it was as common for working-class children to attend college as it was for their fathers to play golf. A strong work ethic and a sense of self-reliance have gained strength: 34 percent of high school boys in 1924 agreed with the statement, "It is entirely the fault of a man himself if he does not succeed." In a 1999 survey, 65 percent did. "We're still fairly conservative," says Larry Lough, editor of Muncie's daily *Star Press*. "Most people believe in a full day's work for a full day's pay."

Today, Muncie, which refers to itself as "America's Hometown," continues to mirror at least some of the changes in American society. Downtown is littered with empty storefronts, as residents take their business to one of the outlying Wal-Marts. The city has watched its factories shut down and blue-collar jobs disappear. Ball Brothers moved its national headquarters to Colorado in 1998. The typical worker in Muncie is more likely to provide services than to actually make anything. The county's largest employer is Ball Memorial Hospital and its associated medical facilities; second is Ball State University. One characteristic that remains the same as in the Lynds' day: the population remains overwhelmingly white (91 percent, according to the 2000 Census) and native born. Meanwhile, locals have grown accustomed to being sampled and polled by outsiders. "Here, it's something of a way of life," says Lough.

Site.) And most recently, the threat and reality of terrorism has, more than any other time in the nation's history, planted fear in the American soil.

We began this book, of course, long before the events of September 11, 2001. But as we reported on that event and watched the nation respond to one of the worst calamities in its history, we felt our humble project assume a new responsibility. In many ways, the war on terrorism helped Americans see a new international foe, replacing the communist threat of the twentieth century with something equally formidable for the twenty-first. The terrorist's philosophy advocates a form of religious tyranny and fears the advance of progress; it seeks to silence the individual voice and squelch the individual will; it abhors compromise and bristles at the rawness of popular culture; it sees "difference" as threatening and tolerance as weakness. In short, it is "un-American."

> **"History does not refer merely, or even principally, to the past. On the contrary, the great force of history comes from the fact that we carry it within us."**
>
> —JAMES BALDWIN

In the days after the loss of so many innocent American lives, we watched the flag raisings like everyone else — the freshly adorned car antennas, the flag lapel pins, and the red-white-and-blue everything. As we did we thought of the hundreds of folk art versions of "Old Glory" that were created in the time before the Civil War, when many people saw not America, but Virginia or South Carolina, Pennsylvania or New York as their "nation" and when a standard alignment of the Stars and Stripes had not yet caught on. We listened to Irving Berlin's "God Bless America," sung by a lone policeman, in full uniform, before the opening-night crowd at New York's Carnegie Hall and by fifty thousand or so at the seventh inning stretch of baseball's World Series and remembered how that song was written by a young Jewish immigrant from Russia at the time of the First World War, became popular with the call to American troops during the Second World War, and was derided as saccharine and jingoistic in the era of the Vietnam War. But, like the flag, it too had survived. We watched schoolchildren once again rise up, place their hands over their hearts, and recite the Pledge of Allegiance, just as they first did in 1892, at the four-hundred-year anniversary of Columbus's landing, the occasion for which a former Protestant minister wrote that ode to acknowledge the primacy of the national identity in the years after the Civil War. We wondered at first how long all the new patriotic fervor would last in this new, twenty-first-century America; then, reflecting on the words of a nineteenth-century American mourning the passing of Thomas Jefferson and John Adams and with them the last vestiges of the revolutionary generation, we recognized how important the patriotic exercise was to American life, how essential it was for all Americans to listen for the ring of old formative truths: "The Republic will cease to be," offered the eulogist, "when it ceases to remember, to revere, and to imitate the virtues of its founders."★

Phoenix, Arizona

Monica Lee (far right) and her sister Kara opened their first wig store, "Judi's Wigs," in Tulsa, Oklahoma, where the hot, dry climate reminded them of their native Korea. "We picked the name Judi because it was a nice American name," she recalls. "People called us 'Judi.' " As their store prospered, the sisters married, raised families, became American citizens, and eventually brought their mother, Sook Ok Park (near right), to live with them. In 1996, they moved to Arizona and opened another store in Phoenix, catering to middle-aged women and the occasional transvestite. They called their Phoenix store (right) Wigs Amor. According to the National Bureau of Economic Research, Korean-Americans have the highest rate of entrepreneurship of any ethnic group in the country; about one in four own their own business. One survey found that in New York City Korean-Americans owned 85 percent of greengrocers, 80 percent of nail salons, and 60 percent of dry cleaners. Yet even after so many years in American business, Monica Lee remains a little on the other side of the cultural divide, perplexed by the ease with which her customers remake themselves. "Americans use wigs like dresses," she says, modeling a wig called "Rachelle." "This is not me. My hair is black. My hair is straight." Her American-born niece, however, feels no such qualms. "My parents and grandparents are always saying Korean kids never do this, Korean kids never do that," says Jamie Lee, twenty-two, trying on a blond "Cindy." "But I'm also an American and I tell them that Americans do things differently."

Watertown, Massachusetts

Americans have an unusual relationship with war. The nation was born from one, but in the minds of the founders, the Revolutionary War was to have been America's last. They saw the republic as breaking with the bloodthirsty traditions of Europe and replacing them with more civilized methods of promoting and protecting the national interest — diplomacy or the withholding of commerce. While that kind of idealism can still be detected into our own time, it has wilted in the harsh light cast first by the Civil War, then by just about the entire twentieth century. Still, no extended foreign war has ever been fought on American soil, leaving boys like Wesley Morgan (left) to imagine what the clash of civilizations must be like in other parts of the world. Morgan, thirteen, who attends eighth grade at the Shady Hill School in Cambridge, Massachusetts, is a military buff of the first order whose interests lean, he says, toward such epic conflicts as the Hundred Years War and "anyplace where Eastern and Western military practices meet." When American soldiers went to war in Afghanistan, Morgan followed their movements as closely as a War College professor, using his pocketknife and sheets of cardboard to build the miniature "Kandahar" seen here. "Kandahar," which is modeled from photographs Morgan saw in the newspaper, took him two weeks to build. Then, after reading the book *Black Hawk Down*, which documents the story of the American raid in Somalia, he replaced it with a model of Mogadishu. Given the sophistication of Morgan's interest, it isn't surprising to learn that he plays alone with his models. "I have only one friend who is into the same stuff," says Morgan, "but his thing is medieval Japanese warfare."

The Woodlands, Texas

"Remember that time is money," Benjamin Franklin advised young tradesmen in 1748. A few years later, the advances of the industrial revolution displayed America's genius for matching personal speed to the pace of its machines. "Have not men improved somewhat in punctuality since the railroad was invented?" asked Henry David Thoreau. "Do they not talk and think somewhat faster in the depot than they did in the stage [coach] office?" No wonder, then, that one of the great selling points of any American product is "it saves time," and that millions of Americans complain, resignedly, that they don't have time to sleep. (The National Sleep Foundation estimates that the average American sleeps 20 percent less today than a century ago.) Working mothers are among the most harried, balancing career with home life. For Kim Larance (center), forty-two, that means an unforgiving schedule centered on the needs of her three children (Jonathan, David, and Jackson) and her own demanding job as the chairman of a school math department. Larance's day begins at 5:15 A.M. when she rises and (when else?) does the laundry, watches the Weather Channel, prepares breakfast, wakes the boys, and, by 6:30, says good-bye to her husband, Jerry, an oil and gas company engineer who commutes an hour to Houston. It reaches a frenzy by the late afternoon (left) when the children finish their commitments to basketball practice, baseball practice, after-school play, choir, and dog-walking while Larance runs the boys to doctors' appointments, grades papers for her next day's classes, and prepares dinner in time for Jerry's arrival home. "When you are stressed, you look at your schedule and think that there is just no way," she sighs. "But I've quit saying I'm busy because it sounds so negative. I say that I have a full life and the bottom line is we're very happy. We're tired, but we're happy."

(opposite page)

Ron and Mary Ames, of Caldwell, Idaho, used to have a computer store, but they gave it up and for the last ten years have sold pies "on the road," working from the back of a commercial cooking trailer or from inside a pitched tent. Here they set up shop at a festival in Quartzsite, Arizona, offering cherry, banana cream, chocolate cream, lemon meringue, peanut butter cream, rhubarb, and, of course, apple. The Ameses and their mobile bake shop, which they call "Ron's Pies," travel throughout the West for six months every year, selling 150 pies a day in some spots; the other six months, the Ameses do charity work and, says Ron, "plan next year's tour."

In Search of America

1 God's Country

The Savannah River Site in Aiken, South Carolina, is one of the few cold war nuclear weapons plants still operating into the twenty-first century, though its five towering reactors, shielded from public view on what is a massive, three-hundred-square-mile nuclear campus, edged by innocent Southern pines, are all now shuttered. Glenn Wilson is a thirty-nine-year-old nuclear technology instructor who works there. By day, Wilson trains workers in the procedures of nuclear waste disposal; principally, the delicate methods by which they will discard over 35 million gallons of radioactive waste still being stored in tanks on the site, the residue of fifty years of production when SRS supplied the killing material for every kind of nuclear weapon in the American arsenal. By night, Wilson tirelessly plots a campaign to have the Aiken public schools adopt a new biology curriculum that would include not only the study of the theory of evolution, as the present program does, but a "scientific" argument for a competing theory as well, the one which argues the world is between six and ten thousand years old, that men once inhabited the earth with dinosaurs, that a man called Noah lived to be 950 years old, and that God began life by placing a fully formed human being named "Adam" in the Garden of Eden. In other words, Wilson is one man of science who rejects the theory of evolution in favor of a literal interpretation of the Bible.

"There is no country in the whole world in which the Christian religion retains a greater influence over the souls of men than in America."

—Alexis de Tocqueville, 1835

Wilson's campaign recalls the celebrated "Monkey Trial" of 1925, when the state of Tennessee, in order to protect its children from "blasphemous" science, actually banned the teaching of evolution in its public schools and the fledgling American Civil Liberties Union challenged the law, leading to America's first nationally broadcast courtroom drama. Then, and particularly later, when the trial was the subject of *Inherit the Wind*, an immensely successful play and movie, it was popularly identified as the moment when religious fundamentalism was defeated by the force of reason. Even though Tennessee actually won the *Scopes* trial — named for John T. Scopes, the teacher who agreed to test the law — it has long been believed that by making a buffoon of fundamentalist lawyer William Jennings Bryan, the famous courtroom attorney Clarence Darrow settled the argument on the side of science: reason triumphing over faith, modernism over tradition. Distinguished historians including Henry Steele Commager, writing in the middle of the twentieth century, saw *Scopes* as just such a turning point in American history. And yet, we now know nothing could have been further from the truth. In defiance of popular culture and the nation's educated power elite, religious traditionalism has refused to die; indeed, seventy-five years later, in the age of the human genome project and nanotechnology, it thrives.

The statistics are clear. While nearly all Americans (95 percent) profess to believe in some kind of God, almost half (47 percent) believe in the biblical story of creation, and more than one third (44 percent, including the current president, George W. Bush) describe themselves as "born again" or "evangelical," statistics which dramatically set Americans apart from the rest of the Western world. Far from ending the central importance of traditional religion in American society, the *Scopes* trial appears to have been a landmark in reaffirming it: after *Scopes*, Arkansas and Mississippi joined with Tennessee to enact laws against the teaching of evolution, while innumerable local school boards, particularly in the South, imposed restrictions on its teaching. Only with the Supreme Court decisions of the 1960s and 1970s, when the political and social turmoil of the day prompted *Time* to ask "Is God dead?" (succumbing, as one writer put it, to the condition of "massive diminishing influence") did the mood change. Religion was forced out of the schools, allowing evolution to creep back in. Yet while it has since become an accepted fact in "enlightened" urban Western society that when it comes to explaining the universe, science takes precedence over faith, that only the uneducated would reject the certainty of the laboratory in exchange for a literal reading of the Bible, it has also continued to be apparent that a sizable part of the American population — if not an outright majority — strongly disagrees.

There are no fewer than seventy churches in Aiken, and on Sunday most of their seats, like those at Town Creek Baptist, above, are filled. "I think there's been a real push back to faith," says Reverend Ken Nelson of St. John's United Methodist Church. "In a world that's constantly changing, there needs to be some place where people can say 'I belong.'"

This is the "shadow" nation, populated by vast numbers of Americans who see so much of the contemporary world we inhabit — Hollywood, the major media companies, the elite universities, the reigning corporations, the popular culture — as anathema to the values they, and their forebears, have always held dear. Disappointed by the drift of society to "godlessness" and "scientism" — and an acute frustration with what they felt was the intolerance of the Left, forcing its ideas upon them and their children — this constituency became a potent political force in the late seventies, eighties, and nineties.

But despite their political influence, religious traditionalists continue to be frustrated by the failure of their agenda to transform society, by their inability to control science, and by the sense that they remain "afloat on a receding wave of history." For many of these people, the effort to undermine the teaching of evolution — like the effort to reverse the 1973 Supreme Court ruling on abortion, to return prayer to the schools, to staunch the trend of popular culture toward sex and violence, and to limit the range of genetic research — is akin to a holy war, representing nothing less than an attempt to recapture a world governed by moral absolutes. They look at twenty-first-century America and feel an overriding passion; like the populist crowds who supported Bryan in the twenties, they want society to take their God back.

Wilson is but one of the many devout citizens of Aiken. The residents of this quiet Southern town have coexisted for the last fifty years with one of the most sophisticated statements of modern science — the "bomb plant" as many call it — literally in their midst. It is where they work. Yet that fact has not shaken their faith in traditional religion. If anything, they say that their belief in the word of the Bible has strengthened over the last quarter century as they watched the moral decline in American life. Most Americans could recite the now familiar list of their worries: abortion, sexual promiscuity, homosexuality, feminism, welfare, drugs, divorce, violence, crime, the disintegration of the family, the replacement of a "God-centered world" with a "man-centered world," and, perhaps the one principle that for them has led to all others, a growing tolerance for "moral relativism" — the measuring of right and wrong in accordance with circumstances — and its philosophical companion, "situational ethics." Not all of Aiken's faithful agree with Wilson that this decline began long ago with the assertion by British naturalist Charles Darwin that man's ancestry could be traced back to "a hairy quadruped, furnished with a tail and pointed ears, probably arboreal in habits." In fact, either because they recognize the constitutional precedents that make it highly unlikely that Wilson will ever succeed or because they have become so discouraged about their ability to genuinely affect the values of public institutions that they no longer even wish to try, most of those who support his campaign to change the Aiken schools' biology curriculum do so only from a distance. Still others feel that chal-

With 172 parks and thirteen dirt roads, maintained especially for horses under a historic ordinance, Aiken is an equestrian's paradise. "There are only two issues that get people to city council meetings," says Mayor Fred Cavanaugh, "horses and trees."

lenging Darwin would be a small and insignificant step in the vast challenge ahead of them to remoralize America. But when Wilson's sixteen-year-old daughter, Halita, a sophomore at South Aiken High School, writes across all questions dealing with evolution on her biology exams, "I do not believe in evolution . . . talk to my dad," her teacher does not mark her answers as "wrong." And most of the people of Aiken heartily agree with Wilson in noting, with increasing despair, the continuing descent of America from its historical position as a bulwark against the sinful world — a "new Jerusalem," if you will. They believe that a return to the moral absolutes dictated by religion, and, more specifically, by the Christian Bible, may be society's only hope for a reversal of a sinister trend. In the fall of 2000, when the local university put on a production of *Inherit the Wind*, some Aiken shopkeepers refused to display posters promoting the production (the publicity showed an ape being transformed over generations into the form of a man) and few tickets were sold. Put simply, it is hard to find an atheist in Aiken.

> **"Despite all the Bible-science confrontations, despite the battles over high school textbooks and controversies about government codes on how and when to teach evolution, the fact is science and religion are both thriving."**
> GERALD L. SCHROEDER
> The Science of God

This is the story of Glenn Wilson, a man who describes himself as a "good old American mutt," related to "Paul Revere's uncle" through his father-in-law; a Boy Scout from Wisconsin who joined the navy rather than go to college, served as a chief petty officer in the Persian Gulf War, and after "a few years of godless debauchery" discovered Jesus Christ and a cause he believes to be nothing less than a fight for the soul of his nation. But if this is Glenn Wilson's story, it is also the story of Aiken Mayor Fred Cavanaugh, a graduate of Virginia Military Institute and a former employee of the Savannah River Site, who, to counter the weakening of moral fiber in his city, instituted the "Character First" program in 1999, in which townspeople are asked to reacquaint themselves with a different moral principle each month, among them responsibility, compassion, courage, patience, forgiveness. It is the story of Reverend Danny Burleson, the associate pastor of Town Creek Baptist Church, whose growing evangelical congregation acts out simple morality plays to "school" Aiken's people in the thorny world of moral conundrums and also of school board attorney William Burkhalter who, while a devout Christian himself, sees grave constitutional issues in inserting the story of Genesis into the Aiken curriculum. It is the story of Rosemary English, a teacher and member of Aiken's school board, who uses science fiction in her high school English classes not so much for its literary merit as for the moral abuses such fiction can demonstrate and of Dr. Alan Roberts, the author of a new ethics curriculum at the Medical College of Georgia, just across the Savannah River in Augusta, Georgia, who deals every day with issues that until recently *were* science fiction. But most of all this is the story of Aiken, a small American city in a fiercely proud and independent Southern state, a state where the Confederate battle flag was only recently removed from atop the capitol and where, even 165 years later, the resentment over the defeat of the South in the Civil War — that battle over what many regard as America's greatest moral transgression, slavery — endures.

In the eighteenth century, Americans debated the line between science and religion, and worried over decline of morality. In Aiken, in the twenty-first century, they debate the line between science and religion and worry over the decline of morality. Just how can a religious nation reconcile faith with science and reason? In a democracy, does the majority have the right to dictate its will even if that will should run against well-established science? Is the freedom to practice religion denied when the state teaches something wholly inconsistent with — indeed, hostile to — mainstream faith? Is science inherently godless; and does its worldview erode the ability to establish right from wrong? In a secular society, what moral authority can take the place of religion? Without moral authority, does society decay? And, finally, the question that makes Wilson's campaign and others like it different from the one that convicted Scopes, if only because science knows so much more now than it did in 1925: When the pursuit of knowledge creates unprecedented, moral dilemmas, of a degree unanticipated by generations before — like that now being explored in fetal tissue and stem cell research, in the mapping of the genome and the experiments in cloning — can right and wrong be addressed without resorting to a higher authority? Can the ideas of a few eighteenth-century intellectuals — those who founded the American republic upon a separation between church and state — still lead?

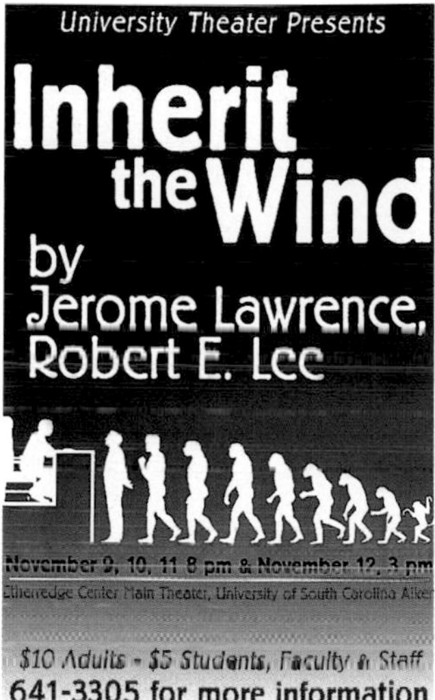

Inherit the Wind, *the play based on the* Scopes *trial, first ran on Broadway in 1955. Above, a poster from the local Aiken production that sold few tickets.*

II

In a way, it would be inaccurate to describe Wilson simply as a religious traditionalist. Though he is a member of Aiken's Town Creek Baptist Church, he says he is not a Baptist, preferring the term "independent" in order to separate himself from those who attend church more out of duty than belief. Though he adheres to the Bible, it is the book of Genesis alone that is his preoccupation, since he believes that all else flows from the essential truths contained there. Wilson does not come from a fundamentalist family. He was raised during the 1960s in a fairly liberal Lutheran church, which accepted evolution. But evolution wasn't an issue for him as he was growing up; neither was faith. He says that he saw church as a family obligation and little more; God as distant and inaccessible. "It seemed as if He were a guy in outer space and if you didn't mess your life up too badly, he wouldn't throw a lightning bolt at you."

Wilson's conversion to his present beliefs came, he says, around 1980, before he was married. He was a young navy cadet at the Naval Training Center in Orlando, Florida, when he met Susan Rahberg, a devoted Baptist. In order to impress her, he agreed to go with her to her church. It was there, at Orlando's Barton Shores Baptist Church, that Wilson discovered that there could be a "personal God" and with devotion to that God, a new vitality to life. It was a notion, he says, that greeted him "like a whack in the eye." Things didn't work out with Susan, but Wilson continued to be interested in a religious life, even as he struggled, he admits, to "stay right with the Lord." Transferred to a base in Norfolk, Virginia, Wilson began attending the Temple Baptist Church there, and confronting the continuing "mistakes" of his private life, among them a relationship with a married woman who, while separated, was, in Wilson's emerging religious consciousness, still bound to her husband by a covenant with God. One night, in a panic over his guilt, Wilson raced to Temple Baptist and began banging on the door, pleading to be saved. Pastor Mark Pullen answered, invited him in, and led him through the "sinner's prayer." It was that moment, Wilson says, that he accepted Jesus into his life.

Glenn Wilson, above, addresses a Sunday school class at his church. He often begins his lectures by holding up the Intel Pentium computer chip he keeps on his key chain and comparing it to the vastly more complex human cell. Neither, Wilson asserts, could have come about by mere chance.

Transferred back to Florida, Wilson took his new faith with him. By then, he had undergone a baptism by immersion and begun to look more closely at the Bible (he claims to have read it cover to cover about six times since). He had also started to consider the disagreements between his schooling in science and explanations for life contained in the Scriptures. At first he continued to believe in evolution, albeit a "theist evolution," guided by the hand of God. Then Wilson came upon *The Lie*, a book by Australian evangelist Ken Ham, which argued that evolution is a scam perpetrated by atheists upon innocent children.

Ham is one of the creation science gurus, a magnetic speaker so in demand, he claims to give three hundred lectures a year, sells videotapes and a magazine (entitled *Creation*), employs a staff of thirty, and recently, in a move that caused considerable controversy, secured the rights to build a $14 million, fifty-acre Old Testament "museum and scientific discovery center" off Interstate 275 in Boone County, Kentucky, at which he has proposed to demonstrate a life consistent with the story of Genesis. It will have, among other things, sixty-five life-size dinosaurs which people will be able to walk among, "just as their ancestors did." Ham's argument is simple. If you believe in evolution, then there is no God and humans are no better nor worse than other animals. Where there is no ultimate authority — no absolute right, no absolute wrong — people are more inclined to do "wrong," hence the proliferation of pornography, pederasty, abortion, homosexuality. With evolution, anything can be justified, because no one need be held accountable. Wilson drank it up.

As it turns out, Wilson is indebted to Susan Rahberg for two pillars of his present life: the experience in Orlando which eventually led him to God and one more. After Susan became engaged to someone else, she introduced Wilson to her fiancé's sister, Justina, who in 1983 became Wilson's wife. Over the next fifteen years, Glenn and Tina Wilson nurtured faith and family (Halita, born 1984; and Megan, born 1988) while Wilson worked as a nuclear technician for the navy and then as a manufacturing technician for Intel. But no manner of modern science, nuclear or computer, would budge his religious convictions. After meeting Kent Hovind, another creationist leader, in Florida, Wilson began building a portfolio as a creationism advocate himself. He developed his own lecture which he gave to local community groups, wearing a white lab coat as a way of mocking the "accoutrements" of science that he says make people give it unquestioning acceptance, and he wrote a "book" which was really a collection of photocopied pages assembled from the ideas he lays out in his talks.

No one was there to observe evolution, he writes, so how can we say that it is the law? Since no one has ever seen God, either, we can only look at the evidence and draw a conclusion as to which is the correct view. He then goes through a host of examples to demonstrate the fallibility of science, particularly on conclusions reached by inference rather than observation and of the "equally plausible" explanations offered by the Bible. He calls his book, which he has published himself, "Lumpy Oatmeal with Raisins," a reference to what the first diagrams of the model of the atom looked like before they were refined by greater study. His own explanations, he offers, may be no more accurate to the biblical truths than those were to the atomic reality we have now achieved. But just as the initial model of the atom led, finally, to the "awesome wonders" of nuclear fission, so his model, he says, can lead people to the "awesome wonders" of a spiritual reality. In the book's final pages, Wilson demonstrates the "choice." "According to the best guess of non-believing men," he writes, "we are nothing but a collection of chemicals which accidentally got together . . . Is it any wonder that evolutionists throughout history, such as Joseph Stalin and Adolf Hitler, have placed little or no value on human life? What you believe about your origin makes a huge difference in your outlook on life."

When Wilson was laid off from Intel in 1998, he and his family moved to Aiken, near Tina's brother. Then, one day, as Wilson describes it, his niece, Andrea, came home from middle school with some questions about the origins of life. Her seventh-grade science class had explored the subject of evolution and, having grown up in a devoted

In the fertile soil of the Hudson Valley: Shards of an "American Monster," long extinct

Larry Lozier takes a break from the mastodon excavation in his Hyde Park, New York, backyard, above. Left, Charles Willson Peale's painting, The Exhumation of the Mastodon, *c. 1806–08. Far left, a sketch of the Brewster Mastodon, which was discovered 155 years before Lozier's. An 1845 poster promoting a circus appearance of the Brewster skeleton was designed to amaze, and it did. "No animal living approaches this in size," it proclaimed. "The weight of the bones is 2002 pounds, and the weight of the animal when living must have been 20,000 pounds!"*

Standing on the deck attached to the rear of his suburban Hyde Park, New York, home, Larry Lozier looks out across his fifty-foot-wide backyard pond and points to "the spot." On an otherwise uneventful day in September of 1999, the ebullient forty-one-year-old mechanical engineer explains, he stumbled over what he thought was a half-buried locust log — just over there, along the pond's far bank, below the tall stand of white pine — and with that small misadventure touched the skeleton of an American original, perhaps *the* American original. "Oh my God," he remembers saying to himself, as he scraped the mud off the log. "It's a bone." But this wasn't just any bone; it was over three feet tall and so thick he couldn't even get his hands around it. Lozier ran to his neighbor's house and begged her to come see. "You think it could be from a Clydesdale?" he asked Marge Tierney, who raised horses. "Larry," she said, "that's no horse."

Some forty miles to the north and three hundred years earlier, a Dutch tenant farmer near the town of Claverack Landing had recorded an experience similar to Lozier's. It is unclear whom he told first or how excited he might have been, but the man's heart most surely raced as he picked up a fist-sized, five-pound tooth. He reportedly sold it to an Albany assemblyman for a half-pint of rum — most of which could fit in the inner recesses of the bone — having no idea that, as it found its way to the governor of New York Province, then, in a box labeled "tooth of a Giant," to the secretary of the Royal Society in London, he was opening one of the more fascinating chapters in American history.

"In the eighteenth century, when dinosaurs had not yet been discovered anywhere, few people were aware of the existence of prehistoric nature," says cultural historian Paul Semonin, author of *American Monster: How the Nation's First Prehistoric Creature Became a Symbol of National Identity*. At first, the Claverack tooth was believed to be from a huge human and proof, as Genesis reads, that "there were giants on the earth" before the great flood. Cotton Mather, the Boston minister whose interest in science earned him membership in the Royal Society of London, extrapolated from the tooth's measurements to imagine 70-foot-tall humans marching the earth. "The Teeth, which are a very durable sort of Bones," Mather speculated, " . . . may serve as well as any Tongues, to tell us What men were once upon it." But as more teeth, and tusks, and toes, and legs, and ribs were found in peat bogs and riverbeds throughout the colonies over the next hundred years, questions abounded about the American *incognitum* — so dubbed by William Hunter, the Queen's physician, in 1767. To exactly what kind of being did these huge bones belong? Carnivore or herbivore? What happened to it? Was it God's will and the Great Flood that killed the beast off? And just what did its existence — or extinction — say about God's universe? About America?

By the time that Benjamin Franklin, George Washington, Thomas Jefferson, and other American founding figures began collecting the bones for their "cabinets of curiosities" and ruminating about their meaning, most serious anatomists and scientists had given up the idea that the 1705 Gyant of Claverack was a giant human. As new bones were found, and their resemblance to an unknown, elephant-like "quadruped" confirmed, the biblical paradigm began to melt away and, with it, an entire world order. "Right up to the time of Thomas Jefferson the conventional wisdom was that there were no extinct animals except what Noah didn't take on the Ark," explains David Burney, a paleoecologist at Fordham University. "God wouldn't allow a species to disappear. He wouldn't make anything he would waste." Now the mastodon challenged that assumption, even though Jefferson, among others, did not give up on the possibility that the animal still stalked the forests (and in 1804, when he sent Lewis and Clark westward, ordered them to look for the American *incognitum*).

By the late eighteenth century, the American *incognitum* fossils became entangled in a fierce debate about national identity that fed the fires of revolution. French naturalist George Buffon had already declared a kind of war on America in his forty-four-volume *Natural History*, claiming the new continent to be a degenerate place, with a naturally inferior landscape and climate. "In general," Buffon wrote, "all the animals there are smaller than those of the old world, & there is not any animal in America that can be compared to the elephant, the rhinoceros, the hippopotamus, the dromedary, the giraffe, the buffalo, the lion, the tiger . . ." Buffon's theory was deemed an attack on the manhood of the American patriots; the discovery, in turn, of an animal that seemed to have been both huge and ferocious was welcomed as a dramatic refutation of Buffon's humiliating theory of American degeneracy.

The founding fathers sought out the bones of the *incognitum.* Washington, who had picked up several grinders in Ohio when he was a soldier in the Colonial army, took time out from fighting the British, in 1780, to visit a mastodon excavation site near his Newburgh, New York, headquarters. And in 1781, toward the end of the Revolutionary War, Jefferson gave Daniel Boone a message to deliver to an American general, asking him "to procure for me some teeth of the great animal whose remains are found on the Ohio." In 1782, as the new ambassador to France, Jefferson asked that he be sent bones of the *incognitum,* "the most desirable object in Natural History. And there is no expence of package or of safe transportion that I will not gladly reimburse to procure them safely." (One wonders if he intended to challenge Buffon, in person.) It was Jefferson who sealed the name of the beast, when he signaled his approval of French anatomist George Cuvier's term *mastodon,* from the Greek, meaning "breast-shaped tooth."

By the early nineteenth century, the search for a complete skeleton became more intense. George Turner, a federal judge in Ohio, told his colleagues at the American Philosophical Society that "the person who shall first procure the complete skeleton of this *incognitum,* will render, not to his country alone, but to the world, a most invaluable present." That honor came to the painter and scientist Charles Willson Peale who, working from bones found at several sites around the Hudson Valley, was finally able to piece together a complete mastodon skeleton in 1803. ("Gracious God, what a jaw!" proclaimed Peale's son, Rembrandt.) With Peale's accomplishment (and his painting of an excavation site, which he unveiled around 1806), a kind of "mammoth fever" swept the nation. "A Philadelphia baker sold 'mammoth bread,'" says Paul Semonin, "and a 'mammoth cheese' weighing 1,230 pounds was sent to President Jefferson by a Baptist minister in Massachusetts."

Unfortunately, neither Jefferson nor Peale lived long enough to see the animal found in 1845 on the Newburgh farm of Nathaniel Brewster. The beast was essentially intact and still in the position it had apparently died in eleven thousand years earlier — standing upright, its front legs stretched forward, its head thrust upward, its mouth in mid-chew of a dinner of local plant. Noting the excellence of the Brewster specimen, the American Museum of Natural History later acquired the skeleton and made it a centerpiece of its collection (where it remains, renamed the Warren mastodon after a Harvard scientist who committed much study to it). From that day forward, the Brewster mastodon became the iconic emblem of the American spirit: natural, proud, ferocious.

By the time Larry Lozier stubbed his toe on his very own mastodon humerus (the upper leg) bone more than 150 years later, the discovery of a dinosaur bone was a less sensational event, but Lozier and his backyard became something of a local curiosity nonetheless. Cornell University paleontologists arrived to search for more bones and an answer to the one remaining mastodon mystery: What caused the animal to disappear? They were joined by hundreds of volunteers. "The mastodon," says Paul Semonin, "maintains this amazing hold on the popular — and scientific — imagination."

More than 180 of the presumed 220 bones in the skeleton were found — including the refrigerator-sized skull — by the time the group closed the dig site and trucked the bones, along with 435 buckets of mud, to Ithaca, for further research. But as yet the Lozier dig has offered no further clue to the crowning mystery of extinction.

To Lozier, who grew up in the house where he, his wife, and daughter now live, the history of his pond had always been about fishing for bullheads in the shallow waters, shooting at frogs with BB guns, ice-skating in the winter. "We swam in it only on dares." Now it has become Hyde Park's very own window into the prehistoric world, and a longstanding American drama.

fundamentalist family, she was confused by the inconsistencies with what she had learned in church. Outraged, Wilson went directly to the school board to raise his objections. He has been raising them ever since.

Wilson's appearances play out like a well-rehearsed script. He arrives on time to each meeting, sporting a baseball cap with the initials "FBI," for Faith Builders International, the "organization" he formed to promote his ideas, though he remains its only member. The nod to the Federal Bureau of Investigation is something of an inside joke. Like many conservatives — and even a few liberals — Wilson remembers the FBI raid on the Branch Davidian complex in 1993 as one of the darkest chapters in the story of American religious tolerance. When the school board's business at hand has been finished, board chair John Bradley moves the meeting forward to a period reserved for public comment. Wilson walks slowly to a desk facing the members, sits down, and, like a witness testifying before a Senate subcommittee, begins his case by first citing the "decadence" of modern life as evidence of evolution's influence upon human behavior. The themes are always the same, but the flourishes change from appearance to appearance. At a moment appropriate to his drama, Wilson has even pulled out a picture of Dylan Klebold and Eric Harris, the two teenage boys responsible for the 1999 massacre of students at Columbine High School in Colorado, and quoted the teenagers who justified their murderous rampage by claiming that they had "evolved" to a higher life form than those whom they aimed to kill. The teaching of evolution leads to such depraved thinking, says Wilson, because it suggests that there is no meaning to life but the predatory cycle that Klebold describes, just the playing out of a biological process in which the strong lord over the weak. If evolution were a proven fact, that would be one thing, but since it is not, then those who insist upon teaching it are filling the minds of our children with dangerous ideas, fraught with dark social implications.

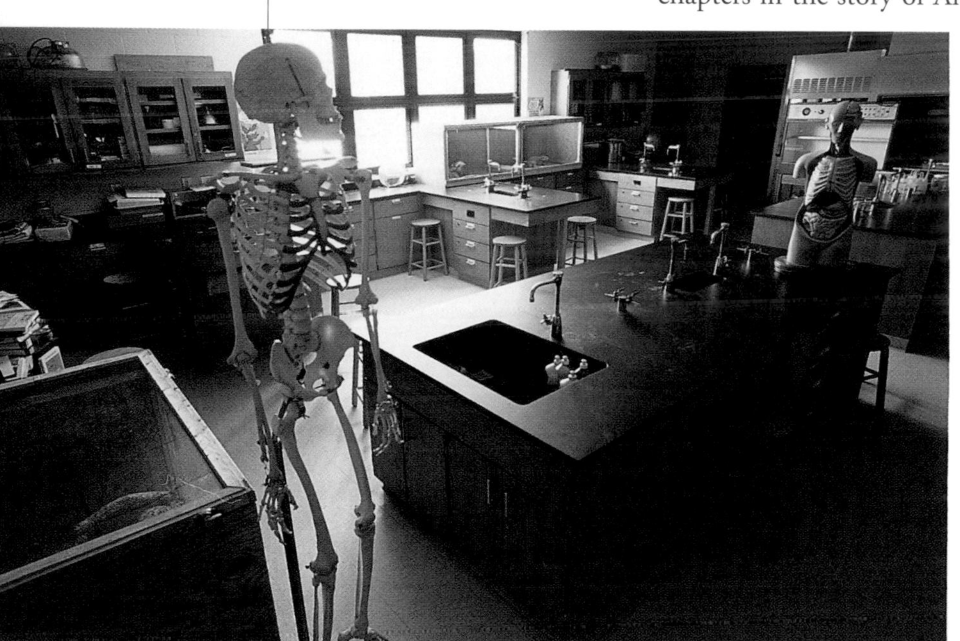

Every sophomore at South Aiken High School is required to take biology, and classes meet here, in the school's biology lab. Students are given only a cursory education in evolution. "There's a problem knowing what to say and what not to say," says Donny Holland, who doubles as South Aiken's biology teacher and basketball coach. "So we touch on it lightly."

Wilson then arrives at the nut of his argument, that creation theory — the explanation of the Genesis story in scientific terms — deserves an equal hearing with evolution. In this, he is following the strategy employed by biblical literalists ever since 1968, when the Supreme Court ruled in favor of Susan Epperson, a Little Rock biology teacher who argued that Arkansas's ban on the teaching of evolution was a violation of the Constitution's prohibition of religious establishment. After *Epperson*, creationists began framing their argument in the language of science. Since no one has ever observed evolution, they say, it will never be anything more than a theory. And if evolution is but a theory, lacking proof, then let the students hear an opposing "theory," too, the one which has the endorsement of most of their parents. Despite the fact that the Supreme Court has since ruled in favor of those who see this as a breach of the line between church and state (in 1987), it has survived as the justification for removing evolution from school science standards (Kansas, 1999), for if evolution cannot be proven, then why insist that biology teachers teach it?

Wilson insists that creation science represents no conflict with the Constitution, and, if necessary, should be heard again by the Court. If creation science is religion, faith more than fact, he says, then so is the equally unproven evolution theory. Despite their claims to be the guardians of the First Amendment ban on the establishment of a state religion, the Darwinists have themselves established a state religion, a secular, "godless" religion.

> **"The attitude that spawned the creation science movement is the same one that made America a leader in world science: a healthy disrespect for authority."**
> KENNETH MILLER
> *Brown University biologist*

III

America was born at "the high tide of eighteenth-century secularism," and its Constitution reflects the somewhat muted religious attachments of the founding fathers. Deism — the belief that the universe, and its physical and moral laws, was made by a God whose influence ended with creation, who essentially set the world to work of its own accord — was the religious creed favored by most eighteenth-century intellectuals, from Voltaire to Benjamin Franklin. George Washington was probably a Deist; and so, most likely, were James Madison and Thomas Jefferson.

Jefferson's story is complicated. He has long been admired by freethinkers and agnostics as one of their own and reviled by believers as an "infidel" (a word with a distinctly modern resonance), if only because it is sometimes asserted that his strong advocacy for a "wall" of separation between church and state was his way of helping mankind escape the tyranny of religion. It is true that Jefferson considered his 1779 Virginia statute for religious freedom, with its disdain for the superstitions of the past and its praise for reason, to be among his greatest accomplishments. Indeed, at his request, it was listed, along with the drafting of the Declaration of Independence and the founding of the University of Virginia, on his tombstone. And he asserted that man had too long been living in the service of dogmatic authority embodied in the alliance of religion with the state.

" Fix reason firmly in her soul . . . and boldly question everything, beginning with the existence of God."

—THOMAS JEFFERSON
as paraphrased by scholar Merrill Peterson

According to scholar Merrill Peterson, Jefferson saw the mission of his times as no longer one of reflecting upon this world or even contemplating another, but changing the life around him. In the spirit of the Enlightenment, Jefferson asserted that man should abandon the gloomy doctrines of the old church, draw from science to discover a new God in the essential laws of nature, and then put those laws to the service of humanity. A century before, Isaac Newton had explained the universe as a mechanistic system, moving in accordance with natural rules that could be apprehended by human reason; similarly, John Locke had pointed the way to a "science" of government. And Adam Smith had declared an autonomous economic order also governed by immutable laws of nature. Now, in America, these revolutionary ideas would be put into practice.

But historians agree that far from condemning religion, Jefferson appears to have sought the barrier between church and state as a way of protecting religion which, if allowed to flower from the private judgment of men, would play an essential role in maintaining the moral character of a community. In this, he was much like America's favorite amateur "scientist," Benjamin Franklin, who insisted that what people believed was their own private business, but the fact that they believed in something — anything — was good for society, because it inspired feelings of good citizenship and morality. "If men are wicked with religion," said Franklin, "what would they be without it?"

In a speech before the Virginia House of Delegates in November 1776, Jefferson raised the fundamental question: "Has the state a right to adopt an opinion in matters of religion?" and then proceeded to demonstrate an argument for the separation of church and state based upon his belief that religion was a private matter of the conscience and therefore outside the domain of civil government. Men turn to the state to secure those rights they cannot secure themselves, he said. But religious conscience is not one of these. Ridiculing the idea of a state-supported religion, Jefferson then declared: "Millions of innocent men, women, and children . . . have been burnt, tortured, fined, imprisoned [in the name of Christianity], yet we have not advanced one inch toward uniformity. What has been the effect of coercion? To make one half the world fools, and the other hypocrites."

The progress of truth in religion, as in science, Jefferson declared, relied upon free inquiry and private judgment. "The opinions and belief of men," he wrote, "depend not on their own will, but follow involuntarily the evidence proposed to their minds." Jefferson went so far as to find in religious freedom a kind of principle of the free market. Religious differences are a boon to both society and to religion, he said, for when religions are forced to compete with each other, they become stronger

Outside New York City: An homage to America's "man of reason"

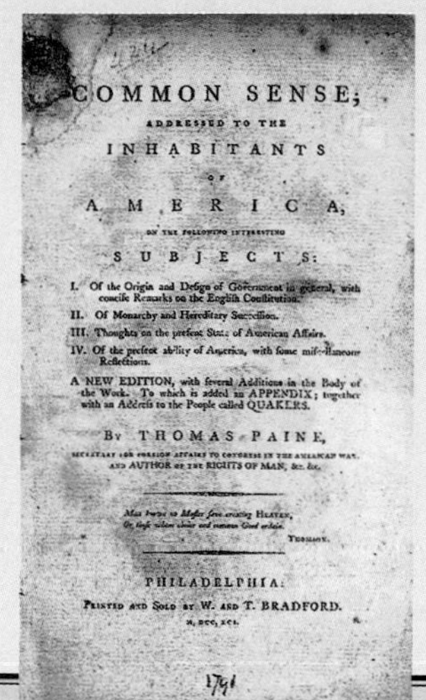

COMMON SENSE;

ADDRESSED TO THE

INHABITANTS

OF

AMERICA,

ON THE FOLLOWING INTERESTING

SUBJECTS:

I. Of the Origin and Design of Government in general, with concise Remarks on the English Constitution.

II. Of Monarchy and Hereditary Succession.

III. Thoughts on the present State of American Affairs.

IV. Of the present ability of America, with some miscellaneous Reflections.

A NEW EDITION, with several Additions in the Body of the Work. To which is added an APPENDIX; together with an Address to the People called QUAKERS.

BY THOMAS PAINE,

AND AUTHOR OF THE RIGHTS OF MAN, &c. &c.

PHILADELPHIA:

PRINTED AND SOLD BY W. AND T. BRADFORD.

M,DCC,XCI.

1791

Paine Association members toast his contributions to history, right. Left, an early printing of Paine's pamphlet, Common Sense, *which helped spur the Revolution. While Thomas Jefferson praised it, John Adams was more reserved. "[He] has a better hand at pulling down than building up," Adams told his wife, Abigail.*

The collection of people gathered for a birthday reception in the main room of a tiny museum in New Rochelle, New York, in late January 2001 was eclectic, to say the least, and yet all there shared something: an admiration bordering on awe for a radical American Colonial patriot named Tom Paine. Paine Museum director Brian McCartin, a portly former high school teacher with an accent honed in the playgrounds of Flushing, Queens, and a blustery manner that befits the memory of the cantankerous Paine, stepped forward, thrust up a plastic cup holding some cheap brandy, and declared the event open to toasts. "To Tom Paine, and the Age of Reason," burst out Jeffrey Block. "To America's first republican, with a small *r*," added Robert Singletary. Margaret Berton saluted Paine's support for "women's rights"; Klara Rukshina, a Russian immigrant, thanked the American for the inspiration he provided to the "first democratic revolution in Russia" (a much-admired, early-nineteenth-century movement that was crushed by the czar in 1825). Margaret Downey varied slightly from the theme by praising the path of adventurous scientists who, if they develop cloning, "can take Paine's DNA and create another." And finally McCartin closed with one last tribute in the form of an appreciation. "To the chance to be a citizen in America," he said, "...the first democratic republic, founded with Paine's help."

Every year, either on or around January 29, fans of Tom Paine gather here at the site of his eighteenth-century farm. They lay a birthday wreath at his memorial, give a series of toasts to his life, and then shake their heads in wonder at the breadth of influence brought to the American story by this one man. As an enemy of taxes and a champion of free enterprise, Paine is a hero to the Right; as an ardent critic of privilege, and an advocate for the poor, he is admired by the Left. And yet Paine's greatest contribution may be deeper still. For more than anyone else in the national pantheon he gave language to the notion of America as a secular haven. In contrast to the tired old tyrannies of the aristocracy, the monarchy, and the Church, Paine declared that Americans would forge a new beginning for all mankind, a nation built from the power of human reason and the possibilities of human progress.

The man whose life and ideas would anoint eighteenth-century America as "The Age of Reason" led a multifaceted life. Born in the British town of Thetford, Norfolk, in 1737, Thomas Paine was first a ladies' corset maker, then a grocer, and later, a customs official. But in 1774, he boarded a ship for a life with a clean slate amid the growing turmoil of Colonial America. Paine was armed with a modest recommendation from Benjamin Franklin. Yet no one, not even Franklin, would have predicted the history that he would soon write for America, and the world.

Upon arriving in Philadelphia, Paine tried teaching, before finally finding his calling in his fifth career, as a rabble-rousing pamphleteer. With *Common Sense*, a radical sheet he published anonymously in January 1776, Paine scored a surprising success. The pamphlet's message was direct, that America should cease its policy of accommodation and declare its independence from Britain. But, significantly, Paine phrased his appeal in the language of reason. "Common sense," asserted Paine, dictated that an island could not rule a continent. That simple insight made his pamphlet a best-seller even by twenty-first-century terms (over 150,000, at a time when pamphlets sold a few hundred, at best) and it touched off the frenzy that led to the American Revolution.

The man John Adams described as having "genius in his eyes" would go on to establish himself as one of the most influential writers in the English language and the poet laureate of the American founding, not least because, in the spirit of democracy, he spoke not to an educated elite, but to farmers, craftsmen, artisans. Paine wrote in a direct style that some contemporary critics derided as coarse, "barnyard." But in fact accessible, unsophisticated, unadorned prose was integral to his philosophy. "As it is my design to make those that can scarcely read understand," he wrote, "I shall therefore avoid every literary ornament and put it in language as plain as the alphabet." Indeed, on Christmas Eve, 1776, in retreat from the British army, Gen. George Washington set camp on the banks of the Delaware River and read aloud from Paine to bolster the morale of his weary troops. "These are the times that try men's souls," Paine had written. "The summer soldier and the sunshine patriot will, in this crisis, shrink from the service of his country; but he that stands it NOW, deserves the love and thanks of man and woman." The following day, the soldiers responded by routing the enemy near Trenton.

Paine relied upon his readers knowing only the Bible and the Book of Common Prayer, which was in itself ironic, since he once told Adams that he viewed the Bible "with contempt" and in one of the last great books of his life, *The Age of Reason*, he took on the church in much the same way that he had earlier taken on monarchy and nobility: as a corrupt and venal institution. It would be his undoing. Paine meant to distinguish between organized religion and a "true" faith which found God in nature and science, but that was lost on the public, which turned on him as an infidel, and his reputation never fully recovered. When he died in New York City in 1809, he was largely a forgotten man. Only six mourners attended his New Rochelle funeral and, in the years that followed, a popular nursery rhyme derided him. "Poor Tom Paine! there he lies, Nobody laughs and nobody cries. Where he has gone or how he fares? Nobody knows and nobody cares."

Thomas Paine, left, circa 1792. Above, the Thomas Paine Cottage in New Rochelle, where in 1805, Paine penned his last pamphlet, on constitutional reform in Pennsylvania. On Christmas Eve that year a gunman fired a bullet through the rear room of the cottage in an unsuccessful attempt on Paine's life.

The first true biography of Paine was not written until 1892 (Moncure Conway's *Life of Thomas Paine*), but even with that, the once revered patriot remained a shunned figure to all but a handful of radical freethinkers. By the beginning of the twentieth century, those who knew of Paine were likely to have adhered to Teddy Roosevelt's characterization of him as that "filthy little atheist." In 1925, thanks largely to the encouragement of Thomas Edison, the Paine Museum was established in New Rochelle, across the street from his cottage. But only in the last couple of decades has Paine's story emerged from the gallows, first when Ronald Reagan began quoting him ("We have it in our power to begin the world over again") as a rallying cry for conservatives, leading to Congress's decision in 1992 to approve the construction of a Paine memorial in Washington; then, when the evangelists of the Internet seized upon him as their philosophical ancestor, the first champion of "the concept of the uncensored flow of ideas." Paine, wrote Jon Katz in *Wired*, the magazine of the new technologies, is "the moral father of the Internet." His words "should be chiseled above newsroom doors and taped to laptops."

Gathered under a portrait of Paine, and amid assorted memorabilia that include Paine's death mask, his angry 1797 letter to George Washington (in another "blasphemous act" he accused Washington of abandoning the principles of the Revolution), and a model of the single-arch bridge Paine designed (like Franklin, he had an interest in science and engineering), Brian McCartin and the others argued that their hero's influence was even more extensive. "Bee" Brown, New Rochelle's deputy mayor and an African-American, pointed out that Paine was among the first to advocate the abolition of slavery.

Gary Berton said that Paine was the nation's most outspoken voice for the principle of equality and, if only by the inspiration he provided, the "true author" of the Declaration of Independence. Sister Beth Dowd, a Catholic nun, announced that she is working with a composer on an orchestral piece based on the words of Paine. And Ken Burchell, a jewelry appraiser who had come all the way from Coeur d'Alene, Idaho, described his visit to New Rochelle as nothing less than a pilgrimage. Noting that Paine stood up for the rights of man at a time when that idea was decidedly radical, Burchell later offered one final tribute. "Paine," he said in earnest, "is the bedrock of dignified existence."

and more self-reliant. They also avoid the coercive (and perhaps corrupting) influence of the state. It was this idea that brought great pride to Jefferson in his dotage; writing to a rabbi in Savannah, Georgia, in 1821, he pointed to what he felt were the two most distinctive accomplishments of the American experiment, one being that man could be relied upon to govern himself, the other that the most effective salve to the raw friction of religious dissension was religious freedom.

But if Jefferson, and his Virginia compatriot, James Madison, were, in a way, the forerunners of today's secularists, enamored of science and highly suspicious of the old European alliance of kings and priests, they are balanced in American history by an equally powerful tradition of religious fervor. Deism may have been the religious flavor of choice among the learned founders, but there were all manner of other, mostly Christian, beliefs among the colonial peoples, too. The Great Awakening of the 1730s had introduced an evangelical, anti-intellectual, spirit-driven church, splintering the traditional denominations and giving rise to a new tradition of revivalist preachers which has lasted straight through to our own time. Like the Puritans before them, many in these sects saw America as the new Eden, a place to correct man's "error" and, presumably, reverse the fortunes of humankind (a point of view consistent with that of many of the founders who felt, in John Adams's phrase, "present at the creation" of a new world). They viewed their lives here as the fulfillment of a sacred prophesy, a "mission into the Wilderness."

Ironically, the idea of a separation between church and state appealed to these sects, too. For one, it allowed for the safe practice of their faiths even if they were in the minority. But there were also many religious people who saw the division of church and state to be fundamental to religious doctrine, who saw men and, by extension, civil authority, as too depraved to be trusted with the sacred mission of the church. Thus, at roughly the same time that the American founders were seeking to establish a secular state, consistent with their own belief in reason and their suspicion of the power of a national church, other, more devout, Americans — some of them anti-intellectual and hostile to reason — sought the same in an effort to preserve their ability to practice their faiths freely. Both found refuge in a Constitutional ban on the establishment of a state religion.

The Virginia statute for religious freedom, which became law in 1786, laid the foundation for the unique American tradition of church-state relations. Its principles entered into the Constitution of 1787 in the form of the First Amendment protection of religion. Given the founders' reverence for science, it was perhaps inevitable that the Constitution would be described in mechanistic terms, in particular as a "machine" or

"Religion is not helped by establishment, but is hurt by it, as is civil society. Establishment would hinder immigration, foster emigration, disturb good social relations, and retard Christian evangelizing."

—James Madison

In the Twin Cities: Where America is still a haven from religious persecution

A Tibetan-American Thanksgiving at John Lundquist's home in Minneapolis, left. Above, an etching depicting Russian Mennonite emigrants aboard a Hamburg steamer on the Hudson River, 1873, en route to their new home in the Dakotas. Many of the Mennonite immigrants who sought religious freedom in America in the late nineteenth century settled in the territory of the Dakotas, home to Mennonite communities that still flourish 125 years later.

The thirty-some people gathered around the Thanksgiving dinner table at the stately, century-old Minneapolis home of Mary Ann and John Lundquist are an odd mix. There are the usual Nordic faces of the northern parts of the American Midwest, people of Swedish, Norwegian, Irish, German and Dutch descent. But scattered among them to celebrate this oldest of American holidays are fourteen Asian immigrants, hailing from places with the decidedly non-Nordic names of Tso-na, Lhokha, and Pemakok. "It started in 1992," Mary Ann Lundquist, a clinical social worker, says of her family's multiethnic Thanksgiving tradition. "We heard through our church about the great numbers of Tibetans who were coming to the area and needed help with resettlement. But we had no idea they would become such a part of our lives."

A few years after the Chinese army invaded Tibet in 1950, incorporating the ancient Himalayan land of 471,000 square miles (more than one and a half times the size of Texas) within its own borders, Beijing began waging a brutal war on Tibetan Buddhism, jailing, torturing, and executing monks and nuns, declaring the Dalai Lama (the country's spiritual leader, who won the Nobel Peace Prize for his commitment to a nonviolent solution to his country's crisis) a "criminal," and, in the words of the Chinese-backed Tibetan Communist leadership, helping "peasants and herdsmen free themselves from the negative influence of religion." In 1976, China's brutal Cultural Revolution — which sought to reinvigorate Communism in China and purge the "poison" of religion — came to an end, but the vast majority of what were once thousands of monasteries and temples had already been destroyed.

Almost from the start of the Chinese invasion, Tibetans began fleeing across the borders in search of a safe haven. Many of them went to nearby India and Nepal. But in the early 1990s the American government granted special immigration status to an initial group of Tibetans, paving the way for more to come to these shores, too, seeking the refuge from religious persecution that has brought so many others here throughout American history.

The Tibetan government-in-exile, based in the northern Indian city of Dharamsala, in an effort to offset the Chinese decimation of Tibetan culture, devised a plan to create cluster communities around the United States, each large enough to sustain their traditions and customs. Besides having a solid infrastructure of social services and a tradition of helping others, Minneapolis was home to a small network of people who were interested in helping the Tibetan cause. They succeeded in having Minneapolis chosen as a cluster site, and in the decade since then about nine hundred people whose lives and traditions were tied to the high Himalayas have been slowly adapting themselves to the land of sweet corn and snowmobiles. Minneapolis now has the second-largest Tibetan population in the United States (after New York City).

The Minnesota Tibetans have powerful stories to tell. Kelsang Lhamo, who left Tibet in 1990, remembers her father being imprisoned after Chinese soldiers found a picture of the Dalai Lama in the family's home; during an uprising in 1988, she was beaten by soldiers when she tried to care for a monk who had been shot. Thinly Woser, the cochairman of the Tibet American Foundation, was seven years old when he left Tibet, in flight from the invading Chinese army. "I heard the bombs being thrown into the monasteries," he says. "The Chinese started broadcasting on a PA system, singing Communist songs, telling people that Buddhism is the poison of society, that we had to be prepared to kill our father and mother for the sake of the state. Of course, we were all very devout Buddhists, and finally we fled. We went first on horseback, then into the Himalayas on foot. It took us months to walk through the mountains to the Indian border. I saw my father shot and killed."

Woser, and others with stories as shocking as his, found comfort from their travails when they arrived in the land of Jefferson and Lincoln. "We were able to come here because America has a tradition of religious freedom," said Wangyal Ritzekura, who works in a men's clothing store and is one of the leaders of the Tibetan community in Minneapolis. "That is something Tibetans have deep respect for because Buddhism believes that all religions are paths to the truth." His experience here has been comforting to him and his family. "I'm often asked what we would do if the Chinese left Tibet tomorrow. I think many of those my age and older would probably go back. But our children are Americans now . . . This is their home."

The Pilgrims, who held the first Thanksgiving in 1621, came here fleeing religious persecution. They were a minority religious sect in England and much maligned for their separatism. Later in the seventeenth century the colonies of Pennsylvania, founded by the Quaker William Penn, and Maryland, founded by the Catholic Lord Baltimore, were established as havens from religious persecution. Then, with the founding of the American republic and the creation of the constitutional guarantee of religious freedom, America became the haven for many vulnerable religious groups. The Amish, the Mennonites, and the Hutterites fled persecution in Europe and sought refuge in the pastureland of Pennsylvania and the plains of North and South Dakota, while Jews fleeing pogroms in Russia and the abuse of the Nazi regime in Germany established themselves in New York City and other urban centers. In the first decades of the twentieth century, Sikhs settled in California, built America's first *gurdwara* (a Sikh temple), and then, in inimitable American fashion, intermarried with Mexican Catholics, creating a distinctive culture blending Sikh and Spanish traditions.

Even in America, there have been pauses in the policy of religious tolerance. After millions of Catholics from Italy and Ireland began entering the country in the late nineteenth and early twentieth centuries, the Protestant majority, in fear that the nation's traditional stock was being diluted, pressured Congress to enact legislation that limited immigration according to country of origin. But once that policy was lifted in the 1960s, a flood of immigrants, many more of them Asian — and largely non-Christian — began to arrive here. In the 1990s, for the first time in history, America made religion a feature of foreign policy. Through a new Office of International Religious Freedom, the U.S. government began monitoring religious persecution around the globe and imposing economic sanctions on the worst violators. While some foreign governments have reacted with scorn at what they see as yet another instance of America imposing its will, the writers of the new legislation used as their justification not only the first amendment of the Constitution but the U.N.'s 1948 Universal Declaration of Human Rights, which borrowed from the American founders' language when it declared that "all human beings are born free and equal in dignity and rights. They are endowed with reason and conscience."

There have been improvements in religious freedom throughout the globe, but America remains the world's most religiously diverse society. The State Department now claims that there are 6 million Muslims in America, which would mean that there are as many Muslims here as there are Jews. In 1996, the U. S. Navy commissioned its first Muslim chaplain. In 2000, the U.S. House of Representatives was opened by a prayer from Shri Venkatachalapathi Samudrala, a Hindu cleric who hails from Cleveland, Ohio. Buddhists, Sikhs, Zoroastrians, Taoists, and Confucians have arrived in record numbers. The face of American Christianity, once decidedly Anglo-Saxon and Protestant, has been changed with the arrival of large numbers of Latin Catholics, Chinese, Haitian, and Brazilian Pentecostal communities and Egyptian copts.

Nearly a decade after it began, the Tibetan resettlement in Minneapolis is proceeding nicely. About 50 percent of the original Tibetan settlers have bought houses; most have applied for U.S. citizenship. A new cultural center is in the works, which will likely include a temple (to date, religious ceremonies are held in churches or community centers). And the people of the Twin Cities have embraced their new Tibetan neighbors. "A lot of us Americans take things here for granted," said Pat Finnegan, a business consultant, "and we see that the Tibetans take nothing for granted, like the opportunity to practice your religion freely. They are a reminder of what we're all about."

an "engine" ("a machine that would go of itself," was James Russell Lowell's eloquent nineteenth-century characterization). But how remarkable that this determinably secular device was established by one of the most religious of societies, that history's first state to disestablish religion did so in a way that actually preserved the nation as a model of religiosity and a magnet for the persecuted.

Still, what would the founders think of twenty-first-century society? And how would they respond to the unique Constitutional challenge formed when it is deemed by many that secularism itself has become a kind of faith, undermining religious doctrine? What would they make of a community deemed by so many to be in a moral crisis? Would they find in that a failure of religion, a failure of the state, or a failure prompted by a too strict reading of language they meant to *encourage* religious and moral advancement?

Ever since 1931, horse lovers have traveled to Aiken to attend the Harness Race, the Aiken Trials, and the Steeplechase, shown here. Georgianna Conger Wolcott hasn't missed a race since she was an infant. "It's a rite of spring," she says. "When I was little it wasn't an Easter dress I'd buy, it was a 'Steeplechase' dress."

IV

Aiken, South Carolina, was born of technology, although a nineteenth-century variety. In the 1830s, the area was established as the terminus of a new rail line between Charleston, to the east, and the Savannah River, dedicated to taking back the river trade from rival Savannah, Georgia. The Charleston steam line — at 136 miles — was, for a time, the longest in the world and, one must imagine, quite a local curiosity. Early drawings show beaming townspeople standing next to steam engines so rudimentary they look like circus calliopes, with hoop-skirted Southern belles gathered around them, waiting for passengers to dismount.

The railroad helped to make Aiken a target during the Civil War, when Union general William Tecumseh Sherman declared that he would loose his men on the Carolinas with such a fury "the devil himself" couldn't restrain them. In the end, however, the Fifth U.S. Calvary was surprised by a Confederate detachment here, and, after engaging in fierce hand to hand combat at what is now the site of the First Baptist Church, the Union soldiers retreated.

In part because it was a Confederate victory and in part because, nearly 150 years later, the Civil War remains a galvanizing event for the people of South Carolina (which was, after all, the first state to secede from the Union, in December 1860), the Battle of Aiken is still remembered proudly. Locals like to point out that graves of Union soldiers appear next to the First Baptist Church and that the flat tops of the stones make them different from the stones at Confederate graves up the street, which rise to a triangle. "The maker of the markers was, of course, a Southerner," explains First Baptist's pastor, Reverend Fred Andrea, with an impish grin, "and he decided that if years later somebody came along and felt like taking a rest they could sit on one of these union soldiers' graves, but they were not going to perch themselves on one of our boys."

Every February, the Battle of Aiken is reenacted in exacting detail by more than a thousand Civil War enthusiasts who pay $600 for uniforms and up to $400 for their muskets. It can be hard, the promoters admit, to find participants who will play the Union side, so hard that there are times when the only way they can assemble enough Union "soldiers" is to promise them that they can exchange their blue uniforms for Confederate jackets and caps the next day, so they can appear where they feel much more at home — on the rebel side of the skirmish. The crowd of spectators for this three-day event has grown to ten thousand, many of them sharing the sentiment of Roy Parrish, Jr., a member of the Sons of Confederate Veterans, who says that the reenactment is "a tribute to our ancestors." But in fact the Battle of Aiken, while a true Confederate victory, mattered little in the end. Coming late in the war, it had no effect upon the impending Southern defeat.

Aiken's "Bee Camp" Sons of Confederate Veterans, named after Confederate general Barnard E. Bee, is one of forty-eight SCV chapters in South Carolina. Bee Camp meets once a month at Bobby's Bar-B-Q, a local favorite, and looks after the nearly twelve hundred local Confederate graves, such as these at St. Thaddeus Episcopal Church in Aiken.

During the late nineteenth and early twentieth centuries, Aiken was a popular winter colony — the "Newport of the South" — with wealthy families retreating here from the frigid temperatures of the Northeast to enjoy polo and tennis. Then, in the middle of the twentieth century, at the outset of the cold war and the atomic age, Aiken's history was once again joined to an emerging technology when it was chosen as the site for a massive industrial complex dedicated to making and processing plutonium 239 and tritium, two elements essential to the hydrogen bomb. Six thousand people had to be relocated from their homes to build the Savannah River Plant, as it was called then, and six small towns on the outskirts of Aiken were leveled.

At the time, some noted the irony: towns destroyed to create room for a factory to process elements to be used to destroy other towns. Particularly after people saw the government offers for their land (a mere $54 an acre, in some cases), there was some resentment mixed with the sentimentality. "We're like the boll weevil," read a sign posted in one town on the eve of its demise, "looking for a home." But for the most part the citizens of Ellenton, Meyers Mill, Hawthorne, Robbins, Leigh, and Dunbarton, and certainly those who lived in Aiken proper accepted their fate with equanimity. The Savannah River Plant was the biggest site in the nuclear program, a mammoth project compared by some with the building of the Panama Canal, and even if it did house tens of thousands of gallons of an exotic and dangerous liquid, the danger was lost in the early frenzy over a revitalized economy and a sense of national obligation.

Today, you can still see some of the old street curbs from Ellenton and Meyers Mill and, occasionally, the pavement of what was once a driveway peeks out here and there from the surface of the property at the Savannah River Site, giving an eerie feeling to a place that doesn't lack for the bizarre, when you consider its mission in the arsenal of destruction. People from the old towns like to reminisce about the swimming holes on Three Runs Creek, the baseball field behind the Masonic Lodge, and what the fishermen say were some of the best places for catfish in all South Carolina, all sacrificed in the name of patriotism. But despite decades of national debate over the morality of the nuclear weapons program and signs that the plant severely polluted area groundwater, Aiken remains firmly on the side of the bomb.

In the earliest years of the Savannah River Plant, as it was then known, signs reminded workers that the slightest slip of the tongue could threaten national security. Conductors of trains passing near the site were instructed to close window shades to shield the plant from passenger view.

The argument that nuclear arms, much more than evolution, represent demon science — great minds put to the purpose of killing people and threatening the health of the planet in the process — still falls on deaf ears. Almost without reservation, most Aikenites see the hydrogen bomb in much the same way as the millennialists of the seventeenth century might have, as a tool for the ultimate holy war, and the fact that America triumphed over the Soviets, that even unused these weapons aided in the ultimate struggle between good and evil, seems to them to only prove their point.

Mayor Frederick Bates Cavanaugh grew up in Aiken and is proud of it. He likes to take visitors by the small ranch house where, in what must have been some long-ago developer's idea of a joke, "Brandy" Road meets "Whiskey" Road. It was here that he lived with his mother and father, a World War II veteran who worked as a maintenance supervisor at the Savannah River Site. Cavanaugh misses the simpler life of those times. "You remember when you came home from school, how you wanted to see your mom?" he asks, bemoaning the advent of the two-career family. "Back in those days, that's how things were done. If no one's home what does a child do?"

After graduating from Virginia Military Institute, Cavanaugh moved through several corporate positions around the country before coming home to work in management at the "bomb plant." He retired from SRS in 1995 to devote more time to his work at city hall, but for him the civic commitment is nothing new. Cavanaugh spent years on the city council; on the boards of local charities; as an elder, Sunday school teacher, and treasurer of the Grace Brethren Church; and as a Cub Scout and Boy Scout leader. As mayor, he receives a salary of just $6,000 a year. But money, he says, is not the issue with him; rebuilding Aiken's character is. For ironically, he says, while Americans — and Aikenites — were winning the cold war abroad, they were losing to the forces of "godlessness" back home.

Cavanaugh holds up a list of newspaper headlines to demonstrate his point: articles declaring a rise in teenage pregnancy rates and incidences of domestic violence within Aiken County. The number of weapons found on South Carolina public school property has doubled in the last decade; drug arrests have increased nearly tenfold, and there are five times as many incidents in which school officials have been threatened. He refers to an oft-repeated saying, usually attributed to Tocqueville (though in fact, the source is unknown): "America is great because America is good. When America ceases to be good, she will cease to be great."

Today, the Savannah River Site, while still in operation, feels more like a cold war relic. The dormant C reactor, seen in the background here, is awaiting dismantling and eventual decontamination as part of the Department of Energy's cleanup of the site.

Cavanaugh's own answer for Aiken is something called the "Character First" program, which he introduced to the city in 1999. The idea originated with the Institute for Basic Life Principles, a nonprofit Christian organization founded in Chicago in 1970 as a way to help gang youth build new lives. Rooted in seven biblical principles, the program was so successful there, it spread to other American urban communities. In 1992, it was adapted to the workplace and, finally, in 1998, to a curriculum for cities (with all direct biblical references removed). The idea goes like this: each month, the city focuses on a different principle (chosen from a list of forty-nine prepared by the Institute and narrowed to twelve by Aiken's "Character Committee"). January 2001 was "sincerity" month; February focused on "respect"; and March was a time for "self-control." During each month, references to the principle can be seen everywhere, in banners hanging across the main thoroughfares, in classrooms, and public buildings. Local companies put aside time for employees to discuss each value and hold workshops in which they are asked to choose the "honest" or "compassionate" or "trustworthy" path. Literature discussing that month's trait is distributed by the town and posted on its website. Even the water bills add a message each month. "Aiken is an *honest* town," they declare, or "Aiken is a *compassionate* town."

Character First feels a bit like an episode of "Sesame Street" played out among adults, but it has been accepted with enthusiasm by the city and while crime has not yet come down, Cavanaugh insists that a falling crime rate alone is not a good measure of the program's success. With the weakening of the family in American life, he says, the role of moral instructor has fallen to the churches and to the government more deeply than ever before. To Cavanaugh, Character First is in essence, then, that "mother" that he says so many no longer find at home.

Aiken Character Calendar

January	SINCERITY
February	RESPECT
March	SELF-CONTROL
April	RESPONSIBILITY
May	ATTENTIVENESS
June	LOYALTY
July	COURAGE
August	CITIZENSHIP
September	TRUTHFULNESS
October	PATIENCE
November	COMPASSION
December	FORGIVENESS

Reverend Danny Burleson is another community member who supports Wilson's cause, but he too feels that much more has to be done. "If this world is survival of the fittest, then, goodness, what are we in for?" he asks. Burleson is the minister of education at Town Creek Baptist, one of Aiken's thriving evangelical congregations. Though it was founded in 1859 and for many years maintained a 270-seat sanctuary at 570 Town Creek Road, the church recently moved to a new building, one which can accommodate eight hundred parishioners at a time. Today, most services are conducted with hardly an empty seat in the house.

One of the reasons for Town Creek's enormous popularity is Burleson and his work with Aiken's youth. Like Cavanaugh, Burleson thinks the answer to the decline of society lies in a stricter moral education. The American belief in self-expression has a dark side, says Burleson, in that it can lead to selfishness. Moral standards become subservient to individual self-realization. "There is a right and there is a wrong . . ." he says. "You can't leave God out of the equation." The books on his office shelf back him up: *Right and Wrong*, *No More Excuses: Be the Man God Made You to Be*, and *I Was Wrong*.

Burleson's work with Town Creek's youth is focused upon "Judgment House," a once-a-year program of "moral theater" performed for the community each October, as an alternative to Halloween. In Judgment House, young parishioners act out a play in which the participants are called upon to make crucial moral decisions. The audience "watches" the drama while moving from room to room, just as they might walk about a haunted house. In a recent production, Judgment House focused on a home where the parents are away and the children take the opportunity to throw a party. After much drinking and smoking, one of the teenagers accidentally drops a cigarette into a trash can. The house burns down, one child dies and is called before God for judgment. Naturally, he does not fare well. The program, which, like Character First, is sponsored by an outside organization that prepares the materials for subscribing churches, makes for entertaining theater. But by demonstrating how moral decisions are a part of every life, Judgment House also delivers a deeper message. "There are choices that we all make in life," Burleson says. "And those choices, ultimately, will lead us to our final destiny."

V

On October 17, 2000, after Wilson had made his case before them no fewer than sixteen times in two years, the members of the Aiken County School Board convened a community meeting in the South Aiken High School auditorium to discuss the merits of his proposal to alter the science curriculum. The discussion was lively and, interestingly, it offered strong representation not only from Aiken's faithful, but from the city's dynamic scientific community, too. As it turned out, the two were not mutually exclusive. The first speaker was Charles H. Hewitt, Jr., who, as he quickly noted, could actually claim considerable authority on both sides of the argument. As a local physician, Hewitt had relied upon the findings of science to heal his patients; but having recently suffered a back injury, he was no longer able to practice and as a devout Christian he intended to make a dramatic shift in his career and enter the seminary. Hewitt scoffed at Wilson's plan, insisting that it was inconsistent with the views of the nation's founders and he maintained that a literal reading of Genesis represented only a minority viewpoint, even among Christians. Evolution is settled science, he said, but that should pose no threat to believers. Science and religion occupy different domains of our world, he argued, as they should. Hewitt then looked directly at the panel. "They accuse the courts of kicking God out of the school," he pronounced, referring to Wilson and others on his side. "But if you as a school board cave into their minority views . . . you will be acting against the wishes of most Americans."

Once a month the 676 pupils in East Aiken Elementary gather for a forty-five-minute "character assembly," in which the children act out skits demonstrating the character trait of the month. Peggy Trivelas, the school's principal, says the results have been tremendous: the children are calmer and more polite, and the cafeteria is quieter.

Roger Rollins, an SRS nuclear engineer, spoke second. He took the opposite view, claiming that far from being settled, evolution was still a highly debatable theory, and yet he did not leave it there. "I believe there is a much more important reason for the teaching of creationism," he said, with emotion. "Our children need to know that there is meaning to their lives . . . [that] we have been created for a purpose. That purpose is to worship and serve the almighty creator, God. When we thwart that purpose and throw God out of our schools, we allow chaos to reign."

Dr. Laura Janecek urged the committee to think of the repercus-

In an Austin, Texas, classroom: Textbooks that simmer with the political heat

Noah Webster, above, while better known for his dictionary, also wrote one of the first American history textbooks. Right, Robert Onderdonk's painting Crockett's Last Stand *(also known as* Fall of the Alamo*), 1903. When it was first unveiled in an art gallery in San Antonio, the painting was decried by Mexican visitors. Slashes in the canvas, since repaired in restoration, are believed to be the work of an angry protester. Opposite, Garraty's best-selling (and edited) history text.*

Mark Edwards and Travis Long remember well the spring day in 2000 when a tall, mustachioed professor from North Carolina visited their fourth-grade class and told them that Davy Crockett wasn't killed in battle at the Alamo. "I was a little surprised to hear that he died in captivity," recalls Mark, eleven, one of eighteen or so children who gathered around James Crisp's slide projector that morning.

Before Crisp's visit, the two boys thought they knew the story of Crockett, who came West from Tennessee in 1835 and helped Texans fight for independence from Mexico. He died, as far as the boys understood, defending the small San Antonio fort against thousands of Santa Anna's swarming soldiers. Travis, also eleven, believed Crockett went up in flames, as John Wayne, playing Crockett, had in a 1960 movie, throwing a torch into the fort's ammunition room in a final gesture of defiance after being fatally bayoneted. Mark recalled Davy's last moments swinging Ol' Betsy, his empty rifle, at a crowd of swarthy Mexicans just as he had seen in the Walt Disney book his parents bought for him at the Alamo gift shop along with the coonskin cap made famous by Fess Parker in the 1955 Disney movie. That was also the scene portrayed by painter Robert Onderdonk in his 1903 canvas, *Crockett's Last Stand*. In fact, the painting, which hangs prominently in the governor's mansion in Austin, was reproduced on page 278 of one of Mark and Travis's history texts.

Unfortunately, said Crisp (an Alamo scholar, in Austin to deliver a lecture at the Lyndon Baines Johnson Library), Disney, Wayne, and Onderdonk got it wrong. Several different eyewitness accounts confirm that Crockett was captured alive. One of the most credible sources, Crisp said, is the diary of Lt. Col. José Enrique de la Peña, a Mexican army officer who described Crockett's execution in gory detail. The diaries, first published in Mexico in 1955, have been well known since then. So why did de la Peña's story not make it into Travis and Mark's textbooks? The publishers of *Texas, The United States and the World* — one of two books used in the boys' class and throughout the Lone Star state — had purposely skirted the issue in order to not offend Texan — or even more broadly, American — sensibilities. But Crisp is not surprised. "I would say that a textbook editor in Texas would handle the Alamo story about the same way someone would handle a basket of hand grenades," he laughs.

In a democracy, the truth often faces a tough competition from popular culture, popular sentiment, and the need, in what has become a $3 billion industry, to satisfy the market. Whether the subject is social studies, history, or even biology, it is sometimes easier (and almost always more profitable) to tell people what they want to know, or at least what those in power *think* they should know. That led Noah Webster when he penned one of the first American "history" texts in the earliest days of the Republic, to tell the American story in a way that made certain that children realized the greatness of their new country as soon as they were able "to lisp the praise of liberty." And, in fact, for most of American history, the story of America, as portrayed in history texts, was the one that the majority of Americans wished it to be: a tale of American virtue contrasted with European decadence, stressing love of country, love of God, obedience to parents, thrift, honesty, and hard work. Minority groups were all but absent from these histories; and when they did appear it was almost always in racist caricature, as in David Muzzey's popular 1911 history, *An American History*. To Muzzey, Aztecs were steeped in "moral degradation," American Indians were "a treacherous, cruel people" and blacks "lazy and in need of protection." Muzzey's book was in print for sixty-five years.

There were some improvements during the 1930s, but the 1960s was the true watershed decade for American history textbooks. As attention was paid to the story of minorities, of women, and the common man, America's sense of itself changed dramatically. Christopher Columbus went from hero (founder of the New World) to villain (insensitive colonialist) in one generation; Thomas Jefferson went from "celebrated idealist" to "racist slaveholder." Yet, ironically, a new kind of rigidity emerged to replace the old. In the interest of focusing on the history of those long ignored, textbook publishers became subject to the enormous pressures of special interest groups and political oversight aimed at keeping the American story even-handed and politically correct.

"By the 1990s there had to be a certain percentage of each race or minority group in the books, either in the text or illustrations," says Tim Paulsen, a Manhattan textbook editor. "By the same token, religion and God all but disappeared — despite the fact that religious beliefs were a key to colonialist exploits as well as the founding fathers' rebellion." The strong narrative of America, guided by God and patriotism, had trailed off into hundreds of separate stories, a nation fractured.

The turmoil may have turned out many nasty habits of history, but now new kinds of errors began to stalk the industry. Columbia University historian Jack Garraty discovered the problem when he noticed that Henry Hudson was missing from a revised edition of one of his popular history texts (first published in 1982). "They had a Spanish explorer named Esteban Gomez as the first European to sail on the river that was named after Hudson," recalls Garraty, who at the time had never heard of Gomez. "But there is no evidence that Gomez had ever sailed on the Hudson," Garraty laughs. "And he wasn't even Spanish. He was Portuguese."

Though he called the publisher and "gave 'em hell," what happened to Garraty's textbook is not uncommon now that textbooks are being increasingly produced by anonymous but powerful editorial machines. Teams of researchers and writers, informed by focus groups and marketing studies,

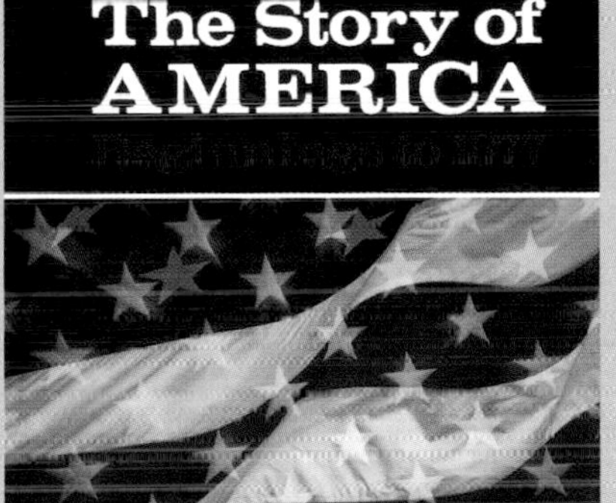

turn out histories that have to meet the increasingly political — and politically correct — demands of state and local school districts. "They wanted to sell the book in Texas and California," explains Garraty of the decision to alter his work, "so they needed Hispanic people in the book. They put a lot of stuff in there that I had never heard of."

Because of demographic shifts in the last twenty or so years, Texas and California now account for 20 percent of the textbook market, and because those two states also observe a statewide textbook adoption system (as opposed to a district-by-district approach), they wield a disproportionate power in the industry. Their state boards of education require companies to conform to detailed curriculum requirements. In 1994, when McGraw-Hill was preparing to submit for approval its *Adventures in Time and Place* — Mark and Travis's other history textbook — the publisher had a one-hundred-page "Proclamation of the State Board of Education Advertising for Bids on Instructional Materials" to use as a road map. The guide specified that fourth-grade social studies texts had to focus on "the multicultural nature of Texas and the Western Hemisphere" as well as "describe the contributions of various individuals and racial, ethnic and cultural groups" and "identify significant leaders, including David Crockett." Such systemization of the process may have made publishers' jobs much easier. They can now comb the Texas list of "Essential Knowledge and Skills" (TEKS) and "correlate" it — using sophisticated computer software — with their textbooks. But critics complain that it has created the kind of problem that John Garraty confronted: the professional historian is all but eliminated from the process.

"We have to realize that children see themselves in history," explains Stephanie Hirsh, who was director of Program and Staff Development for the Richardson Independent School District in Richardson, Texas, when Harcourt Brace Jovanovich tapped her, in 1985, to be the general editor for its *Texas, The United States and the World*, the text still used by Mark and Travis's fourth-grade class. "The more they see themselves in the story, the more they connect. Sometimes you have to sacrifice the real story to be inclusive." Nonetheless, Mark and Travis, invigorated by Professor Crisp's "detective work," seem confused by Hirsh's brand of historiography and let down. "I'm a little disappointed," says Travis, "to think that our textbooks don't tell the truth."

> "Science needs to be truthful with our children. For if our children don't get the truth from their homes, their churches, and their schools, they certainly are not going to get it from television and movies."
> JOHN FRANCK
> *Aiken resident*

sions of denying Aiken's schoolchildren an adequate science education, saying that it would hamper their ability to compete in an increasingly technical world, while Reverend Frank Rottier cited statistics from the Traditional Values Coalition, a Washington lobby group, which has claimed that since prayer was removed from the public schools in 1962, teenage suicide had gone up 450 percent, births to unmarried women, 500 percent, illegal drug use, 6,000 percent; and yet math and science scores are down 10 percent. "It's a record we as Christians should be terribly ashamed of," he said.

Judy Eisenstat, a mother of two, had no objection to evolution being taught as theory, but expressed concern that it was being taught as fact and her children were actually beginning to believe it. To her, it was an issue of choice not only between God and a heartless, amoral system, but between life as it is and those who seek to "perfect" the human situation according to their own wishes and, like Hitler before them, try to build a superior race. Why not let our children hear another point of view, instead of a theory that tells them that life is all about the strong prevailing over the weak? "There are no superior races," she said; "we are all children of God." Countering her, Hugh Hanlin, a professor of biology, quoted Joseph Campbell, the mythologist, who said that every religion is true when understood metaphorically, but you are in trouble if you start thinking that metaphors represent facts. "One does not have to reject God to accept science," Hanlin said. "I have been a scientist for thirty years and I have known very few atheists."

The discussion found two dramatic high points, one when Francesca Pataro, a Unitarian, declared that her children had been ridiculed in school for being non-Christians. "It can be very difficult to be a minority religion in this country," Pataro said, her voice shaking. "[My children] have been told that they will go to hell because Jesus Christ is not their savior." Pataro went on to say that the creation stories of Christians, Native-Americans, Buddhists, Muslims, Hindus all have value and should be taught in the history or comparative religion classroom. "But creationism," she said, firmly, "is not a science."

Yet if Pataro pleaded for tolerance as a member of a besieged minority, Wilson was just as emphatic in claiming the same status for his own people. "I am the infamous Glenn Wilson," he announced, clearly enjoying the attention that had made him something of a local celebrity. "I would like everyone to look around. Tonight we are doing what is not allowed in the science classrooms of this school or any other school in this county. We are comparing ideas and deeply held beliefs." Gathering steam, Wilson then couched his argument in the language of a patriot. "It is not illegal to present an opposing view. It is fully American. It is why I served this country for seventeen years in the United States Navy. I put my life on the line so that others could express their opinion."

Through the entire proceeding, sitting quietly to the side of the school board members, William Burkhalter, the board's attorney, scribbled notes, knowing that when all was said and done, the members would turn to him for an expert judgment on a key piece of the argument: Was it legal? Was there any way for the school board of Aiken County to add creation science to the biology curriculum, satisfying the wishes of so many who saw in that story an issue of sacred significance? Or would that other piece of "scripture," the Constitution, as sacred to some Americans as the Bible is to others, trump their wishes?

As a non-Christian, Francesca Pataro, forty-two, says she's always felt like an outsider in Aiken. Shown here with her children Aili (left), six, and Keelan (right), nine, Pataro attends the local Unitarian church. "People here say, 'I'll pray for you,' and I say, 'Thank you. All prayers are helpful.'"

VI

Evolution was well established in the years leading up to the trial of John Thomas Scopes in 1925. It had become accepted among scientists, social scientists, and even many theologians. References derived from it had entered the language. By the late nineteenth century, even the Constitution, so often referred to as a machine in the days of Jefferson, was being described as an organism, in the process of adapting and evolving, improving with age. But the twenties was a tumultuous decade, the era which thrust America deep into the social turmoil of the twentieth century, and during this time evolution, serving as a kind of metaphor for all the confusion and turmoil that came with the new age, would become a favorite target of those who wished to hold back the onslaught of modernism.

The "Age of Invention," which played out over the forty-some years leading up to 1920, had focused people on the wonders of science and technology and provided excitement about a society made by men for men. It began in 1877, when Thomas Edison created the first phonograph — a machine that could "talk." But that was only the first of a series of creative triumphs that included the telephone, the motion picture camera, the automobile, the airplane, and the radio. The sense of the machine shop as a place of solemn acts gave a new cast to science, albeit practical science, that actually allied it with the heavens. It appeared that no problem was too big for science, no job too large for technology. And the fact that so much of the new science — this transformative science — was being practiced on American soil reawakened that never long forgotten feeling among Americans that their land was the new Eden, American man, the new Adam.

But, however proud one might be of it, the mere news of an invention could never be more than a miracle in a distant lab and it took until the 1920s before all of those same wonders became part of the lives of ordinary people. With the twenties, the automobile became affordable and available; the first motion picture theaters graced the main streets of towns large and small; radio connected communities through the magic of the ether; and at country fairs barnstorming pilots, local Lindys, gave rides through the clouds.

The social upheaval that followed these developments was dramatic, and unexpected. The automobile took people out of the small towns where they saw new sights and heard new ideas; the motion pictures and the radio gave them new and often titillating forms of entertainment; and the airplane encouraged a particularly brazen form of hubris: since the beginning of time man had dreamed of soaring like the birds and now, thanks to his own ingenuity, he was. The new technologies sped up the economy and created a new consumer culture, championed by new and brasher forms of advertising, urging people to abandon their old frugal ways and buy, buy, buy. Almost overnight, Americans went from a life deeply connected to the wonders of nature and an omnipotent God to an artificial environment, throbbing with the creations of man. Looking back on it, it seems only logical that there had to be a backlash.

"The world broke in two," said the novelist Willa Cather of this time, and she was right. For all the excitement of the new age, one could not be unaware of what was being left behind, particularly if you were one of those being left behind, and there were many in America in the mid-1920s who felt that the new age had nothing for them. Where the cities were centers of prosperity and excitement, the farms, anticipating the general economic collapse that would befall the world a few years later, were already in depression. For all those who were thrilling to the new age and its technological marvels, there were just as many who were experiencing it in fearful terms: as a decline of morality, an abandonment of nature, a loss of humanity, an affront to God. "When a mother can turn on a phonograph with the same ease that she applies to the electric light," the great march king, John Philip Sousa, had remarked a decade or so earlier, voicing the anxiety that accompanied technology, "will she croon her baby to slumber with sweet lullabies or will the infant be put to sleep by machinery?" Cather and others wrote of the "vanishing virtues of the Great Plains."

The divide separated Americans on many fronts: urban from rural, old-line American from new immigrant, the elite centers of learning from the anti-intellectuals, and fundamentalist Christians (the term itself was coined in 1921, in a defensive posture) from "modernist" Christians, those who, in the eyes of the traditionalists, had compromised their religion by finding ways to reconcile theology with the findings of science.

In north Jersey: Mining the artifacts of America's "hero" scientist

Thomas Edison (above) in the West Orange chemistry lab, 1904. Right, researchers Robert Rosenberg (left) and Paul Israel, in the same lab ninety-seven years later. To relieve the pressure of long hours at work, Edison and his lab staff sometimes challenged one another to see who could produce the most voltage with a hand-cranked generator.

Deep inside a five-thousand-square-foot concrete vault, buried below the streets of West Orange, New Jersey, lie the artifacts of one of history's greatest inventors: the notebooks, sketches, patents, contracts, correspondence, invoices, prototypes, and blueprints of Thomas Alva Edison and his legendary "invention factory." The collection, some of which remains undisturbed since Edison's death in 1931, includes tens of thousands of artifacts and 5 million pages of notes. It forms a long and winding trail to the mind of the man Americans once called the "Wizard of Menlo Park." Bob Rosenberg, the director of the Thomas A. Edison Papers Project, which since 1978 has been entrusted to sort through these dusty archives, says he knew relatively little about Edison when he agreed to come here eighteen years ago. He knows more now. But both he and Paul Israel, his longtime colleague on this endeavor and the author of a definitive volume, *Edison: A Life of Invention*, say they have a long way to go to fully understand the subject that has become their life's work. Their estimated date for completion is sometime in 2017.

In Edison, the historians have chosen a subject whose image has been well kneaded by legend and worship. In the late nineteenth century, as his reputation as an inventor of genius began to take flight, Tom Edison had been seen as something of a mysterious figure, an alchemist scheming in a laboratory, in touch with "supernatural forces" then so unfamiliar one Catholic periodical ventured that he was the incarnation of Satan himself. But once the stream of machines began to pour forth from his first major laboratory at Menlo Park, New Jersey (the phonograph, electric light, and an improved telephone were all invented there), and people discovered them to be the kinds of inventions that brought them exciting new conveniences — extending the day, saving labor, and affording new forms of entertainment and communication — Edison became nothing less than the benevolent god of the modern world, his work believed to be establishing new rules of nature, his notebooks, the "Edisonian Book of Genesis." Edison's coworkers even described his laboratory, which loosely resembled a New England clapboard chapel, as "the tabernacle." But the place where the snow-crested inventor's freshly burnished image really shone was in the popular imagination.

Encouraged, in part, by Edison himself, who was a terrific self-promoter, the public that had once shied from him grew to see Edison as an American hero, his story as something for the national folklore. Parents exhorted their children to follow his credo of hard work, perseverance, and exploration. By the 1920s, Edison had become an American senior statesman, the Midwestern country boy who, along with his friend Henry Ford, built the modern American city and its vibrant, new, electric culture. Indeed, by the twenties, Edison could witness the extraordinary impact of his labor: cities lit by his light, the sounds of a booming music industry created by his phonograph, a whole new form of popular culture — movies — established by his motion picture camera, grinning back from marquees. Death did not diminish his reputation; it enhanced it. By the mid 1930s, polls ranked Edison's popularity near that of Jesus, Lincoln, Washington.

For young boys in particular, the best part of the Edison legend was its adventurous beginnings, with the young Edison leaving home to ride the rails, selling candy and newspapers while setting up a small lab for electrical experiments in the baggage car. But the essence of Edison's broader appeal was that he had not simply been a "scientist"; he was a peculiarly *American* scientist: because he was largely self-taught, he appealed to that innate American appreciation for the amateur; because he worked 112 hour weeks (and punched a clock just like the other workers), he confirmed the Yankee spirit for diligence and industry; because he focused his work on *applied* science — inventions which had a future in the marketplace — at the expense of the theoretical, he separated his discoveries from those that shattered popular values and beliefs. In fact, Edison derided scientists who spent their lives "studying the fuzz on a bee" as morally suspect and complained when one of his sons began to pursue theoretical physics ("He may go flying off into the clouds with that fellow Einstein, but if he does, I'm afraid he won't work with me . . .").

By studying patents and drawings, ledger entries, and, especially, unbound scraps of paper upon which Edison and his associates recorded ideas in the midst of research, Rosenberg and Israel have exposed some of the innocent fictions that have developed around the Edison story and slowly given human form to a figure who had long been left to caricature. Yet, amazingly, the man they have discovered is no less impressive (so naturally gifted, he is the "Mozart" of invention, says Rosenberg) and perhaps even more representative of the national ethos. While Europeans have always considered invention a refined occupation, in America it was a utilitarian activity, inspired by necessity and dedicated to results. The need to improvise on farms that were a long distance from the nearest city may have been one reason for this humble, yet creative, approach, but even the American telegraph system grew haphazardly, "like a weed," says Rosenberg, an "ugly" network that had one redeeming characteristic: it worked. The papers have revealed Edison to be perhaps the most representative figure of a technological style in the belief that if science is not serving man it is not worth pursuing. "Edison insisted that you have to make an invention work in real life," says Rosenberg. "You have to be able to manufacture it in a way that allows you to repair it and you have to be able to make it cheap enough that people can afford it."

By the 1970s, Edison's name had dropped down on the list of America's most admired, replaced by sports stars and rock musicians. But, perhaps because the waning days of the twentieth century and the first days of the twenty-first have defined a new "age of invention," one as dynamic and transforming as the one that occurred over a hundred years ago, interest in Edison has recently skyrocketed. The inventor's laboratory in West Orange is visited by sixty thousand people yearly and Bob Rosenberg says that the Edison Papers Project's website receives nearly a thousand visits daily, a tribute to the lasting impact of an American original. Before Edison, the image of the machine was as a behemoth, enslaver of men; with Edison, the machine became a slave itself, to man and his mind, an extension not of the muscles, but of the brain, from which naturally followed every major technological event, including the computer. "Edison," says Rosenberg, "was quite simply the best inventor who ever lived."

The world's first film studio, Black Maria, built by Edison in West Orange in 1892. The studio featured a retractable roof and was mounted on a revolving pivot for constant repositioning to receive direct sunlight. Its earliest surviving copyrighted film is Fred Ott's Sneeze, *a recording of an Edison employee sneezing comically for the camera.*

As much for convenience as for conviction, the traditionalists seized upon evolution as the stage upon which to join battle, and to speak for them they had one of the greatest orators in American political history, William Jennings Bryan.

Known variously, through his distinguished political career, as the "Great Commoner" and the "Boy Orator of the Platte," Bryan had chiefly been associated with reform movements in the late nineteenth and early twentieth centuries, when he had championed women's suffrage, a federal labor department, an end to capital punishment, and in general, the causes of "the people" who to Bryan were, more often than not, farmers. Author Edward Larson, whose book on the *Scopes* trial is the definitive work on the subject, has suggested that Bryan was responsible for more constitutional amendments than anyone but the American founders. And in fact, the portly politician with his alpaca suits and string ties, held a combination of beliefs which, while not unusual for the time, would read like a contradiction today: at once forward looking in his enthusiasm for liberal reforms, and yet provincial in his glorification of the farm and traditional religious values. Bryan often employed religious symbolism to his cause (historians have compared him to Martin Luther King, Jr., in this respect), and he was not the only politician who did. "We stand at Armageddon," declared Teddy Roosevelt, the Progressive party's candidate for president in 1912, "we battle for the Lord."

Bryan's most famous campaign before *Scopes* was his 1896 fight against the gold standard, which he believed to be the tool of the Eastern capitalist establishment strangling the farmers of the West. In so doing, he effectively tapped into two deeply held American feelings — that nagging fear of distant power wielded sinisterly and the sense of America (here, rural America of the West) as a place of purity always in danger of being sullied by immoral interests of others. The campaign against the gold standard took Bryan all the way to the Democratic party convention in Chicago where, grabbing the nomination for president, he uttered one of the most famous lines in all American political history, one that dripped with biblical allusion. "You shall not press down upon the brow of labor this cross of thorns," he thundered at the Republicans. "You shall not crucify mankind upon a cross of gold."

The 1896 election, which pitted William McKinley against Bryan, was certainly the most significant since the Civil War and a turning point of its own. The Republicans, standing for the interests of a growing metropolitan America, defeated Bryan and his rural Democrats in a rout. In the years that followed, Bryan never strayed from his theme that urban industrial America was a threat to the farmer and his way of life. Yet by the twenties, with his political career behind him, Bryan began using his

"The majority is not trying to establish a religion or to teach it — it is trying to protect itself from the effort of an insolent minority to force irreligion upon the children under the guise of teaching science. What right has a little irresponsible oligarchy of self-styled 'intellectuals' to demand control of the schools of the United States?"

— William Jennings Bryan

more than two hundred speeches a year and his regular weekly columns in small-town newspapers to focus on another demon: Darwin.

Bryan did not object to evolution in general. In fact, much like Glenn Wilson and others in Aiken who support his cause, he welcomed the idea as "theory." But he saw in it two issues consistent with his defense of the downtrodden masses, two issues which resonate deeply with twenty-first-century America. For one, he believed that the insistence of the evolutionists on inserting their arguments into the American education system was patently undemocratic. "The real issue is not what can be taught in public schools, but who shall control the education system," he said. "The hand that writes the check rules the school." Bryan's other objection was a far graver issue: the acceptance of evolution as fact was dangerous, for its doctrine of natural selection and the "survival of the fittest" invited a belief in eugenics, defended predatory business practices, and even justified war.

The enthusiasm for science at the turn of the century had indeed spawned a movement that advocated applying rational control over the reproductive process and hence the very path of evolution. After all, if everything else was being improved by science, why not the human species itself? "We stand on the brink of an evolutionary epoch whose limits no man can possibly foretell," pronounced Ellsworth Huntington, a professor at Yale and the president of the American Eugenics Society, ". . . consciously and purposefully [selecting] the types of human beings that will survive." Racism was an implicit theme in the eugenics movement, whose members spoke derisively of the "fecundity of mediocrity" and advocated enforced sterilization of the mentally retarded. But so, interestingly, was morality. Science could be used to erase all the flaws of the human species, the eugenicists claimed, allowing for the perfectibility of man, and the true path to righteousness. "Had Jesus been among us," claimed Albert E. Wiggam, a eugenicist and author, "he would have been the president of the First Eugenics Congress."

Evolution had been taught in Tennessee's schools for some time, and without challenge, when the state legislature, in January 1925, went beyond Bryan and considered a bill that would actually declare a prohibition upon "the teaching of any theory that denied the biblical story of creation or the theory that human beings had descended from a lower order of animal." But Bryan had made the subject such a touchstone for argument nationwide and such a folk movement had built up around it, the people rallying to his side now saw the issue as "them" or "us." Ten times as many children were attending high school in 1920 as in 1890; five times more than 1910. The Tennessee law was passed by a margin of four to one to protect them from the intellectuals, the specialists, the urbanites. "Save our children for God," shouted one Tennessee senator.

While he was the son of a socialist and an agnostic and he objected to the antievolution law, Scopes, twenty-four, appears to have had little sense of the important role he would play in American legal and religious history. He was Dayton High's football coach and, in addition, a member of the science faculty, but he was teaching biology in May 1925 only because the regular biology instructor had been ill. Scopes would not have declared such a public challenge to the law on his own and, ironically, he most likely would not have been so publicly challenged for ignoring it either. Tennessee governor Austin Peay had hoped that the whole issue, once aired, would just go away. But with the growing tension between modernists and traditionalists, the American Civil Liberties Union had taken up the cause of academic freedom and, encouraged by a local businessman and evolutionist who was outraged by the Tennessee statute and by a handful of Dayton's civic leaders who saw the spectacle of a trial as a way to bring attention to a farm town in decline, they convinced Scopes to be their test case. When Bryan, and Clarence Darrow, an acknowledged agnostic and celebrated trial attorney, were then brought to Dayton to lock swords over Scopes's fate, the attention of the nation came with them.

"The origin of what we call civilization is not due to religion but to skepticisms . . . The modern world is the child of doubt and inquiry, as the ancient world was the child of fear and faith."

—Clarence Darrow

The legal issue in the trial was whether the state of Tennessee had the right to establish Dayton's school curriculum, but Jefferson's delicate balance between church and state was never far from the discussion. Bryan argued that if the state must not be used to promote religion, it followed that the state must not be used to attack religion either. Still, to the great masses it was a morality play. This was God holding off man; the steady past resisting the mysterious future; the little guy standing up to the monied elites; the farm scolding the city. And the temperature rose considerably with the arrival of Darrow. Only the year before, he had defended two brilliant teenagers, Nathan Leopold and Richard Loeb, who, as advocates of German philosopher Friedrich Nietzsche's belief that some "superior" people are beholden to no moral law, set out to commit the "perfect crime" by murdering a fourteen-year-old schoolboy in Chicago. Using a psychiatric defense and questioning whether right and wrong can ever be definitively determined, Darrow stunned the courtroom and impressed the judge enough to reduce the two boys' sentence from death to life imprisonment.

As effective as Darrow could be, Bryan had an even more tormenting opponent in H. L. Mencken, the Baltimore journalist who covered the trial for the sheer delight, he later said, of holding Bryan and the fundamentalists up to ridicule. Mencken was a true believer in the eugenics movement and an unabashed devotee of social Darwinism whose cyni-

In the rural midwest: Jefferson's "farm" gets fitted with new genes

Francis Alexander's 1822 painting Ralph Wheelock's Farm, *a depiction of the idealized pastoral life that Thomas Jefferson favored, left. Above, Mandy, whose calf was the first-ever clone of a dairy animal sold at auction. Opposite page, the "postmodern" farm, Infigen's tissue cell culture workstation, where cloned embryos are made in a process that splices harvested unfertilized eggs with cells from the adult animal's ear.*

Travelers driving along a certain country road in southern Wisconsin will notice nothing unusual about the farm they pass: just one hundred acres of corn, beans, and alfalfa, and a weathered red dairy barn, with Holstein cattle grazing in the surrounding meadow. Inside the barn, too, things look rather typical for such a rural setting: rows of rubber-matted stalls where the cows munch their feed while hooked up to a state-of-the-art pipeline milking system. This is Wisconsin, after all: a place where dairy farms are as common as the infamous Green Bay Packer "cheeseheads." But the scene is somewhat deceptive. "The animals look normal because they are normal," insists Greg Mell, the farm's livestock manager, acting just a bit disingenuous. "They're perfectly normal clones."

The farm is one of seven operated by Infigen, a biotechnology firm in rural DeForest, Wisconsin (population, 6,656), that specializes in animal cloning and other modern genetic techniques, a business that is at once so commercially competitive and morally charged, the company protects the farms' exact locations in the interest of "bio-security." Back in 1996, Scottish embryologist Ian Wilmut led the first successful animal cloning experiment when he made a genetic duplicate of a Finn Dorset sheep at his lab near Edinburgh and christened the newborn lamb "Dolly." Partly because the procedure suggested that a human clone was both possible and likely, Dolly unleashed an avalanche of opinions on the moral implications of the procedure. Yet despite such handwringing, cloning soon became a growing business for corporations like Infigen, which hope that the biotech "farm of the future" will lead to an avalanche of profits. Infigen produced its first clone, a bull calf named (they just couldn't resist) "Gene," in 1997, shortly after Dolly. Then the company cloned a prize dairy cow and sold the clone at auction in October 2000, for $82,000 (the same cow's non-cloned embryos sold for $25,000 and less). Ever since, Infigen has been attracting considerable attention, particularly from dairy farmers eager to duplicate their highest-producing animals. "We've got more work than we can handle," says Dr. Michael Bishop, Infigen's president. Indeed, by early 2002, Infigen had cloned more than 170 cows and eighty pigs.

From the very beginning, the American identity was tied to nature, and more specifically, the farm. Thomas Jefferson and George Washington were gentleman farmers, as committed to the land as to the principles of reason that governed the Age of Enlightenment. At Mount Vernon, Washington was an early innovator in crop rotation and the use of fertilizers, and he took great pride in the quantities of wheat he sold on the European market. Jefferson's passion for agriculture at Monticello and his five other Virginia farms is legendary. There, he experimented with figs and olives, grew thirty eight varieties of peaches, and was dedicated to cultivating rice, which he imported from as far away as Africa and Indonesia.

Jefferson hailed American small farmers as the bedrock of American democracy, "the chosen people of God . . . whose breasts He has made His peculiar deposit for substantial and genuine virtue." Europe, he offered, was destined to decline further into the evils of tyranny, but the land would save America from such a fate. There was just so much of it here, "courting the industry of the husbandman," nourishing him to a more virtuous way of life that would in itself ensure the triumph of free government.

To Jefferson, the redeeming aspect of the agrarian life was its stress upon independence. Other professions might be more profitable, but they lacked the purity of farming and put man in a dependent relationship with his fellow man, and dependence, Jefferson wrote, "begets subservience and venality, suffocates the germ of virtue, and prepares fit tools for the designs of ambition." In contrast, farming put man into relationship with nature first, and, in turn, with the divine creator.

Inspired by Jefferson's thinking, Americans have made the farm the national homestead. For most of the 1800s, America was truly a nation of farms. As late as 1900, 42 percent of Americans still lived on farms, and even as the percentage declined (to 25 percent by 1930, and 1.9 percent in 1992), popular culture — *Oklahoma, Lassie, Little House on the Prairie*, the pitchfork-holding man and woman in Grant Wood's *American Gothic* — continued to burnish the legend. In spirit, if not in fact, the farm has always been part of the American ideal.

Yet the distinctive American respect for nature has always competed with an equally powerful need to exploit the natural world for man's benefit. When Jefferson idealized the farmer, he was championing both nature and man's ability to use nature to his purpose. He insisted that it was in this interrelationship between the primitive and the civilized, between a natural world and a world shaped by the hand of man, that a better society would grow. By that thinking, biotechnology becomes just another statement of the "frontier" spirit Frederick Jackson Turner described in 1893, a step into the wilderness, a forest waiting to be cleared. But what happens to the old Jeffersonian image of the farm as a pure expression of divine nature, when its very essence can be manipulated by genetic engineering? Is it still God's work or is it man's? Is it still "nature"? "Life, long thought of as God's handiwork, more recently viewed as a random process guided by the 'invisible hand' of natural selection, is now being re-imagined as an artistic medium with untold possibilities," wrote Jeremy Rifkin recently, the author whose critique of the industry has led some to call him the Ralph Nader of biotechnology.

That certainly is how Infigen's high-tech dairy "farmers" see it. (Infigen's name stands for "infinite genetics" — every cloner's dream.) The company is one of several developing cows whose milk would contain special proteins to fight a variety of diseases. Think of a large pharmaceutical factory that consumes enormous amounts of natural resources and emits smelly effluents, says Bishop; now imagine it being replaced by a cow. Bishop expects just such an animal, able to produce $300 million worth of vital pharmaceuticals alone, by about 2009. A herd of cattle could provide therapeutic proteins for the entire world market.

In what would be an even more stunning development, Infigen has also been genetically modifying pigs to make their hearts, lungs, and kidneys compatible with human physiology. Once the next hurdle is passed — altering the surface receptors of the organs so that the human body will not reject them — Infigen and its rival companies look forward to raising herds of pigs whose bodies can be "harvested," providing a steady supply of replacement organs for humans. And while the crops on Infigen's farms are of the standard varieties (a more traditional farmer rents much of the farmland), scientists in other regions of the country have been genetically altering corn, soybeans, tomatoes, and many other crops to make them disease-resistant. In a deft marketing twist, biotech concerns are even encouraging farmers to think of seeds and pesticides as chemical "soulmates." Monsanto not only makes the herbicide Roundup, but "Roundup Ready" seeds, which are genetically altered to protect their plant, and only their plant, from the chemical, thereby creating a Roundup customer for life.

In developing this new frontier, scientists have created enough genuine freaks to inspire considerable concern. There have been warning signs of the potential for catastrophe, too, such as the Australian scientists who, in 1998 and 1999, while experimenting on mice, accidentally created a virus that wiped out their whole stock of rodents, leading to speculation about the possibility of such a rogue virus — perhaps one that has similarly lethal effects on humans — getting loose in nature. Jeremy Rifkin has warned that biotech entrepreneurs could unleash "a biological Tower of Babel" and "the spread of chaos throughout the biological world, drowning out the ancient language of creation." But Dr. Bishop of Infigen thinks much of the criticism is

overblown and is itself a by-product, ironically, of the national shift away from agrarian values. Bishop was born and raised on a farm, unlike most of those, he says, who critique his work, and that has led him to see biotechnology as an extension of the breeding process farmers have been employing for centuries. "A lot of people have forgotten where food comes from," he says. "They are so removed from America's agricultural roots, they think it comes from the grocery store rather than from animals and plants. To me, as a trained geneticist, transferring a gene into the makeup of an animal is simply a faster way of migrating that gene through breeding, which would otherwise take decades."

cism tweaked the sensibilities of the devout and the progressive alike. Yet it was Mencken's version of *Scopes* that first went down in the history books, Mencken's vision of Bryan as an intolerant boob, reactionary in his old age, that made it onto the big screen with *Inherit the Wind.*

The American eugenics movement had long fizzled out, a victim of its own oppressive notions, when the rise of Adolf Hitler, history's most famous devotee of Friedrich Nietzsche, and his vision of a superrace put an even more sinister cast on the idea as a strategy for human "improvement." But seventy-five years later some of the same themes that inspired Bryan to defend the Tennessee statute banning the teaching of evolution have emerged in the discussions over research in genetics.

While he firmly believes in evolution, Dr. Alan Roberts, seen here, agrees with those devout Aikenites who say that modern science is raising complex questions that demand a fresh moral framework. "Is there such a thing as 'sanctity of life,'" he asks, "and how far should we go to preserve it?"

"What worries me most," says Alan Roberts, a physician and author of the ethics curriculum at the Medical College of Georgia, across the Savannah River from Aiken, "is that our ethics have not caught up with our technology." He is waving a copy of the standards of the American Medical Association, which he considers to be hopelessly outdated; then again, what isn't in a world where in just a few years the speed of research has put us face to face with the awesome responsibility inherent in changing human nature itself? The "old" eugenics was Hitler, says Roberts. He describes the syphilis experiments the American government conducted on blacks at Tuskegee in the 1930s and the involuntary sterilization of the mentally retarded authorized by statutes in twenty-some states until the 1940s as examples of America's own abuse of its citizens' rights. Roberts acknowledges that American society has moved away from such practices. "I think the Nuremberg trials and the [awareness of the] Holocaust were the beginning of the change," he says. But he sees a "new" eugenics coming, in the willingness to allow parents to choose the eye color of their baby, to advertise for an egg donor with "good soccer skills," and the host of challenging questions raised by gene therapy. On the one hand, gene manipulation offers the opportunity to wipe out disease; on the other, it could meddle with the human condition. We now have the power to identify fetuses with birth defects in time to abort them, and, as time passes, we will be able to know more and more about the genetic makeup of an emerging child, in effect allowing for what the eugenicists of the twenties dreamed of, control over the evolutionary process itself.

Roberts refers to a group of scientists who recently requested the opportunity to work with bone fragments of Abraham Lincoln's skull in order to extract his DNA and determine if the sixteenth president suffered from a rare disease called Marfan's syndrome (the proposal is still under consideration); he outlines the emerging field of xenotransplantation, the science of moving organs from one species to another, as demonstrated in the practice of genetically designing pigs so that they can provide an inexhaustible reserve of needed hearts, livers, and kidneys to human beings; and he speaks, of course, of the shimmering ethical mysteries inherent in the sensational world of cloning. ("This will be the biggest leap for mankind," one biotech entrepreneur told *Wired* magazine in 2001, "the [Christian] promise of eternal life!") How, Roberts asks, can we address such advances without consulting a moral framework? "We can't let the technology run us . . . We have to run the technology."

> **"Evolution can be very cruel . . . If we could make better human beings by knowing how to add genes, why shouldn't we do it?"**
> JAMES WATSON
> *Codiscoverer of the structure of DNA*

VII

It was a misty evening in early January 2001, the first month of the new century and the new millennium, when Glenn Leonard Wilson, "FBI" hat in hand, climbed into his 1999 green Chevrolet Prizm and drove the two miles from his house on Silver Bluff Road to the administrative offices of the Aiken Public Schools for yet another meeting of the Aiken County school board. As he passed the Shoney's and the McDonald's, the Target store and the Aiken Mall, Wilson recited his speech to himself, wondering which flourish he might employ this time. Then, upon arriving, he took a seat in the front row and listened quietly as Chairman Bradley called the meeting to order.

> **"Once we set about remaking . . . normal genes, then we will have begun the task of remaking man . . ."**
> E. O. WILSON
> *Harvard biologist*

In an Aiken tradition dating back to 1873, school board meetings always begin with a prayer. Tonight it was led by assistant superintendent Nancy Smith, who followed it with an admonition based upon a passage from the Bible, Philippians 3:13, "Reach forward for what lies ahead." Smith then asked all to rise for a recitation of the Pledge of Allegiance. The board always does it in that order — the prayer first followed by the pledge, because that's how they see their obligation, first to God, then to America. Wilson stood, saluted the flag and then, with hand over heart, carefully enunciated each word of the pledge, emphasizing "one nation, under God."

Superintendent Linda Eldridge recognized a teacher and four female high school students from South Aiken High, whose magazine, *Calliope*, had recently been named the best high school literary magazine in South Carolina. They stood for a photograph. Two other teachers were acknowledged as "honored guests." And a football coach and his star player were congratulated for having been named, respectively, South Carolina's coach and player of the year.

Then, as always, Chairman Bradley opened the floor for community comment and, as always, Wilson stepped forward. Three months had passed since the open forum and so, aware that the board was still considering his motion, Wilson chose to focus his talk less on the evils of teaching evolution (though he did take a moment to liken it to slavery and racism), than to encourage the board to take its time before making a decision. He told them that it would take courage to resist the likes of the ACLU, but "it's time to end censorship" and allow the creation story to be told.

Next, Allen Dennis, a professor of geology at University of South Carolina–Aiken, went to the front of the room, to counter the creationist argument. The board looked visibly tired. They had spent so much time and effort on this subject and yet there seemed to be no end to the parade of people who wanted to speak their minds on it. Dennis reminded those in the room that a fragment of a dinosaur skull some 210 million years old had recently been found at SRS, and that the intersection of Martintown Road and I-20 is known as a fossil repository. He invited the board, and Wilson, too, to spend a Saturday with him to learn about fossils and geology. Wilson listened, smiled at Dennis's invitation, then arranged his things and got up to leave. He had made his points and been respectful to the others; now he wanted to get home to his children. But as Wilson started for the door, Bradley motioned to him. "You might want to stick around," he said.

Bradley next recognized William Burkhalter, the school board attorney, who slowly and carefully began to read a statement. "At the request of the Aiken County Board of Education, a comprehensive review of pertinent state constitutional, statutory, and regulatory authority was undertaken," he said. "This research has been focused on the request that the district science curriculum should teach both evolution and creationism or teach neither. Based on a thoughtful analysis of all such legal authority we find no reason to recommend any change." Wilson audibly sighed. "To teach neither," Burkhalter continued, "clearly fails to follow the minimum requirements and testing standards provided for school districts in South Carolina by the State Board of Education. To teach both, would unequivocally violate the constitutional mandate that public school maintain neutrality regarding matters of religion, as concluded by numerous Supreme Court and federal cases which have dealt decisively with these issues."

Wilson planted his right hand on his forehead and looked around at the gathering in amazement. But Burkhalter's report contained more. Citing the legal history of the issue, the attorney retold *Scopes* and the 1968 Supreme Court decision which found statutes like Tennessee's unconstitutional. He then cited all the various compromises that have been tried, including the teaching of creation science along with evolution (rejected in *Edwards v. Aguillard*, 1987), the offering of disclaimers at the outset of instruction saying that evolution is not intended to influence or dissuade biblical teaching (rejected in *Freiler v. Tangipahoa Parish Board of Educa-*

tion, 1999). He examined the idea that a prohibition of the teacher's right to teach creationism is an infringement of academic freedoms (dismissed in *Webster v. New Lenox*) and, finally, the argument that the ban on creation science was a violation of a teacher's right to free speech (also rejected, in *Peloza v. Capistrano Unified School District*). The High Court had been asked repeatedly to find a constitutional basis upon which creationism advocates could amend the teaching of evolution to promote their values and repeatedly the justices had come down on the side of those who wished to protect the schools from even a whisper of religious dogma. To challenge such a wealth of case law, said Burkhalter, would be foolhardy for it would mire the county in a protracted and costly legal battle that it would have little chance of winning.

Like so many American arguments, this one had its day in court, here at the Aiken County Courthouse. Wilson filed a grievance against the Aiken schools but it was dismissed by Circuit Judge Rodney Peeples. Wilson was undeterred. "This is a war between two opposing worldviews," he said, "theism and atheism."

Burkhalter's statement was met at first with silence, then a few members spoke, alluding to the difficulty of the decision and how they had prayed long and hard before coming to the conclusion that Wilson's appeal be denied. Finally, John Bradley himself entered the discussion. He had listened to just about everyone else in the county on this subject; now was his chance to speak. "This issue has been presented as a conflict between religion and science," he said, reading from a prepared text. "The proponents of creationism would have you believe that to accept the theory of evolution as viable is to reject the existence of God. This is not true. I have been a member of the Methodist church for more years than Mr. Wilson has been alive. I resolved my personal conflict between evolution and the biblical creation story when I was about ten years old. We must not allow our various religious beliefs to interfere with exposure to and examination of well-accepted ideas, some of which may be controversial."

Wilson hurriedly left the room, muttering that the surprise delivery of the announcement had been like "the attack on Pearl Harbor." But within a few minutes he had taken the board answer in stride and begun to think of new strategies. He would demand a formal hearing on the matter; he would file a grievance; he would take his argument to the people of the town — something, anything — to see to it that the fight continues. And indeed, one year later there he was again at 1000 Brookhaven Drive, listening to the prayer and reciting the pledge, waiting while a few laudatory remarks about school achievements were read. Then, when John Bradley asked for community comment, Wilson, text in hand, quietly walked forward. "We are in a moral crisis," he said, "the origin of which can be found in our high school biology classes . . ."

EMERGENCY DOOR

Highlands, North Carolina

In Europe, there are families that go back a dozen generations in the same house, but here people like to move along. The typical American will relocate twelve times before he dies, with each move averaging around 120 miles. Clay Creighton (far left), with hand raised, says that he has already lived in three "countries": "Oregon, Montana, and now, North Carolina." His fourth grade pal Nate Brooks (near left and in profile) has moved only once. But it was a "big" move, from the flatlands of Greenville, North Carolina, to the mountains of Highlands (population 1,112), a log cabin and swimming hole sort of place where each day Nate and Clay ride the bus to the local school, a 350-student institution that covers kindergarten through twelfth grade.

Q: *How is it different?*
Nate: Greenville was flat, very hot, and I only saw snow once. Down there the people were a lot easier to know, but you couldn't know a lot of them because, well, there are so many of them.
Q: *Which do you prefer, the mountains or the big city?*
Nate: The mountains, by far. Lots more snow, more fun. It's easier to ride your bike in the mountains because you got hills and stuff. You go up and you go down and take the force from going down the hill to start up the next one.
Q: *What are you and Clay talking about in the picture?*
Nate: About sports or Playstation or stuff like that.
Q: *So what does it mean to be an American?*
Nate: It means being able to start over again like I had to. At least that's what Littlejim said in a book by Gloria Houston that I read. It's about a boy who lived in the mountains, like me.
Q: *Anything else?*
Nate: Well, it's fun, that's for sure. And that's about all I have to say.

Racine, Wisconsin

It seemed at first glance like an open-and-shut case. The defendant, Timothy Ellison (center), a 40-year-old industrial engineer, acceded to the basic facts, that he had shot and killed Chad Pete, twenty-eight, early one morning on a street in Racine, Wisconsin, after an argument over whether Pete's girlfriend, Lisa Baker, could accompany Ellison on a fishing trip. The prosecution was confident but, as always, wary. In America, regardless of the strength of its case, the government is dependent upon convincing a body of independent-minded citizens whose sense of justice is by nature unpredictable. The notion of a trial by jury is not, of course, distinctively American. It goes back to the thirteenth century and the Magna Carta. But the authors of the Bill of Rights made that right "sacred" in the Sixth Amendment to the Constitution, along with the right to a speedy and public proceeding. At the heart of their concern was "the silent, powerful, and ever active conspiracy of those who govern." A corollary principle was the American value of centering decision making with "the people." "The common sense of twelve honest men," wrote Thomas Jefferson, "gives still a better chance of just decision, than the hazard of cross and pile." Yet even with such protections, says defense attorney Mark Nielsen (near left), the defendant enters a jury trial "behind the eight ball." The government has more resources. "They have the power of accusation. They get to start the process at a time of their own choosing, on a charge of their own choosing." The jury system is the great equalizer. "Once people who have nothing to do with the government get a hold of the case, then you've got your shot," says Nielsen. Here, the jury deliberated for nine hours before siding, to the surprise of many, with Ellison. While Pete was not armed, his threatening behavior and history of violence was enough to convince them that Ellison had acted in self-defense.

Near Goose Creek Bridge, Virginia

So much of the American story has been about leaving the past behind. The founders saw their work as a break with much of what came before them. America's preeminent businessman — Henry Ford — once famously remarked: "History is more or less bunk." But the Civil War is different, a "Rorschach blot," wrote author Tony Horwitz, in which Americans continue to find "all sorts of unresolved strife: over race, sovereignty, the sanctity of historic landscapes and who should interpret the past." For Neal Sexton (foreground, at far left), one of an estimated 20,000 Civil War reenactors nationwide, old tensions are best released by spending the weekend refighting the War Between the States. Sexton, thirty-one, is seen here in uniform on the way to the site of a skirmish that occurred in 1862 outside Unison, Virginia. "We do everything as authentically as possible," explains Sexton, a graduate student and salesman, who calls his attempts to recapture the past "living history." For some, that includes marching barefoot and subsisting on Civil War fare. "I was eating some boiled bacon," says Sexton of the photo here. "It wasn't very good." Sexton, whose ancestors fought for the Confederacy, says he is dedicated to "an even-handed portrayal of what went on." But whoever dons the blue or the gray, the real enemy is the threat of development. Seventy-one significant Civil War battlefields have already been plowed under for new homes and shopping malls. Sexton and others have responded by picking up their guns, peacefully. Along with other reenactors, he has participated in a succession of "Preservation Marches," which raise money to buy the sites and save them for perpetuity.

2 The Colossus

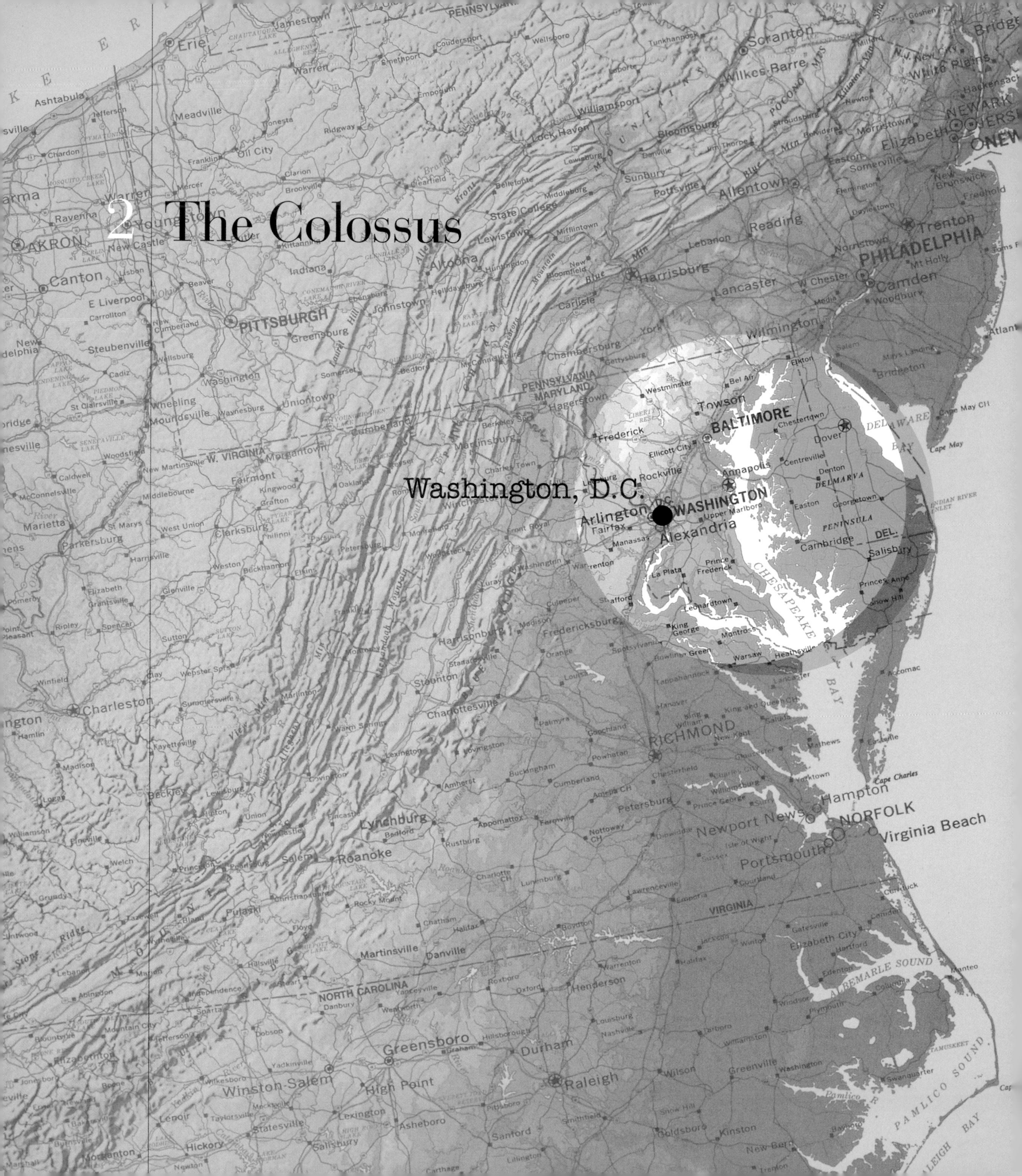

Stephen Moore remembers the moment as one of triumph and anticipation. On February 15, 2001, just twenty-six days after George Walker Bush entered the White House, the boyish, forty-one-year-old political activist was among those at the annual gathering of the Conservative Political Action Conference in Arlington, Virginia, just across the Potomac River from Washington. Rarely had so many of the nation's most active conservatives been in one place at one time, but there they were, thirty-five hundred of them in a mood of giddy excitement. In fact, not since 1994, when the Republicans gained control of the House of Representatives with a campaign defined by the "Contract with America," had conservatives been as filled with confidence as they were at this event. With the feeling that they now had one of their own as the new president, eager to inaugurate a new century in the name of Republican values, they seemed ready to put the bitterness of the 1990s behind them and redirect that considerable energy toward their own agenda. There were no "Where's Lee Harvey Oswald When You Need Him?" bumper stickers, as had been sold at this gathering in the Clinton years; no infighting among competing conservative factions as there had been when they were out of power. At the event's opening night, the mood was unanimously upbeat with speeches from the new vice president, Dick Cheney; from Georgia congressman Bob Barr; from Wayne LaPierre, the executive vice president of the National Rifle Association; and from David Keene, the leader of the American Conservative Union. Indeed, the excitement built with each address until, in a moment that whipped the largely male and nearly all-white crowd into a bubbling frenzy, Charlton Heston stood before them and, in his trademark chant familiar to every gun owner in the audience, raised a rifle over his head and bellowed: "From our cold, dead hands . . . From our cold, dead hands!"

By contrast, Moore's contribution was a punctuation mark, a subtle underscore. In this group, he was not a leader, but one of many faithful members of the tribe, and a man with a passion: tax reduction. Moore participated in a discussion, "Can the Republicans Keep Control of Congress?" but otherwise spent his time at the conference running the booth set up by his group, the "Club for Growth," passing out literature, displaying videos of political attack ads, and barking out tax-cut slogans to passersby as if he were a salesman at a trade show. Still, this event belonged as much to Moore and his fellow antitax advocates as it did to the gun lobby, the antiabortion lobby, the anti–gay rights lobby and administration officials like Cheney. Minutes before Charlton Heston arrived on stage, Steve Forbes, the two-time presidential candidate who had long argued for a "flat tax," addressed the gathering, labeling George Bush's proposal for a $1.6 trillion cut "very small" and calling for other, deeper cuts. "Let's go for broke!" he declared, an applause line which, delivered in Forbes's New Jersey accent, didn't quite match Heston's jungle call, but stirred the crowd nonetheless. Each of those in attendance may have come with a pet theme in mind, but taxes was a subject around which all these conservatives could unite. The hated "liberals" needed tax money to fund gun control; taxes to support the enforcement of the "gay rights agenda"; taxes to stop development and impose regulations on business; taxes to give bureaucrats power over the lives of ordinary Americans; taxes — and here was the overriding principle, line one in the group's catechism — *to grow the size of the federal government.*

In its two hundred-some years as the nation's capital, Washington has been the stage for a predictable battle: those who favor a strong national government against those who do not. When the Bush administration came to power, leaders of the "righteous right," as one local newspaper put it, toasted each other, above, in anticipation of "saddling up to meet the recalcitrant left."

During the campaign, the new president had said many times a tax cut would be the first big legislative statement of his administration, the hallmark of his "first hundred days," and the fact that he was now delivering on that promise only raised the volume of conservative cheers. Moore and the others knew well that every time the White House changes residents, and particularly every time it shifts from one party to the other, the first legislative package of the new presidency carries tremendous symbolic importance. With his proposal, Bush would either grab the imagination of the public and take it with him, much as Ronald Reagan did in 1981 with his 25 percent tax cut, or fail, as Jimmy Carter did with an energy conservation package in the first months of his presidency in 1977.

Some Democratic presidencies — Franklin Roosevelt's New Deal, Lyndon Johnson's Great Society — have successfully established an early bond with the nation by proposing a burst of new social spending. But these were different times. There was less patience with government "solutions" to social problems, and even if he only won the presidency by a whisker (and some Democrats would say that he didn't "win" at all), Bush was making it clear where he stood on that age-old American argument between federalists and states' rights champions; between those who look to Washington for their American identity and those who prefer to claim it in their own backyard. His father's roots might be in the soil of Washington bureaucracy, but this Bush was a Texas conservative to the core.

Indeed, if Bush learned one lesson from watching the presidency of his more politically moderate father, it was to devote more attention than the senior Bush did to the wishes of the conservative wing of his party. Everyone in the Arlington Marriott that night could have recited a "follow the money" capsule history of America in the last forty years, beginning with Democrat John Kennedy's tax cut (implemented in 1964, when the top rates hovered around 90 percent) through the "misery" of Richard Nixon's wage and price controls, the "stagflation" and double-digit interest rates of the Carter years, the much vaunted Reagan renaissance, and finally in the 1990s, when George Bush, Sr.'s capitulation to a Democratic Congress broke a campaign promise ("Read my lips: no new taxes") that many believed brought on the recession of 1992 and his defeat in that year's election. As they saw it, even the prosperity of the Clinton years was the work of Reagan's tax reform; thanks to the ruthless economic climate of the 1980s, American business was able to streamline and retool in a way that allowed it to respond to a new economy built around advancing technology.

The world's most famous presidential mansion was variously known as "the people's house" and the "presidential palace" before the most obvious name — White House — grew of its own simplicity from among the descriptions of the people who first saw it. Thomas Jefferson, its second occupant, added a wall; in 1818, James Monroe extended a fence around the entire grounds.

To the group gathered here, American history contained a consistent truth: the nation has thrived when it has restrained the "greedy hand" of government (Tom Paine's phrase), when it has resisted the urge to expand the federal bureaucracy, when it has followed Ronald Reagan's motto (borrowed, more or less, from Henry David Thoreau) that government is the problem, not the solution, and when it has cocked an ear to listen to the voices of the founding fathers. Hadn't Thomas Jefferson and James Madison spoken of the evils of a powerful and distant central authority, and vigorously opposed Alexander Hamilton's entreaties to grant the new federal government more power to tax, borrow, and spend? Hadn't they resisted Hamilton's attempts to create a national bank, certain that a bank would entangle the people's affairs at the expense of the states, making them beholden to the federal government just as the Colonies had been beholden to Britain's King George? Hadn't Jefferson and Madison's vision of freedom included an unfettered opportunity to

> **"Seen from Washington, America is a country of beginnings, of projects, of designs and expectations."**
>
> —Ralph Waldo Emerson, 1844

pursue personal wealth, meaning without the interference of government? And hadn't President Jefferson himself, after entering the White House in 1801 on the strength of a campaign to reform taxes, set the tone for a model presidency when he reduced the federal budget to $9 million (all but $2 million of that earmarked to pay down the debt), cutting the payroll from 130 employees to a mere sixty-five?

In America, the call to the founding fathers can be a dangerous business, for they defy modern political labels. Hamilton may have sounded like a modern-day Democrat when he argued to center power in the federal government but his pro-business fiscal policy would seem to tilt him more toward modern-day Republicans. Jefferson's small government rhetoric seems perfectly suited to a Republican convention, but his defense of human rights has always made him a hero to the Left. Jefferson himself veered from his small government manifesto when the pragmatist in him prevailed and he raised taxes to fund the Louisiana Purchase. Still, to the CPAC crowd, in this celebratory moment, there was no room for such nuance. To them, government was an object of suspicion, taxes the work of self-serving special interests, and that part of the twentieth century which produced the New Deal, the Great Society, the "Imperial Presidency," and, as they might call it, "a government of entitlements," was nothing more than a deviation from the founding fathers' plan for America, a long nightmare from which, gladly, the nation appeared to have finally awoken. Now, with America poised at the brink of a new century and the Republicans back in the White House, they stood here, on the riverbanks of the nation's capital, to reclaim the national voice. But would they?

For more than two centuries, the immense limestone campus known as Washington, D.C., has been held up to both reverence and scorn, praise and ridicule. And yet, more than any other single place, it has remained America's institutional statement of national purpose. Here the men and women of Congress have gathered solemnly to consider the American way of life, to execute the American way of democracy, and even, as George W. Bush would soon have to demonstrate, to conduct the American way of war. Here the nine members of the Supreme Court have sat in their ebony robes, parsing the 4,543 words of the Constitution, channeling themselves into the eighteenth-century mind of Madison, in particular, but really the minds of all thirty-nine signers, trying to divine the precise meaning of a document more durable than any other of its kind in modern history. And here have come the forty-two chief executives, from eighteen states, to sit, for better or worse, at the head of America's table, and, at the end of the day, to rest their often weary heads in the bedroom of the White House, the burden and the privilege of pre-

Outside Philadelphia: A "gigantic" salute to a revived "Old Glory"

In 1917, just seven months after President Woodrow Wilson called the country to war, ten thousand recruits at the Naval Training Station in Great Lakes, Illinois, took a break from their battle preparations to create a living flag, "the largest in the world," boasted the base newspaper. Eighty-some years later dozens of Downington, Pennsylvania, schoolchildren held on to a billowy eighteen-hundred-square-foot flag, right. "The first thing I think of," said Vietnam War veteran John Peachek, "are the guys who gave their lives for it."

Bunny Welsh is the fifty-seven-year-old sheriff of Chester County, Pennsylvania, the first female to hold that title, and without a doubt, Chester's biggest patriot. It was Welsh who spearheaded the two-year campaign to bring a thirty-by-sixty-foot flag to Downingtown, the county seat, in time for Memorial Day; Welsh who passed the bucket at football games to raise the $50,000 needed to take part in Flags Across America, a grass-roots campaign dedicated to putting giant flags in all 3,065 American counties. Then again, the flag is something sacred to Welsh and her town. "Marines raised the flag at Iwo Jima," she says proudly, "and I think of that every time I look at the flag."

The terrorists strikes of September 11, 2001, may have prompted many across the nation to display the Stars and Stripes with a new enthusiasm. Indeed, the force of those blows woke up countless Americans to the feeling, held off since the Vietnam War, that they are part of a national community ready to embrace as common a symbol as the flag. In Chester they've never doubted that. While self-conscious acts of patriotism were deemed jingoistic in some parts of the country, respect for the flag has always been strong in this old mill town. Here, they love "Old Glory."

The origin of the Stars and Stripes is a subject of debate. Betsy Ross, a Philadelphia upholsterer, is fabled to have designed and sewn the very first flag at George Washington's request. Yet while Ross did sew flags, she likely did not sew the first one, says Whitney Smith, a passionate, erudite "vexillologist" (he created the term — which combines the Latin root, *vexillum*, for banner, with the Greek *logy* for "the study of"). In fact, the Ross legend was unknown until 1870, when her grandson, William J. Canby, presented a paper to the Historical Society of Pennsylvania claiming the honor for her. Canby's tale caught on, says Smith, because people wanted a "great mother goddess of the American Revolution."

Some historians point instead to Francis Hopkinson, a signer of the Declaration Independence, as the flag's originator. Hopkinson designed the Great Seal of the United States, and there is evidence that he did indeed contribute to the flag's creation. In 1870, Hopkinson submitted two bills for his work to the Continental Congress, the first asking for a quarter casket of wine in exchange for eight items of "fancy work" that included the flag's design, and the second for $24 for his work on the flag alone. Congress, however, refused to pay him, arguing that too many hands (and perhaps those of Mrs. Ross) had gone into the design. On June 14, 1777, Congress gave its approval for the basic design, whomever the originator, and declared that the "flag of the United States be made of 13 stripes, alternate red and white; that the union be 13 stars, white in a blue field, representing a new constellation." But in fact, regiment flags were far more important to the Revolution than the American flag, which was not, as fictions have suggested, carried into battle. "In George Washington's day," says historian Scot Guenter, "the American eagle was much more common as a symbol than the flag."

Over the years, the story of the flag has followed the story of American history and in the process appeared in at least twenty-seven different versions. Once Vermont and Kentucky had joined the original thirteen colonies, two stars and two stripes were added. The fifteen-stripe and -star rendition was flown during the War of 1812 and was the inspiration for Francis Scott

Schoolchildren salute the flag in a picture taken around 1900.

Key's "Star-Spangled Banner." In 1818, when a Navy sea captain complained that additional stripes made the flag look unwieldy, President James Monroe signed a proclamation reducing the number of stripes back to thirteen. From then on the additions of stars were to be the only changes, symbolizing the ever-growing union. But these specifications were mere guidelines. Throughout the nineteenth century, the federal government had no specific rules about the positioning of the stars on the field of blue or the number of points on each star. The flags, their varying star patterns subject to the whims of its designer, developed into a type of folk art, and the homespun designs became collector's items.

It was a twenty-four-star version of the flag that Capt. William Driver carried on his ship when he sailed from Salem, Massachusetts, in 1831. Driver gave his flag the nickname "Old Glory" and it traveled with him twice around the world before he retired to Nashville in 1837, whereupon his wife repaired the cloth, and added new stars to bring it to thirty-four and an anchor to commemorate his service at sea. "Old Glory" became a legend throughout Nashville, for its endurance as much as its beauty, and a nickname was born.

Still, it took Abraham Lincoln and the Civil War to bring the American flag to national significance. In 1861, after the attack on Fort Sumter that opened the war, Hartford, Connecticut, declared the first "Flag Day," June 14. When the Confederate states seceded from the Union, Lincoln refused to remove the stars representing those states from the flag, and it became the symbol of a fragmented, wartorn nation. In 1863, a thirty-fifth star was added for the new state of West Virginia, a collection of several counties that refused to secede along with the rest of Virginia. Union soldiers boldly carried that flag into battle. The flag of the United States became a rallying point for the spirited North, and an object of derision for the South. When Union forces captured Nashville, sea captain Driver led them to the legendary "Old Glory," which he had sewn into a quilt for safekeeping. Captain Driver himself then climbed up the tower to hoist his beloved flag over the state capitol. Today, "Old Glory" is in the collection of the Smithsonian.

When the Civil War ended, the flag's popularity continued to grow, particularly in the North, as a sacred symbol of liberty, independence, and justice. "Its prose became poetry," offered historian George Henry Preble in 1880. In the 1890s, Flag Day became a national celebration and *Youth Companion*, a popular magazine for children, launched a campaign to have an American flag hanging in every school in the country by Columbus Day, 1892, the four-hundredth anniversary of Columbus's landing. Francis Bellamy, a former Baptist minister, wrote an ode, "The Pledge of Allegiance," to honor the event and urged all schoolchildren to recite it on that day.

As America's influence in the world grew, the flag's significance as a unifying symbol became more powerful. In 1918, another war — World War I — inspired new devotion to the flag and legislation to protect it. In Montana, a man was arrested for refusing to kiss an American flag; in Michigan, a man caught wiping his hands on a flag was assaulted by automobile workers who tortured him until he apologized. Flag sales soared during World War II, and in 1942, the U.S. government officially recognized the Pledge of Allegiance. Twelve years later, President Eisenhower added "under God" and announced the proper pledge etiquette: "stand upright, remove headdress, and place right hand over heart . . ."

By the 1960s, the flag became, to many, a symbol of conservative politics and defense of the American military policy in Vietnam. Youthful protesters wore flag shirts, painted cars in red, white, and blue and reconfigured the flag with a peace symbol in place of the stars or by displaying it upside down, the symbol of "distress." When Abbie Hoffman, the sixties radical, wore a flag shirt on the *Merv Griffin Show*, the network blacked out his image. But thirty years later, after the attacks of September 11, flag shirts, ties, earrings, and lapel pins offered an opposite message from Hoffman's: now as support for America and its core values. "September 11 made it safe for liberals to be patriots," wrote essayist George Packer in the *New York Times*.

"Memorial Day is not a holiday," proclaimed Bunny Welsh, as the Chester County ceremony started. "It's a *holy* day." Sheriff Welsh, her red, white, and blue scarf blowing softly in the breeze, then invited Chester's children to help her raise their enormous new flag. With a gust of wind, the flag snapped free and whipped in the wind. Then the jubilant sheriff called for quiet, and this disparate group of veterans, scouts, seniors, parents, and schoolchildren lifted their heads, put their hands on their hearts and began, "I pledge allegiance, to the flag, of the United States of America . . ."

serving, defending, and protecting the Constitution falling more to them than any other single man or woman.

America's other great cities developed around the pursuit of profit, but the original hundred-square-mile tract known as the District of Columbia was, uniquely among the world's great capitals, set aside for the single purpose of governing (it was reduced to sixty-nine square miles in 1846 when land was returned to Virginia). In our own time, as in Jefferson's, people come to Washington for essentially the same reasons: to join the national dialogue, to stake their claim to the founders' legacy, and to engage in an essentially creative act that can only be described, even 225 years out, as the making of a nation. You can hear the chattering as soon as you arrive at Reagan National Airport ("Washington," wrote Henry James, "is a city of conversation"), climb into a taxi and cross the Fourteenth Street Bridge, with Arlington National Cemetery, the resting place of national heroes, behind you and the rolling boulevards and sturdy grandeur of what may be America's most beautiful city up ahead. This is a place where even the cabdrivers sometimes debate tax policy and where the words of the founders, etched in monuments that can be seen out of every bureaucrat's and politician's window, echo with every act. Washington is home to 75,000 lawyers, 323,000 bureaucrats, 80,000 lobbyists, 525 legislators, and one president. And every morning, they rise from their beds to either execute policy or debate it, to etch their version of the national identity.

Proposals for a monument to George Washington were made long before there was a Washington, D.C., but they fell victim to that favorite capital pastime, delay. Finally, in 1848, construction began on the 555-foot, 90,854-ton marble obelisk that now stands as a symbol of the nation's capital. The monument was completed in 1884.

Just what is the role of government in the lives of a free and independent people? How should the responsibilities of that government be divided between a defining national center and institutions closer to the people they govern? What interest does Maine have in what goes on in Mississippi, the Great Plains in the morals of New York? What constitutes the common good and how much should government be entrusted to pursue it? Is it the business of government to right the inequities of society or leave them to the free market? In a democracy, how should the government bills be settled? Equally? Or according to the ability to pay? And, finally, whether at peace or war, who speaks for America? What sacred ideals define our shared vision?

Historians looking at the broad sweep of the American story have discovered that the answers to those questions have varied with the demands of the times. The cataclysmic events of the twentieth century called for a dynamic national center, dedicated to protecting the nation from the tyrannies eating up Europe and to establishing a coherent set of national values commensurate with a just and compassionate society. But the two World Wars were won, Communism was defeated, the enthusiasm for an aggressive social policy, directed from Washington, waned, and so, for much of the 1990s, Americans began looking at the federal government with the kind of scowl usually reserved for a house guest who has overstayed. It was a Democratic president, Bill Clinton, who declared, in 1996, that the "era of big government" was over. Indeed, to walk the streets of Washington at the outset of the twenty-first century, in the last innocent months before terrorism galvanized the nation, was to see a country in a mood to retreat to local and regional identities and to re-embrace its original antigovernment values.

II

On K Street, in offices they sublet from a law firm, Stephen Moore and the seven-member staff of the Club for Growth are like wolves in the sheep meadow. Moore helped establish the Club for Growth in late 1999 as a "renegade" organization dedicated to undermining the Washington establishment and — he sweeps his hand in the direction of K Street — "putting all these people out of a job." To that end, the group has spent its money and energy supporting candidates who support lower taxes or, to put it more accurately, to opposing candidates who do not want to cut taxes enough. Other conservative groups might chafe at New York senator Hillary Clinton and House leader Dick Gephardt; Moore's group goes after moderate Republicans. In 2000, the Club for Growth nearly unseated ten-term New Jersey Republican Marge Roukema, by running ads during the Republican primary which claimed that she was a closet Democrat. Indeed, ten of the sixteen candidates the Club for Growth actively backed that year were elected.

With the arrival of the new administration, Moore and his colleagues turned their energy to prodding those Republicans who might be tempted to resist full and unqualified support of President Bush. They ran television and radio advertisements in Vermont, for instance, that mockingly showed an actor posing as an IRS auditor thanking Sen. James Jeffords for having saved his job with his continued support for high taxes. They did the same in Pennsylvania and Rhode Island where Arlen Specter and Lincoln Chafee had expressed reservations about the size of the Bush tax cut. One of the group's favorite commercials, a spoof of the 1950s movie *The Blob*, showed an amorphous red "tax blob" enveloping the Capitol, then causing havoc on Main Street. A giant Club for Growth logo cut the invader off. "We're saving America from the Tax Blob," the ad proclaimed. "Will your congressman side with the taxpayers or the blob?"

Moore calls the American Revolution "the first great tax revolt in history," but he added that "we're refighting it now," attempting to erase a half-century of ingrained thinking on the relationship between the state and the individual. While he, like Forbes, believes that the Bush tax cut doesn't go deep enough, Moore insists that the symbolism of the cut is even more important than the amount. "All Washington debates come down to money," says Moore, and this one was a philosophical fight over the budget surplus produced by the prosperity of the nineties. The historic tendency had been for Washington to incorporate such windfalls into the operating budget and that, says Moore, was the kind of thinking that he and others want desperately to change. The most important message that Bush could deliver, said Moore, was one that could have come straight from Thomas Jefferson's lips: "That money doesn't belong to the federal government; that money is yours."

The city of Washington was born in a closed-door deal, so it only follows that its business would also thrive upon back-room strategizing. Here, Stephen Moore meets in the chambers of one key conservative congressman long after most of the Capitol has gone home to bed.

Stephen Moore has been conservative for as long as he can remember. While growing up in suburban Winnetka, Illinois, he watched his three older siblings fall under the spell of the liberal sixties, and witnessed the family fights over hair length, drugs, the Vietnam War (an older brother, who today runs a successful moving company in Chicago, still has a poster of Che Guevara on his office wall). But when Moore himself came of age in the seventies, the tide had already turned. Watching the gas lines and the rising interest rates, listening to Jimmy Carter and others talk about the need to recognize the depleting natural resources, Moore had an instinctive response: he saw the economic crisis of the seventies as avoidable; the depleting natural resources argument as specious.

One day in 1980, he walked into the economics department at the University of Illinois, where he was already an undergraduate, and asked if there was anyone who shared his point of view. To his surprise, Julian Simon, a world-renowned economist who had long argued that the free market would lead to greater and greater abundance, was teaching there. Soon, Moore became a disciple ("Like a member of his family") and when Simon went to the Heritage Foundation in Washington, D.C., Moore followed the economist east.

Simon, who died of a heart attack in 1998, was something of an intellectual guru to libertarians like Moore and a thorn in the side of the

> **" I heartily accept the motto, 'That government is best which governs least' . . . Carried out, it finally amounts to this, which also I believe, 'That government is best which governs not at all.'"**
>
> —Henry David Thoreau, 1846

Left. His message was simple: that the human intellect and spirit, when left unrestrained, was capable of unfathomable progress. History, Simon said, bore this out, and the future would prove no different. To demonstrate his faith in the free market, Simon made a thousand dollar bet in 1980 with Stanford biologist Paul Ehrlich that five key natural resources would become cheaper (and thus more available) over the next ten years — not more expensive, as Ehrlich had argued. Simon won — proving, he said, that progress is unstoppable.

After Simon's death, Moore took up his mantle. He even finished the writing of Simon's book, *It's Getting Better All the Time,* in which Simon — and Moore — demonstrated that life in America is immeasurably better today than it was a hundred years ago. Their message, however, wasn't in the "fact"; it was in the "why." Eschewing arguments that the growth of environmentalism, feminism, and social welfare were responsible for the vastly better conditions we live with today, the two economists contended instead that the world was a better place and the United States better by far because of the technological achievements of the entrepreneurial and inventive spirit brought forth by the growth of freedom in the twentieth century. Then they added a caveat: even America had shown regressive tendencies in supporting rising taxes and government spending. In other words, America succeeded despite — not because of — the statism of the twentieth century.

> "**Almost every great tragedy of the 20th century has been a result of too much government, not too little . . . unreasonable government control over the lives and liberties of the citizenry.**"
>
> Stephen Moore *and* Julian Simon
> It's Getting Better All the Time, *2001*

After working with Simon, Moore moved over to the Cato Institute, a libertarian think tank, then to Congress, where he joined the staff of Texas representative Dick Armey as an adviser on economic policy, then finally back to Cato. Moore's establishment of the Club for Growth is something of a career departure, more actively partisan, more acutely political than anything he has done in his past. But the shift in strategy demonstrates the frustration that Moore and other conservatives had felt for some time, that they had long ago won the "intellectual war," but continued to lose the political war. "Whether you're talking about welfare reform, the need for tax reduction, the need to have privatization of our Social Security system, or the need to inject competition in the school system, we have prevailed," said Moore, shaking his head. "Yet nothing changes." Or, to put it only slightly differently, if everyone agreed that the era of big government was over, then why didn't it get any smaller?

III

In all of American history, one could not choose two more dissimilar figures than Alexander Hamilton and James Madison. Madison was shy and diplomatic; Hamilton, bull-headed and arrogant. Madison was an aristocratic Virginian; Hamilton, if he had loyalties to any state (he was born illegitimate, in the West Indies), was a New Yorker. Yet the history of the United States — and certainly of Washington, D.C. — owes much to the dynamic and difficult relationship forged by these two longtime friends and collaborators who by the spring of 1790 had become fierce adversaries in a battle over the principles of the infant republic.

Madison and Hamilton had already published their literary masterpiece, *The Federalist* (in language so seamless, it is hard to believe it did not come from one pen) when they became fixed in a standoff so distinctly characteristic of the American dilemma, one is tempted to employ them in caricature — Hamilton, the nationalist; Madison, the emblem of states' rights and fiscal restraint — when, in essence, the appeal of their story is the reverse of such simplicity, a model of human complexity revealed in the most elevated form of intellectual combat, resistant to the modern labels of "liberal" and "conservative."

From the largest greensward expanse to the quietest office corner, the presence of the founding fathers is felt throughout Washington. Since the time of the Civil War, a portrait of Alexander Hamilton — America's first Secretary of the Treasury — has hung outside the Treasury Secretary's office, above.

At first glance, the issues on which the men took exception with each other appear to be simple enough: Hamilton's plan, as the first Secretary of the Treasury, to put the new nation on a firm financial footing by assuming the collective war debts of the various states, and the politically volatile decision being debated in Congress over where to place the national capital. Yet the language of their argument demonstrated a deeper, more elemental confrontation, the importance of which can be demonstrated by its persistence in the American dialogue: the desire, on the one hand, for a strong federal government, establishing America firmly within the community of nations; and the fear, on the other, that the states would be absorbed by just such a behemoth, threatening the hard-fought principles of self-rule and freedom from tyranny.

Hamilton and Madison took up their individual causes when little was certain about the future of America. The War of Independence had only recently been won and the Constitution was a new and untested document. No one yet knew whether a republican government could survive — the language of the time still referred to it as an "experiment" — and indeed, the fear of riot and rebellion was heavy in the air. Only three years before, in western Massachusetts, farmers led by Revolutionary War veteran Daniel Shays had stormed courthouses and state offices in revolt over attempts to foreclose on the farms of those who refused to pay the state's high taxes. When the rioters finally attacked the federal arsenal in Springfield, hoping to procure a few weapons for their cause, federal troops were sent to stop them, but only after Congress concocted the fiction that the soldiers were actually putting down an Indian rebellion. That was the only justification the Articles of Confederation allowed for sending federal troops to penetrate the borders of a state, so determined was the language of the document (which proclaimed itself as establishing nothing more than a "firm league of friendship") to keep the national government small and weak.

Just five months after Daniel Shays gathered his angry mob in Massachusetts, fifty-five delegates took their places at the Constitutional Convention in Philadelphia. They had convened in order to make a stronger government. But just how strong they did not yet know. The Articles of Confederation had been supremely limiting, and not only in the way that it controlled the use of troops. The government had no power to tax, relying for its operating revenue on entreaties to the states themselves, which many states simply ignored. The result was a government that was at best ineffectual; at worst, an agent of its own demise. Throughout the 1780s, there had been talk of splitting the country in half.

While his legacy permeates Washington, James Madison has never shared his more flamboyant colleagues' stardom. Not until real estate developer Marshall B. Coyne built a luxury hotel, above, in downtown Washington in 1963, was America's fourth president memorialized in any grand fashion. The more recent James Madison Memorial Building, a wing of the Library of Congress, finally gave him his due.

Among the delegates, one fear that was constant was the specter of mob rule. Democracy was a new idea to the people of the late eighteenth century, and worries that it would lead to anarchy were rife. Federalists feared what they called "wild democracy." Thus, taking the lessons of Shays's Rebellion with them to Philadelphia, the delegates became more resolute in their determination to establish a more substantial national government. The Constitution they drafted would resist tyranny from two directions, protecting the infant nation from both the whims of a would-be dictator and the unpredictable passions of the people. As Hamilton, in his dark (though perhaps realistic) view of humanity, put it: "Give all power to the many, they will oppress the few. Give all power to the few, they will oppress the many." The Constitution was the delegates' way of achieving a balance.

The Constitutional Convention was a moment of departure for Madison. He had spent most of his professional life as an ally of Thomas Jefferson, on the side of the antifederalists. But now Madison shifted to

At the site of the Murrah Federal Building: Remembering "Oklahoma City"

The memorial's designers created a Wall of Honor, asking each family to contribute mementos of the lives of those killed in the 1995 Oklahoma City bombing. Because Carrie Ann Lenz was six months pregnant at the time of the blast, the diaper pin and pacifier above represent the grandchild Doris Jones would never see; the hoop earrings are ones Lenz often wore. At right, the 168 perpetually vacant chairs, one for each victim.

Every morning before work, Doris Jones, a fifty-two-year-old grandmother of two, puts on a small 14-karat gold pin displaying an American flag overlaid with the Christian cross at its center. Then, after a quick cup of coffee, she climbs into her white Volkswagen Jetta and makes the twenty-five-mile drive to work at the souvenir shop of the memorial to those lost in the 1995 Oklahoma City bombing. Along the way Jones listens to the news on the radio and, from time to time, glances at the pocket-size portrait of a smiling young woman resting on the coffee tray next to the gear shift. "I always take her to work with me," says Jones, speaking of the photo of her daughter as if it were alive. Then again, that picture and a few other personal effects are all that Jones has to remember the life of Carrie Ann Lenz, one of the 168 innocent victims of an antigovernment terrorist act unparalleled in American history.

Jones spends much of her workday at the black marble counter in the center of the store, surrounded by shelves filled with merchandise: baseball caps, T-shirts, sweatshirts, and teddy bears, almost every item featuring an embroidered image of an American elm tree with the words "On American Soil." An elm tree on the site survived the explosion, and it became the logo of the $20 million Oklahoma City National Museum and Memorial, situated here, on the very plot where the Alfred P. Murrah Federal Office Building once stood. With its soft, almost gray natural lighting, Jones's shop is a peaceful working environment — crowded, at times, but never noisy. This is one American landmark that, even in the gift shop, commands a sacred respect.

As she rings up sales, Jones answers questions about the bombing. Most people want to know more detail about the circumstances of the tragedy; a few, after learning Jones's own story, want to know about her personal loss. Carrie Ann Lenz was working for a federal law enforcement agency nine stories directly above where twenty-six-year-old Timothy McVeigh and Terry Nichols parked a Ryder truck loaded with a homemade fertilizer bomb on April 19, 1995. Jones's loss was doubled by the fact that Lenz was six months pregnant with her first child when the bomb killed her. In an effort to deal with her sadness, Jones has devoted her life to the memory of that event, selling books, postcards, and other items that bear witness to the bombing. "My worst fear is that people will forget," she says to anyone who asks her why she is there.

It is unlikely they will. Because it happened in America's heartland, in a city until then best known as home to the Cowboy Hall of Fame, and because it was the work of a young American Gulf War veteran and his Army buddy, not — like the 2001 terrorist attacks on the World Trade Center and Pentagon — the act of foreign enemy terrorists, the Oklahoma City bombing occupies a deeply uncomfortable place in the nation's collective memory. Americans everywhere were stunned, saddened, even shamed by an act that seemed to grow directly out of the long-standing American hostility to authority, and to government in particular. When

McVeigh was apprehended, he was wearing a T-shirt emblazoned with a quote from Thomas Jefferson, whose radical pronouncement in support of the 1787 tax revolt led by Revolutionary War veteran Daniel Shays — "The tree of liberty must from time to time be refreshed with the blood of tyrants" — has become a rallying cry for right-wing militias. Was it possible that tragedy represented some kind of perverted, suicidal extension of the American idea itself? In the first thirty days after it opened on February 19, 2001, more than thirty-four thousand people visited the museum. By that time, the outdoor memorial, dedicated by President Clinton seven months earlier, had already welcomed half a million.

Visitors pay $7 to learn the story of April 19, 1995, in a self-guided tour of the museum, beginning on the third (and top) floor. There, they experience the bombing as Oklahoma City residents themselves did. Entering a dark room with a conference table, they hear a live recording of a meeting at the Oklahoma Water Resources Building, across the street from the Murrah building. Then, suddenly, the meeting is interrupted by the sound and vibration of a deafening explosion. Visitors continue through five rooms of exhibits depicting the ensuing chaos and confusion, and the recovery effort. Near the stairwell leading down to the second floor, the tattered remains of the American flag that flew over the building are juxtaposed with a vibrant flag, flown from a crane as rescue workers dug through the rubble searching for survivors, the workers' own statement that McVeigh's act of evil may have left a trail of carnage, but it would not also claim the national resolve.

On the second floor, visitors are introduced to the bombing victims. An interactive computer offers personal accounts of survivors and their family members. "The Gallery of Honor" displays photographs of the 149 adults and nineteen children in individual clear plastic shadow boxes holding memorabilia given by their families. At the end of the exhibit, visitors enter a room flooded with natural light and called "Hope," where two floor-to-ceiling windows look out over the outdoor memorial: 168 bronze chairs lined up in nine rows for each floor of the building, and in the distance, the jagged walls of the east corner of the building, the only remains left standing. A 318-by-52-foot reflecting pool runs the length of the chairs and is flanked by two thick freestanding concrete "walls of time," one representing 9:01 A.M., a minute before the bombing and the other 9:03 A.M., the minute after. "In between it will always be 9:02 A.M. on April 19," says Doris Jones, her voice quivering. "That's the time the bomb went off and our quiet lives were changed forever."

American history is checkered with violent acts of antigovernment protest. Like McVeigh, who was inspired by what he felt was an egregious abuse of federal power in the 1993 FBI raid on the David Koresh compound at Waco and the 1991 assault on the separatist Weaver family in Ruby Ridge, insurrectionists in the past turned to violence to express outrage against a perceived threat to their individual liberty. Violent expressions of the libertarian spirit in America extend back to well before the American Revolution. Indeed, some read the language of the Declaration of Independence as an endorsement of such violence. "When a long train of abuses and usurpations, pursuing invariably the same Object evinces a design to reduce them under *absolute* Despotism, it is their right, it is their duty to throw off such Government . . ." But that ignores the document's preceding phrase, declaring that "governments . . . should not be changed for light and transient causes" and that man should "suffer, while evils are sufferable" rather than "*abolishing* the forms to which they are accustomed." Jefferson's "tree of liberty" quote was incendiary, and certainly Jefferson's radical views were the most extreme of the founding fathers. But he was writing from Paris, in the days immediately before the French Revolution, with the antiauthoritarian spirit in high gear. When that revolution turned bloody, it shocked even the rebellious Jefferson.

Anyone who wants to learn about Timothy McVeigh won't find very much about him at the Oklahoma City Memorial. This was a conscious decision of the Memorial Committee, which did not want to give voice to McVeigh's views. Ironically, the committee also chose not to seek federal funding for the project. "It would be hard to turn it over to the government now," says Doris Jones. "We feel it's something that belongs to us." From time to time, Jones has tried to understand the motivation behind McVeigh's attack; she comes up empty. "There are ways to make positive change in government," she says. "You don't have to resort to such violence to do it."

A plaque in Pelham, Massachusetts, left, marks the site of the 1787 insurrection known as "Shays's Rebellion." Daniel Shays, the Revolutionary War veteran who led the charge against the government of Massachusetts, had fought at Lexington, Bunker Hill, and Saratoga. He was later pardoned.

campaign for a more powerful national government and afterward famously debated Virginia's Patrick Henry to win narrow acceptance of the Constitution in the Virginia legislature. Madison's active role at the convention led to the description of him as the "Father of the Constitution." Yet, by 1790, perhaps because Jefferson had returned from his stint as minister to France and reclaimed Madison's ear, or maybe because Madison had come to realize the passion with which his constituents viewed any concessions to the nationalists, he began to tilt back toward old Virginia and the argument for states' rights once again.

" There is something noble and magnificent in the perspective of a great Federal Republic . . . but there is something proportionately diminutive and contemptible in the prospect of a number of petty states, with the appearance only of union, jarring, jealous and perverse, without any determined direction . . . ."

—Alexander Hamilton

Madison's seeming turnabout was a surprise to Hamilton (as it has also proved to many historians since, some of whom have come to see the twists and turns of Madison's career as reflecting a discontinuity of vision) and one which did not encourage their friendship. Hamilton had long felt that the most dangerous obstacle to the future of America lay in the "subversion of national authority by the preponderancy of the state governments," which he considered to be a useless relic of the past, and on this, he had counted Madison as an ally. Now Hamilton watched in disappointment as Madison, abandoning the nationalist rhetoric he had embraced in the 1780s, voiced the opposite opinion, decrying the perils of centralization and pushing for a narrower federal authority.

Hamilton had no such ambiguity in his history. Alone among the founders, he was enamored of neither republican government nor democracy (which he later called a "disease"). Though not an aristocrat himself (among the founders, Hamilton's lowly origins were rivaled only by those of Benjamin Franklin), he favored a government run by commercial men of talent and standing. Where Jefferson and Madison were enamored of the agrarian world and a model for national development that essentially allowed economic forces to move according to their natural tendencies (for these, in their mind, would only be good), Hamilton was firmly situated in the world of commerce. He pushed for a system that would manage and guide the economy, in part through the efforts of a strong federal authority, in part by insuring that money was used as a force for development and economic growth. In this, he hoped to establish America according to the design of England, which he much admired. That was an opinion one dare not speak in Virginia, where the revolutionary spirit still simmered in the streets. Even 130 years later, President Woodrow Wilson would reflect that Hamilton was "a very great man, but not a great *American*."

When Hamilton proposed that the federal government assume the debts of the states, he was following this philosophy. If America were to achieve the greatness that was surely her destiny, then it would have to begin by reestablishing respect for its obligations both at home and abroad. Madison objected on two grounds. For one, many of the government notes (payments for wartime service) that Hamilton proposed to "assume" had long ago left the hands of the "patriots" who first possessed them and were now the property of financial speculators whom the debt-ridden Madison, Jefferson, and most of the planter class of the South held in disdain. For another, each of the individual states had paid some portion of their debt. Were those states (like Virginia) that were further along on that process now to be punished by having to also pay the debt for some more delinquent state?

P. J. David D'Angers's bronze of Thomas Jefferson stands seven feet, six inches tall, directly across the Capitol Rotunda from a statue of another larger-than-life figure, George Washington. The relationship between the two Virginians, once filled with respect for each other, ended badly. Jefferson saw Washington as part of a nationalist conspiracy; Washington saw Jefferson as "on the wrong side of history."

Hamilton countered by saying that the transfer of the notes to speculators was a fair and honest transaction; if it was not now to be recognized simply because it did not sit well with Madison and others, then who was to say that any transaction could not be voided arbitrarily? Indeed, what country would trade with a nation that considered its commitments subject to future reconsideration? As for the debt, details could be worked out, but surely it was clear that the federal government needed to establish sovereign power over the states. Hadn't the recent Constitutional Convention demonstrated a consensus on that very principle?

The tension was classic: North versus South, merchant versus planter, urban elite versus yeoman farmer, nationalist versus states' rights champion, the defining clash between the Jeffersonian and Hamiltonian visions of America. And because this contest played out not only over the issue of the national debt, but in the drama over where to locate the national capital, too, these were days of tremendous anxiety. While the Constitution declared that Congress would name a "seat of government," none of the delgates to the convention in Philadelphia had contemplated the political stew this idea would create in a republic so factionalized by state and regional loyalties. There were just twelve states, but by March of 1790, there were already sixteen proposed capital sites (including Annapolis, Trenton, Philadelphia, Baltimore, New York, and, of course, on the Potomac).

Pennsylvania held the upper hand in the argument, for its offer of Philadelphia had the precedent which had been set by the Constitutional Convention; further, it appeared to offer geographic centrality. In response, Madison placed the "center" of the country at a spot of almost spiritual significance: the Mount Vernon, Virginia, estate of George Washington himself. Hamilton preferred New York City, where the government already resided in a temporary home, if only because it offered the opportunity to put the political, financial, and cultural capital of the

At Mount Vernon: Addressing the faded reputation of America's first "action hero"

The two pictures here of the board of directors of the Mount Vernon Ladies' Association were taken in the same spot, the one at right in 1873 when old ship masts were all that held up the portico; the one at left, in 2001, with the house restored to its 1790s grandeur.

"Poor man!" exclaims seventy-eight-year-old Caryl Wilder, leaning carefully over a black metal case in a climate-controlled room in suburban Virginia. The tall, willowy grandmother from Illinois bends lower to get a closer view at — of all things — a set of dentures, nestled securely in a foot-deep pile of soft foam. The teeth, odd-sized, rust-colored, and chipped, are glued to two dull silver curves of lead. Wilder groans. "No wonder he looks the way he does in all the pictures." Those "pictures" are the ubiquitous portraits known to all Americans — indeed to anyone who has pocketed a dollar bill with Gilbert Stuart's rendering of a grim, decidedly clenched-mouth George Washington. Over two centuries, biographers have spent reams of paper trying to make America's cool, distant first citizen come to life, with mixed results. Now it's up to Wilder and the other members of the Mount Vernon Ladies' Association to try their hand.

The venerable organization, which owns and operates George Washington's stately plantation on the banks of the Potomac, has been focused on the first president's physical legacy for nearly 150 years. In 1853, upon hearing that the home had fallen into ruin, Ann Pamela Cunningham, a South Carolina native, began raising funds to buy it. By 1858, her efforts had been joined by twenty-two other influential women who together purchased the property from John Washington, the president's great-grandnephew, and called themselves the Mount Vernon Ladies' Association. The beautiful mansion overlooking the river, the slave quarters, the Washington-designed sixteen-sided barn, the grist mill, even the distillery — all of it — were then carefully preserved by private funds raised by the MVLA. Thanks to them, there is much to learn about Washington from walking the farm, which more than a million people do every year. Here, at Mount Vernon, Washington oversaw what was, essentially, a small village that included a garden and nursery, a distillery that produced eleven thousand gallons of liquor every year, a mill that sold several thousand dollars' worth of flour and a fishing business that netted over a million shad and herring in one season.

But while they have been building up his home, said Mount Vernon executive director James Rees, addressing the board of the MVLA in late 2001, the image of Washington in the public mind has been sliding down. He related the grim news of a recent poll ranking "America's Greatest Presidents." Harry Truman, Ronald Reagan, and even Bill Clinton received more votes than Washington, the man Rees describes as "the most robust, the most athletic, and the most adventurous of all the founding fathers." And so, the time has come, Rees told the group, to rethink their mission. Instead of focusing purely on the preservation of Washington's estate, they must now also undertake the preservation of his reputation, by telling the story of Washington to the citizens of the country he helped found.

In the past, Rees says, they had relied upon the schools and popular culture to do that. But, sadly, both seem to be failing. He recently dusted off his own fourth-grade history text book and found "ten times" more on Washington there than in the texts used in schools today. Popular culture has shunned the glorification of the found ing fathers, preferring to hold their obvious strengths hostage to their occasional foibles (like Thomas Jefferson's relationship with the slave Sally Hemings or John Adams's support for the Alien and Sedition Act). In that regard, Washington is seen as the original and too-revered "dead white male." Rees proposed an $85 million campaign to reverse that trend, including an agreement with Steven Spielberg to produce a short film for a new orientation center at Mount Vernon.

Like many before him, Spielberg, and the MVLA, face an elusive subject. John Adams once described Washington as possessing "the gift of taciturnity," and Washington himself, reacting to a woman who once told him she could see on his face the pleasure of retirement, is said to have shot back, "You are wrong. My countenance never yet betrayed my feelings." Yet since Washington played such an indispensable role in the creation of the United States and was held in such high regard by his contemporaries, it is more likely that his remoteness comes from the fact that it has always been too easy, as one author observed, "to lose the man in the leader." Washington was simply too good, too right, too strong to form an "interesting" biographical subject.

Indeed, no other American was so central, for so long, to so many crucial events. From his stubborn and gallant eight-year command of a ragtag farmer army that defeated the world's mightiest military power, through his master-

In 1796, Washington posed, above, for painters Edward Savage and David Edwin. In the picture, the president is joined by Martha Washington and their two grandchildren.

ful presiding over the Constitutional Convention, and eight critical years as the new country's first president, George Washington was at the forefront of every early American endeavor. For most people in the early republic, Washington *was* the government; in fact, though he was the only president ever to receive a unanimous vote of the electors (and he did it twice), he turned down several offers to become America's "king." Noah Webster, the dictionary man, could hardly contain his enthusiasm for the man. "Begin with the infant in the cradle," he crowed. "Let the first word he lisps be Washington." The editors of the *Pennsylvania Journal* were in equal awe. "If there are spots in his character, they are like the spots in the sun, only discernible by the magnifying powers of a telescope."

Yet for all the monarchical wishes he inspired, Washington was a passionate devotee of freedom and republican government. His support for the Bill of Rights was critical to its adoption and, along with Adams and Benjamin Franklin, he was certain about the evil of slavery: of the nine presidents who owned slaves, he was the only one to free them (though he postponed their liberty until both he and his wife, Martha, died). Indeed, Washington was that rare kind of general who saw battle as a reluctant path to a worthy end (in his case, an independent and democratic republic), not, as so many lesser men of uniform assume, an end in itself. And yet, more than any of the other founders, he did not let the grand language of idealism blind him to the harder realities of life and the business of government. He was, as historian Joseph Ellis has written, the mirror image of Thomas Jefferson: where Jefferson looked forward to a future created out of his own imagination, Washington preferred to situate himself and his nation in the present. While that difference put the two men on the opposite sides of argument in the later years of Washington's presidency, it did not diminish Jefferson's awe for the man whom he saw as "perfect, in nothing bad, in few points indifferent."

That perfection included a physique — six feet, two and one-half inches tall and 175 muscled pounds in his prime — that would not only stop conversation, but, as his fellow soldiers came to believe, bullets as well. Even before he was appointed commander in chief of the Continental Army, in 1775, the twenty-six-year-old Washington was an international icon, celebrated for his wilderness exploits and martial bravery. In one battle during the French and Indian War two horses were shot out from under him and his coat pierced with bullets as he charged the enemy. He had a "cast-iron constitution," as one historian noted, and was rarely sick during nearly two decades of harsh war and wilderness living. "He was an eighteenth-century real-life action hero," says Jim Rees, smiling at the thought of George Washington as the original G.I. Joe. And that is the approach that Rees intends to use for the Mount Vernon educational campaign. Where the other founding fathers were brilliant thinkers and talkers, Washington was first and foremost a doer.

Ironically, Rees and the MVLA will have to fight the "better" with the "very good." All the excessive adulation that Washington received in his lifetime spawned an industry in mythmaking. The lust for Washington lore was so great, the true stories so unbelievable, that, where there were gaps in the record, the popular imagination filled them in. As soon as one year after his death, when Mason Lock Weems published *The Life and Memorable Actions of George Washington,* the author embellished the truth with the most famous of all Washington myths, the childhood story in which Washington, having chopped down a cherry tree, admits to his wrongdoing with, "I cannot tell a lie." Other myths have persevered. Did he wear wooden teeth? No. Throw a silver dollar across the Potomac? No. But he sailed one over the 215-foot-high Natural Bridge in the Shenandoah Valley.

Rees's argument, and the one that he hopes the MVLA and Steven Spielberg will now advance, relies upon the judgment that truth, in George Washington's case, is even more interesting than myth and that the "politically correct" movement has unfairly pushed aside some of America's greatest leaders simply because they were male, white, and, by some contemporary measurements, "unenlightened." That, says Rees, misses the point and robs children — not to mention modern-day adults — of a true American hero. The delegates of the MVLA agree. "This is very exciting," says Mrs. Robert E. Lee IV, who represents Maryland, but is married to a descendant of the great Confederate general from Virginia, before declaring the group's goal with a flourish. "We will bring Washington back."

nation in a single place, where America could build a national center to rival Paris and London. But the Virginians would never agree to that, for it would represent the triumph of "commerce" over "agriculture." To them, there was only one place for the seat of the national government: there by the Potomac, where Virginia could keep an eye on it.

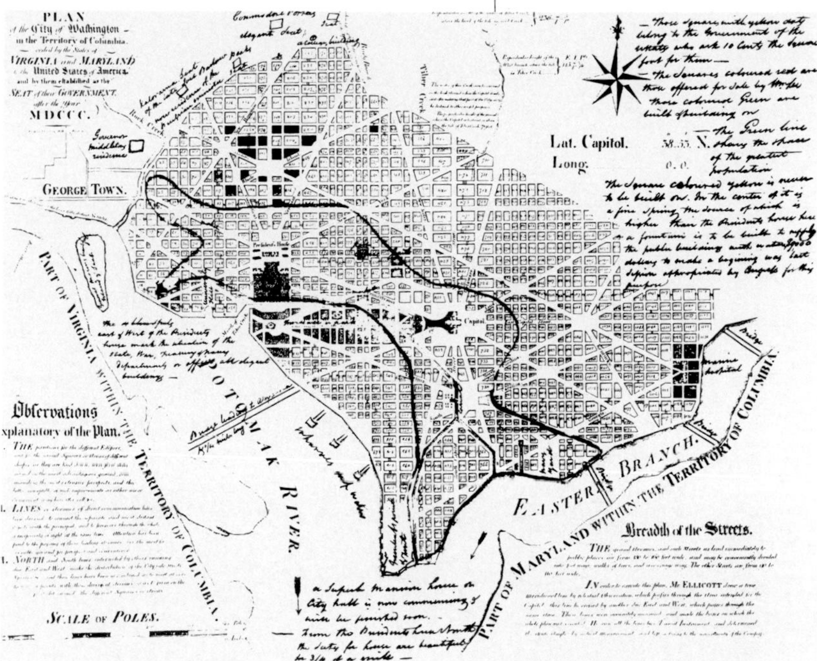

To design the city that would bear his name, Washington turned to Frenchman Pierre L'Enfant, who modeled it after the French capital of Versailles. When L'Enfant was slow to deliver his plan, Washington replaced him with a Pennsylvania surveyor, Andrew Ellicott, who finished the work, above. The choice of "Pennsylvania Avenue" as the name for the central street joining the Capitol and the president's home was probably Washingtons own, in deference to the compromise Pennsylvanians had agreed to in moving the capital from Philadelphia.

By the spring of 1790, the disputes between Hamilton and Madison were so serious that both men feared the loss of the union itself. Then, at a dinner arranged by Thomas Jefferson at his home on Maiden Lane in New York City (Jefferson was serving as Secretary of State in Washington's cabinet), the two men reached a compromise. Madison would not oppose the national government's assumption of the debt, so long as it did not require Virginia to pay more as its part of the debt than it presently owed; Hamilton, in turn, would support a national capital on the Potomac. As in the best compromises, both men thought they had won and, in a way, each had. The assumption of the debt led to the centralization of certain powers in the way that Hamilton had wanted, but the permanent residence of the capital in Washington, so near to Virginia, suggested that Madison and Jefferson would retain their influence over federal institutions, which they intended to keep small.

Since the future Washington was little more than a swamp at the time, many Northerners believed the government would never get established there. While the Potomac plan was being developed, a temporary capital was to be established in Philadelphia for ten years, and many simply assumed that the lawmakers would get bogged down over the Potomac site plans and eventually decide to keep the capital there, in the City of Brotherly Love. But the crafty Jefferson had another idea: he simply proposed that George Washington, the revered general, president, and "father" of the country, be entrusted to make all decisions about the capital site. Since Washington was viewed as something of a demigod by Northerner and Southerner alike, this idea proved irresistible. Soon, Washington was seen walking the Potomac terrain with Jefferson, like two surveyors plotting a housing development.

IV

Four flights up in a dilapidated building on L Street, Robert S. McIntyre holds a candle for liberal America. Steps from Stoney's Beef-N-Beer on one side and the Washington headquarters of the SEIU (Service Employees International Union) on the other, McIntyre serves as the director of what is officially described as the nonpartisan, nonprofit Citizens for Tax Justice, but everyone knows that "nonpartisan" is a bit of a stretch. Ask McIntyre who his heroes are and he will tell you his father and John Kennedy. Ask him who pays his bills, and he will list a roster of liberal Democratic organizations. Ask him who gave him his first job and he will tell you Ralph Nader.

A lawyer by training, McIntyre, fifty-two, was among the many young professionals who came to Washington in the early 1970s to work against the Vietnam War, for civil rights, for environmental protection, for consumer rights — in other words for a strong federal presence in the lives of all Americans. But unlike the rest of them, he said, "I'm still here plugging." Even without the social upheaval of the 1960s, McIntyre would probably have ended up working in some aspect of public policy. One of eight children in a family devoted to the political life, he has a brother who works for a Washington consulting firm, another who teaches tax law at Wayne State University in Detroit, two more who are lawyers in Attleboro, Massachusetts, the family hometown, and a younger sister who teaches at the Naval War College in Newport, Rhode Island. Elizabeth McIntyre occupies the George Herbert Walker Bush Chair in national intelligence. "Yeah," said McIntyre. "She thinks it's funny, too."

Like many old-line liberals, Robert McIntyre, above, continues to argue that the federal government can be a worthy agent of social change. The founders, he says, were suspicious of a "powerful and distant" government; not the "powerful benefactor" that the federal government can be at its best.

Originally a math major in college (he switched to English before ending up in law school), McIntyre described his role in the tax debate simply, and with modesty. "We do the arithmetic," he said, "and then tell people about it." In fact, he is one of the principal sources of information for liberal Democrats on matters of tax policy. And by his lights, the Bush tax plan was simply unfair, because that $1.6 trillion would most benefit the wealthiest 1 percent of the population while 6 million families with 10 million children would get no break. It was a point he has made consistently throughout the first weeks of the Bush presidency, preaching to old-age pensioners, union gatherings, and readers of *The American Prospect*, a biweekly liberal magazine. But in modern Washington, McIntyre felt the political winds blowing against him and, frustrated by the growing consensus around conservatism, wondered out loud just what happened to the political ethic that once put value on providing for the public good.

McIntyre pointed to the successes of the last fifty years: an interstate highway system, medical and retirement programs for the elderly, national parks, a cleaner environment. "All that," he said, "would not have happened without the government's involvement." Even in the modern climate, when people have grown cynical about government and wary of taxes, the call to reduce the size of Washington went largely unheeded because no right-thinking politician would ever attack the two most popular entitlement programs, Social Security and Medicare. "Does it matter if your wages are lower and your taxes are higher?" he asked. Not if you believe the benefits you are receiving are worthwhile and not if you feel some allegiance to the system that allowed you to earn that money in the first place. "You go out and work for a living and make some money," he said, increduously, "and you don't have any responsibility to support the society that made all that possible?"

Our present government system, said McIntyre, was a response to the crisis of the Great Depression, when "capitalism stopped working" and the people decided to "soften some of its rough edges." Indeed, the popular assumption is that the philosophical foundation of modern-day liberalism began with the Roosevelt administration and the New Deal programs of the 1930s. But in fact the antecedent for an active Washington, dedicated to the public good, reigning sovereign over the states, goes back to the middle of the nineteenth century, with a much worse crisis, the Civil War that extinguished 620,000 lives, and the ascendancy of Abraham Lincoln to the pantheon of American greatness. Historians drafting the path of the "colossus" of Washington, are likely to begin with the log-splitting sixteenth president from Illinois.

In 1861, on his journey east to assume the presidency, Lincoln spoke of the task before him as "greater than that which rested on [George] Washington" and few would have argued with him. Seven states had already seceded to form the Confederacy, chosen Jefferson Davis as their president, and begun to build an army. Davis explained that secession was necessary as a defensive move against the incoming Lincoln administration and the antislavery policies it was expected to pursue. Lincoln's predecessor, James Buchanan, who had refused to use the power of the federal government to coerce the confederate states back into the Union, blamed the crisis on the "intemperate interference of the northern people with the question of slavery." Buchanan, who came from Pennsylvania, believed the differences between the two regions to be so intractable, he doubted Lincoln, who had won without a single electoral vote from the South, would even be permitted to take office. "I

" On the site they wanted to make their capital Americans have placed the precincts of an immense city which today is still scarcely more populated than Pontoise [a town in France, near Paris] but which according to them will one day contain a million inhabitants; they have already uprooted trees for ten leagues around lest they should become inconvenient to the future citizens of this imaginary metropolis. In the center of the city they have raised a magnificent palace to serve as the seat of Congress, and they have given it the pompous name of Capitol."

—Alexis de Tocqueville, 1840

am the last President of the United States," Buchanan pronounced, somewhat arrogantly, but it was an opinion shared by many in the Democratic party and among Lincoln's own Republicans, too.

When Lincoln arrived at Independence Hall in Philadelphia, on that same journey east, he raised a new American flag (since Kansas had just joined the union, there were now thirty-four stars, including the rebel states whose decision Lincoln chose simply to ignore) and gave an address in which he drew the nation's future battle lines by citing the Declaration of Independence, with its opening passage on equality, the egalitarian principle upon which he believed the country's future rested. "I have never had a feeling politically that did not spring from the sentiments embodied in the Declaration of Independence," he said. Then he added, ominously, that he would rather be "assassinated on the spot" than surrender such an ideal. Four and a half years later, when Lincoln's coffin was carried down Broad Street, past that same hall where he had so eloquently presented his vision for the nation, the crowd of mourners for "the ideal American character" (as a local priest eulogized him) went on for three miles.

On any given day in Washington, sixteen hundred people walk the steps of 5161 Tenth Street (453 Tenth Street when it was built in 1849), a modest, three-story former boardinghouse where Abraham Lincoln died after the shooting at Ford's Theater. It was Good Friday, 1865, and the coincidence was too much for many to believe. From that day forward, many looked upon Lincoln as America's Christ figure.

V

The importance of Abraham Lincoln to the story of America cannot be overestimated. "Washington's legacy was one nation, perhaps divisible, with liberty for some," historian James M. McPherson has written. "Lincoln's was one nation, indivisible, with liberty for all." The distinction is important, and lasting, for it goes to the heart of the question debated so vigorously among the founders and among politicians today. In seeking to preserve the union, Lincoln established the supremacy of the federal government and, perhaps even more important, the essential binding nature of national ideals, chief among them, that vision of equality.

Lincoln's comments in Philadelphia were, as he said to those assembled there, an "unprepared speech," but it was hardly off the cuff. For several weeks, he had been carrying on a long-distance discussion of the relative importance of the two central American documents — the Declaration of Independence and the Constitution — with a former political colleague, Alexander Stephens of Georgia. Lincoln had been impressed by a speech Stephens had delivered to the Georgia legislature in which he urged that state not to follow the rest of the South by seceding. Lincoln hoped that he might encourage Stephens to join the Lincoln administration and urge Southern cooperation from there.

In return, Stephens voiced his concern that Lincoln planned an attack on the Constitution, which, viewed with suspicion by many states' rights champions back when it was ratified, had come to be seen by the middle nineteenth century as the protector of states' rights and a brake on adventurous federal interference. Stephens and other Southerners feared that Lincoln planned to subvert the rights of the states by taking a federal action on slavery, and he asked him to counter such worries by speaking his intention to stay within Constitutional boundaries. The Georgian quoted Proverbs, "A word fitly spoken by you now would be like an 'apple of gold in a picture of silver.'"

Lincoln demurred, insisting that such a reassurance was wholly unnecessary for he planned no such assault on the law. But he later used the same image to make a different point. "Without the Constitution and the Union," he wrote, "we could not have attained . . . our great prosperity." But "there is something back of these, entwining more closely about the human heart. That something is the principle of 'Liberty to all' that is enshrined in the Declaration of Independence, that 'all men are created equal.'" This, he said, is the "apple of gold" and the Constitution, the "picture of silver subsequently framed around it." But make no mistake about it, Lincoln affirmed: "the picture was made for the apple — not the apple for the picture."

Indeed, the "self-evident" phrase at the beginning of the Declaration, was an abiding problem for the South. In the nearly hundred years since those words of Jefferson's were written (the document is usually credited to him, though it appears to have been a collaboration, involving the labors of Benjamin Franklin and John Adams, as well as considerable revisions by the Continental Congress), "all men" had been understood, at least in the Southern states, to mean all *white* men (and, of course, no women). But since the 1830s, abolitionists had been quoting Jefferson as an "antislavery" advocate, and imploring the nation to take this sacred text of their founding for its literal meaning. In the years leading up to Lincoln's election, northerners in general began to embrace Jefferson, the longtime hero of the South, expropriating his language to their cause. "All honor to Jefferson," Lincoln wrote barely a year before he took office, "who, in the concrete pressure of a struggle for national independence by a single people, had the coolness, forecast, and capacity to introduce into a merely revolutionary document, an abstract truth and so to embalm it there . . . as a stumbling block to the very harbingers of re-appearing tyranny and oppression."

Stephens did not join the Lincoln cabinet. Instead, he became the vice president of the Confederate States of America and only a few weeks later affirmed a belief in direct opposition to Lincoln: that the Declaration was a great mistake, that its ideals were "fundamentally wrong," and that resting the Constitution on the Declaration was the equivalent of building the national house "on a sandy foundation." The Confederacy, he continued, was dedicated to the "great truth that the Negro is not equal to the white man; that slavery, subordination to the superior race, is his natural and moral condition." Given such a bold-faced challenge to the spirit of 1776, it is not surprising to see why many have called the Civil War the "Second" American Revolution.

John Trumbull's The Declaration of Independence *has hung in the Capitol Rotunda since 1826. The artist was said to have carried the twelve-by-eighteen-foot canvas around with him so he could take advantage of a chance meeting with one of the fifty-six signers. Forty-two of them are pictured.*

Over the years, as historian Alan Guelzo has noted, many people have wondered whether Stephens was on to something — not on his ideas of the natural right of slavery, of course, but about Lincoln's devaluing of the Constitution as a mere "frame" holding larger ideals in place, a rhetorical flare that allowed the president to use the Declaration to "demolish" the Constitution "in the name of his own egalitarian ideology" and to "falsify the facts of history and to do so in a way that precisely confuses our self-understanding as a people" (political scientist Willmoore Kendall); "to assume unprecedented and virtually dictatorial powers as president" (historian Gottfried Dietz); to assert the primacy of ideals over the rule of law; to even use the appeal to equality in the Declaration as a way to "put himself in Washington's place as the father of his country" (historian Dwight Anderson).

When Lincoln suspended the Constitution, invaded the South, and instituted the nation's first income tax to pay for the war, he wasn't just saving the Union, he was transforming it. For four years, the wartime Congress, operating in the absence of Southern membership, joined him in pursuing a wholesale widening of federal authority: not only the first system of national taxation, but also the first significant national currency, the building of the first transcontinental railway, the establishment of Lincoln's Republican party as the dominant force in national politics and by turn the establishment of industrial capitalism that would dominate American life through the next century. Here were the seeds of both a politics based upon the pursuit of business interests and the modern liberal state.

Before the war was over, this transformation had even added its own "sacred" document to the American library, the Gettysburg Address. With its stirring phrases, Lincoln's 272-word speech, uttered before twenty thousand mourners and the mounds of freshly-filled graves, asserted, again, the primacy of the Declaration ("Four score and seven years ago" reached back to 1776 — the year of that document — not 1790, when the Constitution was finished) and tied the great civil struggle before him to the question of whether such a nation shall have a "new birth of freedom" or "perish from the earth." "Americans," asserted author Garry Wills in his book *Lincoln at Gettysburg*, "did not know that right before their eyes a decentralized federalist system was being transformed into a sovereign nation-state."

When muralist Howard Chandler Christy was commissioned to match Trumbull's work on the Declaration *with a "companion" painting in 1939, he came up with* Scene at the Signing of the Constitution of the United States, *above, which hangs in a part of the Capitol open only to members of Congress.*

When the war ended with the defeat of the South, the disgraced Confederate leaders conveniently shifted their explanation of the origins of the war away from the now discredited notion of racial superiority and the preservation of slavery, and back toward the cry of their ancestors: states' rights. Both Confederate president Jefferson Davis and even the once boldly proslavery Stephens now took the view that the Southern states had seceded to vindicate state sovereignty. That approach may have been self-serving, but it had some basis in history and, more important, it caught on. The Civil War as the "War of Northern Aggression" became the theme passed down through the years in Southern memoirs, at reunions of Confederate veterans, and it is still embraced by heritage groups such as the United Daughters of the Confederacy and the Sons of Confederate Veterans. To them, the South had been fighting for the pastoral, agrarian civilization and against the overbearing acquisitive, aggressive ambitions of the urban-industrial Leviathan growing in the North. Indeed, visiting a Confederate cemetery shortly after she had been nominated as George W. Bush's Interior Secretary, Gale Norton expressed regret that with the Confederate defeat "we lost too much, chiefly the idea that the states were to stand against the federal government gaining too much power over our lives."

In that view, the war was the clash of two founding principles, both articulated by Thomas Jefferson: the "equality" phrase of the Declaration, on the one hand; the sanctity of individual rights on the other. That is the crowning irony of the Civil War: inasmuch as states' rights and not

The Gettysburg battlefield is littered with private memorials like the one at left, erected by members of the Irish Brigade. Above, Gen. Winfield Scott Hancock and other Union veterans on a return visit to the battlefield in the 1880s. Opposite page, a group of Civil War reenactors fire a cannon to celebrate the demolition, in 2000, of the long-hated observation tower.

John Latschar, the fifty-four-year-old superintendent of the Gettysburg National Military Park, leans back in his office chair, puts his hands behind his head, and offers up a grin of self-satisfaction. Dressed in the drab green uniform of the Parks Service, sporting a beard and a taciturn manner that would fit if he were playing the part of a Civil War general, Latschar is an unusual combination for the service — part historian, part administrator — and since arriving here in 1994, he has called upon his talent for both to restore a site that ranks as a sacred piece of real estate in America: Gettysburg.

More than 1.5 million people visit this tiny Pennsylvania town each year. They arrive in buses and SUVs, school groups and families who enter with the bright enthusiasm of the vacationing tourist, then fall quickly silent as they come under the grip of a spot of singular importance: the final resting place of thousands and the stage for one of the greatest oratorical performances in American history, Abraham Lincoln's 272-word Gettysburg Address. Latschar and his guides say that foreigners who arrive here are likely to have been drawn by their knowledge of Lincoln's talk. Perhaps because they have come to take the address's ideals, and its appeal to unity, for granted, Americans want to know more about the battle. But all walk the grounds in the quiet that accompanies solemn thought. "Gettysburg is the most peaceful place on Earth," says Gabor Boritt, director of the Civil War Institute at Gettysburg College, "because one is surrounded daily here by the story of war, death, misery and, finally, reconciliation."

Gettysburg was a three-day battle, begun almost by accident when a Confederate infantry officer serving under Confederate general A. P. Hill approached this serene Pennsylvania town of twenty-four hundred on the morning of July 1, 1863. About three miles out, the officer and his troops encountered Gen. John Buford's Union cavalry and the battle was joined. (One of the myths is that Confederate troops accidentally stumbled upon Buford's cavalry as they approached Gettysburg in search of shoes and supplies. In fact, both armies were well aware of each other's presence, the network of roads leading to Gettysburg having already drawn them toward each other.) Hill's corps was one of three in the area under the command of Robert E. Lee. In a bold scheme by Lee to invade the North and disrupt the Union war effort, all three had been on their way to strike Harrisburg, Pennsylvania. Lee hoped a victory on Northern soil would demoralize the Northerners and push Lincoln to peace. At Gettysburg, his plan would fail.

Fighting on the first day began west of town around McPherson's Ridge and eventually spread to the north (one of the ironies of the battle is that the South entered from the north and the North entered from the south). But by day's end the Union soldiers had been pushed south. During the night, as the rest of the Union army arrived, they took up a defensive line that resembled a fish hook. On the second day, Lee attacked again and clashes erupted at the Peach Orchard, the Wheat Field, Little Round Top, and Devil's Den. Then on the third, fateful day, Gen. George Pickett led thirteen thousand Confederates in a suicidal charge, known as "Pickett's Charge," at the center of Union lines on Cemetery Ridge. "Up men, and to your posts," cried Pickett before leading the furious advance. "Don't forget today that you are from old Virginia." Despite its short duration, the battle was among the war's bloodiest, resulting in some fifty-one thousand casualties. Afterward, Lee, recognizing Gettysburg as a personal failure, offered his resignation (it was refused).

Four months later, when Lincoln arrived to join those dedicating the new

Union cemetery, the locals had long endured the stench of death (in addition to the human corpses there were five thousand dead horses) and a terrain filled with the "rise and swell of human bodies" hastily buried. A local banker, David Wills, put in charge of all arrangements regarding the cemetery, had first requested that one of the more beloved poets of the age speak. William Cullen Bryant and Henry Wadsworth Longfellow were invited and declined. Harvard scholar Edward Everett, known for his ability to captivate audiences for long stretches, was finally chosen to serve as the main attraction. Lincoln was almost an afterthought; the invitation made only a month before the date. And he would be expected to deliver only "a few appropriate remarks," after Everett had already given the main oration.

Lincoln accepted in part because he worried that Americans had lost a sense of purpose to their ordeal; they had become too engrossed in the mechanics of war to recall what they were fighting for. Even before the war, Lincoln had noted America was at an interesting, and potentially dangerous, juncture in its history, for by the middle of the nineteenth century, the story of the Revolution — so long kept alive by the mangled limbs, scars, and memories of veterans — had faded. The "silent artillery of time" had put the spirit of the nation's founding out of reach.

Gettysburg was thus Lincoln's chance to reconnect the nation with its past and its original ideals. "Four score and seven years ago, our fathers brought forth on this continent, a new nation, conceived in Liberty, and dedicated to the proposition that all men are created equal. Now we are engaged in a great civil war, testing whether that nation, or any nation, so conceived, and so dedicated, can long endure . . ." For years the persistent legend was that Lincoln had written his words on the back of an envelope while riding the train to Gettysburg, a casual toss off which seemed to demonstrate the superiority of the amateur — the largely self-taught Lincoln — to the professional, Everett, whose almost two-hour oration was a studied expression filled with allusion and scholarship. But this was more wish than fact, that American preference for the "natural" over the "learned." In truth, Lincoln dwelled long and hard on his words, and he recognized their power.

For years after the war, school students across the country were required to memorize Lincoln's address and veterans made solemn pilgrimages here to mark the great trauma, and achievement, of their youth. Many of the hundreds of humble monuments that dot the battlefield were the work of no government committee — state or federal — but of the veterans themselves. Then, it was the children of veterans who made the trek and, finally, the children of children. But as time grew further and further out from the event itself, Gettysburg, the site, came under the crass cloud of commercialism and both the battle and the address became obscured. At one point, there was a Stuckey's restaurant in the middle of the Peach Orchard; by 1974, there was also a massive, three-hundred-foot viewing tower at the site of Pickett's Charge. Thomas Ottenstein built the "Tower for One Nation" as a "classroom in the sky," but he came under criticism for marring the sanctity of the site, and, after he began blaring country music through loudspeakers to draw people to his profit-making venture (some called it "the cash register in the sky"), for disturbing the peace. John Latschar was among those who considered the whole venture a sacrilege. If the veterans of the war were still alive, Latschar said, "they would have personally dismantled it themselves."

Instead, Latschar and the federal government did it for them. In 2000, Latschar presided over the demolition of the tower as part of a National Park Service campaign to return the Gettysburg battlefield to the way it looked in 1863. That was only the beginning of their work. Latschar notes that the very building that serves as his office — the Gettysburg site's museum, gift shop, and visitor center — is built on part of the battlefield where intense fighting took place. "We've covered the ground on which 970-some men died with asphalt," he says, with a shake of the head. "You can't do that and claim that you've given them the respect that they deserve." He and the Park Service have devised a plan to move the site off the major battle lines.

The Park Service master plan has met some local opposition from those who fear the loss of business, environmentalists who bristle at Latschar's plan to remove trees that had emerged where there were none in 1863, and, even in the twenty-first century, "antifederalists." When the U.S. Interior Department oversaw the demolition of Ottenstein's tower in 2000, there were letters to the editor of the local paper, asking "if we let the federal government do this, what will they do next?" But the superintendent, who is admired in these parts for his backbone, will no doubt prevail. "When I wake up in the morning, and look out over these fields," says Latschar, who lives in an original farmhouse on the site, "it's not hard to remember what you are supposed to be doing: to see that when your and my grandchildren come to visit here, it still tells them a story, that they come away knowing what was at stake here, and what brave men won for them."

slavery is taken as the impetus for the South, both sides could legitimately claim that they were the true descendants of the language of the founding. Perhaps that is why the surrender was so peculiarly bloodless, and moving, like two brothers reaching out to shake hands before returning to live — together — in their father's house, one defeated, the other in triumph, but each caught up in an abiding respect for the other.

"There was . . . the formal stacking of arms and the last, somber folding of battle flags," historian Jay Winik wrote, describing the closing scene of the War at Appomattox. "Men were not hanged, they were saluted; they were not jailed, they were honored; they were not beaten, they were embraced. Some of this was by design; much of it occurred totally spontaneously. All of it mattered." When the Union officer in charge of the ceremony — the Maine college philosophy professor and Gettysburg veteran, Joshua Chamberlain — spontaneously ordered his soldiers to "carry arms" as a sign of deepest respect for their enemy, they immediately complied, "a token of respect from Americans to Americans," Chamberlain later wrote. Then Confederate major general John B. Gordon ordered his men to do the same, inspiring Chamberlain to poetry. "Not a sound of trumpet more, nor roll of drum, nor cheer, nor word, nor whisper . . . an awed stillness, rather, and breathholding, as if it were the passing of the dead."

VI

The Constitution and the Declaration of Independence may be the most famous American documents, but while decidedly more prosaic, the United States Internal Revenue Code, and its nineteen-volume companion, detailing IRS regulations, describes the most intimate relationship of the citizenry with its nation today. No other civic act is as universal as the filing of the federal return. Wage earners constitute 50 percent of the population. They file 125 million personal returns yearly, involving some 350 million or so forms. The Tax Foundation, a Washington advocacy group, estimates that individuals and businesses spend roughly 4.3 billion hours complying with federal income tax requirements and it is not unusual for a major corporation to employ a full-time staff of eighty or a hundred accountants just to complete the company's filing obligations with the IRS.

As the size and cost of government have grown, so have the size and the difficulty of the return itself. In 1913, the first year that the modern income tax was levied (the emergency income tax levied during the Civil War was allowed to expire in 1872), the top rate was 7 percent and then only for incomes over $500,000. The rate for people making between $3,000 and $20,000 was just 1 percent and anyone making less than $3,000 paid nothing at all. By those calculations (including a $1,000 marriage deduction), all but 1 percent of the American population was exempt from taxes. This was how the original advocates of the income tax had wanted it: a tax to be directed only at excess corporate and personal profits, not the wages of ordinary people. They saw it as a way of reasserting the values of the early republic — which, as reinterpreted by Lincoln, now focused principally on equality — in reaction to the gross inequities brought on by industrialization. In this way the tax fit the mood of the times, for many had come to resent the millionaire industrialist and felt it only right that he be forced to pay some of his earnings back to the society. The income tax was one way to see that he did.

When the income tax was passed in 1913, one frightened citizen wrote the New York Times, *predicting an "army of Federal spies whose nose will be stuck into the affairs of every man . . . having an income of $3,000 or more a year." In its first year, the IRS collected $41 million from 357,545 people; today, working from its central office in Washington, above, it collects $1.37 trillion from nearly 130 million.*

But beginning with World War I and then resuming about fifteen years later with the arrival of the Great Depression, the responsibilities of the federal government began to grow and when the income tax became the favorite way to raise money to pay for them, the number of people called upon to sacrifice some of their hard-earned cash to the common good began to grow, too. Rates rose quickly and took a quantum leap with the demands of World War II when the government not only needed money but could call upon American patriotism to demand it, too. The number of filers rose to the point where it was said that what had once been a "class tax" became a "mass tax," a trend that has continued to today. The April 15 deadline is now something of a negative national rite, dreaded as much as it is observed, the process of filing so complicated, more than half of those who file do so with the aid of a professional tax preparer.

Looking back, it seems remarkable that the income tax could have been extended to include so many people without creating more of a popular uproar. The war helped — after the Japanese attack on Pearl Harbor, people saw the tax as a way of doing their part to defend America — and so did the relatively healthy respect for government that followed the success of World War II and the defeat of the Depression. But perhaps the main reason Americans took so quietly to the income tax was the new way that had been devised to collect it. For that, as Amity Shlaes has written, the IRS can thank Beardsley Ruml, a mid-century

Macy's executive, who came up with the plan to institute what is now politely called "withholding."

Until 1943, income tax was paid out each year in a lump sum and filers were expected to put aside money to make the payment. Yet that year, when the number of wage earners included under the tax grew by nearly 35 million and the Treasury Department became nervous about how many of the new taxpayers were actually prepared to pay, Ruml offered an idea. Aware that customers in his store were more comfortable buying a large item when they could pay for it in installments, he suggested that the government get business to collect the tax by withdrawing it from paychecks in small increments and reporting that amount to the employee and the IRS each year in time for the filer to reconcile the debt at filing time.

In this way, a very large tax might seem significantly smaller and less onerous to an average citizen. For the government, it would also prove much easier to collect, since now the feds wouldn't have to go after citizens; business would have already done the work for them. Business, in essence, would become an undeclared agent of the federal government. Withholding had an added benefit for the government, too: it would get most of its money well in advance of the spring filing date, in effect, a tax increase in itself (since the taxpayer would be denied the chance to invest that money). To get the public's endorsement of the plan, Ruml suggested that a tax amnesty be offered for the past year. And that was precisely what Congress did, forgiving 75 percent of the previous year's tax liability, while putting the machinery in place for the withholding that has operated ever since.

To understand the profound shift that a broad-based income tax brought to the country, one need only consider these numbers: in 1910, tariff and excise taxes brought in more than 90 percent of federal monies, $410 million overall; by the end of the century, the income tax (corporate, individual, and payroll) had replaced tariffs, providing 90 percent of the nation's revenue, $2 trillion overall. More important, the change forced a dramatic shift in the Washington "conversation." Where tariffs and excise taxes had placed the burden of taxation upon regions, industries, or patterns of consumption, the income tax placed the onus more directly upon people and their energies. Now the discussion wasn't about whether whiskey producers or cattle ranchers should pay more, but whether people making over $20,000 should pay more. Class was set against class and a "soak the rich" attitude began to infect the dialogue (with the definition of "rich" sliding rapidly down the pay scale).

As it grew to include much of the nation, the income tax altered Washington in another, even more visible way. It established a whole new

Washington's Most Powerful Lobby Groups, 2001

According to Fortune *magazine*

National Rifle Association
AARP
National Federation of Independent Business
American Israel Public Affairs Committee
Association of Trial Lawyers of America
AFL-CIO
Chamber of Commerce of the United States of America
National Beer Wholesalers Association
National Association of Realtors
National Association of Manufacturers

segment of Washington bureaucracy devoted to tax issues, an industry focused on finding and exploiting loopholes for those "rich" and an even larger industry dedicated to discovering new ways to use government, now that money was so easy to raise. As an elastic source of revenue, the income tax thus became a fundamental part of twentieth-century statism, a tool to be used in the interest of creating a more democratic social order.

You can look around Washington today to see what this wrought: a city bursting at the seams with lobbyists, industry organizations, tax lawyers and political advocacy groups. The work of some of these people is directly related to the discussion of tax policy. Walk into almost any office building in D.C. and you will find on the directory a group with the word *tax* or some euphemism for tax in its title. Citizens for Tax Justice and Americans for Tax Reform are over on L Street; Citizens for a Sound Economy is on H Street, just down the hall from the Tax Foundation, where researchers pore over tax figures to calculate "Tax Freedom Day" (which answers the question, "If all of us — everyone in the country — spent everything we earn on paying our taxes starting on January 1, how long would we have to work before we could keep a buck for ourselves?"). At the Taxpayers for Common Sense, a grassroots organization with offices sandwiched between a video store and a Chinese takeout on Pennsylvania Avenue near Capitol Hill, Jill Lancelot, Cena Swisher, and Steve Ellis carry the torch for former senator William Proxmire, who created the "golden fleece award" to mock the abuse of tax money on endless pork barrel projects. But in a sense, every lobby group is a "tax" group: in trying to affect the way that money is spent, lobbyists argue for the continued flow of tax dollars or tax breaks to their interests.

That growth of the tax bureaucracy could perhaps be forgiven when, in the middle years of the twentieth century, the country still looked to the federal government to provide most goods and services. Yet starting in California, with the Proposition 13 property tax revolt of 1978, Americans began to express their historic revulsion for giving the government money. Over the past couple of decades, with the loss of faith in the federal system, "Washington" became their prime target. In 1980, Ronald Reagan campaigned on the premise that Washington needed to be cut down to size, and, armed with a powerful national mandate to do just that, lowered tax rates and slashed deductions in the first year of his administration. In 1986, Reagan cut rates again, in what was the greatest reform of the federal system since the introduction of the income tax itself. Yet even he failed to tame the beast of Washington, building up deficits that the nation was still paying for into the next century.

The 1998 Reform and Restructuring Act led to a 15 percent reduction in staffing at the IRS and a shift in the burden of proof for tax

When the tax cut seemed to be in trouble on Capitol Hill, the White House turned to K Street, Washington's lobbying district, for help. Influence, an occupation as old as Congress, is a billion-dollar industry represented by everything from the National Grocers Association (which spent $40,000 in 2000) to the mighty Chamber of Commerce (which spent $25 million).

disputes from the taxpayer to the agency. Some complained that the IRS had been gutted; that its powers of enforcement had been seriously diluted, but the public had little sympathy. Even Ruml's time-honored idea of withholding was now coming under attack from a few rogue employers. In the fall of 2000, the *New York Times* published a story that cited twenty-three businesses that had publicly refused to cooperate with the IRS. Informing their employees that the tax system was unfair, they even stopped the practice of withholding taxes from their employees' paychecks. The IRS sent each company a letter of reprimand, but six months later, not a single one of them had changed their practice.

VII

As congressmen go, South Carolina's James Warren DeMint is a rather unorthodox one, modest and unpredictable. DeMint did not inherit his party loyalties, such as they are; having grown up in a Democratic family, he switched to the GOP as an adult, when he found it to be more in keeping with his emerging feelings about freedom and self-reliance. Even then, he has preferred to chart his own path. DeMint has taken no campaign contributions from special interests or PACs and insists that when he completes his third term he will retire from the House, his own self-imposed ethic of term limitations.

Indeed, when DeMint tells his story, it comes out in phrases reminiscent of a Horatio Alger novel. There is the paper route and the job bagging groceries at a local supermarket which earned him enough money to buy a set of drums and start a rock and roll band in the sixties. All the while, his mother was teaching the neighborhood kids poise and pirouettes at her very own DeMint Academy of Dance and Decorum, occasionally calling on little Jim and his siblings to fill in as dance partners whenever students failed to show. DeMint's boyhood heroes were John Wayne (for his "independent spirit") and Andy Griffith ("the perfect father figure"), which seems appropriate when you learn that DeMint hardly knew his own father growing up. DeMint's mother was clearly the most inspirational figure in his life. After an "unpleasant" divorce, she raised him, his two brothers, and a sister on money she made while running her dance school in Greenville. And Betty Batson (she has since remarried) never asked for help from anybody, especially, her son is eager to point out, the government.

DeMint went to the University of Tennessee, then business school at Clemson, and served a stint with the Scott Paper Company as a salesman, before returning home to Greenville to work in advertising. By 1983, he had opened his own firm, DeMint Marketing, which had a somewhat unusual mission: advising institutions not usually associated with the competitive environment — schools, hospitals — how to be more aggressive in the marketplace.

DeMint has said that his politics evolved gradually throughout all this, and indeed one can detect pieces of DeMint's past — the emphasis upon self-reliance, the belief in the competitive spirit, the advertiser's ability to distill complex ideas into a handful of slogans — throughout what is a well-formed philosophy about the future of the American system. In it, he offers an answer to Stephen Moore's question about why, if Americans have this historic aversion to taxes and conservatives have won the intellectual war about the failures of government spending, government never gets any smaller.

The founders envisioned Congress as a "citizen" assembly, composed of men who were called, in James Madison's words, "from pursuits of a private nature and continued in appointment for a short period of time." In an era dominated by career politicians, Rep. Jim DeMint, above, a former marketing executive, has pledged to leave office after three terms.

"This whole democracy assumes that people will resist the growth and intrusion of government because of the personal cost to themselves through taxes," said the congressman in polite tones one can't help thinking he learned at his mother's knee. "It was certainly that way at the nation's beginning. Clearly, the government was seen as a taker of taxes much more than a provider of benefits. And everyone resisted the growth in taxes." But if the money comes from someplace else — and therefore someone else's pocket — the whole equation changes. DeMint points out that despite the historic growth of income tax on the middle class, today one third of the tax load is carried by the richest 1 percent of the population and what flows from that fact is a culture of dependency.

In years past that phrase would have been most commonly associated with the welfare system, but DeMint isn't talking about welfare. He's talking about entitlement programs like Social Security and Medicare and other government services directed at the middle class. His point is simple: when a few wealthy people pay for benefits consumed by the great masses, a dangerous imbalance results, hostile to democratic values. "How can you restrain the growth of government if the people benefiting from it don't have to pay for it?"

The shift of the tax burden to the wealthiest 1 percent happened primarily under the Clinton administration when the top rate was raised from 31 percent to 39.6 percent. But the cycle of "dependency," says DeMint, began long before that, in the middle years of the twentieth century, when Americans experienced a profound change in the relationship between the individual and the state. "When they instituted Social Security in the 1930s," he says, "the biggest worry was that people wouldn't take it. They wouldn't take anything from the government." Now, says DeMint, people expect the government to be their provider. "I see it sitting here in Congress. Every day people are coming through here, from all walks of life, asking the government to do something for them."

DeMint points out that the nation's demographics suggest that the trend he describes will only continue. As the baby boom population enters retirement age, more and more of them will become consumers of benefits at the same time that they are earning less wages and paying fewer taxes, and therefore have less of a stake in seeing that government spending is kept under control. Unless something dramatic is done, he says, the great bulk of the population will find it very easy to vote for bigger government because they won't be the ones paying the taxes to support it. "When this country was being formed," he says, "the critics of democracy said it won't be a permanent form of government because sooner or later people are going to figure out that they can vote themselves more benefits from government without paying for it." They were right, says DeMint, and that moment has come.

Federal Government Civilian Employees

1800 *130*
1900 *239,476*
2000 *2,696,625*

Tax cuts alone will not address what he feels is a flaw so fundamental to the relationship between the individual and the state, it can be addressed only by rethinking government itself. "The issue is not compassion or Republican or Democrat or conservative or liberal. It is that we can't help people by making them dependent. In fact, I believe we can make people more secure only by making them more free. And the way we help them is by building their capabilities and removing obstacles to freedom." How ironic. A generation ago, "freedom" was the herald of the Civil Rights movement. Now it is the conservatives, with their eyes on the "demon" IRS using the same word, and to considerable effect.

To communicate his message, DeMint has teamed up with the Heritage Foundation, one of those conservative Washington think tanks, to show, definitively, the trend that he finds so disturbing. Their work projects out to the year 2030 and it shows a "quantum leap in dependency." Only a wholesale scrapping of the system would change any of this, DeMint maintains. He advocates abolishing the tax code, adopting a national sales tax, and giving Social Security over to individual accounts, invested directly by the owner. In this way, the recipient remains a participant in the national economy and not just a passive beneficiary. For much of American history, the argument has raged over the distribution of power between the federal government and the states. But for DeMint and other conservatives, the twenty-first century defines an even

In Portland, Oregon: Teaching refugees how to be "self-sufficient Americans"

Ten thousand miles from their Ethiopian home, Oriya Tulu Sado and his daughter Nafeesa learn the rudiments of American life from Joe Dunford, a case worker at the International Refugee Center of Oregon. "Any job will do," says Sado. At right, a New York City citizenship class around the turn of the century attracted students representing eleven nationalities. The lesson of the day was on how to use a bank.

Every question seemed to bring Masija Salic to tears. Age? "Fifty-one." Occupation? "Housewife." Children? "Two sons, ages twenty-four and twenty-two." Married? That was the one that brought on a river of sadness as the Bosnian woman said, through sobs, that her husband, Sulejman, had almost died during the Yugoslavian civil war. He spent two years in a hospital and still cannot walk. What, she pleaded, was she to do?

The Salics had been in the United States for only eight days, and it was clear, during Masija's "intake" interview in the Portland, Oregon, offices of the International Refugee Center of Oregon (IRCO) — twelve thousand miles from her home in the village of Zepa — that Masija and Sulejman were, as Victoria Libov, IRCO's assistant director, put it, "challenges" for a staff whose prime mission is helping new refugees become thriving, autonomous American citizens. "But they will make it," insisted Libov, glancing at personnel folders on her desk. "We do magic here."

Though magic is not part of IRCO's business plan, "alchemy" would seem an appropriate term for the task of turning an unemployed gaggle of multinational homeless, emerging from all manner of traditions, into a cadre of independent-thinking, self-starting American wage earners. Since 1982, when a collection of local émigré groups in the Portland area merged to create IRCO, the organization has been taking people of all cultures through a process that could only be called "Americanization." "What we are trying to teach is self-sufficiency," says Sokhom Tauch, who came here as a penniless Cambodian refugee in 1975 and is now IRCO's executive director.

With innovative programs and a supportive local community, IRCO became one of the country's busier gateways for the 1.2 million stateless men, women, and children who sought refuge in the United States in the 1990s. More than forty thousand of them passed through the agency's offices on Portland's east side. With 110 full-time employees (most of them former refugees themselves), IRCO now has a budget of $6 million per year and a building bursting with people who have fled distant homelands for "America," a word that to so many around the world suggests hope for a better life, but reveals little of the travails and transformations that it will take to achieve it once a refugee gets here. Freedom, the refugee learns, is hard work.

Traditionally, refugees from the former Soviet Union have been among those most shocked by the experience of America. Russians have their own word for the United States, *skazka*, says Katheryn Shamrell, one of IRCO's Russian CASE (Coordinated Assistance to Support Employment) workers. "That means 'fairy tale.' They don't believe it when they get letters about what it's like. They throw them away. *Skazka!*" And they often don't believe their own eyes even when they get here. "I've seen families go into a grocery store and simply stop and stare. They

cut in order to meet the demands now facing the federal government. (Bush, characteristically, had a different idea: cut taxes even more.)

The ever-combative Stephen Moore was concerned about the Jeffords defection (for which he took some credit, some blame), "euphoric" about the passage of the tax bill, and, finally, worried that the instinctive response to the terrorist attacks would be, of all things, to grow the federal government. "Government expands rapidly in power and size during war periods," he lamented, "and very rarely gives that power back." He recalled a phrase of James Madison's — "A crisis is the rallying cry of the tyrant" — before asserting, confidently, that the trend away from centralization and the ideas of the Left will prevail. "It's the end of their world," he said, a little presumptuously. For Robert McIntyre, the tax cut was hardly that, more like a rough spot in the road from which he believed liberals would soon recover. But, like the rest of the world, he had not expected the terrorist attacks which would prompt calls for a reversal of the tax cuts so soon. "We couldn't afford the tax cut before," he said, "and we can afford it a lot less now."

For Congressman James DeMint, and many other conservatives, the passage of the tax bill was a little bit of victory, a little bit of defeat. Like Moore, DeMint applauded the cut's focus on reducing the highest rates, but insisted that such cuts did little to alter the basic compact between the state and the individual. The really hard work that DeMint believes is necessary is yet to be done. "In some ways," he says, "the tax cut even made the dependency problem worse." Bush's bill lowered the rates for those making the highest income, but it also took many at the bottom off the rolls completely. To DeMint, taking someone off the tax rolls is like taking away their right to vote. They become only a partial participant in the democracy. Far from being a measure of tax reform, the bill also makes the tax code more complex. DeMint, too, worried that the fear of terrorism would lead to an expansion of the federal government and a growth in dependency. He noted that the attacks had come under the watch of federal agencies — the FAA (whose rules had allowed knives on planes) and the INS (which had allowed the hijackers in) — and bemoaned efforts to federalize airport security by adding thirty thousand new federal employees. "We're just creating more dependency," he said.

But this is Washington, where short of a revolution or a civil war, change comes in small increments, and where past disagreements, like family arguments, linger on in the air that descends from the attic. Over at the Treasury Department, on Fifteenth Street, a statue to Alexander Hamilton commemorates the nation's first Treasury Secretary, a fitting honor for the man who set the nation's fiscal foundation. Yet a mere glance to the other side of the building balances the tribute, for there stands Albert Gallatin, Jefferson's Treasury Secretary, who worked to pay off Hamilton's debt and presided over the shrinking of the government Hamilton had helped build. Hamilton still fared better than his onetime friend and foe, James Madison. The Virginian may be the "father of the Constitution" but there was no monument, no statue, no lasting formal tribute to him until 1981, when the new wing of the Library of Congress was named for him, a drought that could only be matched by the slight to John Adams, the Revolutionary hero and ardent nationalist. Only after Adams became the subject of a laudatory biography in 2001, did the Congress commission a memorial to the nation's second president.

Christopher Columbus, Lafayette, Union generals William Tecumseh Sherman, George McClellan, and Philip Sheridan are all memorialized around Washington. So are a few lesser known veterans of the Civil War: John A. Logan, Winfield Scott, George H. Thomas, John Rawlins, and James Birdseye McPherson, though, for obvious reasons, not a single Confederate. Ulysses S. Grant appears near Capitol Hill, but there is no suitable memorial to the dead of the Civil War. That kind of democratic reflection on the bloody cost of battle is left to the monuments of the twentieth century: the flag raisers of Iwo Jima, the dark scroll of names that lines the walls of the Vietnam Veterans Memorial, and, soon, a memorial to those who served in World War II.

Joggers and commuters alike feel the demanding gaze of Abraham Lincoln, above, from the 1922 memorial to him that occupies the grandest place of all, on the capital's grassy mall.

Still, tourists visiting the capital rarely leave without spending a few, usually quiet, often retrospective moments at two memorials, equally grand in their own way, each a product of its times, each a testimony to the elusive legacies of America's greatest statesmen and their ideas. The Lincoln Memorial, a magnificent Hellenic temple commissioned in 1911 and built shortly after the First World War tested American resolve, welcomes 4 million guests each year. The identification of the Allied cause with the ideals of Lincoln had bolstered the doughboys' spirits. Unveiled in 1922, the memorial was the high point of a resurgence of interest in Lincoln, but it was not erected without argument. House speaker Joseph Cannon wanted a site in Arlington, Virginia, over the favored place, near the Potomac. "So long as I live I'll never let a memorial to Abraham Lincoln be erected in that God-damned swamp," he said. Some suggested a soldier's home in Northwest Washington be set aside for his memory instead. Others proposed a parkway, connecting

"I have sworn upon the altar of God eternal hostility against every form of tyranny over the mind of man."

—THOMAS JEFFERSON,
in a letter to Benjamin Rush, words etched on the Jefferson Memorial

Washington with Gettysburg, a potential gold mine for realty interests. But the Potomac site won out, and the brooding sculpture of the president by Daniel Chester French was met with near-unanimous approval.

On dedication day, Supreme Court Chief Justice William Howard Taft spoke to a crowd of fifty thousand; so did Robert Moton, head of the Tuskeegee Institute, on behalf of the nation's 12 million African-Americans. Ironically, after expressing his "depth of gratitude" for Lincoln, Moton, an African-American, assumed his chair with the other blacks; fifty-seven years after the Civil War, Lincoln's dream of equality, etched in the words of the Gettysburg Address displayed on the memorial's walls, was marred by the persistent insult of segregation.

Over the years, the Lincoln Memorial has become a national cathedral of sorts, where Americans come to cleanse themselves of the sins of racism and war: in 1963, when the March on Washington featured Martin Luther King's legendary speech ("I have a dream . . .") and earlier, in 1939, when Marian Anderson, denied the opportunity to appear at the Daughters of the American Revolution hall, sang instead at the feet of Lincoln, opening with lines that in the context resonated at the foundation of the American soul: "My country tis of thee, sweet land of liberty, to thee we sing . . ."

But Lincoln is not the only eternal presence in Washington. At the tidal basin, Thomas Jefferson stands erect and proud, looking out from the round colonnade of the Jefferson Memorial toward the White House, an image to compete with Lincoln's as much as to complement it. Inside, a frieze shows the third president gathered with his fellow signers of the Declaration of Independence. Across the wall are emblazoned his words: the Declaration, of course, but also quotes from his *Notes on the State of Virginia*, and, in the New Dealer's keen attempt to claim Jefferson for themselves, lines from an 1816 letter in which Jefferson asserted the need for government to keep in stride with the progress of thought.

The Jefferson Memorial has its own ironies. Commissioned in 1939 and dedicated in 1943, the edifice and its design faced a storm of criticism. Modern architects objected to its classicism as inappropriate to the times and to the man: a "pompous pile, barren and joyless, unknown to Jefferson's spirit." Noting that the nation's most vocal champion of limited government was being honored in the time of Franklin Roosevelt, whose New Deal had grown the state to what was to those times mammoth proportions, Republicans declared the idea "blasphemous," unless, they said, Jefferson was to be portrayed "with tears streaming down his cheeks." Liberals, too, thought the memorial wrongheaded — a $3 million extravagance at a time when the country was still suffering the pain of the Great Depression. Let there be a "living memorial," they asserted, in the form of social progress, or a more utilitarian remembrance in the form of a federal agency naming its building after him. To that idea, FDR noted that the "utility" usually trumped the "commemorative" and all manner of memorial was lost.

Of great concern, too, was the proposed size of the original design: twenty-one feet higher than the Lincoln Memorial — to which it was repeatedly compared — and twice the bulk. Would that suggest that Jefferson was more significant than Lincoln? Under pressure from the National Parks Service, the Jefferson designers reduced their plan by one third. No manner of compromise, however, would satisfy the champions of the more than seven hundred cherry trees that would be uprooted to make room for the Memorial. When ground was broken, crowds of women gathered at the site wresting shovels from workmen and chaining themselves to the trees, until FDR himself, displaying some un-Jeffersonian intolerance, ordered them to disperse or be shoveled up bodily with the rest of the earth.

Hovering over both memorials, then as now, were the ever-present issues of American governance: not simply a record of the past, but a guiding hand for the future; not only the veneration of certain historic principles, but their primacy over partisan rancor; not only "who was Lincoln?" and "who was Jefferson?" but, by extension, "who are we as Americans?" Washington — a city born of partisanship — is filled with such grand confrontations and contradictions, the abiding currents of the American civilization.

President John Kennedy once told a gathering of Nobel Prize winners that they were the greatest assemblage of talent in the White House since Jefferson had dinner there alone. Left, an admiring tourist snaps a picture of the third president's memorial, while his family waits, impatiently.

Westfield, New Jersey

It was a Sunday afternoon, and Susan Debbie had just finished hosting a party celebrating her daughter Erin's birthday, when some other children from the neighborhood brought over a present for the six year-old, a hula hoop. Suddenly, for anyone old enough to remember, the America of the 1950s sprang to life. Erin tried the toy, but when she discovered that she wasn't so good at keeping it aloft, she gave it over to her mother. What other country can mark its history by recalling a parade of merchandise? Starting in the 1920s, with the creation of a vibrant consumer culture, America's unprecedented prosperity led to an unusual way to spend money: the frivolous pastime, the inane fad "of the moment" — Kewpie dolls, lava lamps, Rubik's Cubes, pet rocks, beanie babies, and adult scooters, to name just a few. But no fad burned so hot — or flamed out so precipitously — as the polyurethane rings produced by the Wham-O Corporation. Inspired by bamboo toys used in Australian gym classes, hula hoops first became popular in 1958 on local Southern California playgrounds, then rolled eastward (in America, all fads — and jokes — it sometimes seems, move West to East). Twenty-five million $2 hula hoops were sold during the spring and summer of 1958, even if the proper hip swivel necessary to make it work eluded most of those who owned them. Then, a few months after it had started, the fad was over: the *Wall Street Journal* proclaimed "Hoops Have Had It," and thousands if not millions of the rings were relegated to a future behind the boxes in the attic and on the table at the neighborhood tag sale. "The funny thing about this picture," says Debbie, "is that you'd think I was showing the kids how to use it. I don't know how to hula hoop. Who knows how to hula hoop?"

Washington, D.C.

Some 4,500 protestors were marching along Pennsylvania Avenue chanting "No War" to pending U.S. military action following the September 11 attack. Passing the National Archives, the marchers encountered several hundred counterdemonstrators, with their own mantra: "We don't care what you say, we're going to bomb them anyway!" Standing silently between the two raucous factions was Phil Sherman (foreground, near right), a seven-year veteran of the U.S. Park Police, whose job is a daily exercise in the protection of peaceful protest. Nowhere does the First Amendment right of freedom of speech get tested as frequently — or as loudly — as in the streets of Washington, D.C. According to the National Park Service, which oversees federal property, there were 946 permits granted in 2001 for demonstrations in Washington of a political nature, most of them concerned with hot-button issues like abortion rights, gun control, globalization, and gay rights. "As a police officer, you have to remain neutral," explains Sherman. That was never harder than this day, because the antiwar demonstrators "really struck a nerve," admits the thirty-six-year-old Brooklyn native. "I'm a New Yorker, born and bred. I have friends who are firemen, and one of my best friends narrowly escaped the World Trade Center attack. I couldn't believe they were rallying against America seeking justice." But as long as everyone obeyed the law, the only thing Sherman could do was watch; a thick skin helps in his line of work. "You got to protect both parties, so you kind of block it out. They can shout all they want."

GOD BLESS
BUSH
Against
not
your
NO TEARGAS
NECESSARY
WE'RE
CONSERVATIVES
www.FreeRepublic.com
DEFENSE-
A CHANCE
WELCOME
BIN LADEN
FAN CLUB

New Haven, Connecticut

"I started going to the games when the Ravens first came here, about 1995," says Pasquale Sansone, seventeen (left). "The stadium is right down the street from my house so I'd ride my bike there and watch the games and have fun. I used to go every weekend. They had stuff like dizzy-bat races where you put your forehead on the end of the bat and spun around and then ran for the mascot. I never won. But I kept going back. One day in 1997, I was by the clubhouse. The Ravens were a Rockies minor league farm team then and I wanted to meet the players. The clubhouse manager asked me if I wanted a job. I've been doing the scoreboard ever since. It's fun. You gotta climb a thirty-foot ladder. But once you're there it's quite a view. The best time to watch is the first inning, because all the holes in the board are open. By the ninth, they're all full and you have to go back to the first inning where there's a rectangle cut out so you can still see. I've made a whole bunch of mistakes. I've missed a couple of runs because the game got too exciting and I'd just forget to put the score up. The highest score I ever watched was 15 to 7. The longest game was four hours. It went fifteen innings. But even if it goes into extra innings, I still get paid the same, fifteen dollars a game. And there are no bathroom breaks. What I like most is getting to hang out in the clubhouse and, of course, just watching the game. It's a great game. You're out here with eight other guys on the field and yet you've got to work as one. The outfielder can't make a play at home if the catcher isn't there. As a pitcher, you expect your players to back you up. With batting, you're up there individually but you're still working as a team. When you get to climb up here, the game just lights up your eyes. You look down at that green grass, it makes you feel good. You look at it and you think somebody's telling you to come out here and play ball."

3 Headquarters

It is cut to measure five one-hundredths of an inch in thickness and two and a half inches in diameter, a size that fits "easily into the hand" and even more "easily into the mouth." About two thirds of it is pure potato; the rest is a mixture of oil (33 percent), salt (1.5 percent), and water (1.5 percent). To make one, you first slice a whole potato, then fry it in a fifty-fifty blend of fresh and pre-used cottonseed oil for two minutes at a temperature of 350 degrees (when all the oil is fresh, it gives an unpleasant oily taste that sits awkwardly on the tongue), until it arches itself into the familiar shape that chippers call the saddle curl. A flat fried chip indicates the cut is too thick; a chip that curls completely over on itself is cut too thin. To potato chip manufacturer Frito-Lay, the ideal color is golden, though other chip companies sometimes sport a darker, browner look. "We run a light chip," Doug Spearman of Lay's Irving, Texas, plant, explains proudly, because that's what Lay's focus groups have shown that consumers overwhelmingly prefer. A camera at the Lay's plant watches the chips as they come out of the fryer and if it detects a chip darker than the company's rigid standards, it sends a signal to one of sixty-four tiny air nozzles that targets the offending chip and blows it into a waste bin.

Frito-Lay conducts taste tests on its chips throughout the process. Twice each eight-hour shift, the workers themselves "go to the wall," as they call it — actually a tiny, fluorescent-lit room — where they can stand at a counter and eat their own product (a warm chip, right out of the fryer, is a special delicacy). Testers open a fresh bag, filled and sealed only minutes before, and stand in a huddle. Using the old playground hand signals — rock, scissors, paper — they then rate the chips on appearance, taste, and texture. If there is agreement that the chips, say, are too oily, too dark, or too salty, the supervisors then make the necessary adjustment on the computer-directed machinery out on the floor.

Selected bags of chips are also tested by professional tasters at the "headquarters" laboratory in Plano, Texas, twenty-six miles away. There, in the top-secret offices of Frito-Lay's three-hundred-member research and development department, behind a locked door protected by a security guard, eighteen taste "experts" work three to four days a week rating chips with terms that rival those used to describe a fine Merlot. A wall chart lists the foremost criteria: "hardness," "density," "fracturability," "oiliness," "butteriness," "nuttiness," and "tingle." More subjective choices include "mouthfeel," "tooth-pack," the "taste of a Chinese wonton," or even — perish the thought — the beefy flavor of a "McDonald's French fry." No one outside Frito-Lay is allowed in the room during testing, but Lynn Markley, the svelte Director of Public Affairs (one wonders how many chips *she* eats), reports that testers actually use the wall-chart terms frequently as they work. "I'm getting a McDonald's fry," someone might say as they bite into a chip. Or, "This is more of a heavy fry taste, like a wonton."

Finally, the chips are also measured against a "gold standard," in which a limited number of bags are produced by senior officials under optimal conditions, then shipped to the company's plants to be compared by factory workers and focus groups with Lay's own run-of-the-mill product. Random testers chosen to reflect a broad spectrum of the "snacking public" are instructed to take a sip of water, a bite of a plain cracker, and then another sip of water to cleanse the palate. Only then do they bring the chip to the mouth, rolling the crumbs over the tongue, before answering, in writing, a few questions. "How much do you like the appearance?" "Is the chip size too large, too small or just right?" "What is the feeling in your mouth as you eat the chip?" By the time that they are finished with their work, the focus group volunteers have thought about their potato chip "preferences" in greater detail than they ever imagined possible.

American corporate giants of the late twentieth century followed their employees to the suburbs, creating huge, sprawling headquarters where parking was plentiful and office space — like the four-story lobby in the Frito-Lay's main office in Plano, Texas — unlimited. The architect of the 550,000-square-foot building, Dirk Lohan, described his approach as "humanized modernism."

Potatoes are a sensitive vegetable. Once harvested, they react to heat, light, and movement; if they aren't "chipped" quickly, they produce an inferior product. Often they are cooked within a few hours or less of their arrival at the plant. But just as potatoes don't ship well, potato chips (or PCs as the employees at Frito-Lay call them) don't, either. Bagged chips can't travel by air (the pressure will explode the bags), and even the altitude of a mountain road can be too much for the product to bear. Drivers are told to stick with predetermined, low-altitude routes to avoid arriving at their sites with a truckload of broken chips.

Only Procter and Gamble's highly processed Pringles — the most formidable national and international competitor to Lay's — get around such difficulties. With their uniform stackable shape and distinctive, pressurized canister, Pringles are capable of being produced far in advance and "warehoused" until needed, making distribution simpler. Chips manufactured in Procter and Gamble's Belgium plant, for instance, can be stored and sold in deepest China even ten months later. But don't talk to the folks at Frito-Lay about Procter and Gamble's Pringles. "That's not a chip," says Mike White, who directs Lay's operations in Europe, the Middle East, and Africa.

In fact, when Procter and Gamble introduced Pringles in 1968, traditional chip manufacturers tried, and failed, to have the product barred from using the term *chip*, because it is made from reconstituted potato flakes, not an actual potato. Eventually, Procter and Gamble opted, on its own, to use the more vague term *crisp*. Still, White may have forgotten, for the moment, that Lay's, feeling the competitive heat from Pringles, has been developing its own uniform, canister "crisp" — the appropriately named Stax — that is indistinguishable in taste, and perhaps in its makeup, from Procter and Gamble's.

It is only a potato chip — a "delivery platform for salt and fat," as George Will once described it in a commentary on the quantity of chips consumed on Superbowl Sunday (which the Snack Food Association, an industry lobby group, estimates at 2.7 billion chips). But when it is the livelihood of sixty-two thousand people as Lay's and its various sister products are, and offers the potential for mind-numbing profits worldwide, its manufacturing, packaging, marketing, and advertising is an occupation of just such surprising precision and seriousness.

The traditional coffee break at Frito Lay is actually a "snack break," where employees are encouraged to help rate the product. Considered a nice perk by many, such brand loyalty can produce what some staffers call "the Frito fifteen," a reference to the weight that is often gained by new employees.

In the country's earliest years, American business was, of course, the stuff of small merchants, artisans, and farmers. Still, no student of American history can fail to notice that two of the most influential documents of modern times, the Declaration of Independence and Adam Smith's capitalist manifesto, *The Wealth of Nations*, were issued in 1776, within a few months of each other, and that they spoke to a common theme: freedom. All of the founders were familiar with the writings of Smith, a Scot, and they found in them an attitude consistent with their own: the belief that anything that restrained human energy and self-definition — be it political, economic, or religious — was an affront to nature. When America broke off from Britain, it put an end to the mercantile system that had forced the Colonies to act as mere suppliers to the British homeland (the role of the Colonies as a source of raw materials for British industry was one of the chief reasons for the Revolution) and put in its place a system — inspired by the ideas of Adam Smith — that thrived on free enterprise and unrestrained international trade. From that grew the most powerful business nation in human history, a "business civilization," as economist Robert Heilbroner has described it.

Indeed, no country's identity has been more intimately wrapped up with the story of business than America's: in the eighteenth century, with the establishment of free enterprise; in the nineteenth with the rise of the railroad (the first "big" business) and the corporation; in the twentieth with the growth of marketing and advertising and a "consumer" economy; and in the twenty-first, with the exporting of America's "business civilization" to the rest of the world. Even the term *businessman* is an American invention, first used in the ninteenth century, as Daniel Boorstin reminds us, to describe those "men of business" who struck out to establish new cities in the Western states. This American "businessman" was so much more than a merchant — he was a settler, a community maker, and an innovator. Today, no matter the product, American business is a complex enterprise, likely corporate in nature, applying intricate science to every step of the product development and market research process, and executing competitive sales and marketing strategies to challenge the best military models.

"Americans arrived only yesterday on the soil they inhabit, and they have already overturned the whole order of nature to their profit."

—ALEXIS DE TOCQUEVILLE, 1835

Plano, Texas–based Frito-Lay is the nation's snack food giant, in control of 55 percent of domestic potato chip sales, and by far the best performing division of Pepsico, its parent company. More than 60 percent of Pepsico's profits come from Frito-Lay's salty snacks. But the margin for growth in the American market has narrowed (to about 2 percent a year for basic goods) and so, like many American companies, Frito-Lay's sights are now set on the world, where it faces competition not only from Pringles, but from local indigenous brands and — perhaps the greatest obstacle — cultural habit.

Unlike, say, computers, food is a product rich in ethnic tradition and regional nuance. For instance, the brand managers of Frito-Lay have discovered, to their frustration, that the Dutch eat chips during the evening, but never during the day. The Spanish and the British eat them during the day, but never at night. The Indians have an enduring tradition of snacking on a salty fried lentil and chickpea concoction called a "namkeem" (the literal translation of *namkeem*, a Hindi word, is "salty"), so why would they switch to potato chips? The Chinese have long favored a fried and salted rice flour product called a "nyen gao ping," and the Turks prefer seeds and nuts they buy from street vendors. (In fact, the people of Istanbul are so unfamiliar with chips, Frito-Lay's office there found it necessary to distribute pamphlets with recipes and meal ideas just to show them ways to eat their product. "Try a tuna sandwich for lunch," the pamphlets suggest, "and join it with a bag of chips.") By turn, the potato chip is an American original, reflecting so many aspects of American culture, some of them historical, others the invention of American marketing genius, among them the sense of food as an endlessly flowing natural bounty as irresistible as it is plentiful. (Lay's long-standing slogan is "Betcha can't eat just one.")

Frito-Lay has captured 40 percent of the international potato chip market, such as it is. But like any good business, it wants to both inflate the market overall and get an even bigger percentage of it ("growth" is the American businessman's mantra) and when the company looks at the changes going on around the world, it sees the potential to do both at every turn: populations emerging from decades of isolation to hook up to American PCs, watch American television and movies, and, well, eat American potato chips. When some people think of China, they are reminded of a land of ancient tradition and sophisticated culture; others might recall the reign of terror brought on by Mao Zedong or the brutal 1989 assault of the students protesting for democracy in Tiananmen Square. "Every time I hear about China," says Cuban-born Al Bru, head of Frito-Lay North America, "I think for the next hundred years we can have double-digit growth."

From potato to chip to market, the Lay's production process is devoted to consistency. Bags like those coming off the assembly line above are marked with a code that can track the contents back to the plant, the shift, the machine, and the precise moment when the potatoes themselves were delivered.

Bru and Frito-Lay are not alone. American business has become an international affair. Indeed, the most commanding change brought about by the end of the cold war may very well have been the opening of the world's markets to American profiteering and culture. A host of books examined this phenomenon in the last years of the twentieth century, among them *New York Times* columnist Thomas Friedman's *The Lexus and the Olive Tree*, in which he posited his theory that "globalization" — the worldwide triumph of free-market capitalism — was a historical shift as dramatic in its implications for the ways that people live as the cold war had been in its time. Friedman went forward to make a few telling comparisons: where the cold war had been about division (the world's nations chose between the influence and protection of two superpowers, the United States and the Soviet Union), globalization would emphasize integration, with economies interwoven and destinies shared. Where the cold war had been a struggle of ideologies, globalization would thrive on a shared belief in democracy and the natural law of the markets. Where the cold war was about clashing traditions, each rigid in its own way, globalization would favor innovation and change.

In Waco, Texas: Seeing Ben Franklin as the "Founding Father of American Business"

The Universal Instructor in all Arts and Sciences:

AND

Pennsylvania Gazette.

To be continued Weekly. Decemb. 24. 1728.

Baylor professor Blaine McCormick, left, with students, has made something of a career out of promoting the entrepreneurial aphorisms of Benjamin Franklin, whom he considers to be America's "original" businessman. At right, the first issue of Franklin's Pennsylvania Gazette. *Opposite page, Franklin in portrait, as executed by French artist Joseph Duplessis in 1778, long after he quit business to become a public servant.*

"Let's start by going over that second question," Professor Blaine McCormick says, glancing at his notes. "What skills or traits contributed to his success as a businessman?" The students in McCormick's "Great Books for Business" seminar look ready. Dave Heddy, a twenty-two-year-old senior from Flint, Michigan, has an idea of what he would like to say, but he defers to his classmate, Matthew Peneguy, also twenty-two. And Peneguy, who was born in New Orleans, begins confidently: "First, he was humble. Second, he was creative. Third, righteous." McCormick, a popular professor at Baylor University's Hankamer School of Business in Waco, Texas, allows himself a slight grin. "I'm with you on the humility. And the creativity," he says. "But righteous? Sounds holy for Ben Franklin. Help me understand that."

Heddy and Peneguy, six weeks into the semester, had come to look forward to their sessions with McCormick and not just because "Prof Daddy" (as his students at Pepperdine used to call him when he taught there) sometimes held class at Lolita's Tortilleria (located, conveniently enough, on Franklin Avenue), where they could devour both *huevos rancheros* and one of the few business classes that could be said to deal in big, historical ideas. Swept up by McCormick's enthusiasm, Heddy and Peneguy had also come to agree with their young professor's conviction that Benjamin Franklin was the "Founding Father of American Business."

The portly, bespectacled Franklin has a well-burnished reputation in American history as an inventor who experimented with kites and electricity; as a diplomat who served in London and Paris; as a journalist who penned countless essays under pseudonyms; even as a civic statesman who established Philadelphia's first fire company, first public library, and first public hospital. Franklin wrote the proposal that became the starting point for the Articles of Confederation, joined Jefferson to draft the Declaration of Independence, and participated in the Constitutional Convention. Famous long before the "independency generation" had coalesced — in fact, its elder statesman — Franklin seems to have well earned the title so many have bestowed upon him as the "first" American. But Benjamin Franklin, as businessman, is now considered something of a relic of nineteenth-century teaching, when his story was used to promote business as an extension of civic virtue and social responsibility.

Franklin's "business" was printing, and he succeeded at it so grandly, he was able to retire from it at forty-two. But the "wisdom" that makes him worth studying, says McCormick, can be found in a few simple principles articulated in his *Autobiography* (and a handful of other essays) and in the example he set as the quintessential "self-made man." In his writings, Franklin urged "hard work" and "thrift" as well as the display of "honesty" toward customers and other businessmen (competitors included). "Trade [is] not a ball where people appear in masque and act a part to make sport," wrote English novelist Daniel DeFoe, whom Franklin greatly admired and often cited. "But 'tis a plain, visible scene of honest life . . . supported by prudence and frugality." Franklin preached a kind of "democratization" of business when he advocated that it provide the greatest good for the greatest number (foreshadowing mass markets). Business can be an agent to invention, he added, an engine of progress, a benefactor for all.

To the world of his time, these were radical ideas. Yet they were consistent with American principles as they would be articulated at the end of the eighteenth century. In his 1784 essay, "Information to Those Who Would Remove to America," Franklin stressed that America was a land where talent and drive matter more than bloodlines, thereby encouraging the would-be "self-made man." And he demonstrated that a system that promotes incentive and self-interest can be used to create benefit for the larger community. "Up to Franklin's time, the business model was one of force and fiat," McCormick explains. "Franklin invented the freedom model. He said you could be rewarded for good work, and in turn, society would be, too."

Born in Boston on January 17, 1706, Franklin was the eighth child of his mother and the fifteenth of his father, a soap- and candle-maker who had come to New England from the British town of Ecton in Northamptonshire, after having become disenchanted with the Church of England's intolerance of dissent. Though Franklin loved to read — "I do not remember when I could not read," he recalled — Franklin's schooling was cut short at age ten when his father pressed him into service in the candle shop. Two years later, he was apprenticed to his brother, a Boston printer, thus wedding young Franklin's love of reading with the business of making books. A falling out with his brother sent Franklin, still a teenager, to Philadelphia, where, at the age of twenty, he would start his own print shop and begin the path to be coming Colonial America's foremost communications mogul, publisher of the *Pennsylvania Gazette* and author of the legendary *Poor Richard's Almanack,* one of the most successful printers in the thirteen Colonies. He secured a contract to print Pennsylvania's paper currency when he was just twenty-four, in part because of an article he wrote, "A Modest Enquiry into the Nature and Necessity of a Paper Currency," and was soon printing the money of New Jersey, Delaware, and Maryland. (Today, you can find his face on the $100 bill.)

While not fond of organized religion, nor a believer in the traditional sense, Franklin had a keen sense of morality, which he dispensed in pithy aphorisms: "Lost time is never found again," "God helps them that help themselves," "He that's secure is not safe," "Work as if you were to live a hundred years, pray as if you were to die tomorrow," "There was never a good war nor a bad peace." But he lived his own model and he seemed to understand that public probity was not just good — it was smart business, too. "In the middle of the *Autobiography,*" says student Peneguy, demonstrating a command of his subject, "Franklin lists his creed: resolution, frugality, and industry. Those are qualities that make

you a worthy investment, and if you were looking for an investment, Franklin was it. He was the safest investment in Philadelphia. A massive number of people entrusted money to Franklin because they trusted him — not because they thought he was a whiz."

Franklin's *Autobiography* was a must-read in nineteenth-century business circles. The mogul banker Thomas Mellon handed out copies of it to friends and associates. Andrew Carnegie, the steel magnate, wrote at length about Franklin's influence on him. But McCormick believes that Franklin's view of business then became lost, as the corporate model assumed prominence over the merchant model and business became more about making money than providing for the society. Franklin — and the business class he founded and represents — "got a bad rap" when the term *robber baron* began to be applied, with some justification, to a host of businessmen whose practices included indifference to their labor force and ostentatious displays of their own wealth. Both characteristics were antithetical to Franklin's philosophy. "Nonetheless," says McCormick, "it got attached to an entire class of people, Franklin included, who didn't deserve it."

By teaching Franklin's story, McCormick hopes to both introduce a new generation of business students to their native commercial roots and put a fresh face on the culture of commerce itself. He doesn't defend the monopolistic practices of the late-nineteenth-century businessman, but he does call attention to their management skills, work ethic, ambition, and philanthropy, all forms of civic virtue pioneered by Franklin. "Honesty and reputation still matter," he says. Indeed, McCormick sees books like *The Seven Habits of Highly Effective People* as the latest version of a genre of business writing that began with Franklin's *Autobiography* and his 1758 *The Way to Wealth.*

While McCormick's students at Baylor have become more used to a "military model" of business strategy, one that borrows more from the battlefield logic of, say, Sun Tzu or Ulysses Grant, Franklin's melding of vigorous principle and sturdy practice is a message that carries appeal to them. "Righteousness is not a doctrinal or religious thing for Franklin," explains Peneguy, an economics major, responding to McCormick's question. "In fact, Franklin was trying to find a nondoctrinal way of doing right. But he did want to be right." "Good," the professor encouraged. "Perhaps we could say that Ben Franklin invented a secular, wholly American, reason for doing good: it was good for business."

Friedman's vision was, on balance, an optimistic one. He saw globalization bringing about rising standards of living throughout the world and was excited by the prospect of integrated technologies, like the Internet, joining peoples across borders. He advanced what he called the "Golden Arches Theory of Conflict Prevention" in which he noted that no two countries where McDonald's restaurants have opened have engaged in war with each other since their McDonald's opened for business, a clever way of noting that a country with a middle class large enough to sustain American fast food enterprises has reached a level of stability that makes it likely to seek peace in international relations. Even Marxist historian E. J. Hobsbawm has called the recent explosion of wealth brought on by the end of the cold war and the spread of communications technologies "capitalism's golden age," bringing on one of the most important social transformations in history.

> **"National firms are turning themselves into international operators and companies are . . . hastening to create global strategies . . . A technological revolution is creating a 'woven world'. . . making national borders increasingly porous and, in terms of some forms of control, increasingly irrelevant."**
>
> DANIEL YERGIN *and* JOSEPH STANISLAW
> The Commanding Heights

The more than six hundred McDonald's restaurants now spread throughout China are credited with establishing that country's first clean public restrooms (there are now twenty-nine thousand McDonald's overall, in 120 countries). Thanks to McDonald's, the Chinese are beginning to adopt the worldwide custom of the orderly service line — instead of the mad rush — and, despite growing reservations in the developed world about the quality of the nutrition in fast food, a typical McDonald's meal is, to many of the Chinese, a nutritional bounty: water, starch, protein, sugar, vitamins, and fat, all delivered in a restaurant setting which, until fast food came to Beijing, would have been an unaffordable dream.

Still, Friedman did worry about a cultural backlash (the "olive tree" of his title is a reference to the challenge globalization poses to tradition) and he wrote his book, of course, well before Pakistanis, Indonesians, and other Muslims, angered over the American air raids on Afghanistan, expressed their rage by attacking McDonald's as a symbol of "American" culture. Some writers have gone further than Friedman, finding the specter of a single consumer-driven world tacky, at the very least; at worst, an insidious form of American imperialism, disguised in the language of internationalism. In the early 1990s, Rutgers historian Benjamin Barber warned of an emerging American-driven "McWorld," resplendent with neon and logos, mall values and fast-food fat. Others have followed Barber's lead, insisting that "McWorld," the rubric under which Barber meant to include all large, consumer-driven multinational corporations like Coca-Cola, Nike, Reebok, Disney, and even Frito-Lay, describes a new kind of tyranny — a corporate tyranny — profit-driven, nationless, and answerable only to stockholders. The multinational corporation threatens, they said, to destroy local indigenous cultures and replace them with a kind of bland homogeneous life lived the same from Des Moines to Kathmandu, which is to say a future something like the one that Frito-Lay longs for: people of all ethnic stripes and nationalities blissfully engaged in the universal experience of the same salty snack.

Barber joined his vision of McWorld with the rise of a counterforce, equally transnational, equally intimidating, which, long before September 11, he prophetically called *jihad*. But while he used this Islamic term — variously translated to mean either the "struggle of the faithful" or, in its most political manifestation, a full-scale "holy war" — Barber meant it to stand for a wholesale attack upon McWorld joined by peoples of *all* religions and cultures. He predicted *jihad* would rise at the same pace as globalization and gel around a shared enemy: interdependence, homogeneity, mutuality, integrated technology, popular culture, progress — in effect, modernity itself.

"The merchant has no country."
— THOMAS JEFFERSON

Thomas Jefferson and many of the other founders never felt that the principles of democracy and the free market were the exclusive right of the colonies; far from it, they saw the American Revolution as the "opening shot in a global struggle against tyranny that was destined to sweep over the world" (historian Joseph Ellis). Jefferson predicted, prophetically, that history would witness a global clash between ideologies, with all nations of the world aligned either for or against the principles of 1776. Naturally, he expected the American ideals to prevail. Still, it is unlikely that he could have foreseen that in addition to the grand sweep of human freedoms that compelled him forward, he was also paving the way for "Baywatch" and *The Terminator*, Big Macs and MTV, for Funyuns, Rold Gold, and Wavy Lay's.

II

The man who is perhaps more responsible than any other for spreading the potato chip gospel to the world is a forty-two-year-old Pakistani-American, with the grace of a diplomat and a searing intelligence for the nuances of international marketing. Indeed, one imagines that if Ahmed Salman Amin had been born twenty years earlier, he would have been just as comfortable discussing the merits of the nuclear balance of power as he is today on the subject of "stomach share," the somewhat unappetizing term Frito-Lay marketers use to describe the part of any national diet devoted to snacking. It is a number which is rising rapidly around the world as people everywhere replace the leisurely sit-down meal with the quick bite-and-gulp of a snack food life.

Born in Lahore, Amin did not set foot in America until he came here for college at the age of seventeen. Still, he says that he was used to Amer-

brightest — would then receive a full state scholarship to the College of William and Mary. The idea was to find "twenty of the best geniuses raked from the rubbish annually."

Adams saw Jefferson's plans as creating a new privileged class, which was, in fact, precisely what Jefferson intended. In fact, Jefferson's goal was not to abolish the young nation's elite, but to improve its stock, bolster its quality, and make it even better. Adams, for his part, believed that any talk of an elite, regardless of its basis, was suspect and at odds with the dream of establishing true democracy. "Your distinction between the aristoi and the psuedo aristoi will not help the matter," he wrote to Jefferson. "I would trust one as soon as the other with unlimited power."

Their debate would echo throughout much of American history. While the "meritocracy" remained more dream than practice, Americans continued to prize those rags to power stories — Benjamin Franklin's, Abraham Lincoln's, Thomas Edison's, and, in fiction, Horatio Alger's — that gave substance to the belief that in America opportunity was there for the taking. In the twentieth century, the urge to turn the ideal into reality took new force. In the 1930s, Harvard University president James Bryant Conant embarked on a program to remake his college according to meritocratic goals. At the time, Harvard was known as a bastion of hard-drinking, hard-partying graduates of Eastern prep schools with entrance determined by that long-discredited criteria, "birth." To gain entrance to Harvard, one had to be wealthy, Protestant, white, well-born, and male. Conant wanted to open the admissions process to brainy, ambitious high school students regardless of their background. But Conant's ultimate goal was far more ambitious (and Jeffersonian). It was to transform Harvard into a center of scholarship, by finding individuals who would be the kernel of a new public-spirited elite that would

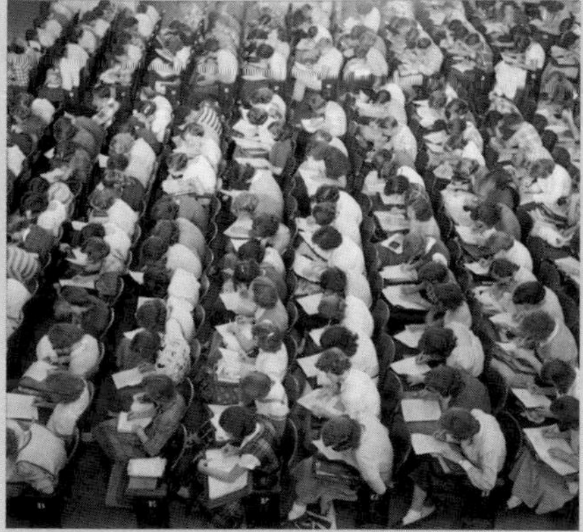

Students tackle the SAT in 1953. Harvard's Henry Chauncey saw it as replacing "sentiment and tradition" with "reason and science."

thereafter lead the country forward.

To discover these students, Conant and his protégé, Harvard assistant dean Henry Chauncey, turned to science, embracing a new standardized test, the Scholastic Aptitude Test, which promised to indicate students' raw IQ. Soon, the SAT had replaced more subjective criteria in judging college admission throughout the country. Yet Adams's old criticism persisted: in choosing who was best qualified to pursue higher education and, in turn, to enter the best institutions of higher education, was the SAT not simply trading one form of elite — the inherited one — for another? "The meritocracy began to look more and more like a means of handing out economic rewards for a fortunate few," wrote Nicholas Lemann in his tome on the SAT, *The Big Test*.

In the years after World War II, when the G.I. Bill helped level the playing field by making higher education possible for all returning veterans, the SAT test was embraced by colleges as a way to screen and sort the tens of thousands of new students. The end of the war also coincided with a new social awareness. Having fought on the side of democracy, Americans now felt a more urgent need to make their own society more representative of democratic ideals. Gradually, large and long-denied segments of the population — blacks, women, Jews, Catholics, and immigrants — were brought into the mainstream of educational opportunity.

Today, American society is, arguably, the most competitive on Earth. The race to get ahead — to ace the big test, to get into the best possible college, to land a better-paying job — permeates American lives. Indeed, while the dominant political debates in most Western European nations have focused on how to redistribute national wealth, Washington's political storms have swirled about how to provide U.S. citizens with equality of opportunity, and successful business executives, like former General Electric CEO Jack Welch, have become popular heroes. (During his tenure at GE, Welch, echoing Jefferson, ordered that the lowest performing 10 percent of employees be fired annually.)

Many Americans, however, instilled from a young age with the virtue of self-reliance, possess an unshakeable belief in their own abilities, coupled with the dream of making it big. In one 1995 survey, citizens of six industrialized countries were polled about whether they would prefer to be paid a fixed salary or receive incentive pay, where their job compensation would rise or fall depending upon their performance. A majority of Americans chose the incentive plan; by contrast, their British, French, Spanish, German, and Japanese counterparts overwhelmingly preferred to receive a fixed salary.

The relentless competition to earn more, to land a promotion or win a corner office, does not come without a price. According to a recent U.N. report, the average American worker logs 1,979 hours on the job annually — 137 hours (the equivalent of about three and a half workweeks) more than even his Japanese counterpart, and 499 hours more than the average German. The term *workaholic* entered the American dictionary in 1968. Erica Chapman and her friend are confident they can avoid that pitfall, that they will able to figure out a way to have a fulfilling career while also taking an afternoon off. But no time soon, of course. "There's a lot of work that has to be done to get to that point," says Sarah Samp.

their parents' native country. Still, neither Salman nor Neelum has any desire to return to Pakistan to live and they are in a constant marvel at their lives here, in the land of the Cowboys and the boll weevil. Indeed, they both recently became American citizens.

"My friends are Southern belles," says Neelum, with incredulity, a tall, dark beauty whose exotic looks make her something of a curiosity here among the legions of suburban blonds. She admits that they have found more racial stereotyping in Texas than they did when they lived in the Northeast and that occasionally she even has to interrupt conversations with friends to remind them that she is a "person of color" who takes offense at their tone. But the exchange is usually a good-natured one and nothing they have experienced in Texas has disturbed their sense of belonging, not even the fear that gripped them from both directions after September 11 — fear for their life here as Americans; fear for their lives here as Muslims living among Americans. Shortly after the attacks on New York and Washington, the Amins convened a meeting in their living room and invited all those in the neighborhood to come talk. It was a cathartic experience for all. "The children went off and played," says Amin, "and we all discussed our feelings. I don't think we've ever felt closer to the people in our community."

Neelum and Salman Amin entered the Immigration and Naturalization offices in Dallas as Pakistani citizens and exited, above, as elated new Americans. "In the United States," Neelum says, "there is no limitation to what you can do . . . The U.S. celebrates who I am."

Indeed, now more than ever, Neelum likes to hear her sons say "we" when they mean "Americans," and believes that her own little suburban enclave has more community-minded values than anywhere else she has lived throughout the world. She says that she found her life stifling when she briefly returned to Pakistan after attending Smith College in Northampton, Massachusetts. ("I was the only corporate banking female in all of Lahore," she says, with disdain.) Indeed, a few years back, when they were living in Connecticut, Neelum undertook a graduate program and now teaches at nearby Richland College, in Dallas. Her subject? *American* history.

Three times a year, Salman Amin hosts the one-week "Frito-Lay Marketing University" out of his offices in Plano. A banner over the podium announces the event, though no one (not even Amin) is quite sure who came up with the idea of a Latin motto scrolled at the bottom of it, *numquam mentit mercatus*, or of what the motto means (a rough translation would be "the market always reveals the truth"). Thirty-some students, representing over a dozen countries attend the event — young, fresh-faced Frito-Lay brand managers with first names like Paulo and Miklos, Shefali and Jeswin, who have come here to learn the tools of business, American style. Only a few years ago, Frito-Lay was likely to send teams of native-born Americans to work in foreign countries, but today it recruits local workers who understand the country and its challenges. They bring culture-specific ideas to Frito-Lay; Frito-Lay gives them time-honored techniques for marketing and manufacturing in return. Nearly half of the "marketing university" students are women, a fact that Amin explains as another by-product of this kind of cultural cross-fertilization. Many of the smaller, underdeveloped countries adhere to male-dominated professional traditions, he explains, and so smart young women eager to mount careers look to American companies to get ahead.

The Amins believe that the United States gives their boys Raza, above left, and Yawer the best of two worlds: material security and a sense of community. Every Friday the family hosts an informal party for neighbors on their front porch.

From his position behind the podium, Amin acts as the senior "professor," joined by three other Frito-Lay Global Development employees: Lay's Global Marketing Director Ahad Afridi, who, while born in Waterloo, Iowa, also has roots in Pakistan; Eepan George, Director of Flavor Development, an Indian national who hopes to some day become an American citizen; and Englishman Peter Harrison, the Global Marketing Director for Lay's sister brand, Doritos, and the "extruded pellet products" which, while sounding like something one would feed the horses, is actually just the industry name for "puffy stuff" like Cheetos.

Amin, a figure of unflagging energy and enthusiasm whose lecture style is like that of a television talk show host — moving about the audience, pulling ideas out of this "student," confronting that one — opens the event with a summary of the company's position throughout the world, using each country's situation as an example from which the marketers can learn. In 1995, when Lay's set up shop in India — a nation with 1 billion people, seventeen languages, eight religions, and one of the world's highest poverty rates — distribution was carried out on three-wheeled bicycles and the potato chip was virtually unknown. Although India has a huge salty snack market with eight thousand tons of product sold every year, Amin explains that Western-style snacks account for only about 15 percent of the market.

Frito-Lay has honed a strategy for such situations: hoping to avert the cost of erecting a new business in an unfamiliar market, they offer to buy up the dominant local chip or other snack food outfit for a relatively modest price and take advantage of their brand recognition, distribution expertise, and knowledge of local custom. If the indigenous company refuses, Frito-Lay moves into the market on its own and, utilizing its superior resources and general marketing experience, quickly makes gains on the local company's business. At that point, Frito-Lay is in the position to make another — often lower — bid to buy the leading brand, which, with its back against the wall, now operates from a weakened bargaining position. With the premier local snack food company now under their control, Frito-Lay can more effectively address the snacking habits of the local culture, gradually introducing Lay's until it becomes the dominant brand.

The Frito-Lay team in India, led by Manu Anand, followed the Frito-Lay approach to the letter. They began by making a stab at buying the leading Indian snack brand, Uncle Chipps, but when the Indian outfit refused to talk, Frito-Lay entered the market, facing off with them "head to head." By 2000, under intense pressure from Frito-Lay, Uncle Chipps gave in, selling for a mere $6.6 million, a long way from the $25 million they originally proposed. In the meantime, Frito-Lay India had worked hard to change the snacking habits of the subcontinent, utilizing what Anand called a "flanking strategy." Knowing that namkeems were the salty snack of choice there, they began to offer up "differentiated" products that look like Frito-Lay snacks, but are seasoned to taste like namkeems. Now, with Uncle Chipps in tow, the unit is ready to "own the category." Indeed, at the Donald Kendall Awards, a Frito-Lay annual event honoring the top company producers, Anand sounded a bit like General Sherman when he declared, to cheers from his audience: "We're taking over Indian snacks!"

At the company's one-week "Marketing University," held three times a year at the Plano headquarters, Frito-Lay employees like Caroline Wu, from Shanghai, above left, and Özant Kamaci, a Turk from the South Africa office, become "students" of American business methods. They then return home to apply the ideas to their own country's markets.

Amin switches the conversation to Thailand, where, he says, Frito-Lay faces a different problem. Large tracts of farmland appropriate for cultivating potatoes are scarce (and potatoes need a cool climate, which is also hard to find in Thailand). The company now has twenty-three hundred farmers with small plots under contract, more farmers than retail outlets. But how can you maintain quality standards when dealing with so many growers? In Mexico, Frito-Lay has grown the market and taken a larger percentage of it. Now they want to see if they are fully taking advantage of the opportunities available to them. Amin asks the group to think about the age and means of their individual markets. "When a twelve-year-old goes to school, how much money does he or she have to spend on snacks? Are we appropriately priced to take advantage of that?"

"The temptation is to do the sexy thing, what the U.S. is doing 2001," Amin says. "But in some countries a more appropriate model may be what the U.S. did in 1965." His push is to have the managers consolidate their approach to advertising, packaging, and marketing, making the Frito-Lay flagship products recognizable globally, while the individual country operations still keep most of their independence. The students nod, with approval. Many are top business school graduates in their countries. Some started at Frito-Lay right out of school; others worked for a local company or another multinational, such as Colgate Palmolive or Procter and Gamble. Then, in the highly competitive hiring environment among multinationals, they were lured away by Frito-Lay.

At Frito-Lay, employees from around the world are courted by the lure of a new identity, not American or Dutch, South African or Chinese, but "Frito." Gatherings of international staff, like the group above posing for a picture on the Plano, Texas, Frito-Lay campus, include dinner, dancing, and sports, all arranged to bond employees together as one multinational corporate family.

The single most important marketing message, Amin reminds the students, is Lay's longstanding association with the notion of "irresistibility." This, he insists, is more than a clever line. Focus group studies demonstrate that once a bag of Lay's is opened, its contents usually disappear in one sitting. Some of this, says Amin, is because bagged chips are treated by consumers as they would treat any other "fresh" food — that is, eaten before they turn stale. Indeed, for all its ease in distribution, this is one of the drawbacks to the Pringles approach. For just as the Pringles canister allows the potato chips to be easily stored in a warehouse, so it can also be easily stored in the home. People eat a few chips, put the top on the canister, and put it back in the cupboard to eat two weeks later.

But the notion of an "irresistible" chip, he says, is also derived from chemistry. Amin defers to Ahad Afridi to explain. Lay's chips are not like other foods, says Afridi. "You don't dream about them. You don't long for them. You don't crave them the way that you might crave chocolate or cake or ice cream." But once you see them, an immediate desire overcomes you. This is stage one. Stage two follows, exhibited by an internal tension— should I have one or shouldn't I? Then the "user" (and they really do use this term, despite the unfortunate resonance with drug abuse) enters the third stage of the "Lay's cycle," when all manner of discipline is lost and the chips start flowing. The marketers call this the "happy surrender." "It's happy because, after all, it's only a potato chip," says Afridi, "nothing to be so worried about and your body is telling you to go on, eat some more, so, having already surrendered, you do."

In the mid-1990s, Pringles encroached on Lay's "irresistibility" theme with its own "once you pop you can't stop" campaign. Prompting some nervousness in Plano. "For forty years we have owned irresistibility," was the message delivered to the troops. "Don't let them take it away from you." Still, Frito-Lay began to study the situation and they discovered that consumers did indeed find Pringles "irresistible" — a troubling thought, at first. But further research demonstrated that they still did not find them *as* "irresistible" as Lay's. It turned out that there was a satiation point which invariably came sooner with Pringles than it did with Lay's (owed, says Afridi, to a host of factors — slice thickness, salt content, oil, potato, cooking temperature — that Frito-Lay has simply refined to an art). Armed with confidence in their product's superiority, the Frito-Lay marketers concluded that they should continue to forge their long-standing campaign and the "truth" of their message would win over the consumers. Or as someone in ancient Rome might have put it, *numquam mentit mercatus.*

"Gentlemen: You have undertaken to cheat me. I will not sue you, for the law takes too long. I will ruin you."

— Cornelius Vanderbilt,
shipping and railroad magnate,
in an 1854 letter to competitors
Charles Morgan and Cornelius Garrison

III

The fried potato was first introduced to America by none other than Thomas Jefferson, who had tasted them as *pommes frites* during his stint as minister to France (hence the American term, "*French* fry"). But the notion of a thin, fried potato "chip" has an even more determinedly local derivation. As the story goes, railroad magnate Cornelius Vanderbilt was dining at a restaurant in Saratoga Springs, New York, in 1853, when he sent an order of fried potatoes back to the chef with the complaint that they were not brittle enough. The chef, a part African-American, part Native-American former Adirondacks guide named George Crum (how perfect is that?) was furious at the criticism and purposely overreacted, slicing the potatoes paper-thin and then frying them to a crisp. To Crum's surprise, Vanderbilt was overjoyed with the result. So was the restaurant, which began offering Crum's thinly fried potatoes on the menu as "potato crunches." Eventually, Crum opened his own restaurant, featuring his invention as "Saratoga Chips."

By the late nineteenth century, chips were being sold in grocery stores, usually out of large barrels. Then, in the early years of the twentieth century, mass production began, with two companies holding the crux of the market: Berwick, Pennsylvania, delicatessen owner Earl Wise sold "Wise Potato Chips" and Bill and Salie Utz of Hanover, Pennsylvania, introduced "Hanover Home Brand Potato Chips." Soon it seemed as if every region of the country boasted its own chip brand: California had "Scudder's"; the industrial Midwest ate "Dan Dee" brand and "Num Num's"; New England went for "Leominster's" and "Tri-Sum." In 1932, Herman Lay of Nashville, Tennessee, started producing his own brand for the Southern market.

Lay was, by nearly all accounts, the quintessential old school American businessman: a born salesman who made his way through life with a grin and a slap on the back. John Ewing, a retired former Frito-Lay vice president, remembers that Lay liked to put his arm around his companion's shoulder when he was talking with him and that when he did, Lay usually walked away with whatever he wanted. Ewing recalls a company maxim — "Herman made millions with that right arm" — that sounds like it is describing the tools of a fine starting pitcher, which is an appropriate analogy when you learn that Lay was an insatiable baseball fan who played third base for his Greenville, North Carolina, high school team.

If Lay was the salesman, the man who would later briefly become his partner, C. E. Doolin, was his opposite, a soft-spoken Texan with high cheekbones, a pencil-thin mustache, and an obsession with quality. Years later, people still recall Doolin as a "country gentleman," whose wife curtsied when she greeted you at the door and who, observing an old Southern custom, set an extra plate at the dinner table just in case someone dropped by. But it was C. E. Doolin's quiet, understated ambition that brought him to the top. In 1929, while having lunch in a sandwich shop in San Antonio, Doolin bought a nickel bag of corn chips and was so taken with them, he searched out the maker, a Mexican immigrant named Guxtavo Olguin, and for $100 bought the corn chip recipe, the equipment Olguin used to make the chips, and nineteen retail accounts. The Mexican, who made the easy deal because he was desperate for money to return home, had already given the chip a name —"Frito," which is Spanish for "fried thing." But it was Doolin who, acting like every American entrepreneur of legend, turned the corn chip into an empire.

"Saratoga Chips," above, appeared when America was a nation of small grocers.

Working first from the ovens in his own kitchen, Doolin, his mother, Daisy Doolin, and his brother, Earl Doolin, began producing Fritos, which Elmer then distributed from the back of his Model T Ford. The control of the product from beginning to end was a Fritos hallmark. Doolin selected the corn, produced the chip, and delivered it to market, a process he called "store-door selling." (That philosophy has endured to this day at Frito-Lay, which maintains its own proprietary seed stock, its own fleet of trucks, and its own drivers, who bring the product into the stores and bargain for shelf space.) Soon, Doolin had expanded his offerings to include Fritos' Peanut Butter Sandwich Crackers, and Fritos'

In an east Oregon penitentiary: Doing time, making money

Serving seventeen years for assault and attempted murder, Brian Godin, above, is grateful for his garment factory job at Prison Blues and glad that most of his $7-an-hour pay goes to support one of his two children. Almost a hundred years earlier, work programs occupied prisoners' time at Sing Sing, right. "It is liberty alone that fits men for liberty," offered the Sing Sing warden.

The bright sun rising over the desert at 6:45 helped wake Erminio Reyes-Aguilar as he walked to work, a $7-an-hour job on the pants line of a garment factory. He carried no lunch box; Reyes-Aguilar came home to eat. In fact, the forty-thousand-square-foot factory building was so close to his bed that the Mexican immigrant could have made it to work in three minutes if he didn't have to stop, just below a ring of razor-wire, to be frisked from head to toe. Reyes-Aguilar may work a respectable forty-hour week sewing waistbands into denim pants and even bring out a reasonable paycheck to show for it, but he is also a convict, who was given a twenty-four-year prison term for murder. The several dozen sober-faced men in blue lining up next to him are also felons — murderers, rapists, robbers, arsonists; all serving time, all making money, in a business run on the grounds of the Eastern Oregon Correctional Institution in Pendleton, Oregon. In America, it seems, even the prisoners are put to the exercise of capitalism.

Thomas Jefferson was among the first to endorse the idea of prison work, Pennsylvania the first state to adopt it. But the first example of prison labor of a commercial nature dates to the early 1800s, when the Auburn State Prison in New York created a prison labor program geared to profit. Auburn prisoners made nails, combs, brooms, tools, threshing equipment, even rifles, all of which was then sold to the highest bidder who in turn took the products to the open market. When Alexis de Tocqueville made his celebrated journey to America in the 1830s, the ostensible purpose of his trip was to study this experimental approach to prison reform being undertaken in the United States: imprisoning criminals not simply to punish them, but to reform them. Tocqueville chose Auburn as a focal point of his study. There he saw a prison dedicated to spiritual and moral change, utilizing two methods of reformation, solitude and labor. Tocqueville was impressed. "It is idleness which has led [the criminal] to crime; with employment, he will learn to live honestly," he wrote in his *On the Penitentiary System in the United States and Its Application in France*, which pre-dated his much more celebrated *Democracy in America*. Tocqueville also endorsed prison labor as a means of making money for the state and defraying the cost of prison operation.

By the end of the nineteenth century, more than 70 percent of American prisoners were involved in some kind of labor, often for profit. Indeed, a few years later, Oregon prisoners were operating one of the world's largest flax mills, turning out linseed oils and fabric for linen; by 1928, their work was netting Oregon $230,000 in sales. At the same time, Mississippi's prisoners were making $500,000 a year for their state, growing and selling agricultural products. To the men who sponsored these enterprises, prisoners formed a (literally) captive workforce, often easier to manage than employees in the outside world; to the degree that prison was a "corrections" facility, work continued to be seen as an appropriate rehabilitative exercise. In fact, American prisoners worked so hard and produced such marketable goods, private businesses and unions began to resent them as competition. In the 1940s, they forced the suspension of American prison business, though prison work on state-owned contracts continued. The making of automobile license plates, for instance, a venerable prison tradition for much of the twentieth century, survived the pause and even today, at the Lebanon Correctional Institution in Lebanon, Ohio, the license plate factory is second only to the state's electric chair as a prison attraction.

The tide would turn back to prison business in the 1970s when a riot at the Pontiac State Penitentiary in Pontiac, Illinois, prompted Congress to enact legislation designed to return some dignity to prison life, including work at the "prevailing" local wage. Now prisoners would actually be paid money to do their work. Over the next twenty years several dozen state prison systems signed on to partnerships with over 145 different private sector businesses, employing thousands of inmates in profit-making ventures. By the end of the twentieth century, there were four thousand prisoners at work in federally certified programs and nearly eighty thousand in state programs, making everything from mattresses to road signs, sheet metal ducts to modular furniture, and earning their partners — private business and taxpayers — millions of dollars of income.

Like so many of their counterparts in the outside world, the sixty Eastern Oregon Correctional Institution (EOCI) inmates punch a time clock, then they go to work producing $2 million worth of jeans, shirts, and T-shirts every year. "Time flies," says Robbie Ferguson, a former Navy seaman serving 15 years for murder. "It's like you're not even in prison." There are no guards in the factory. John Borchert, a short man in a polo shirt and dark slacks, smiles through his neatly trimmed goatee when asked about security. "You're looking at us." Borchert, the general manager of the Array Corporation, which has formed a partnership with the Oregon Department of Corrections to run the prison clothing factory, is a businessman, not a corrections officer. "Never thought I'd be working in a prison," says Borchert's floor manager Nick Hiatt, with a grin. "It's taken some getting used to." On the factory floor, some of the men sit hunched over sewing machines, others stand at sizing tables or push carts of denim fabric from station to station. There is almost no talk as they work. The businessmen insist that as far as their "professional" demeanor, these prisoners form a respectable lot, made more respectable by their prison "professions." "You have to welcome these people back in to the community at some point," says Doug Harder, executive assistant to the superintendent at EOCI. "What kind of new neighbor do you want? The guy that's lived in a box and had his food shoved under the door to him for fifteen years? Or the guy who's been given the opportunity to succeed?"

The factory that is keeping the inmates of EOCI busy turns out fifty thousand pieces of clothing a year — half bought by the state for inmate wear and half bought by five hundred different retail outlets around the world under the label "Prison Blues" and the tag line, "clothes made on the inside to wear on the outside." Thanks to shrewd marketing and an attention to quality — Prison Blues clothes have a manufacturing defect rate twice as low as the industry average — the prisoners' "workware" hangs next to such high-end brands as Carhartt and Woolrich. So successful has the program been that Borchert spends several hours a week giving tours of his operation — to corrections officials from other states, academics, and community groups. They want to know how they can repeat his success in their institutions.

Array pays for materials and overhead. It gives the state a 6 percent royalty on the "branded" sales (those to the retail outlets), which amounts to over $700,000 per year. Even the inmates wages, some $360,000, go to the state, with 80 percent of that figure used for victim restitution, inmate room and board, and inmate child support while the rest goes directly to the inmate. Even though that cash amounts to little more than $11 per day, many prisoners are able to walk out of jail when they've served their time with more than a few dollars and a bus ticket to nowhere. Halfway through a twelve-year prison sentence for aggravated assault, battery, and burglary, Delmar Huston cuts excess padding off of a snow skate, the latest Array/EOCI product, and makes $6.88 an hour; if he qualifies for a bonus, he could make as much as $12.20 an hour. "It's real money," says Huston. "I should have $8,000 when I get out."

Inmates at the state prison in Jackson, Michigan, began making license plates in 1918 and were still making them in 1958, left. Today, Michigan's prisoners also make furniture, road signs, shoes, dental prosthetics, even corrections officers' uniforms.

peanuts, and had established a research and development lab to come up with more products in downtown Dallas. Today's research lab at Frito-Lay headquarters is a direct descendant of Doolin's.

The success of Fritos and Lay's ran against the current of the times. This was the era of the Great Depression, after all, and it was hard to sell potato chips to people who lacked bread. Chips were food, sure, but even then they were understood to be a somewhat whimsical, frivolous food. Many snack food companies failed. David Arthur, Frito-Lay's unofficial company historian, attributes the two companies' success to the unflagging creativity of both Doolin and Lay and their knack for hiring in kind. "Doolin and Lay were entrepreneurs who hired entrepreneurs," says Arthur, "so you had two levels committed to the idea that 'failure is not an option.'"

Business at both Lay's and Fritos exploded after the war years. The companies began buying up regional chip outfits by the dozen, with Lay's controlling the southeastern part of the country, Fritos the southwest. "The two men met at the Mississippi," says David Arthur, and faced a choice. They could either join forces or they could declare all-out war. They agreed to merge, though the deal was not consummated until 1961, two years after Elmer Doolin died.

The new company, which was itself acquired by Pepsico in 1965, was long centered in Dallas but in 1982, it moved to Plano, a place named for the flatness of its terrain. In fact, the town's founders thought that *plano* was Spanish for "plain" (it isn't) but even so it still seems better than the only other name in the running at the time: Fillmore, after Millard Fillmore, the president in 1853. Growth was sluggish until white flight from Dallas began reshaping the city into the kind of corporate park community that surrounds so many large American cities. With that, it took off. As recently as the 1970s Plano's population was eighteen thousand; today it is 200,000 — the fastest growing city in Texas, and the fifth fastest in the country.

Like many modern corporate complexes, the main offices of Frito-Lay are in a pastoral suburban setting fed by interlocking highways like President George Bush Turnpike, above, named after the forty-first president. The nearby LBJ Freeway, memorializing Democrat Lyndon Baines Johnson, the thirty-sixth president, balances the political weight.

Frito-Lay occupies 218 acres of land that was once part of the cattle drive of the Shawnee Trail. The company bought the parcel from Ross Perot, the businessman and 1990s presidential candidate, whose Electronic Data Systems (EDS) is also based here. Perot bought thousands of acres of Plano in the 1950s hoping that the entire area would one day become a business park and, as you look about, it would seem that he has achieved his dream: Plano is home to not only Frito-Lay and EDS, but

High in the Rocky Mountains: Mourning the loss of "Merry Old Olds"

When Oldsmobile was founded in 1897, the mission was to "build one carriage in as nearly perfect a manner as possible" and to its many fans, it did, for more than one hundred years. In 1957, the Olds 98, above, merged luxury and power. At right, the scene at the Denver show featured a 1949 "98" convertible. Opposite page, an ad for Olds from 1904, when the company sold five thousand cars by emphasizing experience in what was then just a fledgling industry.

Along a mountainside near Georgetown, Colorado, a smoke-belching antique steam locomotive creeps on a vertiginous iron trestle past abandoned silver mines, pulling a cargo of tourists. They are friends who have come together from forty states and three Canadian provinces, from as far away as Mann's Choice, Pennsylvania, and Tacoma, Washington, from Ayr, Ontario, and Santiago, Chile. The tone of their conversation, like the contrasting smells of knotty pine and burning coal that linger in the air, is both sweet and laced with bitterness. On this July day, each member has something of grave importance on the mind: Oldsmobiles.

The previous December, General Motors, in what it called a "difficult and painful decision," had announced that it would phase out its oldest brand more than one hundred years after Ransom Eli Olds founded it in 1897. Considering that the demand for the Olds, which once had the company producing 1.2 million cars a year, now had them producing just 300,000, GM might have expected a tepid public response. But for the Oldsmobile Club of America, the decision was nothing short of a betrayal — and the hot topic at the club's annual meet in Denver. "There were no suicides," remarks OCA vice-president Carol Hosey, a grandmother who lives in Springboro, Ohio, "but there was a lot of anger." And how could there not be? To the seven thousand members of the OCA, America had just witnessed the collapse of an institution as integral to the national identity as Coca-Cola: their cherished Oldsmobile.

There are countless "brand clubs" in the United States — joining lovers of Coke, the Edsel, the Brownie Camera, M&Ms, the Stutz Bearcat, Maytag, Chatty Cathy, even International Harvestor — and in each, the dedication of the members to their beloved product is nothing short of profound. Established in 1971, the OCA now has over forty chartered local chapters in the United States and Canada, not including "specialty" groups devoted to limited-edition cars (such as the Rallye 350, manufactured only in the year 1970) and others organized around an idiosyncratic love for a certain Olds model (the Toronado, Cutlass Coupes made from 1973 to 1977, and all 1957 models have devoted followings).

In addition to sponsoring annual conventions and local car shows, the OCA has an extensive website and a network of "OCA Advisors" who handle questions about maintenance, parts supply, and club activities. There is even a monthly magazine, *Journey with Olds*, dedicated to "the entire spectrum of Oldsmobiling" and featuring such articles as "After 27 Years, It's Still My Pop's Olds," and "The Hairy Hurst Olds Story," about a legendary Olds 442 dragster which, after the installation of "not one but two Toronado blown 425-cubic-inch motors into a totally new tubular frame with Toro final drives," became "the first 4x4 all-wheel-drive super smoking–super fast funny-car-type exhibition car in the world." At the heart of it all is an attachment to something more than just a product. To the members of the OCA, the Oldsmobile was a personality, a way of life. "Other cars, like the Buick, had more luxury aspect," says Hosey (clearly unhappy to be speaking in the past tense), but an Olds person was drawn to a vehicle not unlike him or herself, "more laid-back."

Like most brand images, Oldsmobile's was the result of careful business planning. Since 1905, when Dwight Huss and Milford Wigle drove a $650 Curved Dash Runabout from New York to Portland, Oregon, in a race designed by Olds to demonstrate the shabby conditions of American roads, the Oldsmobile stood for economy, solidity, and design savvy. Early ads, which showed a horse and carriage careening wildly around a sharp turn, trumpeted "No Accidents with the Oldsmobile!" and, alluding to the crank-up models popular at the time, bragged that the car "started at will from the seat." The U.S. Post Office ordered a fleet of Curved Dashes to use as its first mail trucks, and on November 12, 1908, in a move meant to strengthen its marketing clout, Olds became the second company, after Buick, to join the two-month-old General Motors Company and take the first step toward a more refined brand identity as engineered by the company's marketing-savvy leaders. As GM grew over the years — acquiring Pontiac, Cadillac, and Chevrolet — the Olds division became associated with practicality and engineering firsts such as the introduction of automatic transmission (1940), front-wheel drive (1966), and the air bag (1974).

Through clever marketing the car solidified its place in the middle of the GM spectrum of cars, which the company designed to take a consumer from low-income beginnings (the Chevrolet) to the height of success (the Cadillac). By the mid-1970s, the Oldsmobile Cutlass was the best-selling domestic car in America. Like many brands, people saw their Oldsmobile not simply as a product of utilitarian value, but as a critical part of their identity, an aspect of capitalism that critics see as almost fetishistic. "The overlap between how you define yourself and how you define the brand keeps growing," says C. B. Bhattacharya, associate professor of marketing at Boston University, whose work involves the strong psychological identification between consumers and brands, "until a large extent of yourself is defined in terms of the brand." As the consumer economy took hold, the middle years of the twentieth century became a heyday for a new kind of American obsession, the melding of personal and even national identity with product. Consumer research was a critical agent to this process: the more the company learned about customer preferences, the more the product became adapted to suit the customer's desires. In the case of Oldsmobile, say market analysts, the company lost that critical understanding of the consumer and, in turn, he took his business elsewhere.

When competition from Japanese and European imports increased and emissions standards toughened, GM

instituted cost-cutting measures — and in the 1980s it began using a common engine among the larger cars across its divisions, alienating many of the older Olds owners, a core part of the brand's following. "It was all corporate greed," says Carol Hosey. "When GM decided to go for one engine for all models, the cars became cookie-cutter. They lost their individuality." Sales started a long slide, and in 1989, acting on a perception that younger buyers in particular were shunning the Olds, GM began an ad campaign that effectively erased the car's long-standing identity: "This Is Not Your Father's Oldsmobile." It was a failure. "The ads were the kiss of death," says Carl Gustin, chief marketing officer for Kodak. "The unintended message was that the Oldsmobile brand stands for 'those old dumb values of your dad.'" Indeed, Larry Ruppel, of the Rocky Mountain OCA chapter that sponsored the Denver meet, was baffled by the campaign. "I always *liked* my dad's Oldsmobile," he says now, plaintively. "I've had one myself since 1975."

The loyalty of OCA members endures. To some, the cars carry the largeness of myth. Members almost inevitably speak of discovering the Olds in their youth. "I had my first car date in my mother's 1974 Delta 88," says Brad Nicholson, a computer specialist in Baltimore. He adds, sheepishly, "And it was the first car I drove up to one hundred miles per hour, coming home late from said date." Roger Green, forty-nine, of Sandia Park, New Mexico, has lived most of his life around the car. "I was born in Lansing, Michigan, home of the Oldsmobile; I was brought home from the hospital in a 1950 Olds; my first car was a 1965 Olds Cutlass; and to this day I own three 1965 Cutlasses and seven Oldsmobiles total."

But few could top the story of Frank LaTorre. In 1969, LaTorre placed an order for a brand new 1970 Olds Rallye 350 in what turned out to be the only year they were produced; then, before he could claim the car, he was drafted and sent to Vietnam. Years later, Vietnam had collapsed, but not LaTorre's passion for the car he'd left behind. On the day his son was born in 1977 LaTorre left the hospital to answer an ad for a Rallye 350, determined to procure it for his heir. To his astonishment, the car's serial number matched that of the one he had ordered so long ago. The LaTorres' son now drives the car proudly and, says LaTorre, "It will remain his for as long as he wants it."

In Spring Lake, Michigan: A passion for Monopoly

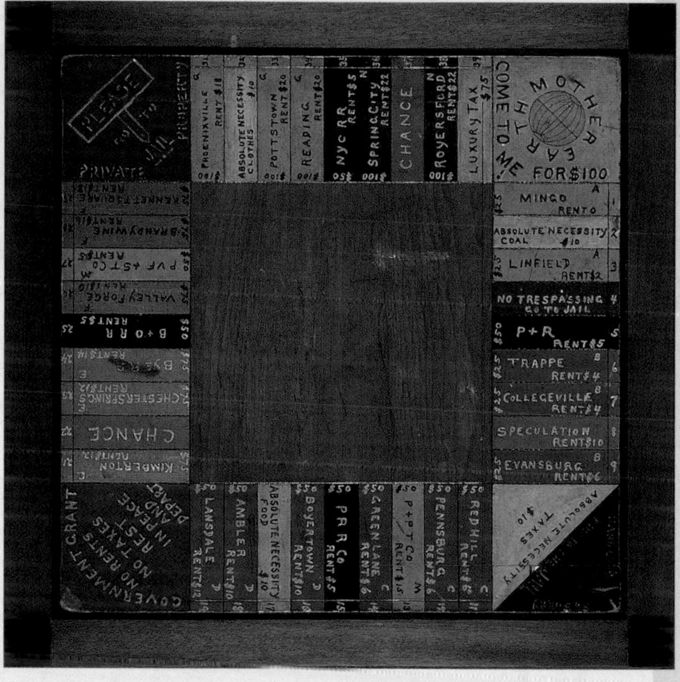

A high school social studies teacher, Greg Wieman, above, in red, won the tenth annual Spring Lake Monopoly tournament in 2001. At right, the game's earliest incarnation, Lizzie Magie's "The Landlord's Game," which was meant to show how "the landlord has an advantage over other enterprisers." The object of the Parker Brothers' board game was simpler — to become "the wealthiest player and eventually the monopolist" — and more popular, keeping Monopoly factory workers in the 1950s, like the one in Salem, Massachusetts (facing page), counting the money.

On a cold gray Saturday in March, Howard Hansen sits anxiously at a card table in the auditorium of the Barber Street School, a nineteenth-century schoolhouse-turned-community-center in Spring Lake, Michigan. Near bankruptcy, with mortgage and taxes due, Hansen has been forced to sell two investment properties. His wife, Terri, stands behind him in disbelief, but Hansen, an accountant for a commercial real estate firm, isn't really in trouble. He's just had a bad day at the board game "Monopoly," something unusual for this fifty-two-year-old father of two. "Believe me, you've earned it when you win here," says Hansen, a Monopoly state champion. "They play hard at Spring Lake."

The annual Spring Lake Monopoly tournament, organized as a fund-raiser for local education and recreation projects in three small communities on the southernmost shores of Lake Michigan, is one of more than a hundred contests held nationwide. But players will tell you that these tournaments are just the most visible; more spontaneous affairs arise in communities throughout America. More than sixty-five years after it was created — ostensibly as a Great Depression pastime — Monopoly remains a nationwide passion.

When Parker Brothers first issued Monopoly (Hasbro bought Parker Brothers in 1991), they promoted it with an appealing story of its origins. The company announced that Charles Darrow, an unemployed engineer from Pennsylvania, had brought them the idea for the game, which he had invented on an old oilcloth to entertain his poor family in the midst of the economic misery of the 1930s. Darrow based the game plan on the spirited streets of Atlantic City, where he spent summer vacations, and created the pawns using the charms of his wife's bracelet. In the original version that Darrow is to have brought to the Salem, Massachusetts, offices of Parker Brothers, he had carved houses and hotels from scraps of wood gathered at a nearby lumberyard.

The timing was perfect: just as people found themselves unemployed — or underemployed — along came Monopoly, a game that put them back in "business," so to speak, and gave them a chance to become a "millionaire" in their own living room. Ironically, Monopoly made Darrow a true millionaire, and more than 200 million copies of Monopoly have sold since. But the true story of Monopoly's beginnings was yet to emerge.

Forty years later, during the economic slowdown of the 1970s, Ralph Anspach, a populist professor of economics at San Francisco State University, decided to speak out against OPEC, the powerful oil cartel, and its control over the rising oil prices. He created a game to teach trust-busting, and mockingly christened it "Anti-Monopoly." Parker Brothers sued him for trademark infringement, which, it was quickly noted, was like claiming that the company had a "monopoly" on the word *Monopoly*.

As the story of the lawsuit was reported in the press, people began calling in and writing to newspapers to tell of parents and grandparents who had played homespun versions of Monopoly that predated Darrow's. Anspach, his lawyer, and a lawyer from Parker Brothers summarily took up the task of finding the original Monopoly. They discovered, much to Parker Brothers chagrin, that Darrow's oilcloth set was not in fact the first version of the game. Thirty years before Darrow arrived in Salem, a liberal young social activist named Lizzie Magie had created a remarkably similar board game. Like Monopoly, "The Landlord's Game," which was what she called it, consisted of forty spaces around a square board, with four railroad properties, a water utility, and an electric utility. Like Monopoly, it featured twenty-two rental properties that increased in value as a player moved clockwise around the board. But there was one crucial difference: in Magie's game the object was not to accumulate property, but rather to weaken the power of evil property owners. Magie was a disciple of the nineteenth-century American economist Henry George, who had been concerned in his own time with the concentration of power and wealth in the hands of the few. George believed that landowners were the most evil of all and in his book, *Progress and Poverty*, campaigned for a property tax of 100 percent on landowners in the hopes of weakening them for good.

It turned out that Magie tried to sell "The Landord's Game" to Parker Brothers in 1924, but the company had turned her down saying the game was too principled to ever gain a hold in the marketplace. Instead, the idea went underground, passed by word of mouth until there were dozens of homemade versions popping up throughout the country. However, in a classic example of the overriding spirit of free-market capitalism in America, each of the spun-off versions of The Landlord's Game transformed Magie's learning tool into a celebration of free enterprise. It was just such a version of the game, based on the valuable property on the streets of Atlantic City, that Darrow had first played.

Noticing a good thing when he saw it and looking for a way to earn money for his poor family, Darrow claimed the game for himself and took it to Parker Brothers executives, who at first turned it down, citing "52 fundamental flaws." But when the entrepreneurial Darrow began to produce and sell the game himself, Parker Brothers quickly changed its tune, buying up his version and patents of similar games which it had heard were circulating around the country, including Magie's, for which they paid $500. They then began using Darrow's rags-to-riches tale, which so fit the Monopoly idea, as a way to sell the game. Some of the fiercest Monopoly aficionados — including many of those at the Spring Lake tournament still recite the Darrow story without qualification, as if it were the whole truth. But most care little about the game's beginnings; they care about the game.

To prevent contests from going on too long (the longest recorded Monopoly game lasted 1,680 hours, or seventy straight days), the Spring Lake tournament is set up in three ninety-minute rounds. Groups of four play at each game, and the players with the six highest scores — determined by totaling the real estate, cash, and mortgage value of all property — go on to play in a final round of the day. Players often bring their own pawns for good luck — a button, an old screw, or their favorite pawn from the manufactured game itself — and a referee, schooled in Hasbro's rules, ensures the games are played fairly. The player with the most points recorded across tournaments in each state is entered into a national tournament, also organized by Hasbro and played every four years. The national champion then plays in the international tournament. Even Monopoly, it seems, has gone "global."

Taking advantage of the game's universal appeal, Hasbro has developed Monopoly to appeal to the specific interests of its fans. Chicagoans can play a game based on the streets of Chicago; New Yorkers, on the streets of their city; and Las Vegans, one based on Vegas. There is a Pokemon Monopoly for children, a National Hockey League Monopoly for hockey-lovers, and a Monopoly.com, created in 1998 for ".com" millionaire wannabes, in which players can circumnavigate the board on a pewter surfboard or mouse and earn $150 million in an IPO. Monopoly has even become a post–cold war novelty: a Soviet ban on the game was lifted in 1992. For all the novelty, the

object — to bankrupt your opponent — remains the same, and so does its popularity.

At Spring Lake, forty-one players, ranging in age from nine to seventy-eight, paid the $15 entrance fee to square off in what has become a much-anticipated community event. A local brokerage firm donated a thousand dollars to sponsor the contest and Stan's Bar gave away lottery tickets as door prizes, a nod, perhaps, to those spectators whose dreams of getting rich quick are wrapped up in chance. As for the tournament players, it's all skill.

It's like life, says Howard Hansen. "You sit at these tables — professionals, kids, tradespeople — and everybody has an equal chance … But to get to the final round, you have to be aggressive."

and hyperbolic in a way that will make people nod and chuckle, because it will resonate with what they think and feel."

Working with Amin and Riskey, Robertson came up with what they call the "No More Mr. Nice Guy" campaign, using the idea that these chips are so irresistible that they can make a "good guy" go "bad." For the Dutch market, they produced a commercial using pop star Marco Borsato. He meets up with a girl at a bus stop. We see they've planned a date, but she has a bag of Lay's. In the next scene, he's riding alone on the bus, she's left behind, and he's happily eating her chips, which he's stolen. There are variations for different countries: in South Africa, it's World Cup rugby star François Pienaar; in England, it's former soccer star Gary Lineker.

The chief executive officer of the venerable Batten Barton Durstine and Osborn North America is Andrew Robertson, above. While Robertson is of Scottish ancestry, he was born in present-day Zimbabwe and grew up in South Africa, all good training for his present challenge: formulating an international "look" for Lay's.

Riskey, Amin, and Robertson went through protracted discussions about these ads, in particular about just how far to go with the "bad-guy" stuff; they liked them to be a bit edgy but didn't want to alienate anyone (with Doritos it's good to alienate people, they say, because Doritos is for a narrow market — the young and the hip — whereas Lay's is meant for everyone). The ads also offered a chance to use local celebrities, who are identified with the country, as a way to suggest the notion that Lay's is a local product, even as they also underscore its universality. Their hope is that consumers will see Lay's as a global product that "they" — the locals — "own." And that, says Robertson, is very different from what McDonald's did, or what Coke did, where they simply took an American brand and shipped it. Still, so much in advertising hangs on the "art" of the medium. "I recently saw Spielberg interviewed," says Robertson, "and he said the reason he enjoyed doing [the HBO television miniseries] *Band of Brothers* was the time he got to spend: ten hours as opposed to two. Well, we're only working with thirty seconds. We have to create a little drama no one has chosen to watch, get them utterly wrapped up in it, and have them get the meaning of it, which is that Lay's is irresistible."

VII

The Pepsico "campus" in Purchase, New York, sits on the site of the old Blind Brook polo grounds, which for years was a playground for the wealthy families of Westchester County and neighboring Connecticut. Indeed, looking out across the 168 acres of rolling fields of grass, one can easily imagine the idle rich playing here, where Pepsi's 400,000-

square-foot Edward Durrell Stone building now stands in the middle of a landscape dotted with outstanding modern sculpture. Every piece in the extensive Pepsico collection, which includes work by Henry Moore, Joan Miró, Alexander Calder, Louise Nevelson, and Auguste Rodin — big, expensive, hulking creations, more like architecture themselves than art — was selected by Donald M. Kendall, who began as a fountain syrup salesman in 1947 and rose to become president of Pepsi-Cola in 1963. Along the way, Kendall became famous for a stunt he pulled in Moscow when, in 1959, as president of Pepsi-Cola International, he maneuvered then–vice president Richard Nixon, who was on a sensitive diplomatic tour of the Soviet Union, and Soviet premier Nikita Khrushchev to the Pepsi booth at the American Exposition. The pictures of the two men sipping Pepsi appeared in the papers throughout the world the next day and foreshadowed the arrival of Pepsi, a little more than a decade later, as the first American consumer product to be sold in the USSR.

The scene at Pepsi's "Ring of Honor" awards, above, which also celebrate the best performers from the company's Frito-Lay snack division, is intended to elevate corporate values in the minds of workers scattered throughout the world. The event is held on the lawn at Pepsico world headquarters in Purchase, New York.

It was Kendall who oversaw Pepsi's acquisition of Frito-Lay in 1965 — the rare blending of a distinctively Southern company (Frito-Lay) with a distinctively Northern one (Pepsi) — and it was Kendall who relocated Pepsi, then based in Manhattan, to the address it now proudly occupies, one of the first such moves in a trend that saw corporations abandon the big cities in favor of the lush life of grass and suburban grandeur not to mention low crime rates and short commuting times that could be found in the land circling America's urban centers. Kendall personally oversaw the drawing of the gardens around the new Pepsico headquarters — "Birch Grove," "Gold Garden," "West Woodland Garden," "Perennial Border," "Lily Ponds," "Stream Garden," and "Iris Garden" — a display so lavish people from around Purchase come to Pepsi's grounds on the weekend to admire the gardens and play around them; some, rumor has it, have even come here to get married. And each year, as the summer begins, the top-performing employees of Pepsi, Frito-Lay, and Pepsico's third division, Tropicana, are invited here, from around the world, to what the company somewhat grandiosely calls the "Ring of Honor" awards, the Oscars of chipping, bottling, and selling.

If there is humor to be found in such an event, it is lost on the participants, many of whom, arriving at Kennedy Airport for what will be a week of celebration culminating in this lavish ceremony, have left their

> "**It was never the Soviet Union, but the United States itself that [was] the true revolutionary power . . . The cultural message we transmit through Hollywood and McDonald's goes out across the world to capture, and also to undermine, other societies . . . Unlike traditional conquerors, we are not content merely to subdue others: We insist that they be like us.**"
>
> RONALD STEEL
> *Professor,*
> *International Relations*
> *University of*
> *Southern California*

home countries for the first time. They come here and witness, firsthand, the enormous corporate wealth that lies at the center of their enterprise and almost all are impressed. The event begins with a salute from the NYC Police Department Emerald Society, in their tams and kilts, with their bagpipes and drums, playing "Shenandoah," "The Boys from Cork," the "Marine Corps Hymn," and, of course, "America." They lead the crowd from the cocktail party on the lavish green outside to the tables under an 80-by-180-foot tent, a scene that must strike many in this audience, particularly those new to America, as nothing short of incredible. Throughout much of the world, the police have been something to be feared, an agent of terror as much as the keepers of the peace. Here, it seems, they are hired to play songs at parties.

Looking about the main event, which honors two-hundred-some employees from fifty countries, speaking twenty-five different languages (there are six hundred people in attendance overall), one feels a bit like one is entering the United Nations General Assembly, with "delegates" wearing headphones to hear simultaneous translation of the various speeches. The men are in coat and tie, the women in formal dress of their native culture, and all are sitting at banquet tables arrayed with a feast of substantial proportions. At the Ring of Honor, which costs Pepsico somewhere around $750,000 (they only confirm that the number is in the "ballpark"), the champagne flows.

From the podium, Pepsico CEO Steve Reinemund offers up the opening comments, his image broadcast over enormous video screens to the right and left of the dais. His is the traditional kind of corporate pride speech — laced with references to the company's history and its future — indistinguishable in tone from an address to a political convention. He is "proud" of the assembled troops, "dedicated" to what the company stands for, "impressed" by the past, but even more "hopeful" for the future ("growth," again, is the all-consuming goal). Reinemund's words form a call to "membership," an allusion to the corporation as alternative nation, requesting the allegiance of the hordes by telling them that here, in the land of wealth and success, here they belong. He takes a moment to introduce Don Kendall who, at eighty, struggles out of his chair and waves to the crowd like the Queen Mum.

Then comes the moment for the individual awards. The Pepsi North America "Bottler of the Year" goes to John Dwaileebe. Dwaileebe's grandmother came to the United States from Lebanon in 1906, and the family business has been allied with the company since 1931, when Pepsi was little more than another soft drink and hardly a serious competitor to Coke. He is praised for his loyalty, and he returns the honor, asking his wife and children to stand for this "momentous" occasion and lamenting that his father was not there to see the success that has come from his long ago decision to go with Pepsi.

The 2001 honorees from Frito-Lay included, among others, Yi-Lung "Jackson" Chiu, thirty-eight, sales director for Frito-Lay China. Chiu got his nickname, which he has shortened from "Action Jackson," at Taiwan's Tamsui Oxford College for being so "open and aggressive." Working out of Shanghai, Chiu helped grow sales 57 percent in the past year, in part by focusing on the "girls" market. "We discovered that girls like PCs," he says, employing the company shorthand for potato chips. "So we market to girls and the boys follow." Chiu, who didn't even speak English when he joined Frito-Lay three years ago, arrived in New York for the Ring of Honor without a coat and tie (he didn't own one), so Frito-Lay representatives took him on a shopping spree to Nordstrom at The Westchester, a local upscale mall. Sudipto Chowdhuri was honored for his work as Frito-Lay sales manager for India and Bangladesh. He spoke about his pride in his unit's launch of a product called KurKure — one of those "bridge" snacks meant to introduce the Western style of snacking while utilizing local ingredients and flavor.

Arnold Selokane, national sales manager, South Africa, was recognized for his work in South Africa. Selokane had come up with the idea of hiring locals to truck Lay's and Simba's (the local brand which Frito-Lay acquired in 1995) into their native townships, making the product feel less foreign. He spoke of the challenge posed by a business where retail outlets are little more than corrugated iron and wood slapped together. And on and on it went, with honorees walking proudly to the stage, receiving their plaques, and waving them in the air.

Then, with the speeches over and the awards all awarded, the dais went dark. Now it was time for entertainment, American style. In the blink of an eye, the curtain went up, the stage lights went on, and the crowd of Pepsico loyalists pushed their way to the front, and there, in the crisp early summer air, unannounced, the Beach Boys — the Beach Boys! — struck up their set, while the Ahads and the Jeswins, the Indiris and the Yi-Lungs, the Samirs and the Sadiptos stood, fists in the air, pumping up and down like a crowd of teenage mashers. "Wish they all could be California, wish they all could be California, wish they all could be California . . . girls!"

While the Beach Boys were off stage getting ready for their surprise performance, champagne flowed with the awards in the main tent. Arnold Selokane, below, from South Africa, issued an appropriate Rocky Balboa–type salute of victory as he accepted his Ring of Honor designation.

Chicago, Illinois

Nineteenth-century European radicals were convinced that the United States, being the most advanced industrial society, would lead the world across the threshold to socialism. But they didn't understand America. Today, only 16 percent of American workers are union members, half as many as a generation ago, and far fewer than in other major industrialized nations. The country has always been too egalitarian, too open, and too democratic to support a large labor movement, and the greater chance for upward mobility here has led workers to view the class system as moveable, not permanent in the Marxist sense. Finally, the founders bequeathed a healthy anti-statism to Americans that has made them reluctant to turn to the government for wage protection and social insurance. "They figure they can handle things on their own," says Bob Roman (near right), a labor organizer for UNITE, the Union of Needletrades, Industrial and Textile Employees. "If they want a raise, they can go to management and negotiate some kind of increase directly." Roman thinks that's naïve. He spent the summer of 2000 trying to improve pay and working conditions for employees of Five Star Hotel Laundry in Chicago. The non-union company's 140 employees, who are mostly Mexican immigrants, wanted representation to fight their near minimum-wage paychecks and what they saw as insufficient benefits. The company hired temporary workers to replace the strikers; this photograph was taken during a prayer vigil in front of the laundry to show support for the walkout. "Losing a campaign is the worst," says Roman. "One time I was organizing an Ohio factory, and the company actually paid the workers off. They gave everybody a dollar raise, and then the workers voted no for the union." Here, Roman had at least a bit more success. After enduring a six-week walkout, Five Star's management agreed to raise employees' pay, grant pension and additional health benefits, and recognize the union. "This group of workers was really good, really strong," says Roman. "They stood up for what they believed. Now they're union brothers and sisters."

ILLINOIS
ON STRIKE
UNFAIR LABOR
PRACTICE

28DM818

Collinsville, Alabama

Barron Deforest Cooper (far left) and his friend and preacher, Ertis Ray Hill, meet every Saturday morning at the Collinsville Trade Day, a sixty-five-acre flea market on the outskirts of Collinsville, Alabama. Thousands come to buy and sell local crafts, antiques, and rusty tools here, and in a section of the market called Coon Dog Hill they come to trade dogs and chickens, pigs and goats, and, well, says Junior (that's what everyone here prefers to call Cooper), "a little bit of everything." Cooper and Hill are regular companions. "Ertis and I hunt together and go to church together," says Junior. Thomas Jefferson would have approved of at least the former, which he described as his preferred form of exercise, one that gives "boldness, enterprise, and independence to the mind." An advocate of the Second Amendment ("the right to keep and bear arms") and a onetime member of the National Rifle Association, Cooper sees the growth of the population and the loss of a rural lifestyle as a greater threat to gun owners than any proposal for gun control. "Even down here where you've got a lot of woods, the people that own the land charge money for permission to hunt." On this day, Hill had brought his beagles and a big pot of peanuts for boiling, a Southern favorite. Cooper had brought his grandson, Chris, and Chris had brought his new dog, Shadow. "He hadn't had that yeller dog very long," says Junior, "and he wanted to show him off." Then someone spotted a bird in a nearby tree. "I had put a scope on my .22 rifle for squirrel hunting — it wasn't loaded — and I was just looking up to see whether that was a hawk or somebody's chicken that had gotten loose."

68

Uniondale, New York

A popular encyclopedia of American history says that America's fall football ritual is "a demonstration of adolescent masculinity," but Anna "Tonka" Tate (number 68), a 5'11", 285-pound "lineman" for the New York Sharks, would beg to differ. Tate has a message on her answering machine that begins, "Hit or be hit, that is the question. It's the Shark thing, don't you know." Though they play on borrowed high school and college fields, have full-time day jobs, pay for their own jerseys, and do their stiff-arming and tackling in front of fans that are counted in the hundreds, Tate and her teammates are part of the continuing democratization of American sport that began with the feminist surge of the sixties (the first Women's Professional Football League was started in 1965, though that league failed after a few seasons) and was institutionalized with the landmark 1972 gender equity legislation demanding equal spending for sports in schools receiving federal aid. "A lot of men don't take us seriously," says Tate, who got her nickname from a fan who remarked that she hit like a truck, "but we do." Indeed, thousands of girls now play sports once reserved for boys — nearly 40,000 on school and amateur hockey teams and over 2,000 on high school wrestling squads — and though the football females once favored team titles like the "Vixens" and "Dolls," the current crop of nicknames in the Independent Women's Football League (which the Sharks joined in 2001) are the more violent-sounding "Warriors," "Blitz," "Tempest," "Thunder," and "Maulers." It would not surprise these women to know that their female forebears worked the fields, rode horses, and hunted with their husbands and brothers. Nor would they be shocked to learn that the first person to ride over Niagara Falls in a barrel and survive was sixty-three-year-old Annie Edson Taylor, a schoolteacher, in 1901. "We play like the men," says 170-pound Kimberly Bishop (number 78), who has a herniated disk from her rugby days. "They're just bigger."

4 Streets

The parade of smiling women in skimpy bathing suits strutting enthusiastically across the neon-framed stage of the "Genesis Center" would feel strange in most parts of twenty-first-century America. In the middle of Gary, Indiana, it feels positively bizarre. Here is a Northwest Indiana city that is famous, essentially, for three things: as the subject of a sweet and simple song in the classic 1957 musical *The Music Man*; as the childhood home of the Jackson Five; and as a perennial candidate for the title of "Murder Capital of America." Just east of Chicago, Gary greets the traveler on the Indiana Toll Road as the sad legacy of America's rich industrial past: to one side, white steam vapors cascade from the imposing refineries of U.S. Steel, to the other lies the heart of a rust-belt city long in decline. Thirty years ago, author Marshall Frady described Gary in *Harper's* as an "endless city of the night" and "an interminable repetition of narrow anonymous streets under wan streetlights." Today it is that and worse. The lineup of dime stores, shoe stores, and jeweler's shops that he saw along Broadway and "the limitless plain of simple homes with flat roofs bristling with a tangle of TV antennas, telephone poles and neons" are now largely abandoned, as if something awful happened, and half the people simply stopped what they were doing, put on their jackets, and left.

Gary has been deteriorating for so long even the name of the city has come to be treated like a curse. An adjacent municipality long known as "East Gary" opted in 1976 to call itself "Lake Station" instead. That same year, the local newspaper dropped "Gary" from its title. (Since most of its readers and advertisers were now in the growing sprawl outside the city, it changed to the shorter and less evocative *Post-Tribune*.) A quarter of a century later, in 2000, the paper gave up nearly all its civic presence when it moved its main offices out of town, too. Perhaps it is an accident of planning, but even Interstate 80 seems to turn a cold shoulder. Not until you are right on top of the Gary city limits do you see signs directing you there. It's as if the transportation department, worried about Indiana's image as a place of corn, soybeans, and homespun values, would simply prefer that drivers pass Gary by.

Gary is a city which, until the EPA ordered it cleaned up a few years ago, was best recognized by the gas-waste fires, the stench, and the orange tone of pollution in the air; a city which at its peak had a population of

180,000, but that is now barely holding on to 100,000; and a place where many of the young residents have come to accept the moniker "Scary Gary," which, in a weird statement of reverse pride, appears on T-shirts sold here. So what is it doing as the setting for, of all things, the Miss USA pageant? Trying, desperately, to sing a revival song.

To judge by the audience in the hall, the event is a roaring success. The people in the crowd stand and cheer and hoot for their state favorites, dancing in their seats to the thump of the music, urging on the mostly white, mostly blond girls. But the crowd at the Genesis Center is window dressing for the real event, the CBS television production beaming Gary's Miss USA pageant into the homes of 8 million. This is what Gary's elders angled for in 2000 when they struck a deal with Donald Trump, co-owner (with CBS) of the show. Gary would spend $10 million to mount the Miss USA pageant over three years. In return, the network would give Gary a few minutes of national television time to sell the "Steel City," as it used to be called: two hours of pretty girls interspliced with commercials telling the world about the "New" Gary for the "New Century." "Thirty minutes from Chicago!" "Pristine beaches!" "Great Shopping!" "World-Class Gaming!"

"Delegates" to the Miss USA pageant were filmed around town, showing off Gary. For the swimsuit competition, the bikini-clad contestants strutted alongside U.S. Steel's blast furnaces, which pageant emcee William Shatner jokingly called "the hottest spot in town."

Even for the usually exaggerated tone of a tourism campaign, the claims are overblown. Yes, Gary is thirty minutes from Chicago, but few Chicagoans are willing to go through the deserted crime-ridden neighborhoods they must pass to get here. And yes, there are beaches in Gary, right next to the steel mills. You can shop in Gary, if what you want is fast food (though you may have to pay for it through a bulletproof barrier). The old jewelry stores and shoe emporiums are now closed. But there are plenty of places to pawn your belongings or sell your blood. There is no decent supermarket in Gary and just four "bookstores": two of them sell only religious books; the other two sell only pornography. And ever since the Sheraton Hotel closed here in 1985, there has been no place to stay in Gary — no place, that is, unless you count the hotel at Trump's riverboat casino, docked at Lake Michigan, five miles from Gary's center. No matter the stunning pageant of youth and vitality being displayed by Miss USA inside the Genesis Center; outside the television picture, Gary, a city that is 85 percent black, is still struggling, mightily.

What would America be without its cities? Revolutions have traditionally needed urban settings in which to find support and encourage unrest, and the American Revolution was no different. Boston, Philadelphia, even New York were the datelines for the American uprising against the British. But the American city, as an entity, really grew and prospered in the late nineteenth century with the rise of industry, the growth of immigration, and the movement of the country away from its agrarian roots. By the turn of the century, many American cities had joined the "City Beautiful Movement," a campaign to turn the growing American urban centers into aesthetic gems, featuring wide boulevards, parks, and distinguished-looking town halls. By the early twentieth century, the city had become an American civic statement, its optimistic steel-framed buildings soaring to the heavens, its ethnically rich populations offering a fresh statement of the American dream. The American city was the nation's cultural center, the home of jazz, movies, publishing, advertising, and the "skyscraper," America's first native form of architecture. The world's future was being molded there and it looked a lot like the best of America: lively, brash, optimistic, and full of energy.

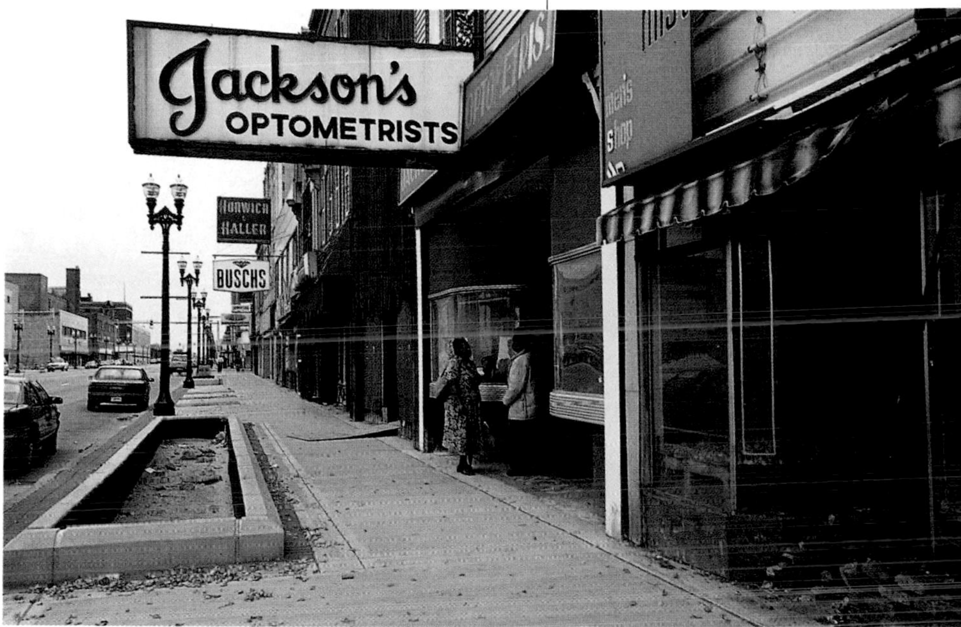

Ghosts of the past linger along Broadway, Gary's main commercial thoroughfare, above, where Jackson's Optometrists, a jewelry-turned-eyeglass shop, is one of only two operating stores on this block. Jackson's once supplied protective goggles to the workers at U.S. Steel. Today, it serves a more modest clientele, about 80 percent of whom receive Medicaid assistance to pay for eyeglasses.

By the 1920s, more people lived in cities than the countryside, certifying the twentieth as America's first urban century. Then came the Great Depression, the Second World War, the rise of the prosperous suburbs, the decline of manufacturing, the movement for Civil Rights, and, in turn, "white flight." In 1950, just 23 percent of Americans lived in the suburbs; by the end of the twentieth century, the number had doubled. Indeed, for much of the last fifty years or so, the phrase "urban America" was likely to suggest a blighted setting, a relic of the nation's rich industrial past, a dangerous place in need of imaginative social policy solutions, occupied largely by an underclass of Latinos and, especially, African-Americans. If the city was still a laboratory of ideas, then those now being offered up by America's cities were the expressions of anger and resentment, deprivation and exclusion, poverty and frustration, despair and resignation. By the 1970s, many American urban centers operated in the language of what one historian called a "riot ideology," the belief that black America's situation was special, that its own very particular history meant that it could not be expected to follow the path of ethnic groups that started out strug-

In an Ohio "laboratory": Concocting the "perfect" suburban grass

A scientist at the Scotts Company greenhouse checks the progress of its slow-grow, low-mow grasses, left. In the 1950s, advertisements for lawn-care products often equated a well-groomed front lawn with a wholesome family life, right. "The observer invariably judges the character of the homeowner by the care that is given to the lawn," read one ad of the day. Opposite page: an 1800 print of Brooklyn Heights, one of the first "suburbs" of New York City.

Like most suburban Americans, Bob Harriman is obsessed with his grass. Harriman, chief research scientist at the Scotts Company in Marysville, Ohio, has for several years been trying to develop a genetically engineered strain of turfgrass that would grow more slowly. If he succeeds, it would be a boon not only to those who mow America's nearly 53 million lawns, but to Scotts, the leader in the $5 billion home lawn-care industry. Harriman had experimented with different combinations of genes, but none was exactly right. Once again, he began the painstaking process: injecting single cells from seeds of Kentucky bluegrass with genes from plants that expressed the "dwarfism" trait, nurturing those cells in a windowless lab equipped with two alarm systems and a computer-controlled climate until they produced a few tiny blades of grass; moving them to the greenhouse where they would be watered by hand and trimmed with scissors.

When Harriman walked into Scott's "Biotech Greenhouse" one recent morning, to check on the strain his research team had nicknamed "No Grow," he could tell right away that this time something was working. Six months after he'd first injected them, the cells were full-fledged tufts. "They looked almost like little Bonsai plants," he recalls, proudly. Harriman brought the rest of his team to the greenhouse, where they shook hands and clapped each other on the back. They were one step closer to creating that quintessential American dream: the perfect lawn.

What is it about a "lawn" that makes so many Americans yearn for it? City dwellers dream of someday owning even a tiny grassy plot. Suburbanites dream of perfecting the plot they already own. Even in sandy Saudi Arabia, the American expatriate community is distinguished by the presence of "front lawns" maintained on desert soil (no easy feat), and no matter the local customs, U.S. embassies throughout the world are almost invariably outfitted with a green carpet of grass, an American emblem as recognizable as the flag. Although there are sociobiologists who suggest a genetic basis for the American passion for lawns — a "Savanna syndrome" that urges one to cultivate domesticated versions of the African grasslands on which our ancestors evolved — the search for the perfect lawn may be rooted less in biology than in culture, *American* culture. No other country is as preoccupied with maintaining expanses of lush, weed-free carpets. Then again, no other country has taken as keenly to the notion of the "suburb," that greensward life which combines a small tract of land and easy accessibility to the city. For so many Americans it has denoted an entire way of life.

As long as there have been cities, there have been suburbs. The word itself — Latin for "under the city" — dates to the Middle Ages, when it referred to the shanties and hovels built in the shadow of the city walls. Medieval suburbs were decidedly inferior real estate, social and economic backwaters frequented by drunkards, prostitutes, and thieves. Even when pre-Revolutionary Boston, Philadelphia, and New York began expanding, it was society's dregs that were squeezed beyond the city limits.

The foundation for the modern American suburb was laid on a spring morning in 1814 when some two hundred people boarded one of Robert Fulton's new side-wheeled, steam-powered ferries in Brooklyn and churned toward Lower Manhattan, inaugurating regular ferry service to New York and triggering what historian Kenneth Jackson calls "the most fundamental realignment of urban structure in the 4,500-year past of cities on this planet." Spurred on by such "mass transit," Brooklyn became, as one 1874 visitor put it, "little more than New York's vast dormitory." Indeed, Brooklyn's own Walt Whitman, who made regular ferry crossings just to watch the tides — he called the ferries "living poems" — provided one of the first descriptions of the commuter rush there. "It is highly edifying," he wrote, "to see the phrenzy ... they rush forward as if for dear life, and woe to the fat woman or unwieldy person of any kind, who stands in their way."

From the nineteenth century on, wherever mass transportation went, the suburbs were sure to follow. When the trolley and the railroad began to expand the range of the American city, the old definition of suburb was turned inside out, as wealthy urbanites settled beyond the city limits and laborers found cheap housing at the city's core. Then, by the beginning of the twentieth century, with the arrival of the single combustion engine, the suburban holy trinity of house, lawn, and car was complete. Now every commuter was his own master, able to go where he wanted when he wanted, the very essence of domestic freedom.

This modern suburb sprang from quintessentially American values. It accented democracy and the access of a middle class to the riches previously held exclusively by elites, and it emphasized the value of property and a home of one's own. (Today, two-thirds of Americans own their own homes, double the rate of most Western European countries.) The "lawn" was central to this, a piece of land from which Americans could both derive a taste of the life of the gentry and connect physically with the earth. Urbanites sought their own sliver of wilderness in communities whose very names — Lake Forest, Glendale, Chestnut Hill — were designed to evoke the call of the wild, albeit sotto voce.

A new literary genre chronicled the challenges faced by the suburban pioneer (including mosquitoes, weeds, lost golf balls, and crab grass). The cylindrical mower, brought to the broad market around 1870, gave suburbanites the means to tame their quarter-acre "frontiers," an event seen then as an experience of rural bliss. "Whoever spends the early hours of one summer day . . . pushing these grass cutters over a velvety lawn, breathing the fresh sweetness of the morning air . . . will never rest contented in the city," rhapsodized Frank J. Scott in *The Art of Beautifying Suburban Home Grounds*, in 1870.

Indeed, the suburban impulse was as much about escape as it was about arrival. As cities, swollen by the industrial revolution, grew ever more congested, polluted, noisy, and disease-ridden, developers portrayed the suburbs as a pastoral panacea. In a sense, they were tapping into the American immigrant impulse. Where the immigrant once fled disease-ridden, "morally suspect" Europe for a fresh start in the wide-open spaces nature offered in distant America, so he now listened to the call of the suburbs as a way out of urban squalor. Citing cities as incubators for "many of the political and social problems of the day," turn-of-the-century demographer Adna Ferrin Weber concluded: "The rise of the suburbs is by far the most cheering movement of modern times." And they continued to rise, developing by leaps and bounds in the 1920s, when Ford's Model T helped to make the car a truly middle-class commodity and commuting a middle-class occupation.

In 1946, the modern cultural symbol of the postwar suburb took root in four thousand acres of Long Island potato fields, where Abraham Levitt and his sons began the largest private housing project in history. "Levittown" and its many imitators made the suburban life possible for millions who could never before afford it. But what looked like a veritable Eden to some looked like a cultural wasteland to others. Suburban bards John Cheever and John Updike documented the alcoholism and the anomie. The suburb, according to its critics, was but a cradle of conformity. In Levittown fences were forbidden, clothes could be dried outdoors only on weekdays, and lawns had to be kept well trimmed, or the Levitts would mow them and forward the bill. Many suburban developers, including the Levitts, refused to sell to blacks. "We can solve a housing problem, or we can try to solve a racial problem," explained William Levitt, "But we cannot combine the two." Real estate advertisements again touted suburbia as a refuge — now from racial tension, crime, and drugs — encouraging "white flight." Between 1950 and 1980, suburban population more than doubled.

Today, more Americans live in the suburbs than in either the cities or the country, making America the world's first and only truly "suburban nation." Some of the overt racism is gone (Levittown long ago began to include African-Americans) and the conformity has given way to the human need to define difference. Even the Levitt houses have lost their sameness, as families added on or built above and otherwise declared their distance from

the stifling uniformity. Nonetheless, the value Americans place on the detached private house surrounded by a small tract of land endures as the quintessential American domestic environment, even if the workload that comes with it is less appreciated. At Scotts, Bob Harriman's "No Grow" — renamed, more realistically, "Slow-grow" — is being tested outdoors, undergoing extremes of temperature and the stress of footprints and lawnmowers. "If we could make a lawn you had to mow only every third weekend," says Harriman, of his quest, "we feel that would be a nice contribution to the American family."

gling but eventually joined the mainstream of American society, assimilating through intermarriage and the exchange of ethnic identification for a new "Americanness." Instead, black Americans had more in common with African colonialists fighting wars of independence, and perhaps even shared more with the founding generation of America as it threw off the chains of Britain. Like Colonial America, black America felt the weight of oppression, the ignominy of servitude, the insult of inferiority, and, in turn, a sometimes unbridled rage requiring the addictive salve of federal monies.

Gary knows this story all too well. Founded at the beginning of the twentieth century as a company town for United States Steel (the official seal still shows a globe poured over with molten steel, and the words "city of the century"), its fortunes rose and fell with the steel industry. At its peak, when American steel was building the world, it was home to a thriving community of German, Polish, and Eastern European immigrants, a rough, but vibrant place (its other nickname was "the Magic City") that thumped with the sounds of pride and achievement. So grand a statement of industrial might was this city, Joseph Stalin once pronounced his wish that his own Magnitogorsk in the southern Urals would become the "Gary of the Soviet Union." But American steel came under foreign competition (even, after the collapse of communism, from Magnitogorsk itself) and at precisely the time when African-Americans seemed ready to inherit the better jobs and — finally — the political power of Gary, new technologies reduced the need for labor at the mills. At one time, U.S. Steel employed thirty thousand here. Now, the company supports only seventy-five hundred, two-thirds of whom live outside Gary.

At 6.5 miles long, U.S. Steel's Gary Works is the largest steel plant in the Western Hemisphere. It produces some 6.5 million tons of steel a year, most of it for the auto industry. In the blast furnaces, above, iron ore pellets are melted into liquid iron at thirty-six hundred degrees, then purified and converted into steel.

You can still see the remnants of Gary's glory days in the long-neglected architecture of this city. There's the once thriving City Methodist Church, built in 1925, which has been empty now for twenty-five years. A film company recently used the building as a setting for a movie on wartorn Bosnia. The city bureau of the *Post-Tribune* still occupies the offices it had when it was the *Gary Post-Tribune*, a 1959 building bordered by City Castle Hamburgers on one side and vacant lots on the others. But with the bulk of the paper's employees at the main office in suburban Merrillville, the space that once housed more than one hundred newsroom employees is now largely empty, the work of reporting on Gary itself left to a staff of five, its entire Gary contingent. "We could have a double or triple homicide and it wouldn't make it into the other editions of the paper," says Richard Grey, the paper's Gary editor. "As long as we're considered the Gary newspaper, no one in the suburbs wants to buy it."

The Palace Theater, on Broadway, was Gary's great movie house. Built in 1925, it went out of business in 1972 and sat in decay until, in anticipation of the crowds that would descend on Gary for the Miss USA pageant, the city took a Potemkin Village paintbrush to it, putting pictures of flower pots on the boarded-up windows and one of a mustachioed attendant in the empty ticket kiosk. Hearkening back to yet another piece of Gary's once distinguished history, they then displayed on the marquee the (false) announcement that the Jackson Five were returning to perform there that night.

No, these days, for the most part, downtown Gary is just a memory imprisoned by interstates: On the northern edge of downtown, I-90 cuts Gary's center off from the steel mills, the casinos, and the Lake Michigan shorefront, a passage of highway that allows Chicagoans to come and gamble without encountering Gary's squalor. To the west, I-65 guards suburban Hobart and Portage, and to the south, I-80 protects suburban Merrillville, Schererville, and Valparaiso, towns where the white citizens of Gary fled from 1960 onward. Merrillville is also home to Southlake Mall and Route 30, the county's main shopping strip. "Have you driven on Route 30?" says Juana Meeks, director of the Gary Enterprise Zone project, noting the number of businesses there that once had a Gary address. "That used to be our *Broadway*."

Opened in 1925, when movies were new, the ornate million-dollar Palace Theater was designed "to make Gary one of the real show cities of the United States." Modeled after "a castle in Spain," the Palace, now abandoned, hasn't shown a film in three decades.

To the rare visitor, Gary seems to be a place that time has completely passed by, segregated by highways from the future that the rest of the country enjoys, a place left to fester in its misery. A couple of years ago, Federal Express announced it would no longer pick up in Gary after dark, so fearful was it for the safety of its drivers, and only when Gary's mayor angrily objected and other civic leaders claimed that racism drove the company's decision, did they reverse it.

Since its decline began in the late sixties, Gary has been through dozens of proposals for renewal, including the one that built the Genesis Convention Center with $16 million in federal funds, the name suggesting, of course, a new beginning, the federal money representing the nation's hope that Gary might serve as a model of urban redevelopment and African-American achievement. Back then, Mayor Richard Hatcher, one of the first black mayors of a major American city, had hoped that the center would help solidify his dream of Gary as a major black landmark, with the Genesis Center drawing conventions and trade shows linked to black American themes, or even more, that Gary would become the center of black culture, a "model city" for black America, the capital of a "black" nation within a nation. But the vision failed. Today, Gary appears to have been as abandoned by middle-class blacks as it has been by whites, and the Genesis Center is a civic money loser, operating at about 50 percent capacity. It serves as home to the Gary Steelheads, a money-losing Continental Basketball Association team established by the current mayor, Scott King, in yet another attempt at revival, and, of course, to Miss USA, a "Miss America" copycat started in 1952 by Pacific Knitting Mills when Miss America refused to provide it with photographs of the contestants wearing their company's bathing suits in the pageant. Even today, at Miss USA, the judging makes little pretense to "talent," opting instead for a somewhat cynical, we-all-know-what-this-is-all-about tone. The women, like the pageant, are here to sell.

> **"The question is whether we blacks can join other Americans — including more recent immigrants — and become the full emotional and civic owners of the place where we were once owned."**
> ROGER WILKINS
> Jefferson's Pillow

Gary's story is the story of much of urban America, in particular, the story of the industrial city, the product of the smokestack world of the early twentieth century, trying to find a new life in the twenty-first century. There are literally hundreds of "Garys" throughout the country — old red-brick furnace towns like Worcester, Massachusetts; Utica, New York; Akron, Ohio; and Waterbury, Connecticut, all plagued by the same unfortunate dilemma. How does a city that rose with a manufacturing economy, producing tires or brass or steel, cope in a world where those operations have been made obsolete by cheaper foreign labor or advanced technology?

Yet over everything and everyone in this beleaguered place hovers another, even more commanding subject, race: the founders' folly, their sin, their silence. No issue did more damage to their reputations. No issue has done more to undermine the stability of American society. In the founders' failure was the seed of the Civil War, the preamble to the segregationist society of Jim Crow, the opening act to Birmingham, the overture to Watts, Detroit, L.A., the roots of modern-day Gary. It led to the bifurcation of the country into North and South, black and white, and delivered a legacy of distrust that has lingered — no, smoldered — to our present day.

Even as they trumpeted the idealism of equality and justice, the founders recognized that they did so in a house of hypocrisy, and yet chose to do nothing about it. For 225 years Americans have lived with their indifference, played out in the steady rhythm of the black American experience, at one moment joined firmly to the national community, at the next cut apart in a stance of bitter confrontation, defining a separate history, a separate America.

II

Ben Clement is Gary's salesman. From his corner office, in an otherwise empty floor of a building that used to house the Gary State Bank (a ninety-year-old Gary institution that was recently sold to outside interests), the forty-five-year-old director of the city's office of economic development sets out each day to bring a positive message about Gary to the world. It was Clement who put together Gary's proposal for Miss USA, Clement who dreamed up the still-unrealized idea of a Gary-based African-American Film Festival, which, because there are no operating movie theaters here, would have to be held in a local high school auditorium (hats that he had made to promote the phantom event lie gathering dust in the corner of his office). It was Clement who helped produce the attractive graphic brochure outlining Gary's future as a high-tech center and Clement who hosts a biweekly local television show dedicated to saying nice things about Gary but that in its title, "Panacea" — a word that means "cure-all" and is derived from the name of the Greek goddess of healing — seems to demonstrate the degree of challenge he, the mayor who appointed him, and all the "Panacea" "correspondents" face. Put simply, Gary is a hard sell.

Gary's director of economic development, Ben Clement, right, meets with Mayor Scott King. "Some African-Americans look at our city having a white mayor as the old slave mentality of 'Master Charlie' . . . but he's got an African-American wife and kids," says an emphatic Clement. "If anybody can empathize with the plight of African-Americans, it's Mayor King."

Indeed, if he wanted to, all Clement would have to do is swing his office chair around to the windows looking out upon the city to feel the inspiration (or, more accurately, desperation) that comes from the ashes of the past. For there, before him, to the east and to the south, are the scars of a quarter century of well-intentioned failures. Straight ahead, next to the Greek-domed city hall, stands the abandoned Sheraton. Built as a Holiday Inn, it had already gone out of business once when the Hatcher administration bought it in 1981 with $2.5 million in federal funds. In an unusual partnership between government and the private sector the city ran the hotel as a Sheraton, building a catwalk to join it with the Genesis Center in the hopes that it would encourage businesses to bring trade shows there. But the lobby flooded on the day the hotel opened — an inauspicious omen, to say the least — and within a few years it had failed. The hotel's cinder blocks were whitewashed and an enormous banner celebrating "Gary Style" was hung in front to hide the façade during the Miss USA pageant festivities.

only to governmental mistakes, to "horse-race" politics, and to personal scandals — and an obsession with "objectivity." The latter affliction, he said, caused journalists to stand on the sidelines of society, poking at it as if probing a laboratory animal. Fallows and others urged editors and reporters to adopt a form of "civic journalism," to care about their community, to respect the public and engage them in a dialogue. They could still point out problems, but they should do so in the spirit of finding solutions. Naturally, Fallows was himself attacked by editors whose work he was holding up for criticism. But some took the ideas to heart.

The challenge of "civic journalism" was especially acute for Juli Metzger, whose *Chronicle-Tribune* was trying to survive in a depressed economic environment that threatened both Marion and the paper itself. Communities facing similar struggles had watched their newspaper fold or move to a more prosperous suburban address and become more "regional." "We would do what a lot of newspapers do," she says, describing long-standing editorial practices. "Something happens and you write a story about it. Statistics get released and you write a story about what the stats say. A factory closes and you write about the factory closing." But it seemed that the paper was chronicling the slow sinking of a ship, one that she and her paper also rode. That didn't seem to Metzger what the founding fathers had in mind when they granted the press its enormous powers. After all, the one choice that Jefferson's maxim failed to suggest was the only one that no one would want: *no* government and *no* newspapers. "People were leaving town, our circulation was declining, and we had an above-average illiteracy rate — definitely not good for a newspaper," Metzger explains. She approached her publisher and said, "Shouldn't we be reporting about that? Shouldn't we be helping people find ways to solve the city's problems? "

All of these concerns were on the thirty-eight-year-old editor's desk when an unsigned letter from a reader landed there not long after the millennium babies story, objecting to the paper running a picture of an interracial couple. For Metzger, who was keenly aware that Marion was the locale, in 1930, of Indiana's last-known lynching, this sign of lingering racism was the last straw. She launched a ten-part series called, appropriately, "Moment of Truth," enlisting all of her nine editors and reporters and several dozen nonjournalist citizens to contribute articles. The first issue set the tone, with a headline, "Time's Running Out for Marion," and a memorable opening: "Marion is increasingly becoming a place where people are born and buried. The time in between is often spent in someone else's hometown." A devastatingly frank discussion of Marion's problems followed, questioning government ("savage politics stifles leadership"), demographics ("the community is growing older faster than the state while the youth continue to move away"), education ("all of Marion is at risk"), and poverty ("one of Indiana's most impoverished counties").

NEW-YORK EVENING POST.

An early copy of the New-York Evening Post, *founded by Alexander Hamilton in 1801.*

"People were angry," recalls Metzger, who invited readers to a town meeting to discuss the first installment. "There were fifty in the room, all loaded for bear." The paper was castigated for airing the town's "dirty laundry," for not being a "cheerleader." Metzger told them that it was not the paper's role to be a "cheerleader." The manager of the local General Motors plant sent some people to the meeting to say that GM hated the series. "I said, 'We're doing this for the people of Marion, not GM.'"

Yet as her staff turned out successive "Moment of Truth" issues — on employment, housing, education, "family and faith," and a half-dozen other pressing subjects — the citizens clambered aboard. The paper offered ample opportunity for community voices, including harsh ones, and guest columns from local leaders. A local businessman offered $50,000 as a challenge grant to build new homes for the poor. And General Motors eventually signed on to the spirit of the community revival project, cosponsoring, with the paper, leadership workshops that grew into dozens of civic projects.

A Pulitzer Prize nomination for the *Chronicle-Tribune* followed. And though it was too soon to tell whether Marion would bounce back, the staff members of the *Chronicle-Tribune* felt proud that they had taken the bold step to tell the "real story" of their city with an eye to solutions. Indeed, in its final "Moment of Truth," the paper revisited millennium mom Stephanie Watkins, the woman whose untold story had helped launch the series. It turned out that a local woman, responding to the call for "community-mindedness," had learned of Stephanie's plight and encouraged her to join a YWCA Mentor Mothers program. Juli Metzger was able to report that a year later Stephanie was off welfare, had a full-time job, and had moved into a new apartment. This was the kind of civic journalism, Metzger thought, that the founders would be proud of.

cause a kid who gets straight A's here actually has to hide his report card for otherwise he might be seen as playing to the white world. That's why I do what I do."

There is something of a swagger to Clement, whose e-mail address is "bossman" and who boasts that Miss USA was a good project for him because, he says, sounding a bit like Trump himself, "I like beautiful women." But while wildly optimistic, Clement's dreams for Gary seem sincere. They draw upon both his proud family background and his long-simmering impatience with the city that is his home.

Like so many of Gary's African-American families, Clement's roots are in the South, though he himself was born in Chicago, where he lived with his parents and two sisters in a housing project until they all moved to Gary when he was four. In Gary, the Clements lived on the far west side in a simple Levittown-style house. It was not a pretty life. Clement remembers being on the football field in his junior high gym class when a gun battle broke out between members of a gang called the Tarrytown Rangers and another called the Kangaroos. The Rangers, which were a spin-off of the Blackstone Rangers, a Chicago gang, controlled Clement's neighborhood, but he resisted the pressure — and the urge — to join. Today, the Gary gangs have been weakened, splintered into a collection of smaller groups called "cliques," mostly because their larger counterparts in Chicago have been broken by the police there. But even now the more than sixty Gary cliques remain dangerous — armed, violent, and deeply involved in drug trafficking — which is why Clement is impatient with anyone who sees something positive in the gang experience, for instance those who argue that the gangs offer an alternative identity and a means of protection for children whose home life has been ruptured. "I grew up in fear of them," he says, "and they nearly destroyed my city."

It's hard for teenagers to stay out of trouble in Gary. Once a high-scoring point guard for Roosevelt High School, eighteen-year-old Chad Knight, above in wheelchair, was shot in a scuffle on the way home from a teenage club. When his foot was amputated, the youth's dream of a college sports scholarship ended.

As hostile as life was at home, the world outside Gary didn't look too inviting to Clement, either, particularly after an incident in 1972, when he joined a group of students on a trip to the finals of the Indiana high school basketball championships in Bloomington. Gary West Side, Clement's largely black high school, was facing off against Connersville High, an all-white school. In Indiana, which has a long and sad history with racism (the Ku Klux Klan effectively ran the statehouse in the

1920s), that alone would have been enough to create a racially charged environment. But in the spring of 1972, with the voice of black power on the rise throughout the nation and George Wallace — the onetime Alabama governor who had stood in the doorway of the University of Alabama, blocking federal officials from enforcing integration — in the midst of a serious campaign for president (his third), a simple basketball game between white kids and black kids took on a whole new meaning. After all, Wallace had stunned Americans in 1964 and 1968 when he garnered a substantial vote here, proving that a racist message had appeal in the North. In 1967, Gary itself had stunned the nation, electing a black mayor, Richard Hatcher, who by 1972 was signaling his sympathies with the black power movement. Indeed, Wallace claimed that the rise of black political strength was so threatening it would "Southernize" the "good common folks" of the country. Among the white citizens of Indiana, he had plenty of people ready for just such a transformation.

In one of the biggest upsets in Indiana basketball history, Connersville beat Gary West, 80-63, but the atmosphere in the arena was tense and the West Side partisans were convinced that the white referees, as Clement puts it, "made certain that the black kids lost." After they lost, some of the Gary players refused to stand for the awards ceremony and then threw their championship game rings onto the floor. In the parking lot outside Bloomington's Assembly Hall, a riot broke out and state troopers armed with "shields and bats," says Clement, harassed and hit the black teens until the teens got on their buses and left. More than two hundred people were injured, leading to a one-year suspension of Gary West from Indiana high school athletics. But Clement says that on the nearly three-hour bus trip back to Gary, he and the other students crouched beneath the seats to avoid the bricks being hurled by Klan sympathizers who had heard about the confrontation and showed up on their route home to send the kids from Gary a message. Afterward, when Mayor Hatcher declared that the fight had broken out because of "geographical" differences separating urban northwestern Indiana from the rest of the state, everyone knew what he meant. "Black" Indiana and "white" Indiana were two incompatible places.

When Clement left Gary for college at Ohio State, he vowed never to return. "The only thing I could think of," he remembers, "was that I was going away and never coming back, and for a very long time, I didn't." After college, he stayed in Ohio and made a brief stab at a career in stand-up comedy, but his experience growing up in Gary continued to nag at him. Why had the "adults" there allowed the city to deteriorate so badly? What had made them lose their self-respect, abandon their civic duty, give in to their worst impulses? Indeed, why had the country allowed this to happen, tolerated the decline of a place like Gary when it was so emblematic of the failure of the American idea? Why had it allowed America to devolve into two "nations," so vastly different and at war with each other? And so, when he gave up on comedy and decided to go into economic development, Clement decided to do it "where I could get some home cookin'." He returned to Gary, moved in with his mother, and started on the path that has led him to his role as Gary's prime cheerleader.

For Clement, there was a psychological journey at work in these years, too. Though his family had remained in the North, they had, like many blacks who followed the path to the great industrial capitals, never gotten the South out of their system. When Clement was a boy, his father regularly regaled the children with stories of growing up in a cotton sharecropping community in Paris, Texas. "T. T." Clement claimed to have met Booker T. Washington and George Washington Carver when they came through town on speaking tours. While the encounter with the former was probably apocryphal (since T.T. was only four years old when Washington died), the pride the older Clement projected about his past made an impression on his son. And so, a few years after Clement returned to Gary, he and a few other family members decided to journey back to Texas and discover their roots.

What they found surprised and humbled them. On the one hand, they discovered that the Clement family had emerged from slavery in the respectable tradition of Booker T. Washington, by emphasizing education and hard work, and that both had served the family well. Unlike many sharecroppers, the Clements were able to get by — indeed, even then they were middle class, says Clement. And the Clements had served as leaders in their small community of Paris, with Ben's grandmother teaching at the local black school and his father working as a county agent, educating other sharecroppers about proper farm management. "My father," says Clement, clearly honored by the thought, "was teaching people how to transition from slavery to sharecropping to independent business person and farmer."

Standing there in his ancestral community, Clement felt odd, like being at home and far away from home at the same time. Mustering his courage, he asked if he and a cousin could be taken to see some cotton plants. Cotton is a big part of African-American history, of course, but Clement was embarrassed to say that as a Northern black and a "city boy" the plant itself had escaped his experience. A local relative took them out to the fields. "He pulled over to the side of the road, ran over and grabbed us some cotton plants," says Clement, "and we held them and thought, 'This is history, *our* history.'"

Clement also went to see the black slave graveyard. On the way, he and his family drove past a white cemetery that was neat and well kept, but the old slave grounds were overgrown and vandalized. There was a lot of racist graffiti and some of the headstones were broken. Clement's own family's markers were untouched, but he found it chilling nonetheless to stand before the grave of his great-grandmother, Maggie, who had been born into slavery and fathered by the white slave master. (Clement has always assumed that the slave master was the source of the light complexion that has been passed through his family.) Standing there, looking at Maggie's grave for the first time, he recalled how he saw pictures of her when she was young and how much she looked like his own sister.

> "I see new business on Broadway, a developed lakefront, and an expansion of the casinos and the airport . . . I see a [white] population moving back . . . and more upwardly mobile African-Americans, too. And after the stadium is finished and people are out enjoying themselves, they will say 'hey, this looks better,' and feel pride in Gary again . . ."
>
> Ben Clement
> *Gary Director of Development*

Clement says he felt no bitterness after his visit. Nonetheless, he took the revelations of his experience in Texas home with him and they have informed his work to the present day. From the clear dignity of his family and its emphasis upon self-reliance, he has derived an impressive work ethic, a rejection of the "victim" mentality that he says pervades much of Gary, that "desire," as he says, "to blame the white man." That's what encourages him, Clement says, to promote something like a "white" beauty pageant, to work for a white mayor, or to pursue other "majority" (he means "white") businesses for Gary's future, even as some in Gary point a finger and call him an "Uncle Tom" for reaching out to the "enemy." But from the visit to the graveyard, Clement also took away the belief that black Americans need to remember that their lives in America remain, sadly, limited. While there has been progress — that sister who looks like Great-Grandmother Maggie is now a practicing doctor in an integrated community in Michigan — it would be foolish to think that blacks have the opportunities of their white counterparts.

"It used to be taught in black families that you had to work twice as long as a white man and twice as hard to make it," says Clement. "Is that wrong? Of course it is. But we can only change it a step at a time." And so every morning, he climbs into his white city-owned Ford Explorer, drives one mile to work, and, like so many before him, plots out the recovery of the place he calls home. "I see new business on Broadway, a developed lakefront, whites moving back into town, and more upwardly mobile African-Americans, too," he says, a twinkle in his eyes. "I see a time when people will feel pride in Gary again."

III

No subject was more uncomfortable for the founding fathers of the American republic than race. One imagines that they hung their heads silently when it came up in conversation, or perhaps looked away as if to find something, anything, to change the topic. It was their great incon-

In historic Virginia: "Getting word" on the slaves of Monticello

Rev. Robert Hughes, above left, was just two years old when Jefferson died in 1826. A slave, he was sold to another slave owner and freed with the end of the Civil War, after which he founded a church in Charlottesville, Virginia. A century and a half later, Hughes's ancestors hold a reunion, above, at Monticello. Right, a 1997 painting by Nathaniel K. Gibbs depicts slave life in the early 1800s along Mulberry Row, where most of Jefferson's household slaves lived in log cabins.

At first look, the quiet, tree-shaded glade near the parking lot for the visitors' center at Monticello seems unremarkable, until you notice the slight indentations in the ground scattered among the tall trees. For the small group of people standing there, those shallow hollows are deeply significant, for research has recently determined that the glade was a burial ground for the slave population of Thomas Jefferson's plantation more than two centuries ago. It's easy to see how the site could have been overlooked; while slaves buried their own, they often used a bend in the road, the trunk of a tree, or even a rock as a marker and never inscribed them. Now, the observers here today are meeting to finally do something about that, to select the design for a memorial marking the final resting place of so many.

Among them is Karen Hughes White, an avid genealogist. For White, an African-American, this moment carries a special meaning. A few years before, she had traced her roots back to her great-grandfather, Wormley H. Hughes. She knew that he had been a preacher in Loudoun and Fauquier counties in the late nineteenth century; that he had performed local marriages; that he had died in 1901 when his son, White's grandfather, was only a boy; and, finally, that he had been an avid gardener. That made sense. Her grandfather and her father were also known for their gardening skills. But beyond that her research had hit a dead end.

Then, a chance encounter with another genealogist began to unlock more of White's past. It was at a convention of the Afro-American Historical and Genealogical Society in Washington that White met Lucia Cinder Stanton, now the senior research historian at the Thomas Jefferson Foundation at Monticello, which is responsible for the restoration and maintenance of Jefferson's home and plantation. White related what she knew about her ancestors and as she did, the name "Wormley" struck a spark for Stanton. A slave named "Wormley Hughes" had been Monticello's head gardener during Jefferson's last years. It was Wormley Hughes, in fact, who dug Thomas Jefferson's grave in 1826. Soon, White and Stanton were mounting the evidence proving that this first Wormley Hughes was indeed White's great-great-great grandfather.

White was thrilled. But for Stanton, proof of White's descent from Wormley Hughes and therefore from Wormley's prolific grandmother, Elizabeth Hemings, was a crucial link in her research. She was in the early stages of an unprecedented project at Monticello dedicated to finding, identifying, and interviewing African-American descendants of the six hundred or so slaves who had lived and labored on Jefferson's plantations. In Karen Hughes, Stanton had found one of them.

Stanton launched her project, "Getting Word," back in the early nineties, at a time when scandal was swirling around Jefferson and his relationship with a young slave, Sally Hemings, with whom Jefferson is believed by many (including, finally, the Thomas Jefferson Foundation itself) to have fathered several children. Indeed, the controversy caused a problem for Stanton when she tried to hire the researcher she wanted to help with the project. Dianne Swann-Wright, an African-American Ph.D. candidate in American History at the University of Virginia seemed perfect for the job, but because of the Hemings fracas and Jefferson's reputation as a slaveholder, Swann-Wright was reluctant to work at Monticello. Only when Stanton explained that the project would be a far-reaching enterprise dedicated to recording the family histories of the descendants of Monticello's slaves, did Swann-Wright agree to sign on. The project would trace the lives and stories of African-Americans as they wound through great events in American history, Stanton explained, and, in short, bear on the whole question of race in America.

Stanton and Swann-Wright's project has focused on the seven families who formed the core of select and well-trained workers at the plantation: the Hemingses, Herns, Hubbards, Gilettes, Hugheses, Colberts, and Fossetts, many of whom were children and grandchildren of two of Jefferson's most trusted slaves, known only as "Great George" and "Ursula." There are only seven images of the slaves at Monticello. Written documents include just a handful of letters and four reminiscences. From these and other materials, the historians already knew that Jefferson's slaves possessed considerable skills in fine joinery, carpentry, masonry, ironworking, and weaving, which they learned from Anglo-Saxon artisans in workshops along Mulberry Row, a mulberry-lined path that stretched from the main house at Monticello.

Lucia Cinder Stanton, left, and Dianne Swann-Wright, Monticello's senior research historians.

They also knew that other members of these families were well trained in household and cultural skills. James Hemings, a cook who accompanied Jefferson to Paris, returned to Monticello with a repertoire of French-American fusion cooking, a culinary skill passed on to Edith Hern Fossett and Fanny Gilette Hern, who helped cook for Jefferson in the White House. The Hemings brothers played the violin for Jefferson and his daughters with such verve that Jefferson remarked: "In music they are more generally gifted than the whites."

What the researchers didn't know was what had happened to most of Jefferson's slaves and their descendants when they left Monticello after Jefferson's death in 1826. Since there were few written records, they could only look to the personal histories that had been passed down orally. That is the meaning of the project's title, "Getting Word." "It echoes the locution of many African-Americans who 'get word' to their relatives about deaths, marriages, and other family events," explains Swann-Wright, "and reflects the importance of oral history in the African-American culture."

The kickoff for "Getting Word" was at a reception in the city of Chillicothe, Ohio. Several of the slaves whom Jefferson freed in his will (he freed only seven of the 130 he owned at his death) had moved to various communities in southern Ohio, a free state, and had prospered there as ministers, builders, educators, and musicians. Stanton and Swann-Wright arranged what they thought would be a small gathering of their descendants. To their surprise, more than forty people showed up, including a young man who seemed so "white" to Swann-Wright that she turned him away. "This is a meeting of African-American descendants of Monticello," she explained to the man who responded, to her embarrassment, that that was exactly what he was.

Convinced that they were on the right track, Stanton and Swann-Wright branched out, following leads that have taken them from coast to coast. Armed with a tape recorder and, finally, a video camera, the two women have traveled more than thirty-five thousand miles in their quest and recorded the histories of more than 135 African-Americans who can trace their ancestry to Jefferson's plantation. Though oral history is dismissed as unreliable by some historians, when it is the only vehicle for people who have few written records to pass information, it is taken very seriously. "Because they didn't write it down, they were very careful to get it right," says Swann-Wright.

The only generalizations the historians have reached so far are simple ones. They have found, for instance, that the descendants of Jefferson's slaves inherited an appreciation for education, freedom, family, and religion. While that may seem unsurprising, and little different from white American families of the time, it is important to note that for slaves any of the four — education, freedom, family, and religion — could have been seen as a harbor from the storms of their situation, a figurative, if not literal, "way out." Many descendants did not know much about the slave part of their heritage. "It wasn't so much that they blocked it out, but that earlier generations did not want to remember the bad time and so it hadn't come down as part of the family's history," says Swann-Wright. "But most everybody, when they realized what we knew about their ancestors at Monticello, was anxious to learn more. Slavery deprived people of their names, their history, their humanity. This is an effort to reclaim what was lost."

After four years of work, Stanton and Swann-Wright mounted a "Getting Word" exhibit in Monticello's visitors' center, dedicated to putting "a face on the African-American presence at Monticello." One hundred and twenty-five descendants of the plantation's slaves showed up from all across the country. Karen Hughes White was there, of course. The weather was fine and warm, the mood a mixture of expectation and trepidation. After all, the "reunion" photograph on the steps of Jefferson's mansion was also a reminder of a shameful past. Still, for many of the slaves' descendants, the return to Monticello completed a life-line. "To walk on the ground that some of my ancestors had walked and toiled on," says White, "that was indescribable."

sistency and they knew it. They lived in a white, Anglo-Saxon slaveholding society, yet they espoused a philosophy of equality and justice.

Not everyone was silent. John Adams and Benjamin Franklin were spirited in their denunciation of the practice. Alexander Hamilton opposed it vigorously. Then again, they were Northerners, each of them, and while the North had its slavery — there were slaves in New York until 1827 — slavery was central to the cotton economy of the South. Even some of those there who were certain that it represented both a moral violation and a violation of the new nation's recently articulated principles were reluctant to abolish it. Any antislavery advocate who wanted to push the issue risked upsetting the fragile North-South alliance that held the infant nation together. "We have the wolf by the ears," wrote a resigned Jefferson toward the end of his life when he had decided that the issue was best left to the next generation, "and we can neither hold him nor safely let him go. Justice is in one scale, and self-preservation in the other."

Early on, Jefferson had harsh words for slavery. He called it a "blot" and a "stain" upon America, "an unremitting despotism" forcing a "degrading submission." It was, he felt, an assault on morality. "Nothing is more certainly written in the book of fate," he penned, "than that these people [slaves] are to be free." Jefferson also saw the issue as social dynamite. In his most famous statement on the subject, he imagined that those so long abused by the practice would eventually rise up against their oppressors, and when they did, goodness, justice, and "the almighty" would be on the side of the slaves. "Can the liberties of a nation be thought secure when we have removed their only firm basis, a conviction in the minds of the people that these liberties are the gift of God? That they are not to be violated but with his wrath? Indeed, I tremble for my country when I reflect that God is just: that his justice cannot sleep forever."

In his initial draft of the Declaration of Independence, Jefferson blamed the American experience with slavery on the king. In his original language for the document, he asserts that the British monarch was waging "cruel war against human nature itself" by "captivating and carrying [a distant people] into slavery." Jefferson then goes on to write that the slave trade is a form of "piratical warfare," an "execrable commerce," an "assemblage of horrors." No doubt, as Joseph Ellis has written, Jefferson was making a stake here for the Declaration as something more than the freeing of a colonial peoples, the kind of break with history that was suggested by the document's stirring opening phrase ("We hold these truths to be self-evident, that all men are created equal . . ."), a call to end every manner of tyranny, and his words have certainly been read that way by people of all causes looking to call attention to injustice. Still, on the issue of slavery, Jefferson may have been getting ahead of his country. It was disingenuous to say that the British forced slavery on the Colonists, and when the Continental Congress voted to strike the grievance from Jefferson's draft entirely, it did so not because it felt it unfair to blame the British, but because so many states were uncomfortable with condemning a practice central to their lives and well-being.

Slavery also posed a personal dilemma for Jefferson. As John Chester Miller has pointed out, it was a part of his life from, quite literally, cradle to grave. Jefferson's earliest memory was of being carried on a pillow by a slave and a slave carpenter fashioned the coffin in which he was buried. Jefferson's beloved home, Monticello, was built by slave labor and even as he was drafting the Declaration of Independence, denouncing slavery with such florid tones, Jefferson was in possession of hundreds of black men, women, and children whom he lovingly referred to as "my family." Where Washington ordered in his will that his slaves be freed, Jefferson's were sold on his death to defray his substantial debt. It is one of the saddest ironies of the American story that the man who gave voice to one of the most compelling and egalitarian phrases in political history — "all men are created equal" — spoke one way and lived another.

" They secrete less by the kidneys and more by the glands of the skin, which gives them a very strong and disagreeable odor. They require less sleep. Their sexual relations are more ardent but lack the tender, delicate mixture of sentiment and sensation displayed by whites. They are much inferior in reason, though equal in memory."

— Thomas Jefferson

How could he abide such hypocrisy? If the long-rumored stories of Jefferson's relationship with the mulatto slave Sally Hemings are now to be believed, then how was he to accept the enslavement of a woman whom he may have loved as an equal? Indeed, of his own offspring? Was he insensitive to such contradiction or was he wracked by guilt over his inability to reconcile his life with his stated ideals? For generations, Jefferson's many fans (and detractors) have looked for answers to those questions and achieved little satisfaction.

One thing seems certain: Jefferson, who delighted in taking the temperature each day outside his Monticello window, had a changeable voice on the subject, and his feelings on slavery seemed to evolve in the direction of despair and hopelessness. In his early writings, he was determinably on the side of equality and emancipation, even proposing in the mid-1780s that a date be chosen — he suggested 1800 — when all newly born children of slaves would be free. In 1784, he proposed to Congress that slavery be abolished in the western territories. But by the time the Constitution was drafted (in his absence), euphemistically sanctioning the practice, and even more so, during his own presidency and after, Jefferson became much more vocal in his defense of the South's "peculiar institution" or, at the very least, in putting aside for later what had become an issue of political intractability.

Even if he had achieved his original goal and slavery had been abolished, Jefferson did not expect an America in which the races lived in equality and harmony. Indeed, in the same *Notes on the State of Virginia* where he had eloquently declared the immorality of slavery, he also argued the incompatibility of the races, a position that became a rallying cry for Southern racists right up to the Civil War. For much of the region, slavery was not only a system of labor deeply imbedded in the local economy, it was also a system of social organization that prevented what many worried would be a grave danger to the white race, the commingling of whites with African-Americans, whom even Jefferson conceded were "probably" inferior. Jefferson also had a more benign worry. Was there not also something cruel in the notion of emancipation, he asked. To free people who had been slaves and expect them to prosper in a society among their former masters would be like releasing children to compete among adults. No, when Jefferson called for freeing the slaves, it was not so that they could join the wider population and enjoy the fruits of the American experiment, but rather with the intention that they be recolonized back to Africa.

Stymied by political realities, the leaders of America's founding generation hoped for a natural solution to the slavery dilemma: noting the winds of change that they helped to initiate were bringing a respect for human dignity the world over, they had reason to believe that slavery would die of its own accord, with the details to be worked out later. But technology would intercede. In 1794, Eli Whitney, a New Englander who had moved to the South, invented the cotton gin, a machine (the word *gin* was short for "engine") that extracted cotton fibers from the seeds. Whitney's gin made the cotton trade dramatically more profitable and secured the slave system for another seventy years. Where there had been about 700,000 slaves in 1790, there were 1 million by 1800, 2 million by 1830, and almost 4 million in 1860, on the eve of the Civil War.

The aristocratic Judge Elbert H. Gary, depicted here in a statue outside city hall, never lived in the city that bears his name. The judge was known as a moralist, says historian Jim Lane, who found even card playing "beneath his dignity."

IV

Gary, Indiana, began as a gleam in the eye of Elbert H. Gary, a former Illinois county judge whose father, Erastus Gary, had founded the town of Wheaton, Illinois, in the 1830s and whose own legal work in the late nineteenth century led to his acquiring an interest in the steelmaking process and the chairmanship of a medium-sized firm called Federal Steel. After helping J. P. Morgan orchestrate the merger of Federal with 212 other independent manufacturing and transportation companies to form U.S. Steel in 1901, Gary assumed leadership of the new company. It was America's first billion-dollar corporation. Eager to grab a bigger piece of the Midwestern market for steel, Gary then chose the marshland site along the south shore of Lake Michigan for the construction of a massive new plant. The geography offered easy transportation by water or rail to the iron ore of Minnesota, the limestone of Michigan, and the coal of Pennsylvania.

The plant needed a town to serve the workers and so, on April 18, 1906, as local history records it, the "first stake was driven into the sand at 5th and Broadway" (the precise location, today, of Ben Clement's office). The mill executives had already laid plans to name all north-south streets east of Broadway after the states and those west of Broadway after the presidents. But Gary discarded a proposal to christen the town in honor of William Corey, the company president, when he decided that it should be named instead for himself. By September 1906, the new community had its first native-born resident, a girl born to the family of Frank Huff. She was named "Gary," too.

Wanting to discourage unionizing, U.S. Steel executives separated workers by class, race, and ethnicity. Men like those in the 1913 shot above, worked twelve-hour days, seven days a week.

It was the progressive era of American history, when many experiments in urban industrial planning were being undertaken. But while Gary was a mammoth project compared at the time with the legendary Krupp Works in Germany, U.S. Steel demurred on any ambition to turn the community into a "model" city. Executives were all too aware of the dangers presented by the "thoroughgoing paternalism" that had characterized the relationship between management and employees at George M. Pullman's railroad car company when it had built a sparkling company town just south of Chicago. There, in Pullman, Illinois, the company was both employer and landlord and in the recession of 1893, when the company imposed dramatic layoffs, it was in the awkward position of putting people out of work and then demanding that they pay their rent. The Pullman Strike of 1894 followed, the one that brought socialist Eugene V. Debs to national prominence. U.S. Steel was determined to avoid a similar situation in Gary. "One twig of experience is worth a whole forest of theory," wrote plant executive Eugene Buffington, borrowing from James Russell Lowell. Yet even as it fostered private ownership of Gary's real estate, the company was said to have vigorously protected its monopoly on local labor by using its power with the city's political leadership to discourage other businesses from achieving a foothold there.

Gary quickly thrived, attracting a flood of European immigrants. By 1910, the population was seventeen thousand; by 1920, it was fifty thousand. Then restrictive immigration laws led the mills to turn to a new source of labor, Mexican and African-American men who since the late 1910s had been arriving in droves from the South (and served in some cases as strikebreakers in the brutal 1919 Steel Strike). In what is often called "The Great Migration," Southern blacks came from migrant farming communities to the nation's big Northern cities in search of industrial jobs. It was a remarkable immersion of an essentially rural population (as late as 1910, 80 percent of black Americans lived in the farm regions of the South) into a new, and shockingly different, urban culture. Chicago was a favorite destination — the "Promised Land" in the biblical parlance of a deeply religious people who had long waited for God to open the doors and "deliver" them from slavery — and Gary was not far from Chicago. By 1930, Gary had a black population of eighteen thousand; by 1950, it was thirty-nine thousand.

200 LEAVE FOR THE NORTH

Selma, Ala., Feb. 9.—Labor agencies are working overtime to secure members of the Race to go north to work. It is not against the law for them to travel in the state, where it is permissible for the licensed labor agency to ship them to various points where they are wanted. Over 200 left here over the L. & N. R. R. for the north. They are constantly leaving and reports are that every one is getting work in the north.

Notices in African-American newspapers, such as the one above from a 1917 edition of the Chicago Defender, *encouraged blacks to work in the factories of the North. The result was the "Great Migration" that led so many to Chicago and, in turn, Gary.*

Even though they were now living in the North, Gary's African-Americans faced a Jim Crow life. The only jobs available to them at the steel mills were the unskilled positions that, not surprisingly, also paid the least. The Gary schools were segregated; so were the beaches and many public services. But the flow of blacks to Gary continued. Indeed, in the years after World War II the Great Migration took on a new urgency — what author Nicholas Lemann described as "one of the largest and most rapid mass internal movements of people in history"— and once again technology was a catalyst. Just as Eli Whitney's cotton gin had led to the expansion of the cotton industry and the prolongation of slavery, the arrival of the mechanical cotton picker in the 1940s curtailed the need for labor and ended the sharecropper system that had supplanted slavery after the Civil War. Up to 1940, about 1.5 million blacks had come north in search of jobs; from 1940 to 1970, another 5 million arrived, nearly all of them semiliterate and possessing few salable skills. Gary's black population swelled.

In the mid-1950s, with the Civil Rights movement in full swing and the Supreme Court reinforcing its call to end forced segregation, the white citizens of Gary began to flee to the suburbs. By 1967, Gary's blacks had reached majority status. That same year the city elected a black mayor, Richard Gordon Hatcher, a soft-spoken thirty-four-year-old lawyer from nearby Michigan City. From our vantage point, thirty-five years later, the demographics make Hatcher's election seem inevitable, but it wasn't. Until Hatcher (and Carl Stokes, who ran a successful campaign to become mayor of Cleveland the same year), no African-American had served as mayor of a large American city. Furthermore, to win, Hatcher needed more than votes; he needed the moxie to beat a well-entrenched Democratic party machine that was dead set against him and the shift to honest government that he promised.

After Hatcher won the Democratic primary, the party's local leadership tried to craft a deal: they would support him if Hatcher would agree to allow the corrupt Lake County Democratic chairman, John Krupa, to install his own choices for police chief and city comptroller. When Hatcher refused, Krupa threw the weight of the party against him and endorsed the Republican candidate for mayor instead. Racial tension then dominated the general election, with Hatcher deriding the Democrats for what he called "plantation politics" and Krupa deriding Hatcher for refusing to distance himself from national black power advocates Stokely Carmichael and H. Rap Brown. Hatcher, said Krupa, was just not "the right kind of Negro" for Gary. When Krupa's last-minute attempt to register fraudulent voters was exposed, Hatcher became Gary's next mayor with a margin of just under two thousand votes. He had not only won, he had honestly won an election that was rigged against him.

When Richard Hatcher, campaigning above, announced for mayor in 1967, few gave him a chance. Even after he had won the Democratic nomination, corrupt local pols worked to register fraudulent voters to block Hatcher's victory, but were exposed two weeks before the general election, which Hatcher won by 1,865 votes.

Nationwide, the excitement that attended Hatcher's election made him something of a celebrity and a symbol of hope. If blacks could succeed in forming a political culture that changed their circumstances, went the thinking, then they might finally shake free of the cloud of their slave past and follow in the path of the Irish who supplanted the Anglo-Saxons and the Italians who supplanted the Irish, on their way to achieving the American dream. To help them do just that, federal aid began to flow into Gary in the form of the Model Cities program, a pillar of Lyndon Johnson's Great Society, and CETA (Comprehensive Employment and Training Act) grants. But in fact all this attention and money may have been a truer statement of "plantation politics." The aid created a measure of dependency on distant bureaucracies that left Gary vulnerable once the money dried up, which it eventually did, and distracted the city from pursuing a strategy that might have encouraged other business to settle there, diversifying the economy and protecting it from the vicissitudes of the steel industry. Furthermore, in retrospect it seems that some of the attention Washington paid to Gary and other cities with explosive black populations in these years was more dedicated to holding off unrest than truly changing the fortunes of a desperate urban people. And, finally, the attempts to hold up Gary as a center of black achievement only made the divide between blacks and whites that much deeper, with white residents and businesses fleeing a city that no longer welcomed them.

Some of Hatcher's decisions should have raised eyebrows, but in the desperate wish for racial peace that dominated the time, they were forgiven. He gave preference, for instance, to black contractors for city projects, slammed the Indiana legislature as the "downstate KKK," tangled with an unsupportive *Post-Tribune,* and tried for a time to co-opt the city's violent gangs to work for him on behalf of the city. With business leaving town at a remarkable rate, a new nickname was coined for Gary, "Plywood City," for all the boarded-up homes and storefronts. In response, Hatcher banned the posting of "For Sale" signs, worried that they were bad for the city's image. But he could not hide the fact that the tax base was eroding, forcing the city to cut its budget, which led to a decline in services and more racial resentment. A common complaint was that "the whites had left and taken all their money with them." Now it appeared that Gary really was just living from the federal till and, remarkable though it seemed to many, even these dramatic outlays of federal dollars did not buy harmony or progress.

"Martin Luther King was gone and the cities were burning, but all was not lost. We were the mayor of Gary now. Gary proved we had crossed the Jordan."
REV. AL SHARPTON

In 1972, Hatcher hosted the National Black Political Convention, a gathering of thirty-five hundred delegates and alternates and several thousand observers, many of whom came to Gary to verbally assault the white power structure and declare an independent political movement driven solely by race. For all its rejection of tradition, the convention itself was organized according to traditional American patterns: the separation of the assembled into state delegations reinforced the federalist system; the internecine battles between radical black "nationalists" and the more moderate "integrationists" suggested something similar to the nation's early (and ongoing) struggle between those with regional loyalties and those who preferred a broader, common American identification. But the thrust of the convention delegates' rhetoric was a direct challenge to some of the most basic American ideas. Some speakers wanted to ban white reporters from covering the convention. Others argued for setting aside part of the South as a new black nation. And when they finished with their own Gary "declaration," it came just short of arguing for an all-out revolution. "We may choose to slip back into the decadent politics of white America, or we may press forward . . . to the creation of our own Black life. We begin here and now in Gary." It appeared that for many of those in attendance, the aim was not so much to "liberalize America" as to "liberate themselves *from* America."

In the end, the convention settled on an agenda that called for the federal government to pay for health insurance, day care, crime fighting, a "guaranteed annual income" three times that already proposed by Washington's Family Assistance Program, and, finally, reparations for the injustice of slavery in both dollars and real estate to be set by a national black commission. In essence, the black power movement was asking for

James Venable, the longtime Imperial Wizard of the KKK, recalled that meetings in Stone Mountain once drew "Greyhound buses full of Klan for five miles long." Above, Klansmen appear atop Stone Mountain, 1934. Now in the majority, Stone Mountain's black population still worships in the 134-year-old church, left, built by freed slaves. Opposite page: The Stone Mountain sculpture featuring Robert E. Lee, Jefferson Davis, and Stonewall Jackson.

Ned Stancliff stood with the controls for a Power Point presentation at his fingertips. At his back, on this February Georgia day, was the world's largest granite mountain, with its ninety-foot-high sculpture of the heroes of the Confederacy — Jefferson Davis, Robert E. Lee, and Thomas "Stonewall" Jackson. In front of him was a room full of people ready to hear his latest proposal. Stancliff, a vice-president of Silver Dollar City, Inc., a company that operates entertainment parks, had long ago contracted with the Stone Mountain Memorial Association (SMMA) to run the thirty-two-hundred-acre Stone Mountain Park and spent three years readying plans for improving the popular recreational area, which already boasted two golf courses, a man-made lake, and miles of hiking and jogging trails. Silver Dollar had proposed adding to the existing antebellum plantation a nineteenth-century town with three opera houses and a re-creation of the historic "Sweet Auburn" African-American business district in Atlanta.

But at today's standing-room-only SMMA board meeting, Stancliff came armed with plans for something even more ambitious, a fourteen-acre "adventure water ride" that would run along the base of the towering mountain. The idea of a man-made river carrying rafters over a waterfall and into a simulated flooded town may have little to do with the history that made Stone Mountain a park back in 1958: its reputation as the Mount Rushmore of the South and as the spiritual home of the modern Ku Klux Klan. But those thoughts are only spoken in whispers around here anymore. Stone Mountain, Georgia, has moved beyond its discredited past; in fact, it has been transformed from one of America's most visible symbols of racism to a statement of middle-class black achievement.

The mountain — two miles long and over eight hundred feet higher than the surrounding flatlands — served as landmark and meeting-place for Cherokee and Creek Indians long before American settlers began arriving in the late 1700s. And it was not long afterward that slavery became an integral part of the local farming and stone quarry economy. In 1839, at the base of the mountain, near the intersection of two former Indian trails, a town sprung up, named, appropriately enough, New Gibraltar. (The name stuck until 1947, when the state changed it to match the name given the rock: Stone Mountain.) The mountain, even then, was a tourist attraction, with a tower on top and vistas all the way to Atlanta, sixteen miles to the west. By the time Union general William Tecumseh Sherman marched through town in 1864, after capturing Atlanta, a third of New Gibraltar's households owned at least one slave. Sherman freed them and, in gratitude, the liberated African-Americans quietly named their New Gibraltar neighborhood "Shermantown" in his honor. To memorialize the event, they even built a church, using the castaway stones from the quarries where they continued to work. Completed in 1868, the Bethsaida Baptist Church is one of the oldest African-American churches in the country.

But in the years leading up to the twentieth century, the resentment of New Gibraltar's white population over their defeat in the Civil War festered. By 1915, that resentment became the driving force behind the vision for the town's future. Helen Plane, an eighty-year-old Confederate soldier's widow and president of the Atlanta chapter of the United Daughters of the Confederacy (UDC), proposed a carving of Robert E. Lee on the side of the giant rock. Then, on Thanksgiving night that same year, a group of sixteen men climbed to the top of the mountain, donned white sheets and pointed hats, and struck a match to a tall cross made of crude pine boards. It was an ugly year in the history of race relations — which also included the release of *Birth of a Nation*, the incendiary movie romanticizing the early Klan — and it began an ugly era, with Stone Mountain its sacred center. Mrs. Plane's sculpture idea earned the immediate support of her UDC sisters, who suggested that New York artist Gutzon Borglum, who had carved a monumental bust of Abraham Lincoln, execute the bold idea. Borglum traveled to Stone Mountain at the widow's invitation, gazed at the mountain, and pronounced the idea of a single hero there silly, like a postage stamp on the side of a barn. Borglum proposed something more ambitious: the gallant Lee on horseback, joined by Davis and Stonewall Jackson, followed by 750 Confederate soldiers, the most ambitious carving ever attempted.

The ladies of the UDC — and much of the old Confederacy — were ecstatic. One New York editor, sympathetic with the Southern cause, wrote that a carving here would "give to the Confederate soldier and his memories the most majestic monument, set in the most magnificent frame in all the world." Delayed by World War I, Borglum's crew began carving in 1923 and by 1924 the artist hosted an unveiling breakfast for VIP guests — on General Lee's massive shoulder several hundred feet above the valley floor. But work would soon stop there: a squabble between Borglum and his men, complicated by disagreements over money, ended the relationship the following year. Borglum wasted no time finding other work — in South Dakota, directing the work on another mountain carving, Mount Rushmore — while work at Stone Mountain continued, hampered by lack of funds and scaled back by two successive artists, before it was completed in 1972.

The Ku Klux Klan seemed to have a better time of it, spreading a white supremacist doctrine and vigilante justice across the country. By 1925, the KKK counted some 5 million members nationwide, with 156,000 of them in Georgia, where some 450 people, most of them black men, were lynched between 1890 and 1940. Stone Mountain honored the hate and bloodshed with annual cross-burning rallies attended by hundreds of white-sheeted men and women who drove through town while the blacks of Shermantown gathered nervously on the sidewalks to gawk, as if at a hellish parade. The Klan's Imperial Wizard, and host of these national hate conventions, was a Stone Mountain resident and the town's mayor. By 1963, in the midst of the Civil Rights movement, Martin Luther King, Jr., in his famous "I Have a Dream" speech, singled out the place — "Let freedom ring from Stone Mountain, Georgia," he intoned — as he urged the nation to quit its racist ways.

"That was a terrible time in this country," says fifty-six-year-old Leslie Breland, of the racist past. "But we're so far beyond that now." Breland, a native New Yorker, is Stone Mountain Park's director of marketing and an African-American. Her recipe for washing away Stone Mountain's dark past is to let the free market cover it over with good times and money. In fact, what has happened to Stone Mountain in just the last ten years would seem to confirm her strategy. A booming Atlanta, which elected its first black mayor in 1973, spread its economic bounty (and progressiveness) to rural Georgia. Because of its history, Stone Mountain at first remained untouched by Atlanta's burgeoning black middle class. But when the economic boom of the 1990s began, even the cross-burning past could not stem the tide. A growing black middle class looked beyond Stone Mountain's history to see a quaint town of seven thousand adjacent to a large state park. Subdivisions with $500,000 homes were built and scooped up by African-Americans. One concerned white minister hired a marketing firm to tell him what to do about a black population that had exploded 200 percent. The pastor brought on a black associate minister and a black music director and soon his congregation, which once counted its black members in single digits, was 40 percent African-American. *Ebony* included Stone Mountain on its list of hot housing markets for upwardly mobile blacks, and by the end of the twentieth century, two-thirds of the town was black and a black man named Chuck Burris had been elected mayor. As if to seal the symbolism of the upset, Burris moved his family into a house once owned by the Klan's Imperial Wizard.

In 1998 Burris found himself sitting behind Hillary Clinton during her husband's State of the Union Address, proving how thoroughly changed the South was. The native Louisianan appreciated the symbolism, but to him the story was not simply that a black population had replaced a white population in a place of such historic dimension; it was that Stone Mountain had gone one step further toward the kind of integrated life that best represented the American ideal. "This was not a campaign about race," he said of his mayoral triumph. "It was about drainage problems, sidewalks, and police. The sidewalk doesn't care if you are black or white." Burris would lose the next election (to a white candidate), but he remained deeply involved in the community. Indeed, he was there in the audience, as a member of the Stone Mountain Memorial Association, when Ned Stancliff pitched his plan for the water ride. Burris found it "garish and a bit over the top," but he agreed with Stancliff that Stone Mountain ought to be a place where people come to have fun.

> **"We are pregnant . . . and whether a doctor is there or not, the water has broke, the blood has spilled. A new black baby is going to be born."**
>
> —REV. JESSE JACKSON, 1972

money, money, and more money to "right" the wrongs of the past, and even though Richard Nixon had succeeded Johnson, the reigning liberal ethos in Washington seemed inclined to comply. The specter of violence instilled by the riots of the 1960s had left many policymakers in a cynical mood, inclined to "give them what they want" or watch the cities get destroyed, and there was, it appeared at the time, some substance to their fears. In the days after the riots that followed the assassination of Martin Luther King, Jr., in 1968, activist (and future mayor) Marion Barry had warned that "when the city rebuilds . . . it might just get burned down again . . . if you don't let my black brothers control the process."

After the 1972 Gary convention, it was hard for many white Americans to separate the image of Gary from the movement for black power, and almost as hard to distinguish Hatcher from Barry and other angry black leaders. It seemed to many whites and blacks that the concept of "integration," so eloquently put forward by Martin Luther King a few years before, was now but a tarnished and essentially abandoned ideal, little more than that short-lived place in time between the 1964 Civil Rights Act and the rise of black power, between a white-dominated city and a black-dominated city, between, as one historian has written, "colored people" and "people of color." And who was to blame for this? The black leaders like Hatcher who treated their arrival at positions of influence as an opportunity to cast aside the white population and make demands for restitution? Or the white federal establishment that treated social policy as a way to assuage their guilt, money as a way to keep the ghettos quiet? The persistence of racism? Or the arrival of racial identity politics?

The 1972 National Black Political Convention brought a boisterous assembly of delegates to the gymnasium of Gary's West Side High School. A then thirty-year-old Jesse Jackson led the revved-up conferees in shouts of "It's Nation time! It's Nation time!"

Throughout the seventies and early eighties, Gary continued to receive substantial federal assistance, but none of it stopped the economic and social decline. Then, as jobs were lost from the downturn in the steel industry and the Reagan administration's cuts in subsidies began to kick in, Gary went even deeper into the abyss. By 1987, Hatcher had served five terms and presided over the spending of more than $300 million in federal aid. But if anything things were worse than when he arrived. Gary stood as a symbol of the failure of liberal social policy, the kind of place about which former New York governor Mario Cuomo once famously said, "the future once happened here." Fed up, the people finally turned

Hatcher out of office in favor of the tax assessor, Thomas Barnes. Then, in 1995, they did something that many within the city and outside of it saw as a sign of defeat, others as a sign of maturity: they installed, in Scott King, their first white mayor in twenty-five years.

V

"Thomas Jefferson was almost a romantic figure to me," says Jacky Gholson, sitting back in a chair in her home. A petite woman with an engaging smile and sad, Marian Anderson eyes, Gholson, sixty-three, is a Gary success story. She grew up here, a generation before Ben Clement did, in the Delaney Housing Community, built in 1939 and named for Reverend Frank S. Delaney, a Depression-era Gary pastor who had an active role in social services. Today, Delaney is a wasteland. But back when segregation joined all classes of African-Americans into a single, self-sufficient community, it was a vibrant and reassuring place to live, a fixture in segregated Gary every bit as much as Roosevelt High School, which sits across the street from it. Wrong though it was, segregation provided some African-Americans with a nurturing and supportive environment that ended when doors were opened and many of the most accomplished members of the community moved on to lives in other, integrated places. When Jacky Gholson speaks of life in segregated Gary, it is almost with a wistful sense of regret for the passing of a life of dignity and promise. "We were poor," she says, "but we didn't know we were poor." And while there was segregation, there was so little contact with whites that Gholson rarely felt the pain of prejudice. The only overt prejudice she recalls in Gary came around the time she began dating. Gholson says that there were certain restaurants in Gary that blacks couldn't eat in and that if they wanted to go to the beach, they couldn't go to Marquette Beach in Gary. They had to drive ten miles down Route 20 to a different one.

Gholson's ancestral roots are in Kentucky (her mother's side) and Mississippi (her father's). Her father came to Gary from Chicago in the 1930s to take a job as a welder at U.S. Steel while her mother worked as a custodian in the Gary schools. In the 1930s, Roosevelt was the primary Gary school for black students; indeed, it had been built as a blacks-only school in 1931 and named for Teddy Roosevelt, who was famous then among African-Americans for daring to invite a black man, the first, to the White House when he requested that Booker T. Washington dine with him in 1901. ("Roosevelt Dines A Darky" and "Our Coon-Flavored President" were some of the racist headlines that greeted the president the next day.) Today, Roosevelt is strictly a high school, but when Jacky

Taylor (as she was known then) attended Roosevelt it was for all grades, kindergarten through twelfth.

Roosevelt's name was on the building, but H. Theo Tatum was the school's guiding presence. Tatum, whose tenure ran from 1933 to 1961, was a strict disciplinarian who believed firmly that he was not just teaching but preparing children for life and in particular *black* children for life in an inhospitable world. It was at Roosevelt that Gholson developed her attraction to Thomas Jefferson for his abiding faith in freedom and equality and for his attempts to write an antislavery phrase into the Declaration of Independence. Gholson admired him for that as much as she admired George Washington as the father of the country and Abraham Lincoln for freeing the slaves. From Roosevelt, Gholson went on to Hampton Institute (Booker T. Washington's alma mater), and afterward returned to Gary to teach in the elementary schools. By then, Tatum was gone and Gary was on its way to becoming a very different place. In 1973, Gholson and her husband joined the exodus from central Gary when they bought a house in the more upscale Miller neighborhood. In 1976, they sold an apartment building they owned in central Gary when they discovered that they simply could no longer find the "right" kind of tenants to live there. In 1977, Gholson's father was robbed and murdered by a gang of Gary teenagers.

Jacky Gholson, left, visits a Gary elementary school with Grace Williams, the school's African-American Infusion program coordinator. "There's a conscious effort here to have black children 'see themselves,'" says Williams. "When an all-black school is decorated with pictures of white children . . . then something is wrong."

The change in Gary was also visible in the classroom. It was gradual, but over the years, what most struck Gholson was the decline in self-respect, the loss of hope. At the height of segregation, Tatum had instilled pride in the Roosevelt students. But now, with segregation gone, so was the pride. Like Clement, Gholson was dumbfounded by the decline of her hometown. How was it possible, she wondered, that with all the achievements of the Civil Rights movement and the subsequent rise of a black middle class, and even the election of a celebrated black mayor, black life in Gary could also include all this crime, bitterness, and despair?

Gholson had served as an elementary educator for almost thirty years when, in 1995, she was tapped to head up a new program dedicated to infusing African-American culture and history into the elementary and secondary curriculum of the Gary schools. For Gholson, her new job was both a personal and a professional epiphany, leading her to emphasize the "African" in "African-American." She replaced the license plate on her Honda Passport with one showing a map of the African continent and the words, "Each one, teach one," the motto of the anti-apartheid movement in South Africa that refers to the passing on of knowledge. At home, she turned her husband's study into an "Africa Room" decorated with artifacts. And every morning, when Gholson is dressing, she adds something "African" to her outfit just to claim that sense of identity.

The "professional epiphany" was much more dramatic. For the more Gholson learned about African-American history, the more it changed her attitude toward the teaching of American history in general and the more apparent it became to her that the black children of Gary were being ill served by a curriculum that brought unqualified respect to the founders and suggested to black children that their history started with the story of slavery. Jefferson may have remained a "romantic" figure to her, but if so, he was not without serious flaws, and Abraham Lincoln may have freed the slaves, but she now understood that the preservation of the Union was perhaps the sixteenth president's primary goal. And what about all that was left out? What of Benjamin Banneker, the black surveyor of the District of Columbia? Why are the children not taught about him? And instead of teaching the story of the transcontinental railroad, how about the story of the "*Underground* Railroad" that extended freedom to the slaves as the abolition movement took hold in the early nineteenth century?

Shauna Wilson, a junior at Horace Mann High School, gives a report to her biology class on Madame C. J. Walker, the millionaire entrepreneur and inventor of hair-care products for black women. At Mann, and every other school in the Gary system, the curriculum — from math to English literature — is taught from an "African-American" perspective.

Gholson didn't stop there. Under her guidance, the Gary schools adopted a program that effectively changed the teaching of all subjects in all schools to reflect an African-American perspective. At its most innocent, this means teaching math by having students plot the words of a Maya Angelou poem on a mathematical graph; biology by doing reports on "underrepresented" (minority) scientists; and English by adding the works of Alice Walker and Langston Hughes to the reading lists. But the Gary "African and African-American Infusion Program" is also informed by the ideas of Dr. Molefi Asante, a controversial academic from Temple University in Philadelphia who has been hired as a consultant to the Gary schools. Asante coined the word *Afrocentrism* to describe a process that rejects the "white supremacy" of traditional Eurocentric American education in favor of an education based upon the history and philosophy of African cultures. Asante's most dramatic claim may be his attack on

" The Negro of the United States has lost even the memory of his country; he no longer understands the language that his fathers spoke; he has abjured their relation and forgotten their mores. In thus ceasing to belong to Africa, he has however acquired no right to the goods of Europe; but he has been stopped between the two societies . . . isolated between the two peoples, sold by one and repudiated by the other, finding . . . only the hearth of his master to offer him the incomplete image of a native country."

— Alexis de Tocqueville
Democracy in America, 1835

Greek civilization, which, he says, stole its ideas from Egypt. But it is his goal, he says, to undermine all European cultural "arrogance" and "expel" the "inferiorization that insinuates itself over and over again in the African-American mind." Asante's textbooks implore students to center themselves in their African ancestry and to resist being mere "renters" of "someone else's information."

Today, Roosevelt High School is a decaying three-story fortress surrounded by the Delaney Community, some small storefront revival churches, and an abandoned building that once housed Shelley's restaurant (the worn and faded sign declares the eatery to be famous for its "soul food"). The 1931 Roosevelt building may be in decay but the addition, which opened in 1973, is in even worse shape; much of it is in rubble. In the summer of 2000, the roof caved in on the math wing. The removal of the debris awaits the outcome of an insurance dispute.

Students enter Roosevelt at the gymnasium, passing through a metal detector on their way to their classrooms. The grand old main entrance to Roosevelt is now closed and a banner that reads "A People Without Knowledge Is Like a Tree Without Roots" hangs there. The sign was the suggestion of Norma Coleman, an American history teacher working under Gholson's tutelage. But the printer got the phrasing slightly wrong, leaving out a critical phrase. It should read "A People Without Knowledge *of Its Past* Is Like a Tree Without Roots," the words of Marcus Garvey, the 1920s-era New York black nationalist who briefly united blacks worldwide into a Pan-African community. Coleman, and Gholson, regard Garvey's admonition as the spirit of Afrocentrism.

Roosevelt is no longer the bastion of discipline that it was under Tatum, and budget cuts have made it hard to hire adequate security personnel, though there are representatives from DADS ("Dads Are Doing Something," an outgrowth of an Indiana governor's conference on fathers) on-site, offering themselves up as mentors. Still, the state of Indiana has had to put the school on probation for its poor academic and student attendance record. Indeed, in 2001, only 30 percent of Roosevelt's sophomores passed the state standards test for tenth graders. In many classes the students are no longer allowed to take textbooks home because, says Norma Coleman, sadly, "with so many dropouts, we'd never see the books again."

Coleman's history classroom is filled with pictures of black American heroes like Frederick Douglass, George Washington Carver, Harriet Tubman, W. E. B. DuBois, and Jack Johnson. In fact, while the basic tenets of American history are taught here, there is not a single picture of George Washington or Abraham Lincoln, or even of the school's namesake, Teddy Roosevelt. "We're Americans first, and we don't want to lose sight of that," insists Coleman. Indeed, she is the ROTC coordinator for Roosevelt, and a diehard fan of the Naval Academy, who sees the military as one way out for Gary's youth. "But I'm not going to teach history that's a lie, either. I am not going to push the negative history under a rug. James Madison and Thomas Jefferson were not *my* founding fathers . . . They owned slaves."

In another part of Roosevelt, Jamal Rasheed teaches African-American history, which is required of all tenth graders in the Gary school system. But perhaps because the motivation for so much of this "infusion" curriculum is to instill self-respect in the student, the class feels more like group empowerment therapy. On the wall, Rasheed has posted a sign reading, "If there's no enemy within, the enemy outside can do us no harm . . . We are not afraid of what the KKK will do . . . Our present enemy comes from within."

Rasheed gets much of his teaching material from a distributor of African-American cultural products called "Sankofa," an Akan word (Akan is the language spoken in Ghana) that means, "We must go back and reclaim our past so we can move forward; so we understand why and how we came to be who we are today." Among the products that Sankofa distributes is a film by the same name, which Rasheed finds essential to his classes. The picture, which was directed by Haile Gerima, an Ethiopian who emigrated to the United States in 1967, is the story of a Ghanaian woman who is possessed by spirits who take her into a slave past where she is abused by her white master. There is much debate among her fellow slaves as to how to respond. Should they accede and collaborate with the slave master or resist him? The woman eventually defies the system and takes her fate into her own hands. But Rasheed uses the film as an exercise in "critical thinking" and as a way for the students to confront the choices available to a people caught in the prison of servitude.

Roosevelt High School makes an effort to sustain its past grandeur, though with declining student enrollment, the task is tougher. Here, John King, the school's assistant boiler operator, takes down the school's flag at dusk.

VI

If black America can be said to have its own "founding fathers," the most logical candidates would be Booker Taliaferro Washington and William Edward Burghardt DuBois. These two men, whose lives intersected in

"The wisest among my race understand that the agitation of questions of social equality is the extremest folly, and that progress . . . must be the result of severe and constant struggle rather than of artificial forcing . . . It is important and right that all privileges of the law be ours, but it is vastly more important that we be prepared for the exercise of these privileges."

— Booker T. Washington
Atlanta Compromise Speech, 1895

the early years of the twentieth century, were the most articulate spokesmen for two well-developed philosophical attitudes and political strategies for black achievement, ideas that to this day continue to animate the discussions of African-American life. They are usually portrayed as opposites — Washington, the accommodating pragmatist; DuBois the agitating idealist. There is in fact something of each man's philosophy in the other, and yet they were also in considerable disagreement and, when seen together, confirm what DuBois called the irreconcilable "two-ness," the "double-consciousness" that characterizes the African-American dilemma, at once American and African-American, "two souls," "two strivings," "two warring ideals."

Washington was the elder, a former slave from Virginia who became a leader among blacks in the late nineteenth century when he founded the Tuskegee Institute, an all-black school in Alabama. There, he advocated that blacks look upon their situation realistically. Rather than strike out boldly where they had never been welcomed before and where abiding racism and black inexperience risked failure, Washington urged blacks to "cast down your buckets where you are" and pursue professions like farming that would not challenge the white power structure. In this, he was pushing for the supremacy of economic self-determination (and self-sufficiency) over the acquisition of political and civil rights. Washington also believed that African-Americans were held back in two fundamental ways, through racism, yes, but also by cultural deficiencies, echoing Jefferson's own fears that once slavery was lifted, black Americans would struggle to cope on their own in a society that had kept them down for so long as "inferior." Washington dreamed of a day when black and white Americans would truly be equal, but he felt that black America would be better advised to pursue a slow pace, chipping away at the edifice of racism and building skills that had been denied them for so long.

There was one other motive to Washington's philosophical pragmatism: survival. He lived in a time when the political fortunes of blacks were growing steadily worse. Jim Crow laws were being passed throughout the South and many of the gains of the post–Civil War era of Reconstruction were being reversed. There were more lynchings in the 1890s than at any other time in America life, and throughout the South, African-Americans were being disfranchised state by state. By agreeing to segregation and encouraging blacks to pursue an industrial over a classical education, Washington hoped to calm fears among white Southerners that blacks might get the "wrong ideas" in their heads and, at the same time, save black lives. When Washington said "in all things that are purely social we can be as separate as the fingers, yet one as the hand in all things essential to mutual progress," he was speaking words that many white Southerners could appreciate, and did.

There were other aspects of the Washington philosophy — its humility, its emphasis upon industry and the self-made life — that seemed consistent with old American values and made him friend to white and black. His role was really as a kind of ambassador, and indeed, for a generation, whites wishing to reach out to black Americans would first visit Booker T. Washington. There is even some evidence that Washington tried to use this role to further the political cause for civil rights, waging a kind of secret diplomatic campaign against racism even as he stood publicly for accommodation. This much is certain: there was no more influential black leader in his time than the man whom villagers throughout the black rural south called, in reverent tones, "Booka T."

Yet by the turn of the century, a substantial black (and white) critique of Washington began to emerge, principally in the voice of DuBois, a Harvard educated sociologist, and the National Association for the Advancement of Colored People (NAACP), which he helped found in 1909. The appearance and manner of the two men demonstrated something of their differences. Where Washington was a Southerner and a big hulk of a man whose very physical presence seemed to authenticate his campaign for a life of hard labor, DuBois was a refined Northerner from the Berkshire town of Great Barrington, Massachusetts, an elitist who made his living with his mind. At Harvard, from which he graduated in 1896, DuBois was a student of the eminent philosopher William James and a classmate of Herbert Croly, a liberal who would go on to become the founding editor of *The New Republic* and one of the most powerful journalists of the time.

DuBois had planned a career for himself in academia and a slow, analytical attack on racism in the form of sociological studies that would disprove what much of white America still believed: that African-Americans were biologically inferior. But he was pushed onto the national stage when he published a book called *The Souls of Black Folk* in which he challenged Washington's public acquiescence to forced segregation and disfranchisement as a moral abomination. To Washington, these examples of oppression and injustice were obstacles, not barriers, to achievement. His 1901 autobiography, *Up From Slavery*, was his own from-the-bootstraps story, which he believed confirmed the viability of his philosophy. But in *Souls of Black Folk* DuBois countered with the view that racism was the overriding fact of black life and argued that because social and political structures built upon such injustice were the primary reason for black failure they must be changed. DuBois was not advocating integration. Like Washington, he also believed that black Americans should work toward

"Men honor Mr. Washington for his attitude of conciliation toward the white South. [But] in failing thus to state plainly and unequivocally the legitimate demands of their people . . . [they] shirk a heavy responsibility . . . to the darker races of men whose future depends so largely on this American experiment . . . There are today no truer exponents of the pure human spirit of the Declaration of Independence than the American Negroes."

—W. E. B. DuBois
The Souls of Black Folk, 1903

self-sufficiency and the establishment of their own, autonomous economic and cultural institutions, but he wanted them to achieve them out of choice not force. Unlike Washington, he cared little about maintaining a harmonious relationship with the white majority.

Washington's influence eventually faded in the harsh light cast upon him by the relentless arguments of DuBois. The older man soon seemed by comparison to be a relic from another age — rural where DuBois was urban, economic where DuBois was political, practical where DuBois was confrontational — and the trends of the twentieth century, which favored social engineering over individual responsibility, were against him. DuBois, who saw racism as a by-product of capitalism and was enamored of the Soviet experiment, was much more in rhythm with the leftward drift of politics in those years.

While he eventually had a falling out with the NAACP and his increasingly eccentric voice became, by the early 1940s, largely irrelevant to the struggle, DuBois's early work had already set the tone and agenda that would become the foundation of the Civil Rights movement that made so many gains in the middle years of the twentieth century. And yet it could also be said that the force of his argument eventually outspent its value and that much of black America has suffered from following his politically driven path to the exclusion of Washington's economic one.

DuBois grew increasingly subversive and bitter. In 1961, he joined the Communist party, declaring that capitalism was incapable of reforming itself. He soon concluded the same thing about America and abandoned the country to spend his last years in Ghana, where he died in August 1963, on the same day when tens of thousands were gathering in the District of Columbia for the March on Washington.

VII

Two projects, from two "warring" constituencies, describing two separate visions for Gary and its future animated the civic argument in the early days of the twenty-first century. One, led by former mayor Richard Hatcher, who now operates a consulting firm, proposed that Gary erect a Civil Rights Hall of Fame at a cost of $15 million. The other, led by Mayor Scott King, asked for additional funding for a downtown baseball stadium. But both were merely new clothing for old strategies.

The Hall of Fame, which had been part of Hatcher's vision for Gary since the late 1970s, not only reasserted his idea of the city as a center of black achievement; it again proposed to rely on public money to do it. Hatcher raised $500,000 in contributions, but he also secured another million from the state of Indiana, a $750,000 grant from Lake

In Northern California: Watching racial and economic demographics clash

"Only in America," says Benyam Mulugeta, left, at Carriage Manor, of the fortune he's made dabbling in the Bay Area real estate market. Above, right, Sister Trinitas Hernandez teaches English to Carriage Manor's Hispanic residents in one of the classrooms she created. Carrie Du Bois, right, was overwhelmed by the poverty of Carriage Manor's residents on her first visit there. "It didn't look like America to me," she said.

University Avenue in Palo Alto, California, is a street with two distinct personalities. At one end it wends under a canopy of magnolia trees and past the stately manors and swanky shops that surround prestigious Stanford University. At the other end, it meets the crime-ridden, two-and-a-half-square-mile lower-class jurisdiction known as East Palo Alto. The street is well traveled. In fact, many of East Palo Alto's predominantly African-American and Hispanic residents (whites form just 27 percent of the population) make their livings tending gardens and cleaning houses in Palo Alto, forming the kind of economic and racial divide that brings people of radically different circumstances into confrontation with each other, courting envy and class war.

All these forces came together in the story of "Carriage Manor," a two-story apartment building in East Palo Alto. There are security bars on its first-floor windows and the thick yellow paint on the outside walls is peeling. Yet it is home to forty-eight Latino families, some living thirteen or fourteen to a room. Robert Perez recalls that when he became manager of Carriage Manor in 1995 there was already an epidemic of overcrowding in the building, double the legal occupancy rate. After that, conditions only got worse.

Most of the Latino families living in Carriage Manor had few options but to stay in their crowded quarters. With the upturn in the Silicon Valley economy of the late 1990s and early 2000s, even housing prices in downtrodden East Palo Alto had begun to rise. When two-bedroom apartments began commanding $500,000 in the valley's most desirable communities and middle-class starter homes all over the Bay Area were routinely fetching more than their already steep asking prices, levelheaded buyers had no place else to push but into dodgier neighborhoods where they promoted gentrification. Between 1998 and 2000, rents doubled and the average sale price of a single-family home in East Palo Alto leaped from $215,000 to $378,000.

Carrie Du Bois had a ringside seat on all this. By day, Du Bois worked as a realtor in the exclusive neighborhoods of the Bay Area, regularly showing million-dollar homes to all-cash buyers. "I saw the runaway wealth and the overbidding," she says. Then, one day each week, Du Bois helped look after the children at a Hispanic day-care center in the Carriage Manor apartments in East Palo Alto.

Du Bois first heard of Carriage Manor in 1998 while seeking more meaningful community service work for the local Junior League. "I asked a friend who worked at a school run by the Daughters of Charity, 'What can the Junior League do in East Palo Alto?'" says Du Bois. At first, the response was cynical and dismissive. But then Du Bois met Sister Trinitas Hernandez, a feisty, five-foot, one-inch, gray-haired Hispanic nun, who had transformed apartment 24, a no-frills one-bedroom just inside Carriage Manor's iron security gate, into an ersatz classroom. "I used to deliver food there," says "Sister T." "One day a lady asked me to teach her English, so I got a grant from the Daughters of Charity," the international Catholic women's service organization to which she belongs, "and I rented the apartment for $500 a month and started teaching the mothers."

By the spring of 2000 the Rosalie Rendu Center, named for a much-admired nineteenth-century sister of the Daughters of Charity, was offering four classes a day, four days a week to nine people per class. When apartment 2 became available, it was converted into the Tot Spot, an activity center stocked and staffed largely by Junior Leaguers for children whose mothers were in Sister T's classes. One of those students was Martha Perez, the wife of Carriage Manor's former manager. A native of Guadalajara, Mrs. Perez spoke scant English when she came to America in 1994. Too shy even to visit the doctor unless accompanied by her husband, Sister T's tutelage opened a new world of opportunities to Perez, who began working as a second-grade teacher's aide. The additional income she brings in has allowed the Perezes and their two young sons to rent a bigger home in East Palo Alto.

But just as the Rendu Center was hitting its stride, word spread around Carriage Manor that the apartment building had been sold to a new owner.

The previous landlord had paid little attention to the rundown complex (and little money on upkeep), but rents were often half of market value. And that, says Du Bois, had actually worked in the residents' favor. "The conditions were awful," she says, "but at least the families had a roof over their heads."

The new owner, Benyam Mulugeta, was more interested in profit. That was, after all, the essence of capitalism, an ideal that Mulugeta wholeheartedly embraced when he moved to America from Ethiopia in 1972. Upon his arrival at New York's JFK airport with but $20 to his name, Mulugeta saw a toilet for the first time in his life, on which he promptly stood for lack of working knowledge. Mulugeta lived with a host family in East Palo Alto, attended community college, and worked nights cleaning animal cages in a local laboratory. When he had saved up enough money, the oldest of fifteen children paid the way for one of his brothers (the first of twenty-four family members Mulugeta brought over from Ethiopia), and the two shared an apartment up the street from Carriage Manor. By 1981, Mulugeta had married, welcomed his first child, and was sharing a small apartment with his new family, his mother, and two of his sisters when they were evicted for overcrowding.

Unfazed, Mulugeta, who had saved some money, bought a house out of foreclosure, renovated it himself, and sold it for a tidy profit. That was first in what turned out to be a series of savvy real estate transactions, the latest of which was purchasing Carriage Manor for a bargain price of $2.1 million in March 2000. Serving eviction notices to families at Carriage Manor posed no ethical conflict for Mulugeta, despite his past experience on the receiving end. "It was one of the best things that ever happened to me," he said. But a month after closing on Carriage Manor, Mulugeta received a call from Carrie Du Bois, who found his phone number on a flyer he had circulated to tenants when he bought the building. On behalf of the Junior League, she expressed a sincere interest in raising the money to buy the complex so as to avert the evictions and save Sister T's center. "It is not for sale," said Mulugeta, who bought Carriage Manor as an investment for his children. "Name your price," replied Du Bois. Mulugeta did and it was more than twice what he had paid for the complex: $4.5 million.

Du Bois did not flinch. Determined, she enlisted the help of a local well-connected philanthropist. He turned her down. The Junior League then turned to the Daughters of Charity, who agreed to meet with Mulugeta and offer him $2.6 million. Insulted, Mulugeta turned them away. In exasperation, Du Bois, referring to the work many of the tenants performed for the Bay Area rich, exclaimed, "We need these gardeners." Mulugeta shot back a brittle retort. Then why, he asked, don't you pay them enough to afford housing at market rates? The confrontation was classically American: a WASP philanthropist, a Hispanic nun and teacher, and a black entrepreneur hashing out their differences, each from his or her own demographic and economic perspective, and all with the lives of the downtrodden hanging in the balance.

Mulugeta's plan for the building included wholesale evictions and increased rents, which earned him an unlikely opponent: his wife, Paula. The many hours Mrs. Mulugeta spent at Carriage Manor fixing up apartments vacated by the families who hadn't waited to be evicted also afforded her the opportunity to meet many of the families, and she grew to like them. Succumbing to her persuasion, her husband wound up serving only eleven eviction notices. But a bigger obstacle proved to be the press.

The newspapers and television caught wind of the story and painted it as a battle between rich society mavens trying to save their servants from an evil slumlord determined to evict hard-working families if a group of nuns did not pay his ransom of more than double his recent purchase price. In truth, it was all about opportunity. Sister Trinitas and the Junior League were trying to help immigrants help themselves, much the same way that Benyam Mulugeta had helped himself climb out of poverty and was now working to pave the way for his children. "They want this to be a charity at my expense," Mulugeta was quoted in the *Wall Street Journal*. "They told me to name my price, and I did. If they don't want to pay it, fine."

For Mulugeta, the only good thing to come from all the bad press was a better offer to buy Carriage Manor: $5.2 million from a Bay Area developer. But a matching offer from the nuns ($4 million from the Daughters of Charity and $1.2 million raised by Du Bois and the Junior League) coupled with a pointed editorial in the *San Jose Mercury News* that read, in part, "Back off, developer," had the intended effect. "The developer did not want the bad publicity," says Mulugeta. "They are not a small fish like me. And they are not an ethnic person like me." Considering the harsh play the press gave an enterprising, self-made minority immigrant, one can only imagine the firestorm that would have ignited had wealthy white owners attempted to exercise what, in the end, is every landlord's legal right.

"Their objectives and my objectives were totally different," says Mulugeta. But in the end, the parties found common ground. In October 2001, nineteen months after buying Carriage Manor for $2.1 million, Benyam Mulugeta sold the complex to the nuns for $5.2 million. Sister T was back at work teaching English. Carrie Du Bois and the Junior League were raising money for extensive building renovations, and Benyam Mulugeta was scanning the real estate advertisements for another opportunity.

County, and a $600,000 grant from the federal government, though all these monies were to be released only after a building had been started. To do that, Hatcher intended to resurrect the designs that had been prepared for the hall twenty years ago when he first proposed it as an extension of the Genesis Center. In those, Chicago architect Wendell Campbell, an African-American, had envisioned a triangular structure with a reflective steel "skin," referencing Gary's history with steel and, even more important, allowing the black people of Gary to see their own image in the building's surface and, in turn, feel pride about being black.

Hatcher saw nothing inappropriate in building a museum that had its original inspiration in the climate of a different time. Anticipating the champions of afrocentrism, Campbell had originally asserted that the foundation of this structure reached back, in a philosophical sense, to slavery and the time before slavery. And, at any rate, the museum's board members openly expressed their wish that the museum would correct what they called an "accident" of history. If the young people of Gary knew more about the story of the Civil Rights struggle, said State Congressman Charlie Brown, then they would never have allowed a white mayor here. Despite such hostility toward him, Mayor King finally endorsed the sale of five acres of abandoned town property to Hatcher's group, even as the *Post-Tribune* noted that Hatcher's board had yet to ac count for the first million or so dollars he had raised, a charge that Hatcher denies.

King's own project fared a little better. When he initiated the proposal in 2000, the mayor announced that the baseball stadium was an idea that he discovered at a governor's conference at Harvard. But, in fact, ever since 1989, when Baltimore built Camden Yards, its beautiful retro stadium on the waterfront, politicians have looked to downtown sports arenas for the kind of economic incentives they hope will help the American city recapture its glory. In this they brazenly borrow from history, believing that baseball, which once thrived in the inner city, can offer the kind of nostalgic associations that will help make the city come alive again. But while the Gary stadium was initially budgeted at $25 million, cost overruns led King back to the voters for an additional $20 million in the fall of 2001. Even with the new money, the stadium will not be ready until the spring of 2003, a year later than planned, which meant that the baseball team, Gary's SouthShore RailCats, would be forced to play its entire 2002 season "on the road."

Nearly every citizen who spoke at a public hearing on the proposed additional budget outlay for the stadium opposed the plan. The close relationship between King and the team's owners was one issue. Two of the owners were attorneys who had done considerable legal work for King

Gary Murder Rate *(per 100,000)*

1950	**12**
1970	**24**
2001	**81**

and the city of Gary, though they insisted that there was no conflict of interest present because the city sought separate counsel for the terms of the lease. Another issue was the fact that a trucking company owned by Jewell Harris, King's campaign manager, received the $1.6 million contract to remove landfill at the site. And then there was the feeling, voiced repeatedly on the street, that baseball was a "white" sport, no more fitting for Gary than Miss USA. Indeed, many considered King's plan for a stadium to be little more than an attempt to bring white people back to Gary. But even if they looked beyond such issues, some who spoke up at the forum insisted that money spent on the stadium — or, for that matter, on the Civil Rights museum — was money lost to the critical tasks of fighting crime, repairing potholes, and educating the young. When casino gambling was brought here in 1996, the city had sold the local people on the idea by stressing their feeling that the extra revenues would turn Gary around. Now, while Gary continued its decay, the city's elders, those from both its present and past, were proposing to spend it all on big symbolic gestures. When, asked some of those at the forum, were the leaders of Gary going to give up on the grand statement and do the simple tasks necessary to make a place civilized? Surely, people don't move to a city because of a museum or a baseball stadium. They look for a place that is safe, that has good schools, and that takes pride in itself as a community. But the city council voted to endorse King's proposal anyway and, looking defeated, which they were, the local opponents went home.

Meanwhile, the misery continued. In late 2001, following another downturn in the steel industry, U.S. Steel began discussions toward a joint venture with struggling Bethlehem Steel and the acquisition of National Steel. But in fact, the entire industry was in trouble and looking itself to the federal government for a bailout. Even as it joined the call for federal assistance, U.S. Steel had already doubled its investment in a relatively new galvanizing facility it had built in Leipsic, Ohio. The news of U.S. Steel's investment in the plant, which takes steel from the mills in Gary and then adds a galvanizing finish for its clients in the automobile industry, seemed a painful reinforcement of Gary's failure. "Without a whole lot of imagination, you can understand that the facility should be in Gary," said Ed Charbonneau, a U.S. Steel spokesman. But with Gary's brutal property tax, Ohio proved to be much more attractive to the company. Now, says Charbonneau, U.S. Steel has a $500 million investment in Ohio, which at even half the present Gary property tax rate would have provided enough money by itself to fund both the stadium and the Civil Rights museum.

As 2001 ended, Gary was named "Murder Capital of America" for the seventh year in a row. There were eighty-four homicides, or 81.55 per

100,000 people, a statistic that placed it well "above" Chicago, St. Louis, and New Orleans. New Orleans, which came in second, had a rate that was roughly half of Gary's. There was a homicide victim in Gary every 4.3 days, and about 77 percent of those victims were black. By comparison, Arlington, Virginia, a city almost twice Gary's size had two homicides all year, and Thomas Jefferson's old hometown of Charlottesville had just three.

Gary's youngest victim was three-year-old Jasmine McClinton, shot by her own brother, who found a gun he thought was a toy in an alleyway near his home. One of the oldest was Mildred Wheeler, seventy-six, who died of dehydration and malnourishment that, because it may have involved neglect, was classified as homicide. But these kinds of stories no longer shock in Gary, where a life of daily peril is the norm.

At 6:30 P.M. on a day in early January 2002, Demetrius Edwards left his home in the Dunes Court Apartments and went out in search of a pack of cigarettes. It was cold and Edwards was bundled up in a suede jacket, black fleecy pants, high tops, and a knit cap that read "No Limit, True Soldier." A dropout from Roosevelt High School, he had just finished a year in a juvenile detention center for stealing a car. Unsure what to do next with his life, Edwards had been drifting. But lately, with a push from a mentor at a local program for troubled youth, Edwards was working on his GED and had taken an interest in joining the Marines. Just as Norma Coleman tells her students at Roosevelt High, Edwards had come to see the Marines as a way out of Gary, a route to a better life. He had an appointment with a Marine recruiter scheduled for the next morning when the Gary police found him lying on his side. He had been shot in the head with a pellet gun. Edwards was seventeen, the murder capital's first murder of the new year.

Teenagers start a pickup game of basketball on an empty lot in Gary.

Office DEPOT

Belmont, California

A few years back, when American business was under fierce competition from the Far East, there was much soul-searching about the methods of the nation's enterprise. Perhaps America needed an industrial "policy," perhaps companies needed to command more loyalty from their workers and develop the sort of environments that tied a Japanese employee, willingly, to his firm for life. Journalist James Fallows took the opposite point of view. Instead of being more like "them," he said, maybe Americans needed to be "more like us." "The force that motivates the country is a vision of people always in motion," wrote Fallows, "able to make something different of themselves, ready for second chances until the day they die." That was 1989, and the 1990s boom, built as it was on the spark of individual initiative, proved Fallows correct. Indeed, his poem to entrepreneurship is an apt description of the lives of (from left) Amalavoyal Chari, Christian Dubiel, Jonathan Goldenstein, and Devabhaktuni Srikrishna, who gave up well-paid positions in the tech industry when they decided to launch FHP Wireless in the summer of 2000 (the name refers to an obscure technical standard and not, as some have joked, "Fool Hardy Professionals"). For the three foreign-born partners, going off on their own to start a company represented the kind of prospect that brought them here in the first place. "Back in Guatemala, I certainly would not be able to do what I'm doing now," says Dubiel, who graduated from Stanford in 1995. "The scale of opportunities in the United States is enormous." Their new company aimed to develop improved wireless computer networks based upon research done by Amalavoyal and Devabhaktuni, but at the time this photograph was taken, FHP didn't have much to show just yet for its efforts: The quartet had been living off their savings for six months and had yet to complete their initial prototype. "I don't think any of us went into this thinking that it was our only opportunity," says Goldenstein. "We said, 'Okay, we'll give this a try.' But if it doesn't work out, we'll do the next thing."

San Diego, California

Americans are born joiners, a nation of two-legged Elks, Lions, and Moose, not to mention Masons, Rotarians, and the occasional Oddfellow. Arriving here in 1831, Tocqueville observed that Americans "make associations to give entertainment, to found seminaries, to build inns, to construct churches, to diffuse books, to send missionaries to the antipodes." He explained it by noting that while a democratic society values individuals it nonetheless leaves them "powerless if they do not learn voluntarily to help each other." Whether people pursue charity, community, or politics, strength, he said, depended upon forging bonds with other individuals to create voting blocs and political factions. Tocqueville was writing about white Americans, but after Emancipation his observations could be extended to black Americans, too. Indeed, a mere forty-five years later, the nation's first black college sorority, Alpha Kappa Alpha, was established at Howard University in 1908. (The "Greek" system is also peculiarly American; the first college fraternity, Phi Beta Kappa, was founded at Virginia's College of William and Mary in 1776 by undergrads sympathetic to the Revolution.) AKA's nine young founders conceived the sorority as a social club, but over the decades its mission became channeling the energies of its 150,000 members into volunteer services and good works, too. Most of the sorority's founders ended up working as teachers and administrators in the segregated schools of the era, thereby helping generations of African-American children enter the mainstream. In San Diego, the local AKA chapter has sponsored a debutante ball for deserving teenage girls since 1955, not simply introducing them to society but honoring their achievements in volunteer service, academic achievement, or athletic prowess. For Jasmine Moore (center, facing camera), the 2001 party was among the biggest nights of her life. Along with twenty-seven other girls, she was to be presented as an "Ebony Pearl" to 750 guests, representing the top tier of the local black community. For months, they had been preparing by attending classes where they were taught which fork to eat their salad with, the proper way to curtsy, public speaking, and ballroom dancing. "That was a new challenge for me," says Jasmine, then a sixteen-year-old Eastlake High School senior. "Every Saturday morning we would practice with our escorts and try to get down the steps and everything." The process instilled the "joiner" ethic in Moore. When she went off to college the next fall, she planned to pledge AKA herself.

Marshall, Texas

Americans have always had an active relationship with nature. The sheer abundance of it was inconceivable to the European settler of the eighteenth century and may have planted the seed for the nation's unique attitude toward waste: Why worry about polluting this valley, when there's another one just over yonder? Americans preferred their woods raw, their mountains majestic, their streams rough, Nature as God made it. They liked to sit in contemplation of what writer James Fenimore Cooper called "the holy calm of Nature" every bit as much as they liked plotting to conquer it and carving it up to better suit their commerce. One of the triumphant moments of the nineteenth century was the completion in 1825 of the Erie Canal, connecting the Great Lakes to New York Harbor. God had His streams; now Americans added their own. Derek Johnson, a Texas high schooler, didn't have Cooper or Henry David Thoreau in mind when he joined in on Senior Mudding Day, here, with a frightful leap from the back of a pickup truck that could only be envisioned by the immortal spirit of youth. "When it rains," says eighteen-year-old Derek, "Grapevine Lake spills out into the flat area, creating big mud puddles all over the place." Historian Vernon Parrington once described Thoreau's philosophy as an attempt to "order life so that the primary things should not be lost amid the superfluities." Derek Johnson has a simpler evocation of the same idea: "We like mud," he says.

5 The Stage

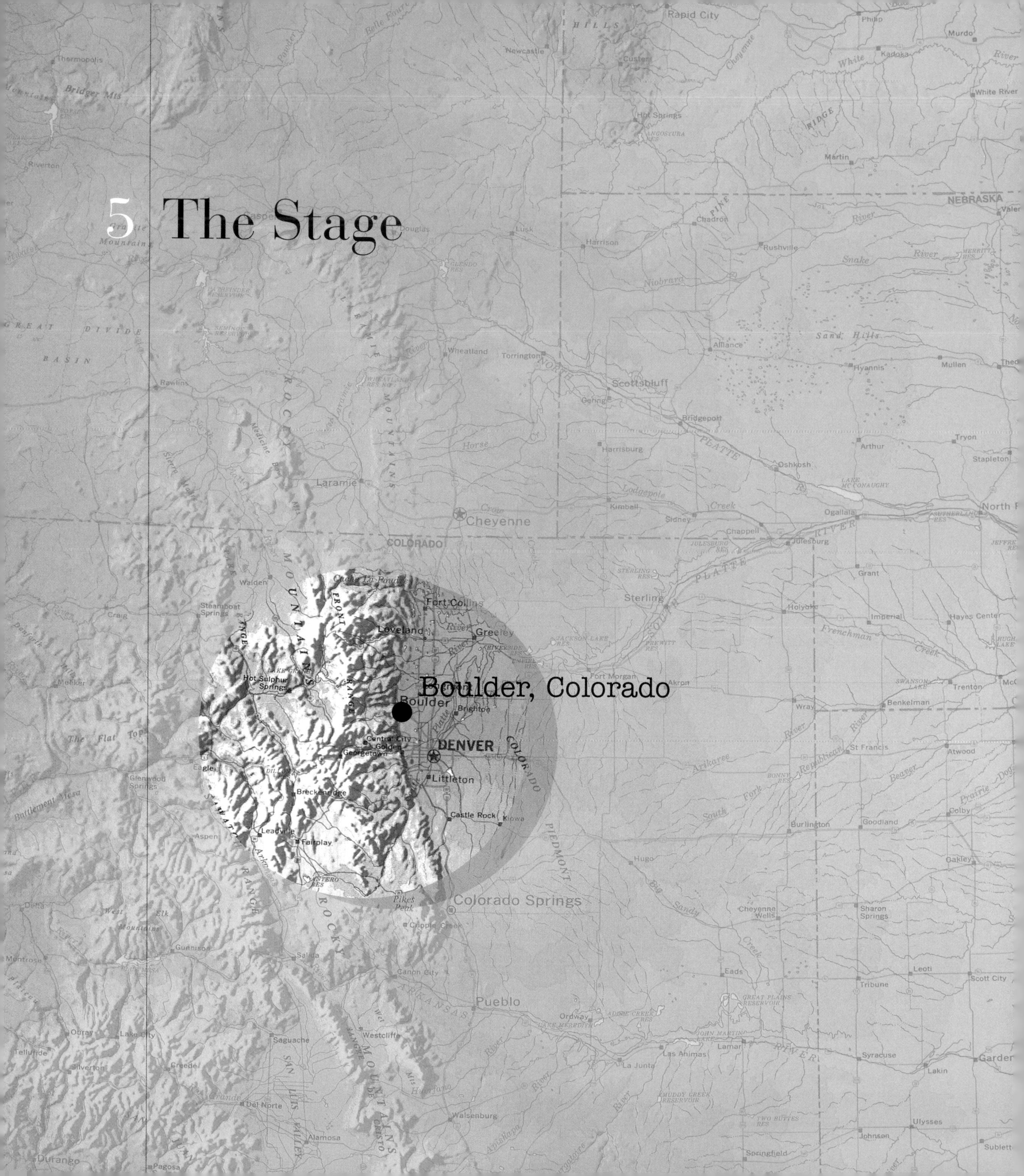

The first idea that this collection of teenage actors had to get used to was the notion of a "tribe." Not a "troupe," not a "group," not a "company." A "tribe." The musical *Hair* called for that, for the performers to see themselves as a single group of people, marching in lockstep around a set of ideas, much the way that the youth of the sixties seemed to march lockstep around the ideas of "rebellion" and the questioning of "authority," around "peace" and "love" and "acceptance." Indeed, when Gerome Ragni, James Rado, and Galt MacDermot wrote *Hair* the nation was in the throes of the most dramatic youth uprising in its history, one in which the young took psychedelic drugs, practiced something they called "free love," accused the "establishment" of being recklessly militaristic, and pushed for the reordering of priorities appropriate to the arrival — the "dawning" was their organic term — of the "Age of Aquarius." Not everyone from the sixties generation participated in its revolution, of course, but those who did held sway over the public argument and popular culture for some time. Some think they still do. And so, thirty-some years after *Hair* first appeared on Broadway, thirty years after Woodstock and the student riots at the Democratic National Convention in Chicago, after the rise of the Students for a Democratic Society (SDS) and the antics of Abbie Hoffman, thirty years after the "be-in" and the "love-in," here we were at Fairview High School in the onetime hippie enclave of Boulder, Colorado, watching the children of Boulder's sixties generation mount their own production of one of the crowning statements of their parents' once-radical culture, and just maybe, in the process, discover something about what it means to be an American.

The idea of a teenage musical is not unusual. Most high schools in America mount some musical stage work each year, though it is more likely to be one of the romantic Rodgers and Hammerstein chestnuts, *Oklahoma!* or *South Pacific*, *Carousel* or *The Sound of Music*, than the still-controversial show which opened on Broadway in 1968, billing itself as "the American tribal love-rock musical" and became, almost overnight, a clarion call to the young (and some who merely yearned to be young) throughout the world. Adolescence, as a separate stage of life, is an American invention.

The term *teenager* entered common usage in the 1940s. In the years before that, when most "teenage" children worked on family farms, they went from childhood to the life of an adult in one leap. But with the extension of high school education to the great majority of the American young, the advent of a popular culture (driven by the arrival of the radio, the recording industry, and the singing sensation Frank Sinatra), and finally, with the achievement of middle-class prosperity in the 1950s, a whole new era of life was "created," a period characterized by overactive hormones, unchecked idealism, rebellion, and self-discovery.

Today, the teenage theatrical production has become a kind of rite of passage for American high schoolers, the first time many adolescents get to grapple with big, adult issues using only their voices, their feet, and their ability to imagine themselves into a character by immersing themselves in the nuances of a script. That old adage describing the only essential elements of the theater — "two planks and a passion" — applies here. No matter how crowded the chorus scene, one is essentially alone on a stage, vulnerable, at the mercy of one's wits, which, no doubt, is one of the reasons educators see theater as good preparation for life.

Seventy-seven people auditioned for Boulder's Fairview High School production of Hair. *They were asked to read a monologue, sing a few bars of the song "Age of Aquarius," and demonstrate some dance steps. Riley Haemer, singing the song "Frank Mills" at a callback above, would win the role of Crissy.*

But the high school musical remains another rite of passage, too. Like the movies (which eventually supplanted it in the broader culture) and jazz (from which it has often borrowed), the musical is an American art form rooted in central aspects of the American idea, a "mongrel" medium, combining the influences of light opera, the patter speech and comedy of Gilbert and Sullivan, vaudeville, burlesque, the minstrel show, and what turn-of-the-century people called "Negro music." Like most American culture, it has always put entertainment before enlightenment. Indeed, Americans, in general, have never had a feeling for high art, but they have excelled at the creation of a "popular" culture, one dependent upon the box office for success, one that appeals to the taste of a mass audience. In this sense, it could be said that America's is, quite naturally, a rawer, more "democratic" form of culture, and while democracy is not known for its cultural sophistication, the history of the American musical and its cousin, the American popular song, shows that occasionally the chemistry between the artist and the whim of the marketplace can produce something extraordinarily beautiful and enduring. It may not be anything on the order of Caravaggio or Beethoven, but something of lasting significance nonetheless, reveling in its popularity. The classic American songwriter Irving Berlin could have been speaking for the entire American musical theater establishment when he said he did not so much care what critics, his peers, or even the history books thought of his work, only what the audience — he called it "the mob" — thought, an opinion he felt was best gauged by going into the lobby to spy on the audience and find out if anyone was humming his music as they left the theater. They did hum, of course, and they are still humming Berlin, just as they are humming George Gershwin, Cole Porter, Richard Rodgers, Frederick Loewe, and Jerome Kern the world over.

No composer of the quality of those men has worked for the stage in decades and, with the possible exception of the now seventy-two-year-old Stephen Sondheim, Broadway no longer has a resident theatrical genius. Still, the musical theater remains a vital part of American cultural life. Nearly sixty years after it was introduced, there were around six hundred productions of *Oklahoma!* throughout the United States and Canada in 2001 (and a big Broadway revival in 2002). A show almost self-conscious in its simplicity, set as it is at a Midwestern American picnic, *Oklahoma!* continues to thrill audiences in dozens of foreign countries as well (among them Kuwait, Malta, China, and Saudi Arabia), and it has been translated into Danish, Norwegian, Swedish, German, French, Dutch, Japanese, Polish, Hungarian, Hebrew, Spanish, Italian, and Greek. Other American musicals have such broad appeal and staying power, too. There were several hundred productions of *The Music Man* in 2001 and just as many of *Guys and Dolls* and of *West Side Story*, to name just three which continue to please audiences the world over with their "American" character.

"People move to Boulder valley with the thought that they want their children to come to Fairview," says the high school's principal, Dean Palmer. The performing arts program is legendary, with a full one-third of the school's students participating in choir alone.

The history of the American theater song is filled with ironies of a particularly American flavor, not the least of which is the immigrant's flair for reinvention. Who better to write "White Christmas," the quintessential secular hymn for the Christian holiday, and "Easter Parade," celebrating the day of Christ's resurrection, than Irving Berlin, a Jew, the son of a cantor, who arrived here in 1893 as Israel Baline from a part of Russia that neither he nor anyone else was ever quite able to confirm, speaking only Yiddish? Berlin left his Lower East Side New York home at the age of thirteen to slum it in the sordid bars of New York City, singing for pocket change to audiences of Irish and German laborers, and it was

"Democratic peoples have only a very mediocre esteem for erudition . . . They mean to be spoken to about themselves, and they demand a picture of the present . . . they like to find on the stage the confused mixture of conditions, sentiments, and ideas that they encounter before their eyes; the theater becomes more striking, more vulgar, and more true."

—ALEXIS DE TOCQUEVILLE
Democracy in America, 1840

there, at a place called Nigger Mike's Pelham Cafe, which was owned not by an African-American, but by a Russian Jew, that Berlin wrote his first song, "Marie, from Sunny Italy." Ethnic caricature was all part of a day's work for Berlin, who, it was said, could croon "with equal facility as an Italian, a German, a Jew," even as the shameless depiction of a black man that the saloon's title promised (historian Ann Douglas). Or consider how countless couples of the 1920s and 1930s fell in love to the lyrics of Lorenz Hart, Richard Rodgers's first collaborator (they met and began working together in 1919 when Hart was twenty-three and Rodgers just sixteen), who, in contrast to many whom his words serenaded ("My Funny Valentine," "Isn't It Romantic?" "My Heart Stood Still"), was a decidedly unhappy man — alcoholic, painfully short (under five feet), and a closeted homosexual. Cole Porter, America's most urbane composer and lyricist, came from the very un-urbane Peru, Indiana (and Fred Astaire, who made many Porter songs hits, from the equally unsophisticated Omaha, Nebraska). Years after Rodgers quit working with Hart to join up instead with Oscar Hammerstein, the composer used to delight in the number of times that people would approach him and offer congratulations for his artful use of their favorite old German folk song, "Edelweiss," in *The Sound of Music*, which was not an old folk song at all, but had, like everything else in their astonishingly varied oeuvre, come completely out of Rodgers's and Hammerstein's very fertile imaginations.

The musicals that have been the medium's biggest hits are those that strike closest to the heart of the American experience: in 1927, Jerome Kern and Hammerstein made a success of *Show Boat*, which looked at the complicated issue of race and miscegenation; in 1943, *Oklahoma!* examined American farm life and the settling of the West; in the 1950s, *West Side Story* treated immigration, gang life, and the streetscape at the same time that *The Music Man* looked at rural innocence and the redemptive power of music; and in the sixties, *1776* mined the founding drama of the Declaration of Independence while around the corner *Hair* offered a fundamentally American piece of advice: question authority.

"Give me a head with hair
Long beautiful hair
Shining, gleaming,
steaming, flaxen, waxen
Give me down to there
hair."
—Hair

The authors of all these works cast their songs and stories in a manner that could be called the single greatest compliment to a democracy: they showed that the lives and language of simple, ordinary people are rich material for art. To the American stage director, cowboys, riverboat workers, small-town folk, street gangs, sailors, salesmen, political revolutionaries, and a wandering band of hippies are the stuff of great drama. The common man, they showed, is not really so "common"; he sins, he succeeds, he murders, he loves, he climbs, he falls, he cheats, he learns every bit as much as his operatic counterparts. More important, the

In Springfield, Massachusetts: Listening for a distinctive American language

An 1860 cartoon in Vanity Fair *(detail shown at left) spoofed the mid-nineteenth-century "war of the dictionaries" between Noah Webster's, then owned by the Merriam brothers, and Joseph Worcester's slightly more conservative approach. The magazine titled the cartoon "Sporting Intelligence." Bolstered by sales from its edition of the Bible, the Merriams mounted an advertising blitz, right, for* Webster's, *complete with government and celebrity endorsements. "Superior to All Others," barked Ralph Waldo Emerson. In the end, Webster, and the Merriams, won.*

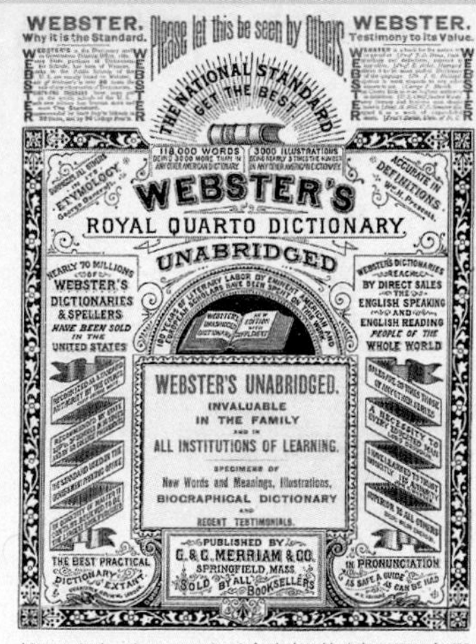

There is no American academy to train the budding lexicographer, but perhaps the closest thing to it can be found on the second floor of a red brick building in a slightly threadbare section of Springfield, Massachusetts. Here, in a room so quiet you can almost hear a consonant drop, Tom Pitoniak, forty-one, and twenty-nine other dictionary "definers" try to divine the special characteristics Americans bring to a language that has roots stretching back to the migration of Germanic tribes to Britain in the fifth century.

It's not your average job. Every day Pitoniak and his colleagues, employees of Merriam-Webster, the country's oldest dictionary publisher, settle in to do what people inside the company describe quite formally as "reading and marking," but which looks to an outsider like nothing more than what most people do when wasting time. They skim magazines and other periodicals both mainstream (*BusinessWeek* and *Better Homes and Gardens*) and obscure (*Bulletin of the American Fisheries Society* and *Australian Geographic*). They surf the web and listen to the radio (both AM and FM), prowling for new words and new meanings for old words, hoping to catch some of the neologisms created by technology (*megapixel*), science (*nutraceutical*), business (*etail*), current affairs (*bioterrorism*), and popular culture (*cybersex*). "It's not enough for a word to be used once to be included in the dictionary," Pitoniak explains. "There've got to be clear signs that it is gaining widespread acceptance."

Once a year, working from what Pitoniak and his colleagues discover, Merriam-Webster updates its most popular lexicon, the 170,000-entry *Merriam-Webster's Collegiate Dictionary*, which defines words in mainstream use (the entire dictionary is revised cover-to-cover every ten years). Among the words that made the cut for 2002 were *treehugger* ("an environmentalist"), *hottie* ("a physically attractive person"), *roadrage* ("a motorist's uncontrolled anger that is usually generated by an irritating act of another motorist and is expressed by aggressive or violent behavior"), and *dollarization* ("adoption of the U.S. dollar as a foreign country's official national currency"). Deciding which words deserve to make the cut is the challenge of Pitoniak's job. Although he earned a Ph.D. from Columbia University in American literature, Pitoniak explains that the only skill a dictionary reader must have is what Germans (Americans, apparently, don't yet have a word for this) call *sprachgefühl*—a feel for language.

English is perhaps the greatest legacy America inherited from Britain (and certainly the longest lasting), but even before independence Americans were busy making the language their own, modifying the mother tongue to suit themselves. "The new circumstances under which we are placed call for new words, new phrases, and for the transfer of old words to new objects," remarked Thomas Jefferson. The variant of English that evolved here reflected the people themselves: direct, energetic, inventive, and wildly acquisitive. As early as 1782, J. Hector St. John de Crèvecoeur wrote in *Letters from an American Farmer* that "our dictionary . . . is . . . short in words of dignity and names of honor."

Indeed, it did not take long for English to go its own way in America. Confronted by a variety of flora and fauna for which no English word existed, the earliest English settlers responded by eagerly lifting Indian words to describe them: *moose, raccoon, caribou,* and *hickory*, among other words, had all entered the settlers' expanded lexicon by 1620. Later encounters with Dutch (*cookie*, *boss,* and *landscape*) and Spanish (*coyote*, *buffalo*, and *ranch*) speakers yielded hundreds more words. By necessity a practical and innovative people, the colonists fashioned new words by mashing together two existing ones, coming up with *rattlesnake, copperhead, catfish, timberland, bluegrass, backtrack, cookbook, underbrush,* and *hillside.* Such compound words are an enduring characteristic of American

English. If they got lost in a *snowstorm* (an Americanism first recorded in 1771), the colonists worried about *frostbite*. Many old English words received new meanings, too. In Britain, a *creek* described an inlet of the sea; here, it signified a stream.

The language reflected Americans' democratic ideals in subtle ways, avoiding the many Latin and French forms (such as *aubergine* for eggplant) prevalent in British usage. And when it came time to name the government's chief executive, Congress choose the austere title of president (from the Latin *praesidere,* to guard or preside over) after mulling more grandiloquent monikers, including *His Highness, His Mightiness, His Magistracy,* and *His Supremacy.* During the decades before and after the Civil War, Americans coined a multiplicity of expressions to describe wealth: *well fixed* (1822), *well-to-do* (1825), *in the dimes* (1843), *in the clover* (1847), *heeled* (1867), *a high roller* (1881), or *a money bag* (1896). In Britain, a *businessman* was someone engaged in public affairs; in America it signified someone hoping to *strike it rich* (1850s) in the world of commerce.

In Noah Webster, a severe, humorless Yankee lawyer born in Hartford, Connecticut, in 1758, American English found its first great champion. "Why should we permit the survival of the curious notion that our language is a mere loan from England, like a copper kettle that we must keep scoured and return without a dent?" he once wrote. In 1806, Webster published *A Compendious Dictionary of the English Language,* credited as the first truly American dictionary, but with only twenty thousand entries, Webster was only warming up. Over the next twenty years, working alone, he compiled and wrote his magnum opus, *An American Dictionary of the English Language*, which defined seventy thousand words (Webster claimed to have learned twenty-three languages for the task).

Webster documented and defined such conspicuously American words as *skunk* and *chowder*. His dictionary also contained his rather ambitious notions of how to reform English spelling. American spelling conventions had already begun to diverge from British usage, dropping the *u* from *honour* and *colour* and turning around the *re* in *theatre* and *metre.* Webster listed hundreds of his own preferred spellings, such as *groop* for *group*, and *wimmen* for *women*, each of them demonstrating a preference for the practical: a word should look the way it is pronounced.

Webster's American dictionary was a critical success, but at $20 a copy — equivalent to about $300 today — it was a commercial failure. Upon his death in 1843, the rights to the dictionary were bought by two brothers, George and Charles Merriam, who ran a print shop in Springfield, Massachusetts. The Merriams scrapped Webster's bizarre spellings and, by squeezing the type, shrank the multivolume dictionary into a single book, which they published in 1847 for only $6 a copy.

It was an immediate success, but there was competition. In 1846, Joseph Emerson Worcester, who once worked for Webster, published his own lexicon, *A Universal and Critical Dictionary of the English Language.* The differences between the two men's works were minor. Worcester's spellings were more conservative than Webster's, but the number of disputed words only numbered about one hundred. Still, a twenty-year-long "War of the Dictionaries" was fought between their partisans. The rivalry seemed to be more about the intellectual allegiances — Worcester was a Harvard man, while Yale claimed Webster — than anything else. Many of the leading literary men of the day — Herman Melville, Washington Irving, and Nathaniel Hawthorne among them — followed Worcester. But the Merriam brothers successfully lobbied legislators to buy thousands of copies of Webster's dictionary for state schools. During the 1860s the lexical slugfest ended, with Webster triumphant.

In time, the American language reflected the arrival of millions of immigrants. Few groups had as much impact as the Germans, who, arriving in droves during the middle of the nineteenth century contributed such words as *ouch*, *loaf* and *loafer, fink, delicatessen*, and *scram*. Later, millions of Jews from Eastern Europe and Russia introduced *kibbutz, keister, glitch, nosh,* and *phooey*. Ironically, each new wave of immigrants absorbs the linguistic gifts of earlier arrivals: Today, outside of New York City, a Korean-owned takeout advertises bagels with a schmear of cream cheese for $1.25.

Webster's single-handed effort at dictionary making is inconceivable today. "Language is developing and changing more rapidly than in preceding generations," says Pitoniak. Each month Merriam-Webster's definers generate as many as fifteen thousand citations of new words or usages. It turns out words fall out of the dictionary, too. *Tattleltale gray,* a phrase popularized by TV commercials for Fels-Naptha Soap during the 1950s and 1960s — it referred to the smudge left around shirt collars by inferior soaps — entered the eighth edition of the *Collegiate Dictionary* in 1973. Twenty years later, however, the commercials were forgotten and the phrase had fallen from favor, so it was removed. "There is no way a dictionary can stand still," says John Morse, Merriam-Webster's president and publisher.

At the end of the day Pitoniak leaves the Springfield office and prepares to drive home to his wife and kids with the satisfaction that comes from bringing clarity to the dynamic, wonderfully unruly language spoken by 280 million Americans. "A good day is one when you can really disentangle a word, when you can point to clear meaning of a particular meaning or usage, and clearly mark a word's borders," he explains. He's aware it's a task that can never be pronounced truly finished. What one word would Pitoniak use to define his job? "Unending."

American musical shows us that the common man's life has every bit as much *right* to the immortality of the stage.

Seen in this way, the "rite of passage" represented by the high school musical production is the one that burnishes the child into an American, brands him or her with the preoccupations will be carried with him throughout life — freedom, individuality, mobility, equality, rebellion, justice, democracy, and a life tied close to nature — a treasury of stories that form a cultural foundation for a country too young to have its own "myths of origin." *Hair* made its first mark on theater history in 1967. It opened then as an Off-Broadway eccentricity before going uptown to shock the tired sensibilities of the Great White Way. The show had little plot (the *New York Times* critic described *Hair* as "a musical with a theme, not with a story"), essentially a single dramatic question: Will Claude Bukowski, a teenager from Queens who has just received his draft notice, go to war in Vietnam or will he listen to the antiwar pleas of George Berger and his "tribe," a cult of wandering youthful agitators who take drugs, sleep on park benches, steal food, and in general confront New York City's establishment with a taunt and a raised middle finger? Broadway's *Hair* included a group nude scene, a lusty tribute to "black boys" ("chocolate-flavored love") sung by white girls and another to "white boys" ("skin as smooth as milk") sung by black girls, as well as a celebration of the high produced by marijuana, LSD, hashish, even "shoe polish." Wearing its irreverence on its sleeve, it alarmed with a song describing a multitude of sexual positions, pairings, and groupings; another which had a black character defiantly reciting every racial epithet known to Americans ("black nigger, a jungle bunny jigaboo, coon, pickaninny, mau mau, Uncle Tom . . .); and a third called "Abie Baby" in which a black character, dressed up to look like Abraham Lincoln, recites a hipped-up version of the Gettysburg Address ("conceived in liberty and dedicated to the one I love") while a white character polishes "Lincoln's" shoes. Before there was an "Earth Day" *Hair* pointed the finger at polluters ("Welcome, sulphur dioxide"). And long before Rosie or Ellen, even before the Stonewall Riots of 1969, *Hair* offered tacit acceptance of homosexuality and mocked the traditional family.

In the end, Claude defies the "tribe." He goes to war — and dies there. But *Hair*'s story was only one reason for its success. The show's appeal was also in its engaging score, which produced several popular hits ("Aquarius" "Good Morning, Starshine," "Easy to Be Hard," "Let the Sunshine In"), and in the sense that the authors had captured the zeitgeist of their time. Many who lived through the sixties imagined themselves at a special moment in history, a spiritual awakening for which *Hair* was the morning reveille.

Hair, *which opened in 1968, had a 1,742-show run. Above, the original Broadway poster.*

> "**The draft is white people sending black people to make war on yellow people to defend the land they stole from the red people.**"
> —Hair

Compared to *Oklahoma!* or, say, *The Sound of Music*, *Hair* is not a great work. Its lyrics do not measure up to or possess the timelessness of Hammerstein's or Hart's, Dorothy Fields's or P. G. Wodehouse's, all early century masters. To many, it now seems dated. But Roz Boatman, Fairview High School's fifty-three-year-old theater director, had a keen sense that a show that focuses so directly upon the joys and strains of youth, upon that period of time when one is caught somewhere between the whimsicality of the child and the earnest responsibility of the adult, was appropriate for her students. "It's about them," she says. She also felt that the musical, which preaches love and tolerance, accepting people even if they are different, and suspicion for tradition and authority, could be productively provocative at a largely white school in a sheltered and prosperous suburban American community which once embraced the *Hair* ideas as their own. Known for its liberal inclinations ("The People's Republic of Boulder" some proudly, others sarcastically, still call it), Boulder has rarely had them tested. But what Roz Boatman could not have predicted, of course, was the historical accident of the production's timing: in the wake of the terrorist attacks on September 11, 2001, the very cloistered young citizens of Fairview High confronted through the special power of art some of the same questions their parents faced decades before. What about America is worth fighting for? Worth dying for? Worth killing for? What separates Americans from the rest of the world's people? What makes us different? What makes us "better"? Do we practice the freedoms we seek to protect? Do we take our freedoms for granted? Have they been respected through our history? Or have they been distorted, even perverted, by our own complacency? And is there an inspiration to be drawn from that era of disturbing social turbulence in the 1960s that we have lost sight of? Or were the sixties just a time of naiveté and self-indulgence from which we still sadly suffer?

II

As soon as she committed Fairview to producing *Hair*, director Roz Boatman was inundated with questions from the school's students and their parents. *Hair*? For high school students? Was she crazy? "They all wanted to know if I was going to cut anything," says Boatman, whose excitable nature and dramatic locks are enough to assure that she would be picked out in any police lineup as the "arty" one. "And I always said 'Well, we're not doing the nudity.' And then immediately, the next question would be about drugs. Am I going to cut the songs that deal with drugs? And I would just say, 'No,' and tell them that's the history of 1968, and you cannot cut drugs from the story of 1968. And then they would finally ask about the song 'Sodomy,' and I would just say, 'Well, okay, we probably won't do that one.'"

Boatman had trouble convincing some people that this was theater, not advocacy. She said over and over again that she wasn't asking the students to get on stage and promote drugs and sex and rebellion, just portray a group of people who did. In the end, she toned down many lines in the script, substituting "populate" for "copulate," "make love, not war" for "lay, don't slay," replacing some of the four-letter words with rhyming substitutes so that, technically speaking, the teens wouldn't be cursing on stage (even if the rhymes made it sound like they were) and deleting altogether lines like the one where the pregnant "tribe" member Jeanie says "I got knocked up by some crazy speed freak, wouldn't ya know?" But even thirty-some years later you can't take the shock out of *Hair*, particularly when high school students are the ones standing before you slowly chanting "hashish . . . cocaine . . . cannabis . . . opium . . . LSD" in a foggy reverie articulated by facial expressions of sheer bliss. As early as 1934, Cole Porter wrote "some get a kick from cocaine" in the song, "I Get a Kick out of You." But by 1968 drugs were seen by many not merely as fun, but as an acceptable route to a "higher consciousness" or at the very least a legitimate form of rebellion.

Following guidelines of the 1995 Federal Protection of Privacy Act, the final cast list was posted with numbers – not names – even if everyone would eventually know who made it and who didn't. Above, Robin Wallace, a senior, checks to see if she is one of the thirty-four who survived the cut. She did, as a member of the ensemble, or "tribe."

Boatman could do *Hair* just about any way she wanted to and still be faithful to the work because, unlike more traditional musicals, *Hair* is meant to be staged almost as improvisation. The show certainly opens that way. There is no curtain-raising. Instead, the script, such as it is, calls for the "tribe" to emerge from the wings as the audience is being seated, to wander aimlessly about the theater, uttering birdcalls, passing out flowers, and moving in slow motion toward the stage, before launching, seemingly spontaneously, into the song "Aquarius." The choice of this January birth sign came from nothing more than the fact that Ragni's son, Erick, four years old when *Hair* came to Broadway, was an Aquarian. But the idea that the play would begin organically, rising up from all parts of the theater, as if growing out of the earth itself — more like a weather event than a composed work of drama — was the assertion of a common American theme, that image of a "new beginning" that is so central to the immigrant experience and that also, in another sense, describes youth's emerging self-awareness. "When the moon is in the seventh house," sings tribe member Ronnie, "and Jupiter aligns with Mars, then peace will guide the planets, and love will steer the stars."

There have been many versions of *Hair*. Before it moved uptown, *Hair* was essentially a rock music revue. On Broadway, it got its thread of a storyline and a more committed sense of irreverence when the director added the nude tableau and Galt MacDermot, the composer, penned a few more songs. But some elements are consistent. The introspective Claude and the in-your-face Berger are usually portrayed as two sides of the same character — Berger, the ego; Claude, the id — and Claude is sometimes seen as the Christ figure, the conscience of the play who is eventually sacrificed for the ideals the "tribe" represents. The script calls for two girls to emerge at the outset and place an altar cloth in the center of the stage; at another point, Woof takes "communion," though he uses drugs, not the traditional wafer and wine, to stand for the body and blood of Jesus Christ. Boatman deleted these scenes, and, for that matter, any other references to Christian symbols with the exception of the finale, when Berger forms a cross in the air with drum sticks and holds it above Claude's dead body, for the Fairview performance. She worried that a "hippie" portrayal of Christian ideas — however sympathetically one might interpret it — could offend Christians in the Boulder community.

In recent years, Boatman had directed Fairview students in musicals having to do with 1930s Germany and the rise of the Nazis (*Cabaret*), with a turn-of-the-century Yonkers, New York matchmaking service (*Hello, Dolly*), and in a spoof of British high society (*My Fair Lady*). But introducing twenty-first-century high school students to the nuances of the sixties revolution was a tall order. In early *Hair* rehearsals, the students were the very picture of innocence, largely unaware and certainly unmoved by the ideas that prompted the cultural effusion that was so integral to their parents' lives. Some of the attitudes of the sixties have become so accepted in American life, it was hard for the students to believe there was a time when the right to wear "long hair" was something to be fought for, when young boys were sent to an unpopular foreign war and agreed to go out of a sense of national duty, and when homosexuality and out-of-wedlock pregnancy were shocking. But others have been rendered into cynicism or caricature. In America, time tends to undermine even the most sincere cultural trend, turning it into a salable commodity, and the sixties are no different. Boatman, the child of a Texas preacher, says that she herself watched the sixties revolution from the sidelines (and made up for her indifference in the seventies). But for these students, none of whom were even born until Ronald Reagan was

Inside the Dallas party scene: Fighting for a right to "pursue happiness"

Thousands paid from $10 to $30 to attend the all-night Texas Zen Festival, left, held at a 3,200-acre ranch in Grandview, Texas. Once through the gates, ticketholders danced, walked through tiki torch trails, played "lasertag," and enjoyed abstract performance art.

Twenty-one-year-old Sean Anderson had booked an old Dallas movie theater months in advance, distributing hundreds of colorful invitations to his second annual techno music dance party. Then, several hours before the event, one of his sound men called to say the party was canceled. "The situation isn't nice," he told Anderson, a part-time biochemistry major at the University of Texas. "They came in force." The "they" were Dallas policemen, a dozen vice officers who, concerned about drugs, warned the theater owner that if the party went on, they would shut it down and arrest him. It was the frustrated police force's latest tactic in a war on "club drugs," a group of mind-, body-, and emotion-altering substances that in the years beginning the twenty-first century had become the drugs of choice at nightclubs and big blowzy all-night music festivals known as "raves." The most popular of the club drugs was Ecstasy which, while illegal since 1985 (and classified a Schedule I dangerous drug, like heroin), had nonetheless, by 2000, been tried by an estimated 6.5 million people.

Despite Ecstasy's classification, the drug's advocates maintained that it was only dangerous if abused. Even while millions were ingesting it, fewer than a dozen deaths a year had been attributed to Ecstasy, many fewer deaths than can be attributed to some prescription drugs. And its benefits were not limited to the kind of high appreciated by denizens of the club scene. Psychotherapists argued that Ecstasy was a worthy tool for their work. So why should it be illegal? Just what is the state's interest in policing "personal freedom"?

Though they could never have even imagined something called a "rave" culture, the founders of the republic ignited the long-burning American quarrel on this subject when they boldly asserted in the Declaration of Independence that individuals were born with "unalienable rights" to "life, liberty and" — to many minds, here was the relevant phrase — "the pursuit of happiness." The words were no idly tossed-off literary flourish. "Happiness" was an important ideal to the founders. "As all divines and moral philosophers will agree, " wrote John Adams, "the happiness of the individual is the end of man." But just how far did the founders' enthusiasm for "happiness" go? And just what did they mean by the term? To them, did "happiness" include "pleasure"? Or, if it did not, just what value of the state did they feel was abridged if the pursuit of pleasure was not uniformly allowed?

First synthesized — and patented — in the early 1900s, MDMA (for methylenedioxymethamphetamine), Ecstasy's official name, was virtually unknown until discovered by chemists in the 1970s, one of whom found that the psychotropic chemical produced an "altered state of consciousness with emotional and sensual overtones" and passed it on to some psychotherapist friends in California. That's when MDMA developed its quiet but loyal following among therapists who found that its euphoric and calming effects allowed patients to confront fears and anxieties. At higher doses, as some Texas entrepreneurs soon discovered, the drug increased the feeling of self-satisfaction and empathy to such an extent that one could dance all night and find even normally repugnant thoughts, like perhaps joining up with the person next to them, pleasant. And so, the multicolored pills, renamed "Ecstasy," began rolling off the assembly lines at the rate of one thousand a day.

The drug was sold openly, throughout Dallas and many other cities with lively party scenes. But the legal fun ended quite quickly when parents, police, and emergency room doctors began reporting problems associated with overdoses — rapid heart rates, high blood pressure, and hyperthermia. In 1985, the DEA, at the suggestion of Lloyd Bentsen, Texas's powerful U.S. Senator, declared Ecstasy a Schedule I drug — prohibited for every application, including medical.

Among the founders, John Adams,

for one, would probably have approved of the ban. While the therapeutic applications of Ecstasy may have given him pause, the Massachusetts attorney would have frowned on the legalization of any substance for the sole purpose of intoxication. Adams never considered the protection of "happiness" to include "un-virtuous" acts. In 1787, the year the Constitution was drafted, Adams wrote that "happiness, whether in despotism or democracy, whether in slavery or liberty, can never be found without virtue." And to Adams, the form of virtue which led to true happiness came from qualities like "humanity and general benevolence, public and private charity, industry and frugality, honesty and punctuality . . . sincerity, good humor, and all social affections."

Adams also worried that the notion of virtue and self-interest could become corrupted by "intoxication, extravagance, Vice and folly." He and the other founders were perfectly aware of the effects of alcohol on the behavior of the common man. George Washington experimented with varietal grapes and had a distillery at Mount Vernon, and Thomas Jefferson, among his many interests, was a serious wine connoisseur. In 1785, Benjamin Rush, a Philadelphia doctor and friend to both Jefferson and Adams, said that excessive imbibing was a national "disease," and estimated that four thousand people a year were dying from drink — out of a population of just 6 million.

In essence, Adams felt that without some controls put upon it, human nature would tend toward the corrupt. To Adams, the state's interest in controlling personal freedom was twofold: to encourage more virtuous behavior which, in turn, would lead to a more industrious society, and to discourage less virtuous behavior, which, in the form of crime, slothfulness, and degeneracy would only cost society and in the end lead to more government in order to make up for the people's failings. But Adams was not the only voice on this subject. Jefferson maintained the opposite: that human nature had a natural tendency toward the virtuous which could only be corrupted by governmental interference. The freer people are, the more they revert to their natural state, which, to Jefferson, was the definition of God's will.

John Adams, above, was the voice of self-control among the founding fathers.

The founders' "resolution" came in a combination represented by the two essential founding documents: the Declaration of Independence declared the American faith in human nature, even as the Constitution provided the controls on its darker behavior. There would be freedom, but with rules to protect the common good. Adams spoke for the majority, arguing that "the best" government was one that "communicates ease, comfort, security or, in one word, happiness, to the greatest number of persons, and in the greatest degree." Adams argued that a strong Constitution, ably and intelligently constructed, could help form the kind of virtuous individual which would, in turn, make the union stronger. Nature indeed "throws us all into the world equal and alike," he said, but that didn't mean that you could allow any man to "endanger public liberty."

Striking this delicate balance between personal freedoms and "public liberty" has never been easy, and in the republic's earliest days there was considerable doubt that it could ever be achieved. In a letter to a friend, George Washington expressed his worry that perhaps the British were "wiser than others" in their prediction that self-government would lead to chaos. No wonder Washington felt such tremendous relief, then, when the Whiskey Rebellion of 1794, an eruption of violence in Pennsylvania over an excise tax on the "drug of choice," ended. Washington was able to quell the dispute with an overwhelming show of military force wherein not a drop of blood was spilled. "Republicanism is not the phantom of a deluded imagination," he exulted. And the lesson he drew was that in no other form of government would "the laws be better supported, liberty and property better secured, or happiness more effectually dispensed to mankind." But Jefferson was not impressed. He, predictably, saw Washington as squelching a benign expression of popular discontentment.

Drugs have often posed a special challenge to the "delicate balance" since they can contain both the Enlightenment promise of perfection — delivering both physical and mental health — and, put to the wrong use, the dangers of indolence and death. At the end of 2001, in fact, while the Senate Caucus on International Narcotics Control heard expert testimony regarding Ecstasy's harm, the Food and Drug Administration decided that the drug might help victims of rape or post-traumatic stress syndrome.

For Sean Anderson, the Dallas vice squad's warning seemed a ham-handed way to conduct the discussion, but he recovered to rent another theater in a nearby town for his party — and to launch a lawsuit against the Dallas police for violating his Constitutional rights. "I have friends of mine who have gotten really messed up on it," he says of Ecstasy. Even though he doesn't condone the use of Ecstasy, Andersen says, "it shouldn't be classified as a dangerous drug. It's less dangerous than alcohol. You don't go violent on Ecstasy. And you can usually drive yourself home."

president and who matured well after the collapse of the Soviet Union, she even had to explain something as simple as patches on jeans because their idea of "hippie" clothing had been shaped by years of designer fashions, of $50 bell bottoms with neatly sewn on "protest" insignias. "They had no idea that the original patches were to cover holes," says Boatman. "We had to start really basic." But once she did, she watched the play, and its relationship to the world around it, transform the students.

For senior Kate Stratton, a sweet brunette whose innocent twinkle has made her the envy of Fairview's theater crowd, the ideas and mood of *Hair* were at least familiar. The show may have rattled the theatrical establishment in the sixties, and there was no doubt that it still rattled a few parents and administrators at Fairview in 2001, but for Stratton, *Hair* was more of a historical artifact. In fact, says Stratton, she might as well have been playing her own mother at that age, because Kate's mom, Susan Stratton, was a college student and a protester, a member of the radical Students for a Democratic Society, a self-described "left-wing pinko commie."

The first rehearsal, above, was a simple read through. Others, like the musical itself, were more unorthodox. "Okay, we're going to pretend that we're smoking marijuana," said director Roz Boatman, during one run-through. She then turned out the lights, told the cast to sit still and feel "mellow," and had them sing the song "Hashish."

Kate Stratton had grown up listening to her mother talk about politics and about her lack of trust in the government because, quite simply, it "lies to us." Still, standing on stage, trying to conjure up the idealistic vision of a street hippie in 1968 was, for Kate, a challenge. At first she felt "cute" saying lines like "What do we want? Freedom! When do we want it? Now!" The language had lost some of its revolutionary resonance; it felt trite. But it helped when, with Boatman's encouragement, Stratton began to "internalize" the sixties, to ask, as every theater beginner is told to ask of him- or herself, "What is my motivation here? What is my character feeling?" And Stratton discovered that one motivation of the sixties radical was to make a truly democratic statement, one suspicious of those in power, a desire to change things, and the belief that youth's opinion should count, too. "Here were these kids being shipped off to die for a cause that they didn't really believe in," says Stratton of the Vietnam generation, "and I don't think they felt that they were being heard. When the hippies grew out their hair and went around protesting and started to be loud and obnoxious, I think it was their way of saying, wake up and listen to me."

For Dan Kohler, playing Berger, *Hair* was also about individuality, something the curly topped senior had witnessed in his own family when his parents divorced and his mother entered into a lesbian relationship with a woman who has become a kind of third parent to him. The experience made Kohler sensitive to the disapproving attitudes some people bring to homosexuality, certainly a *Hair* theme; it also convinced him that you should do what comes naturally to you and not keep up appearances for others. Indeed, if his friend Kate Stratton could claim that she was in a sense playing her own mother, well, then Kohler found his way into his character by realizing that he was playing himself, or, more accurately, himself as he might have been had he lived thirty years ago. Kohler already had a love for sixties music; now he began to embrace the sixties ideas. "I was Berger before I had to play Berger," he says, demonstrating the somewhat overbearing confidence appropriate to his role. "I'm loud and out there . . . That's why I like *Hair*."

Much of the rehearsal time was spent getting the students into the mood of the sixties. "Don't get a haircut," implored Roz Boatman, above, feel "earthy," and become a "family" with the rest of the cast. "Every single person who is in this show," she told them, "will say 'It changed my life.'"

Given the racial makeup of Boulder and, in particular, Fairview High (there are only thirty or so African-Americans out of a school population of about two thousand), Boatman had a hard time recruiting black students for a play that demanded black characters. She found herself walking up to people in the hallways and pleading with them to audition even if they had never had an interest in the stage. One "person of color" who responded, Ali Hammett, is a dramatic blend of Korean, Hispanic, and black ancestry and the adopted child of white parents. Hammett, who would go on to play Hud, had never even heard of *Hair* before. But once she became familiar with it, she decided that *Hair* was, for her, about racial tolerance. "The first song I came across," she says, " was 'Colored Spade' (the song which includes a recitation of racial slurs) and it seemed to me to be in bad taste. It reminded me that the first time I was called 'Nigger' was when I was eight years old. But I grew to like the fact that *Hair* is so shocking."

Rebellion, individuality, freedom, racial equality, the list of ideas that came rolling out of the students from their reading of *Hair* was a litany of American values, certainly, yet in this sixties guise they still felt foreign, like something they had to "learn." When the group wondered why Claude seems so lost, Boatman reminded them that many youths in the sixties felt lost. They had been raised by the World War II generation in mostly prosperous circumstances and more of them had gone to college than in any generation before them, yet they felt uncomfortable with the world they were now expected to join. It seemed empty, arrogant, materialistic, insensitive, even cruel.

When the students were put off by the raunchiness of the lyrics,

Boatman pointed out that the words were meant to be freeing, that they were to be heard as a challenge to the kind of conformity that the hippies saw around them, that they believed was stifling to their own sense of free expression. Boatman brought her husband to talk to the cast about Vietnam. Joe Boatman is an environmental scientist who helps his wife by building the sets for Fairview's theater productions. He described high school gym classes that were meant to prepare boys in his generation for the drills of boot camp. Joe Boatman then told them that he himself was drafted but received a physical deferment. But schoolmates of his went to Vietnam and several of them died there. Susan Stratton, Kate's mom, said that she had lost six friends in Vietnam — two who had died there and four who returned deeply traumatized. They have never been the same.

Dance is part of most of the Fairview musical productions, but for Hair, *the cast was asked to improvise movements. Director Boatman worried that a show that looked choreographed might seem too "pretty" for the sixties sensibility. Above, Camille Harris, left, and Ashley Howard strike a pose.*

Roz Boatman told the students that even more than most plays this one required that they meld as a group of people. They must take the image of a "tribe" seriously and see themselves as a unit which, under the stress of a dangerous world situation (she had to remind herself that the cold war was like ancient history to these kids) and a host of other factors, had decided to seek comfort in one another and form an "alternative" family. To convey that idea to their audience, the students needed to feel that sense of comradeship, too. "Until you do that bonding," she said, "until you feel that sense of tribal love, you haven't done the work that this piece demands."

Ironically, their work (and Boatman's) became much easier after September 11. The rehearsal scheduled for that afternoon was canceled, but rather than going home, the cast went to senior Nathan Cooper's house just to be together and share their feelings on an awful day. Like much of the nation, the students were bewildered by the tragedy. They felt inarticulate, unsure whether to express anger or sadness, so they did both. Some worried about what might follow from the terrorist events. Almost immediately they made the connection to the sixties. Many Fairview seniors were just turning eighteen. If the world situation deteriorated and required the establishment of a large American standing army, would they be drafted? If drafted, would they go? Others simply decried the violence in the world ("What is it about the human race that makes people want to destroy one another?" asked Stephanie Ablowitz) and a few, anticipating that Americans of Arab descent would be looked upon now with suspicion, voiced concern that old stereotypes would be given new justification. But Kate Stratton seemed to speak for the group when she posed a difficult question and answered it herself. Given the gravity of the event, given the awful display of hatred and evil, she said she had been wondering all day about what they could do to respond to it, how they could express some counterforce. "And you know what I realized?" she asked. (Like a good actor, she then paused for effect.) "We're already doing something. We're putting on this antiwar, pro-peace musical called *Hair*."

III

"What pity is it that we can die but once to serve our country!"

— *From Joseph Addison's* Cato, *a popular Revolutionary-era drama*

Thomas Jefferson is recorded as having spent money to see "a learned pig" and a rendition of "Dutch dancing" and to hear a performance of "musical glasses." But in general, the theatrical entertainments preferred by the founding fathers, like those preferred by most aristocratic Americans of the eighteenth century, were of an elevated, and inherited, nature. Jefferson was an accomplished violinist who played on his own Amati instrument, one of the finest of his day or any other, and he appreciated the music of Corelli and Vivaldi as well as light musical theater. As president, Jefferson encouraged the Marine Corps Commandant to send to Italy for musicians who might improve the sorry state of the Corps' band (which, Jefferson felt, had played poorly at his inauguration). But, in contrast, he expressed his wishes that the general citizenry of the new nation focus on cultivating the practical arts — gardening and architecture were those he cited — rather than the "less useful" arts that appealed more to the mind and soul.

John Adams shared Jefferson's love for the stage. While serving in France, Adams was appalled by the extravagances of European aristocracy ("I . . . would cheerfully exchange all the elegance, magnificence, the sublimity," he sighed in a letter to his wife Abigail, "for the simplicity of Braintree and Weymouth"), but he loved the theater, where he sometimes watched from a box next to Voltaire's. And George Washington, while not usually mistaken for a man of letters, was a staunch advocate of the stage drama. He was profoundly moved by Shakespeare and other playwrights and even encouraged idle soldiers at Valley Forge to put on a performance of the Englishman Joseph Addison's 1713 *Cato* (which they did, in between games of "bowls" played with cannonballs).

Washington and Adams were fond of the Romans in particular. As Richard Brookhiser has noted, all the founding fathers preferred them to the Greeks because "they had done what the Americans themselves hoped to do — sustain an extensive republic over a course of centuries." *President, congress,* and *senate* are all Roman terms. The play *Cato* is the

> **"The Puritans who founded the American republics were not only enemies of pleasures; they further professed an altogether special horror of the theater. They considered it an abominable diversion . . . The opinions of the first fathers of the colony left profound marks on the spirit of their descendants."**
>
> —Alexis de Tocqueville
> *Democracy in America,* 1840

story of the last great hero of the Roman republic, who was defeated by Caesar. But while it was written by an English classical scholar without any particular political message in mind, the work took on extra meaning in the Colonies where the word *Caesar*, with its whiff of tyranny, was a Colonial euphemism for "England," and Cato, as one who died in the pursuit of liberty and justice, was an example that served as a model for the American patriot. *Cato* was among the most performed dramas in eighteenth-century America and sentiments lifted from it were prized as maxims. Both Patrick Henry ("Give me liberty or give me death") and Nathan Hale ("I regret that I have but one life to lose for my country") derived inspiration for their most famous utterances from the play, and Washington, who saw it numerous times from youth to maturity, is said by many to have modeled his life on Cato's.

American musical theater took longer to develop than did the stage play. Yet throughout their early histories both faced random condemnation by conservative clergy concerned about the impact of the stage on the nation's morals. During the time of Washington and through the first few decades of the nineteenth century, several states employed laws against theatrical performances, though there is little evidence that they were vigorously enforced. And as late as 1865, when Abraham Lincoln was assassinated at Ford's Theater while watching a performance of the popular English comedy, *Our American Cousin*, the president's pastor, Dr. Philip D. Gurney, who was present in the bedroom when Lincoln died, offered, rather indelicately, the thought that Lincoln had let down his "Christian friends" by being shot in "a school of vice and corruption through which thousands are constantly passing into the embrace of gaiety and folly, intemperance and lewdness, infamy and ruin."

Despite Dr. Gurney's protestations, a far more raucous stage genre, the musical, was born just a year later. If one is to believe the apocrypha, a New York theater producer, saddled with a commitment to *The Black Crook*, a tedious drama set in Germany, stumbled upon the news that a Parisian ballet company visiting New York had been rendered stageless by a fire and needed somewhere to perform. The producer stuck the dancers into the play, had some songs written for them to dance to, and *The Black Crook* went on to have a long run. With that, Broadway, a street in New York that follows an old Indian path, became Broadway, the street of American dreams.

At the time of *The Black Crook*, the theater was still the province of the well off. But beginning in the late nineteenth century, with the rise of a prosperous middle class and a labor movement to protect their interests, leisure became a mass activity and, quite suddenly, the stage and other public venues began to speak in a democratic voice that blended

In northern Utah: Making Americans laugh

Writer Constance Rourke's three archetypes of American humor included the backwoodsman, right, the minstrel, opposite page, and the Yankee. The amateur comedian Walter O'Neal, left, at the Wiseguys Comedy Cafe, draws on all three for his stand-up routine. Still, he says, "The primary rule of comedy is you got to make fun of yourself first."

"Don't worry. I'm not here to rob you," says Walter O'Neal, a twenty-seven-year-old African-American car salesman, standing before an audience of about forty. "I've got the homeboys in the parking lot taking care of that for me right now." O'Neal squints through the spotlights, smiles nervously, then, knowing that timing is the essence of good comic delivery, pauses. "I just hope they beat the Mexicans to it." There's laughter and O'Neal is off and running on this Wednesday, amateur night at the Wiseguys Comedy Cafe in West Valley City, Utah.

O'Neal is one of a half-dozen or so aspiring comics on the slate, which includes two college students, a man who makes his living juggling for children's parties, a Coca-Cola deliveryman, and a man in a wheelchair who suffers from cerebral palsy. One by one, all of them make their way to a small stage in a large, dimly lit room that once served as a storefront church. There they stand and chatter on with jokes and stories, impersonations and confrontations, on the chance that they might get someone in the audience to smile, chuckle, or, dream of dreams, roar. Surveying the scene, Rodney Norman, the deadpan manager of Wiseguys, offers a colorful description for the evening of hit-or-miss acts. "I call it sausage night," he says. "Everyone likes sausage but no one likes to see it made. But if you want to be a comedian, this is where it starts." Or doesn't. A few minutes before O'Neal appeared on stage, the evening's host warned the audience to refrain from heckling. "Not laughing is enough to get the message across," he assured them. At a comedy club, silence is the "sound" performers dread most.

Every night, across the country, on well-worn city stages and under the unforgiving spotlights of backroom rural grill joints, thousands of aspiring comics aim to do something as elementary as it is endearing: make someone laugh. In America, comedy has taken many forms including, most notably for our time, the stand-up, an American creation which in its very posture — a single person standing before a crowd, looking for a laugh — emphasizes the primacy of the individual in American life. The great traditions of American humor can be detected there as much as they can in the comic stage drama and the newspaper comic strip, in the madcap film or television situation comedy, and in the idle joke passed to colleagues by word of mouth. In each, Americans laugh when their own particular fears and insecurities are revealed, when the high and mighty get their comeuppance, when the habits of new immigrants or other racial types are — sometimes cruelly — parodied, and when Americans' own gargantuan ambitions are gently mocked. Throughout history, American humor has encompassed the tall tale and the leveling insult, the ethnic caricature and the dethroning of the powerful. "I am a greater man than George Washington," offered one of America's best humorists, Mark Twain, felling moral righteousness and the deification of national leaders with one swoop, "because Washington said 'I cannot tell a lie.' And, well, I can tell a lie. I just choose not to."

One might say that the Revolution started with a practical joke, when, one night in 1773, a few dozen colonists donned Indian garb, walked through a crowd, boarded British ships, and tossed several hundred crates of Darjeeling into Boston harbor. The English would get another dose of the colonists' humor when the song they themselves had once sung to ridicule Americans — the one about "Yankee Doodle," the rube who rode a pony to war and stuck a feather in his hat thinking it would make him a "dandy" — was caroled back at them, embraced by the colonists as if it were a national anthem. Thus was born, in the heat of rebellion, America's plainspoken hero, the one with rustic intelligence, simple virtue, courage, and a sense of humor.

Among the founders, Benjamin Franklin possessed the most impressive wit, which he usually employed to some larger purpose: tweaking the British or, among his own countrymen, the defenders of slavery. But in 1790, it was George Washington who marched into a Philadelphia theater to witness one of America's first comic theatrical productions, *The Contrast: A Comedy*, written by Royall Tyler, a Revolutionary War veteran. The republic was but an infant, yet Tyler had already created a new American character in the form of the play's "hero," Jonathan, who, a mere valet to a military officer, nonetheless declared himself to be "a true blue son of liberty" and demonstrated a sense of self-respect when he insisted on being called a "waiter" not a "servant."

For Constance Rourke, whose 1931 book *American Humor: A Study of the National Character* would became a classic, Tyler's Jonathan was an American "aboriginal character" who had "sprung suddenly" from the spirit of the fledgling republic. Unlike previous historians who studied the expressions of the educated and powerful, Rourke detected culture also in the folk traditions and the basic myths belonging "to the mass of the people." She identified a comic trio of characters which arose in the early years of the Republic and has lasted in one form or another throughout American history: the "Yankee," the "backwoodsman," and the "Negro minstrel." Each was an original American type, Rourke argued, though the three shared common comedic traits, utilizing the homespun metaphor and the earthy simile, telling tall tales, and inventing stories that mocked accepted norms even as they imparted political and moral lessons. Long after *The Contrast* closed in Philadelphia, "Yankee" characters could be detected in comic stage performances throughout the country. The touring Yankee performed as a "peddler," a "sailor," or a "Vermont wood-dealer" with names like Jedediah Homebred and Jerusalem Dutiful. He often dressed in a white bell-crowned hat, a coat with long tails, usually blue, and eccentric red and white trousers, making him look a bit like Uncle Sam. "Half bravado, half cockalorum," said Rourke, "indefatigably rural, sharp, uncouth, witty." The Yankee was always winning by losing and usually had the last laugh.

Rourke's second type was a variation on the theme of irreverence and homespun intelligence. But where the Yankee spurned blue-blood society and tradition, the backwoodsman spurned all society and anything but his most natural instincts. Davy Crockett was a backwoodsman: a pioneer with civilization at his back, always looking outward for "more elbow room," oblivious to danger and lucky to a fault. Even the Negro minstrel, the third type in Rourke's comedic trinity, was originally fashioned to be heroic, though with the odd dissonance created by the fact that in a slave society he had to be portrayed by a white man in black face. Early "burnt-cork" impersonators told tales that were just as outlandish as the Yankee's and the backwoodsman's and his character was just as buffoonish. "Ole Dan Tucker" combed his hair with a wagon wheel and washed his face in a frying pan. "Jim Crow" could be found on the Mississippi, falling in the river, and ending up in New Orleans, so "full of fight" that when he hit a man there was nothing left of him, "'Cept a little grease spot."

The great wave of immigration in the late nineteenth and early twentieth centuries opened up a new venue for humor, the ethnic caricature. Country bumpkins of the Yankee and backwoodsman type were present on the vaudeville stage, but so were acts that billed themselves as "Irish" or "Hebrew" which, as historian David Nasaw explains, didn't describe the ethnicity of the performers, but the nature of the act itself. The Marx Brothers, who started in vaudeville, represented a blend of these types, with Groucho as the "Hebrew" tossing off rapid-fire irreverent jokes, Harpo as the "knockabout, slapstick" warmhearted "Irishman," and Chico, the "happy-go-lucky Italian." Italians, Irish, and Jews were all present in vaudeville audiences and they laughed at their own stereotypes — so long as it didn't go too far. By blending types, vaudeville was doing its part to achieve a new American man. But the mocking of blacks was different. Fueled now by the resentment brought on by their freedom, blacks were portrayed by the late-nineteenth-century minstrel cruelly: as wooly-haired fools who were lazy, frightened, overly sexual, and dangerous.

You can see the bits and pieces of Rourke's types throughout American comedic history, just as you can see the abiding presence of ethnic humor. Mark Twain was a tall-tale teller whose characters have a simple, native intelligence that reveals itself over time; Red Skelton gently mocked the rube with his portrayal of the country bumpkin "Klem Kadiddlehopper"; and Jackie Gleason was the "poor soul." "Beverley Hillbillies" portrayed a family of simple country folk who, like Rourke's "backwoodsman," stumble on good luck, and in the 2001 cartoon movie

Shrek, Mike Myers gave voice to a character who is ugly and simple-minded and yet charmingly sincere, while black comic Eddie Murphy is the voice of a donkey who is frightened and lazy yet goads his "master" toward the right moral choices. When it comes to comedy, Americans remain Americans. Indeed, when Wiseguys Cafe comic Walter O'Neal slurs Mexicans, he is, like so many comics before him, making fun of his outsider status and helping to remove the sting of ethnicity in a multiracial society. "Hey don't worry about it," says O'Neal to the crowd. "I'm a black guy. I can get away with doing that." Then, grabbing a lackluster fifth-place finish in the night's competition, he puts aside his dreams to return to his day job.

the bizarre with the stunning and (very occasionally) the refined. Jefferson could never have imagined a theater for the masses (and probably wouldn't have enjoyed it), but the democratic revolution that he helped start had led to precisely that. By the late 1800s people of all stripes were, for the first time, sharing a common, commercial culture, arriving at places of entertainment where, as historian David Nasaw describes it, "there were no restrictions as to gender or ethnicity, religion, residence or occupation . . . Unlike the landsmen's lodges and union halls; the saloons and church socials; and the front stoops, parlors, and kitchens, the new entertainment centers held more strangers than friends. 'Going out' meant laughing, dancing, cheering, and weeping with strangers with whom one might — or might not — have anything in common." Only blacks and prostitutes were segregated or excluded. The rest of America sat together, as near a definition of a cultural "democracy" as had been experienced anywhere to that day.

There were soon more theaters in New York City than any other city in the world, and, with their wide-ranging clientele, the acts really did now seem to dance on the edge of propriety. Vaudeville, a new form of revue which offered "something for everyone," had elements of the circus sideshow blended in with the theater. A Boston promoter, appropriately named Benjamin Franklin Keith, featured one bill, historian Nasaw notes, that included a "Brooklyn Miss" weighing over five hundred pounds, a "demon dwarf," German midgets performing on a zither, the biggest frog in the world, a puppet show, some Guatemalan musicians, a comedy duo and a stage farce called *Murphy's Fat Baby*.

It is hard to believe that an art form of considerable depth and substance could evolve from such an eclectic blend of cultural expressions, but it did, thanks to the imagination of a handful of men, most notably George M. Cohan, Irving Berlin, Jerome Kern, Oscar Hammerstein, and Richard Rodgers. Cohan's life story has the air of a musical plot itself and was in fact made into a musical, in a classic 1942 movie starring Jimmy Cagney as Cohan (*Yankee Doodle Dandy*) and a 1968 stage work called, simply, *George M!* What dramatist could resist the robust tale of an egotistical Irish-American song and dance man who succeeded in creating an American musical stage genre brimming with flags and patriotic filigree, accenting the common man and standing up to the stodgy Eurocentered theater elite? Given his penchant for writing jingoistic songs, many of which rightfully passed into the night, and his knack for self-promotion ("Whatever you do, kid, always serve it with a little dressing," was his advice to a young Spencer Tracy), it is not surprising that people have questioned whether Cohan was indeed "born on the Fourth of July," as he claimed. But several of his biographers have confirmed it and Cohan

In northeast Florida: Honoring "America's troubadour"

America's first popular songwriter, Stephen Foster, right, in a daguerrotype circa 1861, had a melancholy disposition, which his ballads often demonstrated. Foster's music harkened back to the Old South, though ironically, he likely never visited there. Left, the "Jeanie" finalists pose on the veranda of the Civil War–styled house at the Stephen Foster Culture Center State Park in White Springs, Florida.

On the veranda of a white antebellum house framed with Spanish moss, Bridget Sanchez stood fluttering a lace fan, cooling herself in the thick Florida air. She had already sung a rousing "Oh, Susanna" that won her the applause of the audience. Now it was her turn to be serenaded. A college tenor, resting respectfully on one knee, gazed at her lovingly and sang a tribute. Feeling flattered, Sanchez composed herself. Then, after gracefully bowing her head to receive her crown, she flashed what she later called a "huge cheek-hurtin' smile." She was the new "Jeanie" — "Jeanie with the Light Brown Hair," that is, winner of a fiercely fought annual White Springs, Florida, vocal competition to honor Stephen Foster, the songwriter some have called "America's Troubadour."

Like many Americans, Bridget Sanchez, "Jeanie 2002," grew up singing such classics as "Camptown Races" and "Oh! Susanna" without even knowing that they were Foster songs. Only when she began rehearsing for the Jeanie contest did she come to realize the mid–nineteenth-century Pittsburgh native's profound impact on American music. Foster has a way of surprising people like that. His music is so familiar, so basic to the American story, and it is learned so early — often at the knee of a parent — that many people assume that it could not have been composed, that it must be folk music of the purest kind, passed down in the grand oral tradition. Yet in fact, the imagination of one man came up not only with "Jeanie" and "Dreamer" and "Camptown" and "Susanna" but "Old Black Joe" and "Old Folks at Home" — nearly three hundred songs in all, many of them American classics, an oeuvre big enough and varied enough to be described by some as the foundation of popular music, and he did it all before he died tragically at the age of just thirty-seven.

The life of Stephen Foster had an auspiciously American beginning. Like the great stage patriot, George M. Cohan, he was born on the Fourth of July, and in Foster's case it was no ordinary Fourth — July 4, 1826, to be exact, the date marking both the fiftieth anniversary of the Declaration of Independence and the passing of two great American giants, Thomas Jefferson and John Adams. Foster came into the world as they left it. Like most children of his class, he spent many afternoons playing and singing at the piano in the family parlor. But Foster was also interested in music he heard outside the home, in the growing popularity of the minstrel, the white men in black face performances of the 1830s and 1840s which dominated the theaters and, at a time when the nation was still emerging from its Colonial past, worked to establish a distinctive American culture.

At once racist and "patriotic," the minstrel exaggerated for humor's sake the mannerisms and cultural traditions of the African American and allowed white Americans from different ethnic backgrounds to join in expressing their superiority to the black man, a unifying event in a nation of immigrants. But to the young Foster, who would often return home from the theater and put on minstrel shows of his own with his friends, there was also something fascinating about the black music and lyrics he heard there (even if they had been twisted for derogatory effect), and he carried that sympathy forward years later when, as a bookkeeper in his brother's steamboat business in Cincinnati, Ohio, he decided to become a professional songwriter.

From his office window on the docks of the Ohio River, Foster marveled at the music of immigrants arriving from Germany and Italy, Ireland and Scotland, and, especially, the blacks who had come to Cincinnati to work on the docks. Now Foster could hear real African-American music, not just the caricatures of the minstrel men, and it continued to hold his fancy. Locked in complete silence in his study, Foster carefully incorporated the diverse melodies he'd absorbed from the many varieties of music he now heard, first working through them note by note on the flute, then playing them full-out on the piano until they became the raw material for his own music. In the end, Foster's lasting appeal would rest in his ability to draw on this fascination, from which he created a uniquely American sound, borrowing from elements of Irish and Scottish ditties, German lieder, Italian opera, minstrel music and black spirituals, to create simple melodies with lyrics that spoke to simple human needs: a longing for family and for home and the heartbreak of love and loss.

"Oh! Susanna," Foster's first minstrel song, written in 1846, was also his first "smash hit." Arriving at a time, just before the Civil War, when national pride was just beginning to grow and new technologies — the railroad and, soon, the telegraph — were uniting people across the nation, it caught on like no song before it. The most popular piece of sheet music before "Susanna" had sales of about five thousand. "Susanna" would sell over 100,000 copies and instantly become part of the national cultural heritage. California miners hummed it as they dug for gold out west and, in 1849, New York journalist Bayard Taylor reported that black rowers sang it as they guided him up stream across Panama to California. Indeed, "Susanna" was probably the single most sung song in all of America in the middle 1800s, the first genuine "popular" song, owned by the masses.

After the success of "Susanna," Foster became serious about making a living in music and publishers began billing him as "The Songwriter of America." In 1850, he wrote sixteen songs; in 1851, he wrote sixteen more. The refined parlor ballads were there, demonstrating Foster's ever more sophisticated use of language ("Jeanie," written in 1854, includes the glorious line, "Borne, like a vapor, on the summer air"). But the really successful works were still the minstrels, which became a controversial emblem of his music. In fact, for as long as Foster's music has stoked the popular imagination, his fascination with the black experience has encouraged debate over whether he contributed to racism, reflected it, or, by treating black life with humanity and understanding, fought it. Even "Susanna," in its original form, was written in an ignorant black dialect and included a verse (rarely sung today) in which the singer

The original sheet music to Foster's "Jeanie," which he wrote for his wife.

declares that he "jump'd aboard the telegraph and trabbled down de ribber" but "De lectrick fluid magnified and kill'd five hundred Nigga." (Minstrel songs often portrayed blacks as frightened of technology — the "telegraph" here refers both to the machine and the name of a steamboat. But the more Foster wrote, the more complex, and sympathetic, even this "Ethiopian Music" became. He dropped the term *minstrel* and began referring to these as "plantation songs." He toned down the dialect and blended the ideas and images together with white phraseology so that the black experience began to serve less as an object of ridicule and more as a metaphor for all manner of American yearnings, most importantly, the one for "home." Indeed, that instinct led in 1853 to one of Foster's greatest songs, "My Old Kentucky Home," a plaintive ballad which, only after it has grabbed hold of the listener's emotions, reveals itself to be about the selling of a slave down the river.

It was a "home" song that brought the Jeanie contest (and a Stephen Foster Memorial) to White Springs, Florida, more than fifty years ago. The connection is slight, but true: "Swanee River" — more familiar to some as "Old Folks at Home" — is one of Foster's many enduring songs and the real Suwannee River (Foster had changed the spelling to sound more lyrical) flows south through the edge of White Springs. In fact, "Swanee River" is Florida's state song, at least for now. Citing the song's black dialect, a group of Florida residents recently called for retiring it in favor of something less controversial. But they were turned back, in part by the efforts of the Florida Federation of Music Clubs, a group of women who organize the "Jeanie" contest and who vow to keep the spirit of Foster alive.

To compete both for the title and a $1,500 music scholarship, "Jeanie" contestants must be no older than twenty-three, come dressed in an antebellum style, and then perform one Foster song. Twelve singers are chosen to compete each year. Sandra Lopez, a recent Jeanie, now sings with the Metropolitan Opera in New York City. But even after she won, Bridget Sanchez, the 2002 champion, claimed no grander ambition than what she already does, teaching music to elementary school children in the heart of Miami. The majority of her students are Haitian immigrants, just getting to know life in America, and to help them learn something about both music and American history Sanchez intends to teach them Stephen Foster. "Foster wrote the songs that are important to America," she insists, before adding, with a lilt, "and they are such singable songs."

himself said that the date of his arrival into the world bestowed upon him a patriotic duty which he willingly embraced. "If it had not been for the glorious symbol of Independence," he remarked, "I might have fallen into the habit of writing problem plays, romantic drama or questionable farce . . . The American flag is in my heart and it has done everything for me."

Cohan lived his life in the theater. He started performing at seven when, with his sister and parents, he was part of the much loved act known as The Four Cohans, and he ended in his own failed play, *Return of the Vagabond*, in 1940, two years before his death. But it was his writing, even more than his performing, which would make Cohan a legend. On this, Cohan worked with an uncanny speed, writing songs for his shows in an afternoon, sketching out dance numbers by the following morning, and directing the entire production at the same time, a no-nonsense approach that in his mind distinguished American theater from European high art. Indeed, in the early years of the musical theater, Cohan made it his job to rend the American musical from its dependence on European influences such as operetta and, in particular, Gilbert and Sullivan. And while most of Cohan's forty-some plays are deservedly forgotten, it was the attempt at something "American" which made him significant. As Hammerstein once commented, "Never was a plant more indigenous to a particular part of the earth than was George M. Cohan to the United States of his day."

George M. Cohan, above, succeeded on Broadway at a time when America was developing a fierce national pride. "I'm the kid that's all the candy, I'm a Yankee Doodle Dandy," sings the lead character in his Little Johnny Jones.

Cohan had something of Irving Berlin, his younger contemporary, in him. In fact, while the name Cohan, which was derived from the more obviously Irish "Keohane," was pronounced "Co-*han*" by the rest of his family, George preferred to accent the first syllable and shorten the last, as in "*Co*-en," because it sounded more "Jewish," an advantage in a stage world that was already seeing the rapid success of Jewish immigrants. Like Berlin, Cohan was fond of ragtime music, or as much of it was more crudely known back then, the "coon song," and not only for its syncopated rhythms, which he employed to good effect in his music, but also for its use of vernacular speech. While European immigrants Franz Lehar and Rudolph Friml were writing works employing the elevated language of society, Cohan created a new sort of theater character, a fast-talking "jaunty" New Yorker who preferred slang to slower, more formal speech, had common tastes like the racetrack, and projected a fierce pride in the USA.

Cohan's 1904 *Little Johnny Jones*, about an American jockey (played by Cohan) who goes to London to ride in the Derby and is falsely accused of throwing the race, included two of his most famous songs, "Yankee Doodle Dandy" and "Give My Regards to Broadway." It is often cited as the first truly "American" musical even if it didn't exactly succeed at the box office. ("What makes the American so proud of his country?" demands one character. The answer: "*Other* countries.") But his *George Washington, Jr.* is even more typical of Cohan, chock full as it is of an even brasher form of patriotic symbolism. The show is the story of George Belgrave, an American whose Anglophile father wants him to marry up the social ladder and suggests a good English lady of title as a candidate. George (again, played by Cohan) refuses because he is in love with an American — a Southern belle, to be more precise. When in anger his father then disowns him, the boy in turn disowns his father, changing his last name to match that "of the only father I know . . . the father of my country."

Cohan's 1906 "You're a Grand Old Flag," above, was a sprightly tribute to, as its lyrics read, "that patriotic something that no one can understand."

Well before Cohan staged *George Washington, Jr.* he had written its hit song in a moment of inspiration. While riding in a funeral cortege one day, Cohan sat next to a Civil War veteran who held a tattered flag in his lap. The man had helped defeat the Confederacy at Gettysburg in the slaughter known as Pickett's Charge. "And it was all for this," he said, stroking the cloth. "She's a grand old rag." Cohan's gifted ear picked up the line instantly (as well as the pun it provided for the word *ragtime*), and when *George Washington, Jr.* opened on Broadway, the song that electrified the audience was "You're a Grand Old Rag," which would go on to become a patriotic classic, even if Cohan was regrettably later forced to change *rag* to *flag* when a critic claimed that the use of the vernacular was, in itself, an offense to the red-white-and-blue.

George Washington, Jr. was idle patriotism, offered at a moment when the nation was at peace. But a decade later, Cohan's nationalist instincts were called upon more dramatically when, after years of reluctance to engage with Europe's troubles, President Woodrow Wilson brought America into World War I. Cohan had none of the ambivalence that would burden Claude Bukowski and the cast of *Hair* fifty years later. Indeed, the Broadway star's first instinct was to enlist, but he was too old to serve. Instead, after hearing Wilson's announcement, he locked himself in his study and began feverishly working on a new hymn to the cause, which the president had described as making "the world safe for democracy."

By Sunday morning, two days after Wilson's declaration of war, Cohan was finished. He called his family together in the parlor of their Manhattan home. For effect, he put a tin pan on his head and threw a broom over his shoulder. Then, marching around the room, he sang them the lines to his newest song. "Over there, over there," Cohan burst forth to a musical line reminiscent of a bugle call. "Send the word, send the word over there, / That the Yanks are coming, the Yanks are coming, / The drums drum drumming everywhere . . ." Irving Berlin wrote a ballad then, too, and christened it "God Bless America." But Berlin's song would have to wait for the next war and the voice of Kate Smith before it would become popular. Cohan's "Over There" was the song of this day, the one destined to become the rallying cry for the American soldiers headed across the Atlantic to defeat the kaiser.

"Whenever we get too high-hat and too sophisticated for flag-waving, some thug nation decides we're a pushover all ready to be blackjacked. And it isn't long before we're looking up, mighty anxiously, to be sure the flag's still waving over us."

— JAMES CAGNEY, *as George M. Cohan, in the movie* Yankee Doodle Dandy

IV

Long before there was a "tribe" of "hippies" preparing for the Fairview High School production of *Hair,* there were real tribes of Indians in Boulder. What is now known as Colorado was home to the Arapaho, Ute, Comanche and Cheyenne Indians in the early nineteenth century. Then, in 1861, while the rest of the country was on the verge of the Civil War, the Treaty of Fort Wise was signed with the Arapahos and Cheyennes "extinguishing their land title," except for a small reserve in what is now the southeastern part of the state. That same year, the Territory of Colorado was recognized by the United States Congress and, in 1876, Colorado became a state. Boulder, a tiny settlement named for the large rocks lining the canyon, grew rapidly after that, principally as a supply base for miners searching for gold and silver, but also, later, as a tourist center, and then as the main campus of the University of Colorado.

For his 1917 "Over There," Cohan said he had merely dramatized a bugle call, but the song meant much more to a nation nervously heading across the ocean to fight the Germans.

Several events drove the growth of Boulder in the twentieth century: the opening, in 1952, of a highway connecting the city to Denver, thereby allowing Boulder to serve as a bedroom community for the Colorado capital thirty-five miles away; the establishment that same year of the Rocky Flats Atomic Plant just south of here; the opening in 1966 of the National Center for Atmospheric Research and the rise in college enrollment that made the University of Colorado campus the center of life in this city. There are now about 100,000 people in Boulder, but a full quarter of them are university students. Both the highway and the growth of the university helped to confirm the image of the city as a well-defended hamlet, nestled in the comfortable protection of the Rocky Mountains, a beautiful place to be young, pursue enlightenment, to raise children, and avoid the perils of the world.

You can still find the remnants of Boulder as it was in the 1960s and early 1970s, when it was the hippie capital of the Rocky Mountain region. The Arts Bar and Grill, which thrived as a music venue, is here, but it now is a topless bar called The Bustop. And there are still no display windows at the Colorado Bookstore, which were filled in after antiwar riots and looting broke out in 1971, even if these days the only riots

"**I ask myself, 'Where did all those free-spirited people go?'"**

Fairview senior Kate Stratton, on the changes in Boulder since the 1960s

in Boulder are drunken beer revelries held by college students who, if they should be inspired to loot at all, would not be going after books. After all, *The Princeton Review* ranked the University of Colorado fifth on its 2001 list of the "top twenty party schools" in America, just above Alabama and just below Florida State.

The city is still the home of Celestial Seasonings teas, and of White Wave, which produces tofu and soy milk products ("business without guilt" is the company's motto), both of which began doing business in Boulder in the seventies. And Boulder is not only the home of the University of Colorado but also of Naropa University. Naropa describes itself as a school grounded in Buddhist traditions, practicing "contemplative education," which combines the meditative traditions of the East with the scholarly traditions of the West. "Where East meets West," said the school's founder, "sparks will fly . . ."

Four blocks of Boulder's Pearl Street shopping district were turned into a pedestrian mall in the late 1970s. Today chain stores, like Banana Republic, have joined what's left of the city's once-vibrant street life. Above, a lone guitarist plays for pocket change.

There is a Vietnam veterans memorial in Boulder, near Boulder Creek. It displays the names of twenty-four Boulder County residents who died in Vietnam and one who remains missing in action. For those in need of it, there are plenty of opportunities for drug rehabilitation, even as the Boulder County sheriff's department recently found it necessary to raid the studio of a local glassblower whose ornamental pipes, sold at Boulder tobacco accessory stores, were of the kind the officers find "when making drug arrests" (the manufacturing of such pipes is a second-degree misdemeanor). But with the average house price nearly $500,000, Boulder has certainly moved on from the sixties.

Fairview High's students certainly see it that way. Putting on the musical *Hair* was, for many of them, like finding old pictures in the attic showing their parents in the days of their own dreamy youth: dad in shoulder-length hair carrying a joint in one hand and a Grateful Dead album in the other, mom pregnant in a peasant dress and flashing the two-fingered "peace symbol." The students' response to what they learned was mixed. As they entered more deeply into the ideas advanced by the musical, some found themselves casting a critical eye at what became of their parents' generation's many dreams. "Since the 1960s I think people have been regressing back into their smaller, more conservative . . . habits," says cast member Mia Van de Water. "It's sort of

In Massachusetts: Struggling to hold on to the bonds of family in a nation of "independents"

The Keefe family gathers for their third reunion, left, at Jiminy Peak, Massachusetts, in 2001, a tradition started ten years earlier by Leo Keefe's grand-nieces. Right, a Keefe family wedding, circa 1935.

Seventy-five-year-old Leo Keefe looked out over the crowd at the Jiminy Peak ski resort atop the Berkshire Mountains and beamed. It was June and there was no snow, but there was family, lots of it: his two sisters were there; so were his eight children and their spouses and their children, a couple of dozen's worth; and dozens more Keefe nieces and nephews and their spouses and children. The various "Keefes" had come from far away to be here, some 150 strong, packed into seventy-five rooms at this western Massachusetts resort where they spent three days talking, hiking, playing games, eating, reminiscing. "Who could ask for anything more than to be surrounded by your family?" said a proud Leo. "What the heck. That's what life is all about."

In America, the family reunion is big business. At Jiminy Peak alone, there are more than forty such gatherings every year, some modest in size, others, like the Keefes', assembling relatives in the hundreds. But the mere fact that Americans have "family reunions" may be a sign of the strains experienced by the family institution here. "People in other countries cannot even grasp the concept of a family reunion," says Tom Ninkovich, author of books on how to plan family reunions. Europeans live among their families, as they have for generations; Americans scatter themselves across the Earth.

Mobility is, indeed, one factor that has put stress on the American family unit, forcing the kind of artificial gathering that a family reunion represents. Given that nearly all American families began with an act of immigration by someone from somewhere, one could argue that the population is self-selected toward those who want to leave home. But it may also, ironically, explain that yearning to "return" home, whether it be in the manner of a family reunion or the nostlagia for reclaiming ethnic roots. "What genius so defined the essence of what we're after by calling it 'home plate'? Why isn't it 'fourth base'?" asked Bart Giamatti, the one-time Yale president who also served as commissioner of Major League Baseball. Whoever it was understood that Americans often seek to leave home only to spend their lives trying to find their way back to it.

Perhaps because they lack the cohesive bonds of a homogeneous society, with its strong traditions and practices, Americans, more so than other people, have looked to the organizing principles of their institutions to find clues on how to structure family life. "A family is a little Church and a little Commonwealth," wrote an early colonist. Once the republic was established, the family was a "little nation," too, a place where the American values of self-sufficiency and independence, even democracy, reigned supreme. The best families, said James Madison, represented a "class of citizens who provide at once their own food and their own raiment"; and Madison insisted that those that did would be "the most truly independent and happy." In describing the family as the basis of "public liberty," Madison meant to suggest that the more the family served as its own governing unit, the less necessary government itself, with its tyrannical tendencies, would be. In this way, says historian Stephanie Coontz, early American families were "the silent partner in America's cult of self-reliance." Indeed, to encourage the institution, some local governments imposed fines on men who lived alone.

But it did not take long before the founders' passion for democracy and individual liberties also clashed with the ideal of family cohesiveness. One of the first things state legislatures in the new republic did was outlaw "primogeniture," the practice by which families passed property, including huge estates, from generation to generation by leaving it all to the eldest son. Abolishing the practice, as Noah Webster said, was a way to throw "a vast weight of property into the democratic scale." But by stripping fathers of one of their most reliable sources of paternal authority — the right of passing property to their children — it also sent an unintended message, that in America the rights and needs of the "individual" trumped those of the "family."

By 1831, when Alexis de Tocqueville was traveling about America, he was startled by the family structure that he saw. "In America," he wrote, ". . . the family does not exist . . . .[except] for the first few years following the birth of children." After that, he implied, it became a group of individuals, each pursuing his own fulfillment, supported by the companionship offered by the family unit. The family model that Tocqueville was most familiar with was the one that existed in Europe. There, men were superior to women, parents were superior to children, older children held sway over younger children, and government had power over them all. Here, such hierarchy was abandoned, leading, as Tocqueville noted, to a casual relationship between father and son and an emphasis upon developing the child's self-reliance, preparing him to leave the family, to gradually loosen "the ties of filial obedience" until he becomes "master of his thoughts" and then "master of his conduct."

That urge to encourage the formation of the individual and, in turn, to protect his rights has been manifested in small and large ways throughout American history, from the imposition of mandatory school laws (removing responsibility for the schooling of children from the home to the state) at the beginning of the twentieth century and the creation of "family courts" at roughly the same time, to the landmark and controversial Supreme Court decision in 1967 that children enjoyed the same constitutional rights as adults. To this day, says Tom W. Smith, of the University of Chicago's National Opinion Research Center, "Americans emphasize individualism much more than European [and other] societies." In fact, says Smith, of five traits Americans were asked to evaluate as important to a child's development, 50 percent said "to think for one's self" was most important and only 18 percent chose "obedience." These values are imparted even in infancy. Recent studies of infant-mother attachment show that in America progress toward autonomy is prized much more than in other societies.

A Scottish-American family gathers for a reunion in 1870, above.

The counterweight to all this is the way that America's stress on the individual produced the need for the kind of protective environment that the family represented. The free-for-all created by unregulated capitalism at the beginning of the nineteenth century fostered a frontier image of the family, a powerful "cult of domesticity," where the family became a safe harbor from the storms of the new American economy. "Idealization of family . . . seems to have grown in direct proportion to the spread of individualism and market principles in the rest of society," declares Stephanie Coontz. Women became the de facto rulers of this sanctuary. "The cult of the Self-Made Man required the cult of the True Woman."

The nuclear family with its strict gender-defined duties was an American ideal long after that, intensely focused on nurturing independent, productive, and democratic citizens. "My dad worked really hard outside the house and mother worked really hard in the house," recalls Gerry Keefe, Leo's oldest son, who was born in 1953. "She ran a tight ship." There was an implicit social transaction there. The stay-at-home mother provided the essential emotional and psychological support that was needed for men to function in the free-market world.

Ironically, the intense nurturing of individuality in the 1950s produced expectations of individual liberties that completely transformed American society — and the family — during the succeeding decades. The youth rebellion, the Civil Rights battles, and the feminism movement, far from being a rejection of American values, were the concentrated and confident calls for freedom and liberty learned in the idealistic world of fifties families. The results were a staggering change in family structure. As late as 1972 a majority of traditional families had a father working outside the home and a mother working at home; by 1998, only 27 percent of such families worked that way. While divorce rates were exploding, so were out-of-wedlock births. In 1960, only 5.3 percent of births were to unmarried women; by 1996, it was 32 percent.

These changes have challenged the family. But the threat also calls to mind one of the American family's most enduring characteristics: its adaptability. "The family itself is a very tough institution and has survived a long time," the anthropologist Margaret Mead wrote in 1945. Mead observed that people worry about an institution "as if human beings were made for institutions and not institutions for them" and suggested that people would figure it out. Indeed, by 2000, divorce rates were leveling, work rules were changing to allow parents more time with their children, support systems for single mothers were emerging and one state — Vermont — even passed a law recognizing homosexual marriages. It is not a world that Leo Keefe necessarily likes. "I don't like this divorce bit one iota," he says. "You buckle down and you live through it." But when his son Gerry told him that he was getting a divorce, Leo resigned himself to it by recognizing that it was a statement of individual choice. "That was his decision and I have to respect that."

funny," adds Kate Stratton. "Boulder is a place where people are still politically active and where they like to protest and fight for causes, but then we go home to our large mansion houses, with our Jacuzzis and our tennis courts and our SUVs."

Indeed, *Hair* provoked many of Fairview's thespians to see their own world as out of step with the values their parents still promote but which, as their children see it, they no longer seem to practice. The musical advocates racial diversity, yet Boulder is still a decidedly white community with, the students believe, decidedly provincial ideas about race. In the entire city, there are little more than one thousand African-Americans. "I think all of Boulder needs to be dropped off in a third world country," says cast member David Little, "loaded into a plane and dropped off in Africa somewhere."

Kate Stratton, right, learned a lot about the sixties from her mother, Susan, who insists that "young people back then really did believe they were going to change the world." Susan Stratton bemoans the loss of idealism, but has no respect for that decade's attitudes toward drugs. "If one of my kids came home stoned," she jokes, "I'd know it . . . and I would kill her."

Hair preaches "free love" and condemns jealousy and bitterness in personal relations, yet Boulder, like many upper-middle-class American communities, is rife with divorce. *Hair* rejects materialism, but, if anything, Boulder has become a pampered environment, where many who once preached the evil of the profit motive seem now to delight in the advantages afforded by wealth. *Hair* asks people to seek peace and harmony, and yet here is America, thirty years after Vietnam, again caught up in a violent struggle with people of the third world, and this time Boulder is largely in sympathy with the rest of the country's newfound, flag-waving patriotism. "There are so many things that send chills down your spine about how related the play and this new war are," says Robin Wallace, a senior. "People say, 'Oh, they were just hippies.' But I think now we understand what they were about. They were saying that you can't conquer hate with hate, but you can overcome hate with love. And that's such a strong message right now."

The combination of the play and the new war on terrorism prompted the students to look differently not only at their parents' generation, but at their country, too, and some of them did so from that dangerous place that youth knows well, where idealism exists unencumbered by responsibility. For Brian MacDonald, it was a chance to see America for its strengths, and weaknesses. "We should be proud of our country because it is built on incredible beliefs like tolerance and respect for all races. And yet some people, I think, have reacted to September 11 by demonstrating the opposite. They go around like, 'Here's our flag and it's going to bash your flag.' Why do I never see a car with a peace flag on it?" For Ali Hammet, the word *American* has become nothing more than a "title," a geographical description. She sees herself instead as a "citizen of the world" and insists that "peace and love are things that should be universal rather than stuck in a particular place." For Dan Kohler, *Hair* showed the importance of the value America puts on free expression, on being able to look about you and comment on the world you live in. His favorite song in *Hair* is "What a Piece of Work Is Man," which borrows its text from Shakespeare's *Hamlet* to make a comment on the killing in Vietnam. Kohler now sees the song as applicable to America's present terrorist dilemma.

The cast of Hair *sings "Let the Sunshine In" at a dress rehearsal. For Stephanie Ablowitz, center, the thrill of the theater is "the rush of being on stage, having people watching you and being someone you're not."*

Even as they questioned their parents' devotion to the once-prized ideals of the sixties and looked upon their country with a critical eye, many of the students also thirsted for the kind of meaningful adolescence that the *Hair* generation once enjoyed and for the chance to participate, if only through rebellion, in the making of their country and its ideals. Many of them felt frustrated by the comfortable life they enjoy in Boulder, in part because it is *so* comfortable. How amazing, they thought, to stand for (or for that matter, against) something, to care so deeply about a cause that you would risk your life for it.

After a while, there was even some newfound respect for their elders. By doing *Hair*, the cast realized that there was a time when mom and dad didn't represent "authority," but the *challenge* to authority. Looking at their parents now, noticing how that once-bright idealism has been tempered by experience, they could recognize that, no matter the strength of one's convictions, life does not always follow a straight path and that in America, especially, there is always a productive tension between the individual and the group. "One of my favorite songs from *Hair*," says Sheeba Ibidunni, "says 'Where do I go, follow the river / where do I go, follow the gulls' because that really is Claude's dilemma." Claude doesn't know what he should do, and so he looks for guidance from nature, and when he finally does go to war, says Ibidunni, he doesn't quite know why he has, he just knows that he must.

Finally, for at least some of these teens, the lesson of *Hair* was radically different from the lesson that *Hair* projected back in its day. Thirty years of history have passed and they have not been kind to the ideals of the sixties. Support for peace has, in general, proven to be anything but its guarantor. "Free love" has been revealed as a utopian fantasy. Drugs, it turns out, lead to degeneracy much more often than they do to enlightenment. Racial harmony, we've discovered, cannot be legislated and, as the politically correct movement has demonstrated, a "tribe" can be simply another form of tyranny. Indeed, it was another sort of tribe — exclusive, intolerant, and barbaric — that attacked Americans on September 11.

V

If anyone in American musical theater has a longer and more colorful stage life than that of George M. Cohan, it would be the handsome, unassuming Oscar Hammerstein II. America's two greatest musical stage works, *Show Boat* and *Oklahoma!,* were written by two different composers, Jerome Kern and Richard Rodgers, respectively, yet they shared a single lyricist, Hammerstein. Just about every great American musical of the last sixty years derives its spirit, if not its form, from one or both of these seminal works, sealing Hammerstein's legacy as the most significant American musical theater man of the twentieth century.

"Let me go 'way
from the Mississippi
Let me go 'way
from de white man boss;
Show me dat stream
called de river Jordan,
Dat's de ol' stream
that I long to cross."
— *"Ol' Man River,"* Show Boat

Like Cohan, Hammerstein was more or less born to the theater, being the grandson of Oscar Hammerstein I, a theatrical innovator who for a while around the turn to the twentieth century built and then ran a sometimes-bawdy vaudeville stage called the Victoria Theatre and Varieties on Times Square while at the same time challenging the august Metropolitan Opera House with energetic productions of Europe's finest masterpieces at another theater. The first Oscar Hammerstein eventually quit the opera when he ran up an intolerable debt, all of it under the eyes of William Hammerstein, his son, who, besides being the younger Oscar's father, is credited with having invented that staple of the simple stage comedy, the pie-in-the-face, when he served as manager of the vaudeville performances at the Victoria.

William Hammerstein had experienced enough of the instability of theater life to encourage his son to find a more dependable profession. Oscar Hammerstein II first planned a career in the law and enrolled at Columbia University. But genes won out. Yet another Hammerstein, Oscar's uncle, Arthur, who was managing a stage on Broadway at the time, took him on, assuring that the Hammersteins would dominate the theater for yet another generation. As the late essayist Clifton Fadiman once wrote, recalling the eighteenth- and nineteenth-century influence of John, John Quincy, Charles, and Henry Adams, "the Hammerstein

sense of a time long past than if the students had donned powdered wigs, waistcoats, and britches and marched about pontificating about original American ideals as the actors do in *1776*. That musical, which tells the story of the brutal rivalries and passionate arguments that attended the writing and signing of the Declaration of Independence, was *Hair*'s biggest competition on Broadway back in the late 1960s and, like *Hair*, it also featured a band of revolutionaries, some off-color jokes, a brash in-your-face moralist (John Adams), a comic character who acts as the show's wise man (Benjamin Franklin), and a doubting, introspective protagonist (Thomas Jefferson).

Both *1776* and *Hair* examined a classic American dilemma: In a society that values the individual, just what is the place of the group? Or, put the other way, in a society that values the democratic compromise, just what is the place of the individual? The central dramatic moment in *1776* occurs when John Adams (and, to a lesser degree, Thomas Jefferson) challenges the Congress to include a phrase in the Declaration condemning slavery. When the South balks at the idea, Adams, with great disappointment, finally accedes to them. In *Hair*, of course, it is the opposite, with the "tribe" at first in control, then giving over to the individual will when Claude makes the decision to go to war. It was *1776*, not *Hair*, which won the Tony award for Best Musical that year. But while the music was dramatically different (*1776* had a more traditional Broadway score), the two shows were, in a sense, about the same thing: they both challenged the audience to think about what it means to be an American and they both showed how that challenge, if taken seriously, can be a life and death matter.

As George Berger, Hair*'s lead, Dan Kohler was the most visible "hippie" in the cast and among the hardest-working. "I used to think that my mom was pressuring me [to excel]," says Kohler. "Then I realized that I was doing it myself." Above, he embraces his fourth-grade teacher after a performance.*

There was no doubt among any in the Fairview auditorium on opening night, or those of us who saw one of the five other performances, that the world had changed since the days when *Hair* first appeared on Broadway. The news of the week was confirmation of that. A group of Afghan rebels had taken the Taliban stronghold Mazar-e-Sharif while American airstrikes were thought to have killed a key deputy of Osama bin Laden, the mastermind of the World Trade Center and Pentagon attacks of September 11. Only two months before, the word *Taliban* and the name "bin Laden" would have been unrecognizable to most in attendance, and it is likely that no one, even looking at a map, could have found the Afghan city of Mazar-e-Sharif. But as every commentator had been saying for weeks now, to the point of cliché, the world had become a very different place after September 11. Even in this audience, filled with graying onetime hippies, few questioned the president's resolve.

With the national mood still one of revenge, it was hard for the cast of *Hair* to advance the timeless, if unrealistic, appeals for peace and love with any sincerity. But somehow, they succeeded. On this Colorado high school stage, the sixties, removed from the sixties, lost their sting, but held on to their earnestness. The idealism appeared attractive, like something American life has been missing out on for too long. Indeed, when the closing number came ringing out there was hardly a person in the audience who was not on his feet clapping, shouting, laughing, crying, and more than a few had joined the actors on stage. Tomorrow's news might return them to their resolve that America needed to root out the terrorist networks with as much force as necessary, but for now, at least, it felt right to remind oneself, even if only from the fantasy world of the stage, that peace is still the ultimate objective, the one that will preserve human civilization.

After two months, forty-five rehearsals, and six performances, Fairview's Hair *was just a memory. Cast and crew alike struck the set, above, but the experience had left its mark. "No matter how old we are," said performer Brian MacDonald, "we'll still be members of this 'tribe.'"*

For the young players, there were many lessons learned. When they began to engage this piece of theater history, they were just a collection of teenagers, some of whom had never done drama before and who may never do it again. When they stood on stage, they had come together around their understanding of one of the largest social movements in American history. In the process, they had discovered something about America, about the theater, and about themselves, and the fact that they did so at this moment, as many of them prepared to leave home and go off to start new lives, made it that much more poignant to watch. Like the river in Hammerstein's *Show Boat*, they too were about to "roll along" to their own "new beginning," and several sets of parents, perhaps aware of the irony, had arranged for messages to be printed in the program, wishing them bon voyage. "Nathan, our 'Flower Child,'" read one, "you are an important part of our tribe! We wish you love and peace!" "Kate," read another, "you've come a long way. Fly well, baby bird, and always let the sun shine in!"

BOC GA
MARKETPLACE
35

Washington, D.C.

Though it has always been burdened by a reputation for exclusivity, the 112-year-old Daughters of the American Revolution (DAR) boasts a membership of 170,000 women. There is that "little" genealogical requirement, of course: all members must be able to trace their bloodlines to an ancestor who worked on the side of the Revolution. For an organization that dedicates itself to "preserving the memory of those who secured our freedom," this has always seemed slightly odd. The notion of an aristocracy developed from bloodlines was abhorrent to those freedom-seekers, particularly Thomas Jefferson. But the directors of the DAR insist that their numbers and their variety — not to mention their dedication to educating people on the Declaration of Independence and the Constitution — should counteract such criticism. "We have American Indians, Mexican, Spanish, Italian, French. We have Jewish members, absolutely," says Linda Tinker Watkins, president general. Along with three dozen other members, Watkins carried a gigantic flag at the 2001 Washington July Fourth parade (she's in front dressed in blue, third from left). A candidate's ancestor need not have fought in the Revolution, Watkins insists, just been on the right side of it. "If your family gave a cow or something to feed the troops . . . then that would count." So would a relative who was a minister or a town clerk or, today, even a slave. Thirty years ago, the society dropped the requirement that all ancestral marriages had to be documented, presumably to account for unions between African-Americans that were not legally recognized. But the organization has long recognized the descendants of foreign troops (French and Spanish) who helped to defeat the British. About 8,500 people apply to join each year, assembling the thorough documentation that the DAR requires. All but around 500 make it. "We won't close anyone's application," says Watkins, "until they tell us that they are tired of working on it, and to just forget it."

Los Angeles, California

To so many people in the world, this is America. In one word, "abundance," dozens of brands and flavors of foods, from sodas to produce to breads and meats in a plethora of options that the businessman describes as consumer choice and the consumer describes as confusion. At the hundred or so "99 Cent Stores" scattered throughout California, Nevada, and Arizona, they make one part of shopping easy: everything is, well, 99 cents. "We have ten-packs of Kit Kat candy for 99 cents; two gallons of bottled water for 99 cents; a six-pack of Shasta Cola for 99 cents; brooms, mops, trash cans and even underwear, all for 99 cents," explains Thang Dang, the manager of the Hollywood, California, store on Sunset Boulevard, right. Arriving in America as a war-weary thirteen-year-old a few days before South Vietnam surrendered to the Communists in 1975, Dang remembers being overwhelmed at first by the sheer quantity of consumer goods that occupied store shelves in America. "Back in Vietnam, the setup was completely different," says Dang. "We had open-air markets, everything was so disorganized. And the variety of products was not very wide. We had only basic items. Now, I have customers that come in and buy two or three carts full of merchandise." To Amartya Sen, a Nobel Prize–winning economist, that is no accident of geography but a byproduct of political freedom. In the history of the world, argues Sen, there has never been a famine in a system with a democratic press and free elections. Indeed, in Sen's observation, the most democratic countries take care of first things first: they make sure that there is enough food, or the government will suffer retribution.

Thanks...!
99¢ ONLY
Rolo
slice
Spree
mr. Goodbar
Krunch
3 for 99¢

Selma, Alabama

In America, the right to vote is a cardinal right. The founders' devotion to the cause of American independence flowed from their absolute belief in self-government. "The powers vested in Congress are little more than nominal; nay real power cannot be vested in them, nor in any body, but the people," wrote Noah Webster in 1787 in *A Citizen of America*. Still, it was not until 1965 that the landmark Voting Rights Act finally extended the franchise to millions of Southern blacks. Sam Randolph (center, in dark suit), born that year, grew up listening to his parents' memories of Selma's "Bloody Sunday," when hundreds of civil rights sympathizers were beaten and teargassed by state troopers and sheriff's deputies. "People were harassed because they wanted to vote," says Randolph, a driver for Federal Express. Today, two thirds of the 16,000 registered voters in Selma are black. Yet long after gaining the vote, many of Selma's blacks still felt locked out by the political establishment. Joe Smitherman, a former segregationist who took office shortly before "Bloody Sunday," ruled City Hall for nearly thirty-six years, winning whites' votes and just enough blacks. James Perkins, a computer company executive, tried unsuccessfully to unseat Smitherman in 1992 and 1996 (allegations of voter fraud against the Smitherman camp could never be substantiated). But Perkins's 2000 campaign was different. Black Selma voters were organized like never before; young men and women stood on downtown street corners with placards proclaiming "Joe Gotta Go!" Volunteers helped voters travel to the polls on election day. "The night Perkins won, they had about ten thousand people in downtown Selma celebrating," says Randolph. "They were blowing horns and everything. Perkins had to come out and tell people to go home, thank you." On the morning Perkins, forty-seven, was inaugurated, left, the cheering started all over again. "A lot of people say, 'I just don't feel like voting today,'" says Randolph. "But that one vote counts."

6 Homeland

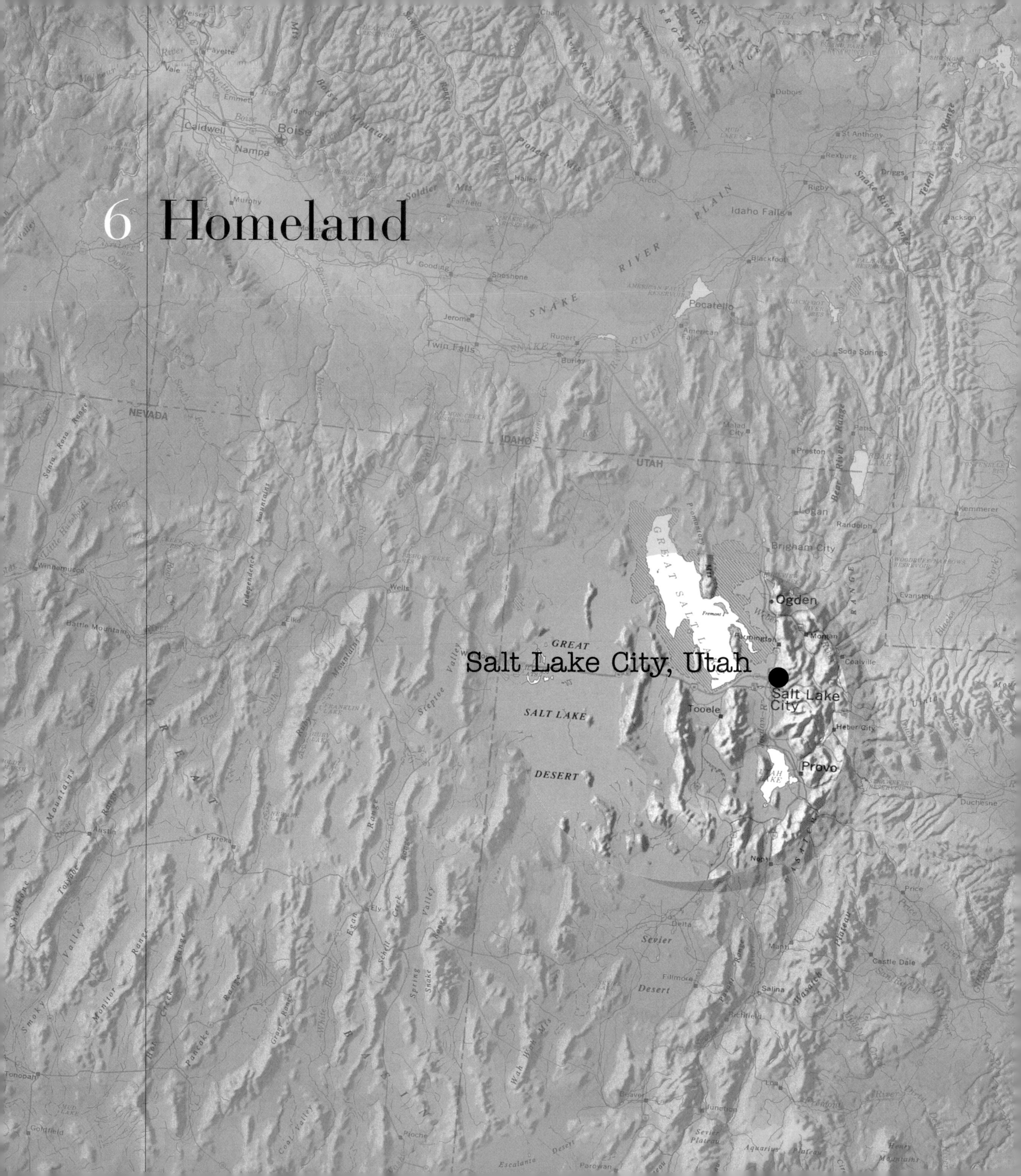
Salt Lake City, Utah
Salt Lake City
Ogden
Provo
Tooele
Brigham City
Logan
Pocatello
Idaho Falls
Boise
Nampa
Caldwell
Twin Falls
Winnemucca
Battle Mountain
Elko
Wells
Austin
Eureka
Ely
Tonopah
NEVADA
IDAHO
UTAH
SNAKE RIVER PLAIN
GREAT SALT LAKE
GREAT SALT LAKE DESERT

Law enforcement officials called it "Operation Safe Travel" and, since the raid by several federal agencies on employees of the Salt Lake City Airport came exactly three months after the terrorist attacks of September 11, that seemed like an appropriate title. But for many of the 208 workers who lost their jobs and the sixty-three others who faced deportation proceedings as a result of the raid, the thought that acts of terrorism on American soil had made them suspect and exposed them as illegal aliens (or, their preferred term, "undocumented") felt like an odd turn of events. While a handful of them were working as cargo handlers, none of the arrested had a history of terrorist activity or anti-American associations. Most were janitors or food service employees. They were, almost to a man or woman, good, steady workers, or so said some of their employers who complained that hiring Americans to do the kind of work done by what often turned out to be illegal Mexicans and other Latinos was either impossible or impractical. Indeed, it was well reported after the event that the undocumented worker was essential to the Utah economy. Even the head of Utah's Office of Homeland Security, Robert Flowers, who coordinated the raid, admitted that there was a regrettable human cost to it. Indeed, on the face of it the rounding up of airport employees now looked a little extreme. For all the urgency attending the flushing out of terrorists from their hiding places inside America, Flowers (whose own ancestry is English) had, for all intents and purposes, corralled a couple of hundred people with a simple, unthreatening, all-American aim in life: to work hard, make money, and raise their children here.

Of course, the issue was more complicated than that. Maybe there were no terrorists sugaring the crullers at the airport bake shop, no whispers of *jihad* between the stalls as the airport janitors moved about with their mops and pails. But the fact of the matter is, there are millions of people in America who arrived here illegally and whose falsification of identity papers by itself constitutes a felony. Many of these people maintain no particular loyalty to America and do not, certainly in their illegal status, intend to develop one, and all of those arrested from the Salt Lake City Airport had daily access to secure areas. Desperate to keep their jobs, living in constant fear of being exposed, they could, especially in an age of terrorism, be vulnerable to the casual bribe. Even many of those who sympathized with the arrested and were outraged at the severity of the charges admitted that there was a problem in that. But the irony here was that the response to one desperate situation — terrorism — had cast a harsh light upon another: America, an immigrant nation, has an abiding problem with immigration.

It begins at the border, that line in the sand or the mud, the one formed in some parts by the natural drift of the Rio Grande, in other parts by the shifts of politics and history, and which in the Southwest has always, no matter the quality of the water, been murky. More than 800,000 people cross the border legally every day, engaging in the growing commerce between America and Mexico. Another five thousand break the law daily, slipping under barbed wire, gripping the underside of a car, wading through miles of dirty water filled with rattlesnakes and scorpions, before they are caught and turned back, or "VR'd," border parlance for "Voluntary Removal," which is allowed so long as the person seized was not caught in a crime. But thousands more — no one knows the real number — are never caught. They join the tide moving across America, forming an "invisible" nation, neither Mexican nor American, undocumented, unappreciated, unrecognized.

Technology, improved transportation, and the robust Western economy have precipitated a global migration crisis that in America consists largely of great numbers of Latin American, and especially Mexican, immigrants. Above, a maid dresses a bed at a Salt Lake City area hotel. One local employer estimates that 70 percent of the service jobs in Salt Lake are held by undocumented workers. But Utah is emblematic of a national trend.

The illegal alien has long been a part of American life. Now he is a deeply important part of the American economy, a growing population dedicated to the jobs it is said Americans will no longer do — the nation's gardeners, maids, nannies, dishwashers, taxi drivers, and day laborers. Chances are, he arrived at work with a Social Security card he bought in a park for a few dollars, a stolen card, or a reproduction of a card made on a color photocopier (or, occasionally, on a very sophisticated printing press), but in any case a card with a number, *some* number, and for most employers, who are not required to verify identification — only make a "reasonable" effort to do so — that is enough. From there, he proceeds to a life perpetually in the shadows. For the undocumented worker, the "border" is never really crossed. He lives a game of pretend, working, even paying taxes, sending his children to American schools and money back home to Chihuahua or Tijuana or Guadalajara, yet always in fear of the knock on the door or the unanticipated visit from his boss, joined by an INS inspector who has every right to start proceedings to send him packing.

Any illegal immigrant caught committing the felony of identity falsification will likely never be allowed to enter the country legally again, and anyone caught returning illegally to the United States after deportation can face a prison sentence of up to five years. But except for extraordinary circumstances, these have become hollow charges. The INS admits that it lacks the staff to enforce immigration laws and has adapted by, essentially, going after criminals and anyone whose continued presence is likely to embarrass the agency, while leaving the others to go about their lives, for the moment at least, unimpeded. The political will to take any further action is simply not there. Knowing how important these workers have become to American businesses, and knowing that the sheer numbers of illegal aliens in the country now (officials estimate it at 8 million) make it impossible to do anything but selective enforcement, politicians from both sides of the aisle, whether in Congress or the Utah state house, have decided to look the other way, rather than watch American immigration agents adopt a pose they feel will smack of a "police state."

Many Americans face a classic dilemma with immigration: it's how they, or their ancestors, got here, and it feels wrong to keep those behind them out. Above, a farm outside Salt Lake City. "When the pioneers first came here to Utah, we all helped each other," says rancher David Ure. "Why all of a sudden has it changed? Why don't we have the same concern for these 'illegal people'?"

The result is that the relationship between the alien and the society that labels him "illegal" has become a peculiarly vague one, neither this nor that, neither here nor there, destructive of all manner of American principles, and injected with the ambivalence of a nation caught between two compelling (and often competing) ideals: on the one hand, the tradition of respecting and encouraging immigration, and on the other, the tradition of respecting the law and, through it, protecting society from the kind of disruptions that lead to chronic social instability.

The American economy depends upon the undocumented worker; indeed, it preys upon him. It takes Social Security taxes from his income, billions paid into the system that, because of the worker's undocumented status, will never have to be paid out. It withholds federal and state taxes from his paycheck, too, and perhaps too much tax at that, since he may not have the will to file a return (fearful that an income tax return would get the INS's attention) and the government may not have to pay him a refund. Since he is undocumented, the illegal alien will probably be prevented from following the path of upward mobility that has characterized the story of new immigrants throughout American history. In other words, he alone faces here in America something decidedly un-Ameri-

> **"North of the U.S.–Mexico border, brown appears as the color of the future. The adjective accelerates, becomes a verb, 'America is browning.' South of the border, brown sinks back into time."**
> RICHARD RODRIGUEZ
> Brown: The Last Discovery of America

can: an immovable hierarchy, barring him entry to the places of power, making him part of a permanent underclass.

American public schools educate his children. Indeed, in a controversial 1982 ruling the Supreme Court has determined that they must (many Court observers believe the same case would be decided in reverse if it were put before the more conservative Court presiding today). Yet those very children, studying in what is for most their second language, sometimes encourage the resentment of legal Americans by bringing down the level of education taught in the public schools and by causing overages on budgets crafted to accommodate population figures that do not account for the tremendous influx of children recorded only in estimated terms on census roles and other official documents. Most illegal aliens do not speak English in the home and, in a largely misguided effort driven by the trend toward multiculturalism, the alien has recently been encouraged to hold on to his previous cultural and linguistic identity, which in a society where business is conducted in English, translates into holding on to his — usually lowly — economic and social identity. And yet, on the other hand, why wouldn't the alien cling to his Hispanic roots? He has no assurances that he can stay here, no guarantee that he is part of a new American culture. He is a straddler caught between two worlds, the one he sought to flee and the one he may or may not seek to join, but which very often sees him as a burden, a parasite, a threat.

During the cold war, when the stories of people escaping communism came forth from behind the Iron Curtain in much the same way — they, too, clung to the underside of cars ramming through barbed wire fences, lied or cheated or paid someone off — Americans cheered them as heroes and embraced them as new citizens of the free world. But this is different. While immigration remains a cherished national value, the illegal alien as an idea is abhorrent to the ordinary American even as he may hire him to weed the garden, dine in a restaurant where he will wash the dishes, or hail a cab driven by him. The removal of him from the economy would risk running the country into recession.

So many of the trends and traditions we have documented in this book are part of the immigration debate. To those who worry that America has lost its moral compass ("God's Country," Chapter 1), efforts at forging an amnesty for the undocumented are a travesty. To them, as well as others, amnesty (or "regularization," as proponents call it, semantics being an agent of argument here) would reward people who have broken the law and encourage others to do the same, even as it also in effect would punish those who are waiting in long queues lined with paperwork, dutifully following the legal guidelines for entrance to this country. To at least some of those who value freedom as the sacred principle of American life and see government restrictions and regulations as anathema to the founding principles ("The Colossus," Chapter 2), the image of a powerful bureaucracy in the form of the INS is just as hard to tolerate, a violation of the free movements of people, the natural right to choose where one wishes to live, and a discouragement to what has traditionally been the lifeblood of the American story: the regular infusion of people from around the world who break with old traditions, sever ties with old tyrannies, abandon old corruptions, to come here and make a new life. "Send these . . . to me," beckons Lady Liberty.

To the multinational businessman ("Headquarters," Chapter 3), the influx of undocumented workers is merely another example of the flow of the free market that he finds so sacred, of the increasingly blended national economies collapsing borders around the world. Even more important, the illegal alien is a source of cheap labor that allows the modern businessman to compete in that global environment, for it is not just that Americans will not do the jobs that illegal aliens are willing to do, but that they will not do those jobs at the wages being paid for them. And to anyone feeling the pain of racism, or simply aware of the acute dilemma that race has posed for America ("Streets," Chapter 4), there may be something analogous in the story of the illegal alien. Like many black Americans, he lives in two worlds, carries with him an abiding sense of a split identity, not willing to part from his ethnic associations, particularly in a society that he is not sure will welcome him as one of them. Encouraged to see himself as part of an abused minority group, he looks upon assimilation not as the exchange of his past identity for a new, American one, as many previous immigrants did, but as the dominant, white Anglo culture's assault on his cultural and linguistic heritage. And yet more so than any ethnic group in American history, his presence is rapidly changing the ethnic makeup of the American population, in the short term making Latino-Americans the nation's largest minority (eclipsing the African-American) and in the long term, leading America away from its roots as a country formed by people of European origin. And finally, to many who detect and endorse an essential "Americanness" in the nation's popular culture ("The Stage," Chapter 5), there is something unyielding about the Hispanic, something threatening about having to accept a bilingual society,

"We wouldn't have the kinds of resorts we have in Utah today without the Mexicans and other Hispanics who have moved into the area and performed much of the labor," says Utah congressman Christopher Cannon. Above, the kitchen of a resort hotel in Deer Valley, east of Salt Lake. "You can't get a taco or a hamburger without getting it from someone who is recently from a Latin American country."

something peculiar about a culture from south of the border that remains as vital and powerful north of the border.

The Mexican has discovered Utah. In 1990, this famously white, famously Mormon, famously friendly state had just 57,000 Mexicans, or at least that was what officials thought. The illegal alien problem, such as it was, was something for Los Angeles or Chicago, Houston or New York. But in the last decade or so that has all changed, not just here, but across the nation. Now there are at least 136,000 Mexicans in Utah, and even that dramatic increase is exceeded by the increase in other states: in the same ten years, Georgia went from a Mexican population of 49,000 to a population of 275,000, New Jersey from 28,000 to 102,000, and North Carolina from 32,000 to 246,000. You can see the newcomers at the nation's train and bus stations in the morning, day laborers looking to get hired to build a rock wall or frame an attic, to pick strawberries or paint an apartment. And you can read about the growing worries over their arrival in the minutes of town meetings or school board hearings, in crime reports and complaints about the abuse of welfare.

> **"We have a problem in American society. We have demanded these people, we have brought them in, we're paying these people, and they're contributing to our society. We may be able to root them out, but at a terrible cost to the principles that make America America."**
>
> REP. CHRISTOPHER CANNON, *Utah*

The last great immigration wave, the one that stretched from 1870 to 1920, changed American society dramatically. Driven by developments in industrial technology that demanded an influx of unskilled laborers to run the nation's factories, it, too, was led by people who were ready to do the jobs that old-line Americans didn't want to do. Comprised mostly of the poor of southern and eastern Europe — Jews and Catholics, both — it, too, changed the demography of the American population, unsettling old Puritan values. Capped by the First World War, it, too, became entangled in worries that lax immigration laws were allowing an opening for enemies to get inside America. America survived, but only after a protracted battle between assimilationists and nativists, which resulted in the adoption, in 1924, of the strictest anti-immigration laws in American history.

A kind assessment of that episode would conclude that America needed a breather from so much social turmoil, that there remained a public consensus that immigration was a good thing, but that too much of a good thing — whether it be chocolate cake or work-starved Italians — can be bad for everyone. A darker analysis would recognize that the presence of different peoples, driven here more by economic than political motivations, chafed with traditional American values in ways that fed prejudice and incited violence.

The immigration laws changed again in 1965, lifting national quotas and infusing the process with a new democratic spirit. We are living with the product of those reforms today. The modern immigration wave (both legal and illegal) dwarfs the overall numbers of the past (even if by

In California: Preserving the memory of the migrating "Okies"

Earl Shelton, right, is helping save the few buildings still standing at the former Arvin Farm Labor Supply Center in California's San Joaquin Valley, a migrant labor camp built during the Great Depression to handle the influx of migrant workers from the parched Midwest. The simple setting felt like "paradise" to Shelton when he arrived there with his family in 1941. At left, the Sheltons when they were still struggling in Oklahoma, 1933, and Earl's mother was pregnant with him.

The three shabby buildings surrounded by chain-link fence hardly look like a spiritual oasis, but for Doris Weddell it is her shrine. The sixty-eight-year-old retired librarian comes almost every day to this tumbledown lot. "When there is no one here, in the winter, and the sky is gray and there are no leaves on the trees, the ghosts walk, I tell you," she says. "I can see Woody Guthrie and Tom Collins and John Steinbeck and Dorothea Lange." She can also imagine the voices of the thousands of less famous men, women, and children who passed through this same spot, the Arvin Farm Labor Supply Center, and found there, in tents and tin shacks, some respite from the drought and depression of the 1930s. Known to the world as the Weedpatch Camp, thanks to Steinbeck's 1939 novel *The Grapes of Wrath* (Steinbeck used the Arvin camp as a model for his fictional setting), the Arvin migrant center contained the story of an enfeebling national crisis, the Dust Bowl, and its remarkable cultural outgrowth, the Okies, who came to fertile California by the tens of thousands in one of the largest peacetime migrations in our history. It is the lingering power of that episode that has spurred Doris Weddell and a group of crusading friends to form the Dust Bowl Historical Foundation to save the few remaining buildings at Weedpatch.

"It was heaven to me," recalls Earl Shelton, a retired oil-refinery machinist who arrived at the Weedpatch Camp in 1941 and has stayed in these parts. Shelton was only seven, and he and his family had just completed a three-month trek west from a parched and dead Scipio, Oklahoma. Before they decided to move West, Earl and his dad and three brothers — and their mom, until she died of cancer when Earl was four — had lived in a log house, seventeen miles from the nearest asphalt road, subsisting on revenues from farming twelve acres of cotton and selling skunk and possum hides. Then came the drought. "The clouds appeared and went away, and in a while they did not try any more," Steinbeck wrote. "The surface of the earth crusted, a thin hard crust . . . Every moving thing lifted the dust into the air . . . The dawn came, but no day." It would be the most devastating drought in U.S. history, scorching more than 75 percent of the country — twenty-seven states. But the worst-hit area was a swath of some 150,000 square miles of land across Oklahoma and the Texas panhandle and sections of Kansas, Colorado, and New Mexico. That was where the "black blizzards" ravaged the land, covering cars and cattle and houses with dust. "They thought the world had ended and thought it was their doom," Woody Guthrie sang, describing successive gusts "so black you can't see your hand before your eyes, or a light in your room or a dollar in your pocket or a meal on your table."

Men, women, and children fled toward California. Between 1930 and 1940 more than a million piled into cars and into buses and even went on foot, mostly along Highway 66, headed to a land that, since the Gold Rush, had meant prosperity. The population of the San Joaquin Valley, where cotton, fruit, and vegetables were plentiful, increased by 50 percent in the 1930s, most of it with people from the Southwest. "They said in California, that money grew on trees," went one popular ditty, "that everyone was going there, just like a swarm of bees." Indeed, Shelton, now sixty-eight, remembers to this day when the old Model A that his dad was driving turned off Route 466, at the top of the Tehachapi Mountains, and pointed toward the valley below. "It was like the promised land," he says. "Green as far as you could see."

Compared to what they had left, California was indeed a land of plenty. But it was not an evenly distributed plenty, and the swarm of migrants tried to find work and shelter, turning many parts of California into communities of tents, tar-paper shacks, and tin shanties, "boom towns of destitution." Poor when they left Oklahoma and Texas and Missouri and Arkansas — the four states hit hardest by the natural and economic disaster — they frequently found more desperation in California. Hunger was a constant. A study of children in the San Joaquin Valley cotton camps in 1938 found that 17 percent of them suffered from malnutrition. And there was a native population — as "native" as one could get in a state that was barely a hundred years old — which was decidedly unsympathetic to the "Okies." In 1936 the state legislature considered a bill to close California's borders to "all paupers and persons likely to become public charges." It failed to pass, but that didn't stop Los Angeles police chief James Davis from sending a squad of 125 officers to form a "bum blockade."

Thanks to the Farm Security Administration, migrant camps like this one in Shafter, forty miles northwest of Weedpatch, had showers, laundries, community halls, even newsletters produced by the "farm workers' community."

As harsh as this California welcome was, there was no turning back. The newcomers dug in, in part because they had no choice. "We're hard hit, we're hard hitters," wrote Guthrie, "but it's a dern cinch, we ain't quitters." In their "Little Oklahomas" and "Okievilles," they created a brand new American culture, rising out of the dust, filled with the language and song of survival and migration and hope, a reinvention of America itself. It was characterized by a sense of dignity in the face of poverty, of hard work for little pay, of tough resiliency under a steady rain of misery. One camp resident wrote a poem that began, "Forget the grouch, erase the frown. Don't let hard luck get you down . . . It does not take great wealth to laugh. Just have the grit to stand the gaff." In their Southwestern drawl, their raw poetry, their evangelical religion, and their music, they gave voice to a purity of spirit that captured the awe and respect of the entire nation — white-man's blues, expressing rootlessness and loneliness, but also honesty and simplicity, original American virtues. The Okie culture was a well-developed event before Steinbeck arrived, but the Salinas, California, writer helped draw attention to it. He wanted his story of the Joad family, which he wrote in just five months in 1938, "to rip a reader's nerves to rags," and he succeeded. *The Grapes of Wrath* was an immediate best-seller, and it stayed at the top of the list for most of 1939, the same year that Darryl Zanuck and Henry Fonda showed up at Weedpatch to begin making the movie. "In the movie this was the manager's office," explains Doris Weddell, giving one of the many tours she now conducts around the former Arvin camp. "It's where Tom Joad registers and where he finds out they have showers and laundry facilities." Weddell knows the line by heart. "Tom says, 'I can't wait to tell Ma. She ain't been treated decent in a long while.'"

Earl Shelton, who is a member of the Dust Bowl Historical Foundation and helps with the tours by telling stories about his time at the camp, remembers his feeling of awe when he arrived at the Arvin Center. "They may have put men on the moon and all that," he says, "but there's been nothing in my life like the day I got to use a flush toilet and took a hot shower instead of having to bathe in a number-three bucket." Like most of the three hundred–plus families that lived in the camp, during the day the Sheltons would work in the fields — picking grapes, potatoes, peas, cotton, tomatoes, apricots, peaches, and plums — and relax at night, usually in song. "In the evening we'd go out on the lawn and someone would be playing music," recalls Shelton. "Someone was always pluckin' something." The Farm Security Administration (FSA), which would open seventeen migrant camps like the one at Arvin, sponsored regular entertainment and Saturday night dances. Okies from miles around would come. It "cleared your head up," said Woody Guthrie, a Texas native who traveled the Okie highways and sang in the camps. "Caused you to fall back and let your draggy bones rest and your muscles go limber like a cat's." Radio stations in Bakersfield, the heart of Okie country just north of the Weedpatch Camp, were filled with the new workingman blues, soon to be called "country" music. A young Buck Owens, son of Texas "fruit tramps," learned his music in the San Joaquin Valley and created from its raw and rough life the "Bakersfield Sound," sometimes called "hard-knocks country."

The music that filled the Weedpatch Camp is part of what Doris Weddell and the Dust Bowl Historical Foundation want to preserve, but first they must save the buildings. Three have been put on the National Register of Historic Places, including the big, barnlike Community Hall. "It was used for everything," says Weddell. "Basketball, church on Sunday, dances on Saturday. Well-baby clinics. They did canning there. They had community parties and a stage for plays. Weddings. Graduations. You name it." Earl Shelton, for one, wishes Wedell and her team godspeed. "It would be good," he says, a bit wistfully, "if everybody knew what happened here."

percentage of population, today's influx remains slightly behind the levels of the late nineteenth and early twentieth centuries). It has skewed the immigrant population in the direction of those from Latin America and from Asia and has prompted the arrival of a greater percentage of illegal immigrants than any time in history. About a third of annual immigration numbers — roughly 300,000 — represent those who entered illegally. But the questions remain the same ones that have riddled the leaders of the American republic since its inception: Who among the world's population should be allowed to live in America? Among those who we deem as qualified, how many should be let in? Just what should be demanded of them to stay here? Is there a reason to preserve an ethnic balance in American society? What can a state built upon freedom do about the incessant barrage of its borders by those whose only crime may be that they, too, want to enjoy the opportunity that Jefferson once argued, powerfully, was the right of all peoples? Whose interests should immigration policy serve? Those of the citizens already here? Or those of the prospective citizens who wish to come? The past or the future? And finally, the question that pervades all others in this book, just what is an American?

II

When Ana Maria Castro de Amaya, thirty-two, awoke on December 11, 2001, she had a whimsical thought. After getting her children — Ana, eleven, and Ismael, fourteen — off to school, Castro, a petite woman with a warm manner and engaging brown eyes, asked herself: Should I go to work today? Her grandmother was visiting from California and Castro wanted to see her. Anyway, it was an "office day," as she describes it, a day when she wasn't required to go to work, but often did, just to catch up on supply orders and to reorganize the freezer at the Ben and Jerry's ice cream shop she managed at the Salt Lake City Airport. She could easily put that off and tell her assistant to watch over things. Then, even before she could decide, there was a knock at the door. When she opened it and looked outside, six armed federal agents confronted her.

There was a time when Castro worried daily about just such an event, but that was long ago, back in the first few months after she entered the country illegally in 1989. Since then, she had settled into a reasonably comfortable existence, first in Los Angeles, where she and her husband, Jose, and the then-infant Ismael, lived for a while and where she gave birth to young Ana; then in, of all places, Salt Lake City, Utah, a strangely dissonant location for a Mexican, with its mountains, Mormons, and money.

They had come from Guadalajara, a city of 4 million or so that dates to the sixteenth century but is perhaps most famous as the capital of mariachi music, and while their passage here was unpleasant and at times frightening, it was easy compared to that of many others. Urged on by her husband's sister, who is married to a naturalized American and was living then in Los Angeles, Castro and her husband had made the decision over Christmas, 1988, to come here. Like most immigrants, they imagined that in America they might find a better way of life, not only more money and perhaps the chance to enjoy the things that money can buy, but also a chance to "show who I am," as Castro puts it, in essence to "become someone." In the first days of the new year, 1989, they set out, carrying a change of clothes and bottles for Ismael, but nothing else.

When Ana Castro, above right, was arrested and entered into deportation proceedings, her daughter, Ana, eleven, above left, was outraged and took matters into her own hands. She composed a letter to President Bush on the family's home computer. "Mom, he's my president and he will have to listen to me," she said. But Castro stopped her from sending it.

The first leg of their trip was a thirty-eight-hour bus ride to Tijuana, close to the California border. They arrived there at five in the morning, already worried as they milled about the crowd, that they might be raising suspicions. Castro's sister-in-law had phoned some smugglers to let them know when Castro and her family would arrive in Tijuana and indeed, after a while, two men emerged from the crowd, holding a picture to identify them that the sister-in-law had forwarded. Castro and her family were taken by taxi to a house outside town where there were hundreds of others waiting to do the same thing as they were. The house had no furniture, just people crowded into every room. All of them had been told to remain silent since there was considerable fear that any noise might draw attention to the house and spoil their passage. Then, at twilight the next night, Castro and her family were loaded with about twenty others into the back of a windowless van and off they went.

Castro could tell when the driver was following an "off-road" route. She felt the car leave the smoothness of the payment and enter a bumpy area; then after about an hour, he whispered toward the back, "*Ya estamos al otro lado,*" or "We're on the other side now." She felt the van land on a freeway and uttered a tiny inaudible sigh. "Okay," she thought. "We made it." But they weren't safe yet.

Castro and the other passengers noticed a burning odor. Fearing fire, some screamed. The driver said something was wrong with the transmission and pulled the van to the side. He opened the back and told them to run. In the darkness, Castro, holding her infant, scampered up a hill and over a tall chain-link fence. The fence wasn't the border marking; that was long past. But it and the hills that followed would prove to be the most formidable challenge to their journey. Castro's sweater got caught and she momentarily tried to free it without tearing the fabric. Then a woman next to her, part of the group, became frustrated that she would delay them and ripped the sweater free. On the other side of the fence, the group found some bushes to hide in and lay there for two hours. It was cold and the baby was wet and they didn't know what would happen next. But eventually another van came, they piled in, and continued their journey to Los Angeles.

In L.A., they were taken to an apartment where, again, there were hundreds of others. Border-passing is a lucrative business. Indeed, the black market that has arisen to ease the passage of people like Ana Castro is a way of life for thousands of Latinos who feed on the desperation of their former countrymen. After a few hours, Castro and her family were driven to her sister-in-law's home. The sister-in-law gave the smugglers $1,200 in cash to free them — Castro says she felt like she was being reclaimed out of hock from a pawn shop — but now she was truly here. The money was a huge sum to Castro and her husband, equivalent to four months' work for Jose back in Guadalajara, where he drove a city bus, and they made a pledge to pay the sister-in-law back, which they did, quicker than they ever thought they would.

In Los Angeles, Castro was guided along at first by the enormous, informal community of undocumented aliens there. It was they who told her that she would need a Social Security card and an alien registration card (known popularly as a "green card") to work here and where to get phony ones, how she should show up at a specified street and hang out there over a period of days just so that those in the loitering crowd could get used to her. She was told that she should walk up to people and ask if they are selling cards and not be surprised if they at first turned her back, because they must guard against undercover federal agents. Castro went to the street near MacArthur Park in South L.A., followed their advice, and eventually found someone who took her name and then, for a fee of $40, met her at an assigned location the next day with her cards. Only two years later, after her daughter Ana was born here and, as an American citizen, received an official Social Security card, did Castro realize what a bad reproduction she had bought that day. Comparing the two, she and her husband chuckled: the bogus card was flimsy, the ink was a lighter shade of blue, and if carefully examined it looked definitely fake. Yet that card and the number on it would go unchallenged for twelve years and six jobs.

It did not occur to Castro during all this — the stolen entry, the underground purchase of "official" identification, and all the secrecy that attended her arrival — that she was doing anything really wrong. She sees her journey here instead as an act of courage. Sure, she "jumped the queue" past all those people who were trying to come here legally. Sure, she took a job that could have gone to an American (though in point of fact it would more likely have gone to another alien). But she insists that she assumed a risk to do it, riding that van, climbing over that fence, and, for that matter, living a life apart from the law for twelve years. And if she hadn't done it, she says, someone else would have. "It's like finding a hundred dollar bill on the road," she says of the opportunity to steal their way here. "Do you take it or pass it by?"

Schools across the country have been forced to adapt their curricula to meet the needs of the children of newly arrived immigrants. At Brockbank Junior High in Magna, Utah, many new arrivals are taught by an instructor trained to teach English as a Second Language. But so far, Utah has resisted the push to teach Mexican children in Spanish. Above, the class takes a break from academics for a year-end celebration Mexican style.

Castro acknowledges that in an ideal world, people should not subvert the system, but she, like many Mexicans (in fact, many Third World peoples in general), had grown up in a society where the government was understood to be corrupt and law enforcement often susceptible to a bribe. She had at first assumed that the same conditions would apply in the United States; that one must learn to manipulate the system to get what one wants. It was not, after all, idealism that drove her here, not some dream of living in a society that respected rights but, primarily, prosperity and the chance that she could achieve a better way of life for herself and her children. She had not yet understood that one of the reasons why there is such prosperity in America is because the society is so free and because the institutions here provide recourse to the suffering of injustices and that her breaking of the law was an injury to that free society. She has since become impressed by the honesty and the openness of American life, and the decency of officials. Indeed, she had her own peculiarly ambivalent feelings toward the officers that arrested her on December 11. They don't wish me harm, she thought, as she looked warily at their guns. They're just doing their job and it is a job that they have to do.

Castro's first experience with Utah dazzled her. The grass was so green, the surrounding mountains glistened so brightly with snow, and everything seemed so wide open and inviting. She came first from Los Angeles to visit family living here and then, falling in love with Salt Lake City's friendliness and natural grandeur, decided to move here herself.

In a Philadelphia suburb: Bringing the "melting pot" home

Playwright Israel Zangwill (on the cover of a 1923 edition of Time, *left) saw America as the place where races and religions would blend to create a new race formed of all peoples. His 1908 play* The Melting-Pot *was a popular interfaith love story. But nearly a hundred years later, people still struggle with the challenges that such a union presents. Olga Guerra (left, in picture on right), a convert to Judaism, leads an interfaith marriage support group at Beth Or synagogue in Spring House, Pennsylvania.*

Kate, a teacher, and Steve, a lawyer, had been dating for seven years, falling steadily and more deeply in love, while trying to avoid the one subject that persistently blocked the way to a wedding: their respective religions. Steve (they withhold their last names in the interest of privacy) may have only attended synagogue four or five times a year, but when he thought about their future together, he grew increasingly uncomfortable with Kate's weekly church attendance. Kate, a Lutheran who grew up Catholic, knew, in turn, that she couldn't give up her beloved Christmas tree, much less her faith in Christ, to follow the detailed laws that some Jews required of their faithful. "God doesn't care what kind of yogurt you eat," she said dismissively. Maybe not, returned Steve. "But if my children are not raised Jewish, I will be betraying the whole line of ancestors who preserved my heritage for thousands of years." The couple struggled on their own to negotiate a compromise of their religious differences before seeking help at a support group in a leafy Philadelphia suburb. There, they reasoned, they could talk with other men and women facing the same challenge: how to make an interfaith marriage work.

The five couples and two counselors — and a mother-in-law — that gathered one spring Sunday at Congregation Beth Or in Spring House, Pennsylvania, were an eclectic mix, which included a lawyer, a teacher, a counselor, a musician, a businessman, an engineer, a singer, and a nurse. They ranged in age from their late twenties to seventy. Some were veteran parents, some had no children. One woman was pregnant with her first child; another danced her youngest, who was eleven months old, on her lap. They had ancestors from Ireland, Russia, Scotland, Poland, and a half dozen other nations. But each of these twenty-first-century couples was engaged in a decidedly American struggle: by blending deeply held religious and ethnic traditions, the interfaith or interracial marriage brings the challenge of "Americanization" into the home. Every marriage is "a negotiation of love and tradition," says sociologist Egon Mayer. "Interfaith ones make the negotiation more difficult." Indeed, Emmy Livezey, a 911 dispatcher, informs the group that when she told a rabbi that she wanted to marry a non-Jew, "he basically trashed me."

From the earliest days of the republic, American literature is filled with references to a "composite" American character, "amalgamated," "fused," or "blended" from different ethnic and religious peoples. Still, it was not some early American, but a British Jew of the twentieth century, named Israel Zangwill, who popularized the term "melting pot." Zangwill, the son of Russian immigrants, grew up poor in a London ghetto and was one of Britain's best-known writers by the time he became enamored of American life as the wave of the future and unveiled what he called his "American" drama as a way of heralding it. When *The Melting-Pot*, a four-act play about David Quixano, a Russian-born Jew who marries Vera Revendal, a Russian-born Christian, opened in the Columbia Theater in Washington, D.C., on October 5, 1908, Zangwill made it clear that the marriage could not have happened in Russia, but was possible only in the "the great Melting-Pot" where "the great Alchemist melts and fuses" a multitude of races and nationalities "to build the Republic of Man and the Kingdom of God." In the audience that night was Theodore Roosevelt, who shouted from the presidential box, "That's a great play, Mr. Zangwill, that's a great play."

Perhaps because it emphasized the heroic nature of the American mongrel, *The Melting-Pot* became an immediate hit, running for six months in Chicago and five in New York and traveling the country for nearly a decade. Still, the work was not always greeted favorably. Some critics complained that Zangwill was devaluing old American stock by suggesting that the only "real" Americans were those who were the offspring of the current wave of immigration, uniting cultures from around the world. Even tougher claims emanated from the American Jewish community, which saw Zangwill as working toward the extinction of the Jewish race, "cast into and dissolved in the crucible."

Zangwill himself appeared to be a mass of contradictions. Even as he praised the American idea of absorption, he presented himself as a Zionist, working in favor of a Jewish homeland in Palestine. He explained the paradox, not entirely satisfactorily, by saying that American Jews should accept their integration into an American identity ("the Jew . . . Americanized and the American Judaised"), but those Jews who wished instead to be part of a separate Jewish state should work for that. He saw no need to formulate "a panacea for the Jewish problem, universally applicable."

The general enthusiasm for Zangwill's *The Melting-Pot* finally ran aground in the anti-immigration backlash of the 1920s. With great sadness and disappointment, the playwright watched America, his ideal republic, burn not so much with the fire of the melting pot as with the hate of the Ku Klux Klan. Reacting to the return of that organization to American life and with it the patronizing spirit of "Nordic dispensation," Zangwill complained that Christ himself would now be turned back at Ellis Island. When immigration restrictions, forging ethnic quotas, were imposed by the Congress in 1924, Zangwill reacted with disgust. He died in 1926, his once-mighty ideal of the melting pot revealed, as the *New York Times* editorial put it, as so much "pious belief."

The group meeting at Beth Or temple is proof that nearly a hundred years after the premiere of Zangwill's play, the image of the melting pot, battered about not only by nativist impulses but by pluralist ones, too — remains a compelling image of American life. None in the group had ever heard of Zangwill, but all have been drawn to the challenge of blending diverse backgrounds and beliefs every bit as much as they have shrunk in fear of losing their identity in the alchemy of intermarriage.

"The melting pot is certainly one of our strengths as a country," says Steve. "My great-grandparents came here from Lithuania and Poland in the late nineteenth century." He was the first in his family to consider marrying out of the faith. Amy Small-McKinney, a poet who works as a counselor for homeless women and a member of the Beth Or group for one year, congratulated Steve on his strength of conviction. "I feel we are very courageous for doing this," she said. The men and women sitting around on old sofas and chairs in what is normally the "youth lounge," nodded in agreement. Then Amy, who is Jewish, went on to talk about "the minefield" that she and her husband of eleven years, Russ McKinney, a Presbyterian, have crossed. "There were times I felt like I was betraying my ancestors, too," she said.

Betrayal, and the guilt that accompanies it, is not an uncommon feeling among people who have decided to marry someone of another faith, says Olga Guerra, a member of the Beth Or support group for three years before taking over its leadership in 1998. Guerra, a psychotherapist, was married for seventeen years to a Jewish man before she converted to Judaism, raising two Jewish children even though her own background was Catholic. "It is very similar to the grieving process," explains Olga Guerra. "There's anger, then sadness, then denial as you give up a part of yourself." But then come children, which, as Zangwill implies in his play — "peace, peace, to all ye unborn millions, fated to fill this giant continent" — are the true products of the melting pot. "Children are the big question," says Guerra. "You have to face all the questions again. And without being able to ignore them or agree not to deal with them."

"We thought that the kid question would be one of presenting a united front," says Emmy Livezey. "But it turns out not to be that easy." "Will I be in heaven because I've accepted Jesus Christ as my Lord and Savior?" Guerra says is a typical question, "while my spouse and children go to hell?" "Children are the core issue," explains Guerra as she looks at the twelve adults around her, some of whom already have children. It was the issue that stopped Steve and Kate and the one they struggled with for seven long years before deciding finally to get engaged. At this meeting, Nancy Gazan, a Methodist who agreed to raise her children Jewish, congratulates Steve and Kate on their recent marriage. Steve explains that they have agreed that Kate will keep her Lutheran faith but that they will raise their children Jewish. Kate smiles wanly, then blurts out that there are still challenges. "At Passover it hits you in the face," she says. "I truly don't believe in this. How can I look a child in the face and say, 'You can't eat off this plate'? God doesn't care what plate you eat off of!" "I have the same problem with that little wafer thing," says Emmy, who immediately realizes her own insensitivity. "Excuse me. I hope I didn't offend anyone." Actually, everyone laughed. The American crucible had held another day.

The Melting-Pot *featured the marriage of a Jew, David Quixano, and a Christian, Vera Revendal. Above, the drama's Washington premiere.*

Castro had been in Los Angeles for three years, but living there as she did in the largely illegal, largely Mexican community, she insists that her experience as an American began instead here, where she had to learn English, make change for customers at a cash register, and send her children to a school that is largely old-line American. She and her husband even bought a house here, a small split-level in Magna, Utah, a working-class community of 22,000 about thirteen miles west of Salt Lake City. In essence, then, it was in Utah that Ana Castro, an illegal alien, began, slowly, to assimilate.

Her first job was as a housekeeper at Salt Lake City's Doubletree Hotel. But by the time she was arrested, Castro had gone through four other positions, each one better than the last, invariably impressing her employers with her work ethic, her honesty and ambition. She had become the principal breadwinner in the family, a role she relished for the sense of accomplishment that it afforded her. This is what she had dreamed about back in Mexico when she thought of coming here, the opportunity to "do whatever you want because you can do it here."

Ana Castro and her husband, above, have embraced life here, though their home country remains dear to them. "Most people would probably criticize me for not wanting to choose one country over the other, but I have my heart in Mexico and America," she says, adding with a sigh, "I wish this were a borderless world."

When Joe Lambert, who is director of operations for a firm that runs restaurants and ice cream parlors in the Salt Lake area, first hired Castro it was as a supervisor at the airport Ben and Jerry's. But Castro quickly moved on to a position with more responsibility. Ironically, it was that promotion, to manager, now, of Lambert's Ben and Jerry's airport shop that, because it required her to go through a secure area to move inventory, put Ana Castro on the road to deportation.

Lambert (Scottish, French, and English heritage, with family going back to the seventeenth century, near Boston, Massachusetts) says that he didn't have any extraordinary suspicions that Castro was illegal. Like many area employers — like many employers nationwide — he has stopped worrying about whether the people he hires are legal or not. So long as they have the proper identification, he is content to employ them. While the INS requires that he have a prospective hire fill out an I-9 form and show him documentation (on the form the employee must also sign that he is "aware that federal law provides for imprisonment and/or fines for false statement or use of false documents"), Lambert is not encouraged to challenge that documentation. "Ten years ago," says Lambert,

"Born in other countries, yet believing you could be happy in this, our laws acknowledge, as they should do, your right to join us in society, conforming, as I doubt not you will do, to our established rules."

—Thomas Jefferson

"you were afraid that if you hired illegal people, you would be put under scrutiny, but now it's so prevalent . . . It's like that thing with gays in the military, 'don't ask, don't tell.'"

Lambert felt like he was losing a good employee when Ana Castro was arrested, so much so that he assisted her in her search for a good immigration attorney, even went to see the attorney with her and testified to Castro's good character and standing. Castro was touched by her employer's concern (she had worried that he would have felt deceived by her), but in stories like this, Lambert is not unusual. Many others in the community offered assistance to those arrested in the December 11 airport raid. Indeed, a few months after the event, Salt Lake City Mayor Rocky Anderson (Norwegian and Scottish, dating to the late 1800s), who had initially supported the raid and then had second thoughts about its political implications, began a family-to-family program, hoping to match each potential deportee with a member of the community who could offer financial, emotional, or legal assistance. The mayor even set the tone for the program when he himself became the sponsor for Gilberto Rejon, a baggage handler, who faces deportation.

In Castro's case, there was both a criminal charge — the felony of document falsification — and an immigration violation. Her criminal charges were eventually dropped. U.S. Attorney Paul Warner (English, German, Danish, and a little Cherokee Indian) had said that he might, for "humanitarian" reasons, dismiss the charges on some of those arrested at the airport raid and in the end he had apparently been impressed by Castro's upstanding life here. But her immigration case remains active. Castro's attorney sees one chance. Since her daughter, Ana, who was born here, is a citizen, Castro has applied for "cancelation of removal," a status granted to those who have lived here for ten years or more and whose deportation is deemed to put their citizen child, spouse, or parent in extraordinary hardship. Few are granted such status; it is reserved for those whose children have some need that cannot be met anywhere but here. Indeed, of the hundred thousand or so applications handled each year, only about four thousand are awarded. Ironically, while she waits for the ruling on hers, a process that could take two years, Castro has been given a work authorization that has made her "legal" for the first time in her thirteen years in America. Five months after she had been arrested as a security risk and held in jail for nine days, Castro was back at work at the same airport Ben and Jerry's shop, wearing a kelly green "please don't forget dessert" shirt, ordering new supplies of Chunky Monkey and Cherry Garcia.

III

From its earliest days as a republic, America was a multi-ethnic state. While the Colonies had been decidedly English in the years leading up to the eighteenth century, their population more than tripled in the 1700s, with newcomers arriving from Ireland, Germany, Scotland, Wales, France, Switzerland, and, in the case of slaves, from Africa. Among the revolutionary generation some took pride in the great variety of American ancestry. "Europe, and not England, is the parent country of America," wrote Tom Paine. In 1776, a committee of the Continental Congress suggested that the emerging nation adopt a Great Seal that would show all the major lands from which the American people had come. Thomas Jefferson himself boasted in the opening of his autobiography that he wasn't simply of English stock; he was also "Welsh," from "near the mountain of Snowdon," on his father's side.

"Why should the Palatine Boors be suffered to swarm into our settlements and, by herding together, establish their language and manners to the exclusion of ours? Why should Pennsylvania, founded by the English, become a colony of Aliens, who will shortly be so numerous as to Germanize us instead of our Anglifying them and will never adopt our language or customs any more than they can acquire our complexion?"

— Benjamin Franklin

There was, to be sure, some resentment of "strangers" and their tendencies toward exclusive communities. Benjamin Franklin was concerned that the Germans settling in Pennsylvania were "the most ignorant and stupid sort of their own nation" and worried that the Germans "will soon outnumber us." The influx of Irish and Scottish to parts of Virginia led to the derisive term "Mac-ocracy." But the Revolution helped to discourage such attitudes and center the discussion on a new "American" man, to be revealed not in the blood, but in the mind. Joel Barlow, a Connecticut writer of the time, declared that what Americans think is what they are. Indeed, all the founding documents of the United States were written to stress the word *people* over *nation*. *Nation* was too artificial and, as historian Arthur Mann has explained, "too static" for the vision of the founders, "too captive of the parochial past." In contrast, "people" was of the present, "unfettered and dynamic, endowed with the power to choose and to change, to break the crust of custom if need be." It also had the quality of universality: with the tragic exception of the African slave, *people* meant those of all races, religions, and histories.

In such a climate, immigration was not a pressing issue. Indeed, except as it refers to procedures for naturalization, the subject of immigration is hardly touched upon in the writings of the founding fathers. To the degree that the question of entry into the United States was considered at all, it was in the eagerness of the revolutionary generation to welcome people who could populate the new country. English law was focused around the concept of *jus soli* (right of the soil), which granted citizenship according to the place of birth. It did not recognize naturalization. In fact, in the list of grievances contained in the Declaration of Independence, Jef-

"To admit foreigners indiscriminately to the rights of citizens, the moment they put foot in our country would be nothing less than to admit the Grecian horse into the citadel of our liberty and sovereignty . . . [They must first] get rid of foreign and acquire American attachments . . . learn the principles and imbibe the spirit of our government . . . and [feel] a real interest in our affairs."

—Alexander Hamilton

ferson accused King George III of endeavoring to "prevent the population of these States . . . [by] obstructing the Laws for Naturalization of Foreigners, refusing to . . . encourage their migrations hither."

This was an important point for Jefferson. He considered emigration, or "expatriation," to be the natural right of man to depart "from the country in which chance, not choice" had placed him and go "in quest of new habitations." In his "A Summary View of the Rights of British America" (1774), he wrote of this as the inevitable flow of history, the one that had brought England's own Saxon ancestors to the island of Britain, and America's ancestors to the Colonies. The Declaration of Independence was itself first and foremost an act of expatriation. And Jefferson also had an ulterior motive in supporting the flow of people here. He believed that the arrival of "free white laborers" could help diminish the economic impact of the end of slavery, which he hoped to see.

Yet even as they opened America's doors, and held firm in their belief in the rights of people to leave the nation of their birth and come here, the founders were keenly aware of the need for a limiting principle, too: they had, to their great credit, a historic accomplishment in this establishment of a nation-state centered on the rights of mankind and they needed to protect it. No church tied the people of America together, no shared folklore or literary tradition, no history to speak of, and no ethnicity. But a few central ideas of the Enlightenment, now being put to the test for the first time in American politics, did, and it seemed logical, in turn, to demand from those who wished to live here a commitment to those same democratic and egalitarian principles.

This was the other voice of Jefferson, the one that spoke to his worries that immigrants arriving from "absolute monarchies" would settle in America for the wrong reasons and bring with them all those city-bred vices and tyrannical notions of government that they had "imbibed in their early youth." In this he agreed with Franklin, whose criticism of the Germans was based in part on what he saw as their "not being used to liberty" nor knowing "how to make [even] modest use of it." "They are not esteemed men," declared Franklin, emphasizing that Americans need to break with the past, "until they have shown their manhood by beating their mothers." Jefferson preferred to think of the American population growing from within, with freedom-loving people begetting more freedom-loving people. But he never argued to curb immigration, for that would be counter to his belief in that natural right of expatriation. Instead, he urged that immigration simply not be fueled by "extraordinary encouragements." In this, he was making yet another claim for the essential freedom of the human spirit, which he believed should be left to its own impulses, both unimpeded *and* unpersuaded.

Jefferson's seemingly contradictory attitudes demonstrate a tension that has attended the immigration issue throughout American history. On the one hand, America prides itself on being an asylum from the brutal regimes and corrupt economies of the world; on the other, it sees itself as a special and, perhaps, fragile experiment in human history, one that demands from its citizens a certain loyalty lest it, too, fall victim to the designs of the tyrant. "The last hope of human liberty in this world rests on us," wrote Jefferson in 1811. "We ought, for so dear a state, to sacrifice every attachment and every enmity."

Yet it was during the presidency of John Adams, not Jefferson, that America suffered its first serious "crisis" with immigration, even if the furor over the Alien and Sedition Acts of 1798 was actually more about domestic political rivalries than immigration, per se. During Adams's presidency, American politics was caught up in a ruthless clash between Jefferson's Republicans and the ruling Federalists over America's relationship with revolutionary France. Jefferson and his party tended to support France and downplay both the recent seizure of American cargo ships by the French and the affront that America had suffered from Paris in the XYZ affair, a diplomatic fiasco in which representatives of the American government, seeking to establish peace, had been told by French agents (designated X,Y, and Z) that talks could not begin until the United States granted France a $12 million loan and paid the French foreign minister a $250,000 bribe.

When news of the exchange was made public, it enflamed the nation. The conservative wing of Adams's Federalist party, led by Alexander Hamilton, was ready to declare war. The Alien and Sedition Acts were then advanced by the Federalists to curb the infiltration of disloyal "foreigners." They extended the period of residency required to become a naturalized citizen (from five to fourteen years), demanded that aliens declare their intent to pursue citizenship five years before it would be granted, and made people from enemy nations ineligible for naturalization. The acts, which also put restrictions on speech and association, were roundly condemned by Jefferson as "in the teeth of the Constitution" and "worthy of the eighth or ninth century." He pinned the blame on Adams and the Federalists, whom he accused of using the threat of a foreign force as an excuse for trampling the freedoms of innocent people at home.

"What think you of terrorism, Mr. Jefferson?" —John Adams

Jefferson had rightly detected that the Federalists saw these acts as a way of limiting the influence of the Republican party, discouraging the "hordes of wild Irishmen" who had brought a revolutionary spirit to the republic, and assuring their own place in power. A Federalist rallying cry of the time made it explicit by heralding Adams: "May he like Samson

In Santa Cruz: Tasting an American cuisine

Tony LeBourveau, right, a former pipefitter for the county water district, followed decades-old family kitchen secrets to win the Santa Cruz Clam Chowder Cook-off. LeBourveau might have succeeded without Fannie Farmer's 1896 best-seller, left, but the "Mother of Level Measurement," opposite page, helped make quality cuisine a democratic art, with recipes for goodies like "rolled wafers tied in bundles of three with baby ribbon," from page 410 of her book.

When Tony LeBourveau awoke one February Saturday, he had clams on his mind — as in clam chowder, that is, and a recipe that has been in his family for several generations. He reached deep into the corners of his memory, back to 1949 when he was thirteen years old and working on a water taxi on Catalina Island. That was around the time when LeBourveau first learned his family's "secret" seasoning, the one that flavors the best soup he says he has ever tasted and made him something of a celebrity in these parts. This morning, LeBourveau's chowder is one of forty-six entered in the Santa Cruz, California, Annual Clam Chowder Cook-off, a decades-old contest that attracts ambitious chefs from roadside motels, from mom-and-pop luncheonettes, from fishing boats, and, of course, local home kitchens. The variety is astounding: there's a chowder with chiles and Mexican herbs from Watsonville, California; a chowder with Thai lemongrass from San Jose; and, of course, the traditional milk-based recipe from Boston. That would be the one made by LeBourveau, who has adapted and refined the old family favorite for fifty-three years now, personalizing it with a delicate blend of cheeses that seems, each year, to meet with greater success. Indeed, LeBourveau's recipes have won more awards than any other in the Santa Cruz cook-off's history.

A study of the eating habits of the American "mainstream" presented to the American Medical Association in the 1970s offered a grim picture of the national diet: "Oreos, peanut butter, Crisco, TV dinners, cake mix, macaroni and cheese, Pepsi and Coke, pizzas, Jell-O, hamburgers, Rice-a-Roni, Spaghetti-O's, canned pork and beans, ketchup and instant coffee." Still, there is an American cuisine and not all of it is all canned and prepackaged. Some of it borrows from indigenous produce, like maize, squash, potatoes, peanuts, tomatoes, and pumpkins. Other recipes hail from early American history, notably the interaction with Native Americans who introduced the English settlers to a repertoire of corn dishes. Colonial cookbooks demonstrated a surprising sophistication: "All things that are green should have a little crispness," reads a Virginia chef's *Art of Cookery* (1747), "for if they are over boil'd they neither have any sweetness or beauty." They also reveal the impact of new cultures: West Indian and African, as well as German and French.

In fact, the American dish clam chowder has its own origins as a French stew made in a *chaudière* (cauldron) on the beaches of Brittany. Adapted on these shores to include local fish and New World foods like potatoes (and in Manhattan, tomatoes), then served with hardtack biscuits, it became a one-pot staple and sustained generations of American laborers, café diners, and soon, the great masses of an emerging people. Critics often point out that American cooks tend to "bland down" sharp, pungent, or assertive ethnic flavors in order to "Americanize" them. From tuna casseroles to hamburgers, meatloaf, baked ziti, lasagna, and chowder, Americans' favorite dinners are almost always straightforward and easy. But that fit the premium placed upon fashioning food for a democratic society, available to all levels of cooking experience and all kinds of palates.

The person most responsible for the development of an American form of cookery was born in 1857, in the middle of the national journey. By 1896, when Fannie Merritt Farmer made her mark on American cookery, there were as many chowders in America as there were cooks. Farmer included five in her seminal edition of *The Boston Cooking School Cook Book* (now known as *The Fannie Farmer Cookbook*), and codified the version that most Americans know today, the one which forms the base of the soup that Tony LeBourveau concocted for the Santa Cruz Clam Chowder Cook-off. LeBourveau didn't exactly follow a Fannie Merritt Farmer recipe for his chowder, but he is aware of the debt all Americans owe to this remarkable woman.

The story of how American foods originating in the Colonial era, in the pioneer West, on the plantations of the rural South, and in the Heartland breadbasket all met and became a national cuisine is intricately intertwined with the story of how this young invalid woman overcame stereotypes and obstacles to become a powerful unifying force in shaping American cookery.

In her fifty-eight years, Farmer did for American cookery what Henry Ford did for industry: she created a uniform method of operation, a language of measurement, and instruction that could be in every burg and hollow.

Farmer's life started with an early struggle, when a paralytic stroke right after high school prevented her from attending college. But when her strength returned, Farmer grasped onto a position as a "mother's helper" for a Boston family and let her penchant for precise measurement of ingredients build her a reputation. As she shared her recipes, her contemporaries began to notice that they were easier to reproduce than the sketchy instructions most cooks passed among themselves, which often specified "a pinch" of one ingredient, and "enough to thicken" of another. Not content to specify "butter the size of an egg," Farmer measured, using the graded devices mostly employed by retailers. She was encouraged to seek schooling and enrolled in the Boston Cooking School. That fateful decision, and her outstanding performance at that institution, changed the course of American culinary history.

Farmer earned a position as assistant director of the school in 1889. Increasingly self-confident, young Farmer also took summer courses at the Harvard Medical School, which would later fuel her passion for nutrition and dietary guidance for the infirm. In 1891, Farmer was named director of the school and began reshaping the school cookbook, infusing it with her own passion for precise measurement and her views on what a properly prepared cook should know to prepare the dishes typical of the American table. Her edited volume, released in 1896 as *The Boston Cooking School Cook Book*, consolidated the country's up-to-date ingredients, techniques, and dishes in an accessible and standardized way. It was not the first volume to collect popular recipes of America (Library of Congress records *American Cookery*, from 1796, by Amelia Simmons as the first truly American cookbook), but Farmer did some unique things with it that made it a survivor: her book, for instance, listed ingredients separately from the instructions, a standard followed to this day.

Here, in one volume, was the wide range of American cookery. Chowders and Indian pudding drawn from Farmer's native New England region shared space with fried grits, Virginia waffles, pumpkin pie, butter taffy, and other flavors from the Deep South. Western stews and preparations for wild game common in the West found their way to the Atlantic in her first 1896 edition. In the effort to keep her book up-to-date, Farmer was said to have made forays down to the Boston docks in the hopes of meeting arriving French chefs who could tell her the latest dishes and ingredients in Paris.

She's said to also have surreptitiously secreted away samples of dishes she liked at restaurants, and then worked to re-create the food in her own kitchen.

Farmer's personal peccadilloes enriched her cookbook's periphery. She devoted whole sections to skills like boning poultry, building a fire, what "doneness" means, and most famously, the proper way to measure ingredients precisely. For the latter, she acquired the somewhat grandiose nickname "Mother of Level Measurement," but this was actually a very significant achievement: by taking the guesswork out of cooking, Farmer's measurements — level cupful, teaspoonful, and tablespoonful — allowed people of humble means to cook fancy dishes and introduced an array of food to every American family that previously would have been out of their reach.

The Boston Cooking School Cook Book became an instant success all over the country, with twenty-one editions printed before Farmer's death in 1915, selling second only to the Bible for most of that time, and reigning as the top American cookbook until *Joy of Cooking* was published shortly before WWII. The book has never been out of print since her 1896 edition.

As for Farmer, she remained director of the Boston Cooking School for eleven years before establishing her own school in 1902, focused more on practical cooking than on theory. Fannie Merritt Farmer, an unmarried, self-made woman, became a national celebrity, and as she did, she used her public role to promote special therapeutic cookery for the sick and handicapped, becoming the foremost authority on the subject and lecturing nurses, women's groups, and notably the Harvard Medical School. Indeed, her name carried such a positive connection with food, an ambitious chocolate manufacturer licensed it from her family, and became one of the most well-known confectioners in the nation.

Farmer embodied what American cookery represented in her time and in ours: an amalgam of world influences, forming a wholly new cuisine. In Santa Cruz, California, Lisa McGinnis, one of the organizers of the chowder cook-off, says she sees America's immigrant heritage in every bowl at every booth. She calls chowder "an ever-changing stew of cultures and flavors — a metaphor for America." Indeed, Santa Cruz's chowderfest organizers have found it necessary to define "chowder" as narrowly as they can, to avoid being inundated by soups so diverse that judging them would be like comparing apples and oranges. As for Tony LeBourveau, the basics are enough, plus a few cheeses. And in 2001, that was enough for the judges, too. LeBourveau walked away with the prize, for the thirteenth time.

slay thousands of Frenchman with the jawbone of Jefferson!" But Jefferson's own supporters were not without blame for the contentious mood of American politics in the 1790s. Looking back on it later, Jefferson referred to the whole sorry episode as the "terrorism of the day." But while Adams would live to regret his support for these measures and blame them on the extremists in his own party, he could not abide Jefferson's claim of the moral high ground. After citing episode after episode in which the nation had come close to disunion, in which threatening Republican mobs had surrounded the president's house in Philadelphia, while Jefferson "was fast asleep in philosophical tranquility," Adams demanded to know: "What think you of terrorism, Mr. Jefferson?"

In the United States alone, there are 5 million members of the Church of Jesus Christ of Latter-day Saints. Most Mormons live in Utah, where they comprise 70 percent of the population and hold a majority of the statewide offices. Above, Salt Lake City's Temple Square, home to the Tabernacle.

In the end, the Alien Acts were never enforced. Indeed, on news of their passage, most Frenchmen and other "dangerous aliens" had already fled. The Sedition Acts, however, were another matter, leading to twenty five arrests, fourteen indictments, and ten convictions, every one of them a Jefferson Republican. Three years later, when Jefferson succeeded Adams in the White House, the new president gave voice once again to an open-door immigration policy. "Shall we refuse the unhappy fugitives from distress that hospitality which the savages of the wilderness extended to our fathers arriving in this land?" asked Jefferson in his First Annual Message. "Shall oppressed humanity find no asylum on this globe?" By 1802, the Republican majority had let the acts expire. Still, a precedent had been set and over the course of American history, whenever the nation has been threatened by a foreign enemy or engaged in a foreign war, suspicion of foreigners living within the nation has been ramped up, and calls for restrictions on immigration and naturalization have been issued.

IV

Before Mexicans were a minority in Utah, Mormons were. In fact, the history here is enlightening. The Church of Jesus Christ of Latter-day Saints was founded at Fayette, New York, in 1830 by Joseph Smith, Jr., who claimed to have experienced a visitation from God and Jesus telling him to abandon all other creeds and several visitations from an angel urging him to turn instead to the writings in an ancient book of golden plates that was to be entrusted to him and him alone. Smith translated the writing on these plates from its original language and then published them as the 588-page Book of Mormon, and it, along with the Bible and various revelations recorded by Smith, became the sacred basis of the Mormon religion.

The Book of Mormon features the story of two competing groups from the tribe of Joseph, one light-skinned and good, the other dark-skinned and bad, who eventually take their battles to the Americas, where the resurrected Jesus appears to them encouraging their repentance. The book's setting is, along with the religion's homegrown beginnings, the reason that Mormonism is often identified as a peculiarly American faith. So is its focus on the divinity of the individual. Indeed, Mormons assert that God himself was once a "mortal man" and that Jesus Christ is God's literal son. Yale Professor Harold Bloom regards Mormonism as possibly the world's next great religion, a post-Protestant, post-Christian faith, centered in the belief that one "finds God in herself or himself." Originally, says Bloom, every Mormon was taught to believe that he, too, was a "mortal god."

Proselytizing throughout the Northeast and the Midwest in the middle years of the nineteenth century, Mormons sought to establish a government in which the godly ruled, but everywhere they went they ran up against the American tradition of separating church and state and were literally run out of town. In Illinois they achieved their greatest numbers and faced their most violent opposition when Smith and his brother Hyrum were murdered.

Brigham Young, a church official, was named the sect's new leader and in 1847, under pressure from anti-Mormon forces, he took them west to the great Salt Lake Valley in what was then, ironically for our story, part of Mexico. Young supposedly stood looking out over the desert and pronounced, "This is the right place." But if so, it wasn't yet their place. "They were trespassing on Mexican territory," says Armando Solorzano, a professor of ethnic studies at the University of Utah. "They were here for nearly a year without permission from the Mexican government." Had they asked for permission, they would probably not have received it. In its early days as a republic, Mexico had encouraged Americans to come live in their northern province of Texas, provided they become Roman Catholics and swear their loyalty to their new country. Only when the Treaty of Guadalupe Hidalgo was signed in 1848 — ending the Mexican-American War and awarding present-day Arizona, California, New Mexico, Texas, and parts of Colorado, Nevada, and Utah to the United States — did the Mormons, who now comprise a full 70 percent of Utah's population, achieve legal status.

The treaty remains a sore subject among some Latinos who have

> **"Most of the traditions which we associate with the American West were invented by pulp writers, poster artists, impresarios, and advertising men; excepting, mainly, those that were imported from Mexico, whose vaqueros had about a three-century jump on our cowboys when it came to handling cattle . . . many of the skills associated with American cowboys were Mexican skills moved north and adapted to Anglo-Saxon capabilities and needs."**
>
> LARRY MCMURTRY
> *"Inventing the West"*

settled in the West, not because it made the Mormons legal, but because it is viewed as an act just short of thievery by the United States. The war was fought over the status of Texas (which had recently broken free from Mexico) and the corrupt Mexican government's outstanding debt to American nationals. It was seen by many Americans of the time as a romantic adventure in which their largely volunteer forces would serve as an army of democracy set to restore republican values to a people overrun by dictators. Indeed, when Gen. Winfield Scott and his forces triumphantly entered Mexico City, the general wore a plumed hat and had the military band accompany his march with a stirring rendition of "Yankee Doodle." But more than 150 years later, at least some Mexican-Americans look back at that war as little more than a land grab by the United States and proof that they belong here, perhaps even more than the traditional American population does. Some other Americans, in turn, fear that the arrival of great numbers of Mexican immigrants is the first step in a movement toward *reconquista*, the reconquering of American land by Mexican peoples to create a greater Mexico stretching from the Yucatan north to Colorado.

As more Mexicans move to Salt Lake City, Mexican markets, bakeries, and bodegas are opening in the city's largely Hispanic West Side to cater to them. La Diana, above, a grocery wholesaler and tortilla factory, sells Mexican breads and confections, laundry detergent, and hard-to-find spices for authentic cooking.

One reason for these suspicions comes from the geographical proximity of Mexico to the United States. Unlike the Irish or the Italians, the Germans or the Koreans, Mexicans do not have to make as unyielding a commitment when they come here. No ocean has to be crossed, no transcontinental travel has to be undertaken. It remains easy to visit relatives back home and hard, at times, to distinguish life in the American borderlands where a city like El Paso, Texas, is not that different from the Mexican border town of Ciudad Juarez. But recently the Mexican government became aware that a further blending of the line between the United States and Mexico has enormous benefits for them, whether it be in commerce, with the North American Free Trade Agreement (NAFTA), or in encouraging dual loyalties and dual citizenship. The Mexican-American who remains devoted to Mexico is more likely to send money home, invigorating the Mexican economy. Indeed, many do, to the tune of $9.3 billion a year, the third largest source of revenue for Mexico (after oil and tourism). The government of Mexican president Vicente Fox has created a "Presidential Office for Mexicans Abroad," to undertake the paradoxical task of helping Mexicans living outside the country to prosper outside the country, but never forget where they came from. That office's first director, Juan Hernandez, a Mexican-American who until his appointment was teaching at the University of Texas, uses "we" when he talks about Mexico and "we" when he talks about America. He bridles when asked if Mexican-Americans are being encouraged to create a "nation within a nation" (America, he says, echoing a phrase of Walt Whitman's, is "the nation of many nations"), but he agrees with Vicente Fox that a "successful Mexican in the United States is a successful *Mexican*."

If there are Mexican-Americans in Utah whose loyalty remains south of the border, there are also plenty of Chicanos (the term used to distinguish Americans of Mexican descent from recent émigrés) who are firmly rooted here. While Andrew Anthony Valdez, a juvenile court judge in Salt Lake County, can trace his ancestry in the Southwest back three hundred years, he is still sometimes treated like an immigrant. "If I walk into a high-end department store and I am not wearing a suit and tie," he says, without a trace of bitterness, "I have been followed by security." But like many Chicanos, he sees himself as an American first and foremost. "I don't even like Mexico," says the carefully coifed and mustachioed fifty-year-old. "The government doesn't treat people well there." The Valdez family counts veterans fighting on the American side of the Spanish-American War, in World War I, World War II, and Vietnam. Valdez's son James, a member of the U.S. Marine Corps, is in training for a possible deployment to the war in Afghanistan.

Andrew Anthony Valdez, above, a juvenile court judge, hopes to inspire immigrant teens to find a place for themselves as Americans, but with pride in their Hispanic heritage. Here he talks with a group of youths at Salt Lake City's Jordan Park.

Valdez has become something of a celebrity among Chicanos living in Utah, particularly since he moved from a wealthy neighborhood where he was "the only brown person on the block" back to Salt Lake's largely Latino West Side, among the bodegas and the taco shops. The Hispanics in the neighborhood there are divided roughly half and half between Chicanos and recent Mexican immigrants, some of whom are no doubt illegal. Many of their children end up in Valdez's court, having joined a gang (Chicano and Mexicano gangs regularly face off against each other here) or otherwise ended up somehow on the wrong side of the law. Valdez does not lecture them about their illegal status. That, he says, is something for the parents, not these innocent kids, though he adds that

"The gates will not be closed; the wheels of industry will not retard; America is in the race for the markets of the world, its call for workers will not cease." —PETER ROBERTS
The New Immigration, 1912

the parents are often afraid to come to court anyway because they fear authority and fear being deported. But Valdez makes a point of telling the children his story and that of his family and showing them, he hopes, by example that they can belong here and maintain their ethnic identification with Latin America.

V

Out of the enormous industrial growth of America in the middle of the nineteenth century — the countless new factories, with their belch and bang, forging new standardized products at record speed, the imposing new steam locomotives passing through city and countryside alike — came the overriding image of the American late nineteenth century. It sealed the triumph of the industrial north over the agrarian south: the machine. It was seen by the generation that first witnessed it as nothing less, writes Robert Hughes, than a "big dumb superslave, a Negro without the moral criticism attached."

You could see the growing enthusiasm at "Machinery Hall" of the 1876 Philadelphia exposition, marking the centennial of the American idea. There people could stand as if in the middle of a fulcrum, looking to one side at Ben Franklin's old hand press, and then to the other to gaze in awe upon the new thirty-foot-diameter Corliss stationary steam engine which looked for all the world as if some wild beast had been netted — a woolly mammoth sporting a fifty-six-ton flywheel — and harnessed as the sign of the American future, the agent of mass production, the harbinger of the assembly line. Inspired by that fair, Walt Whitman, who occupied the unofficial role of national poet, told the hordes of Europe to look west, to America, "for a better fresher, busier sphere" the kind of place where "a wide, untried domain awaits, demands you."

Yet far more prosaic appeals than Whitman's were soon at work on the European masses. America's new factories needed unskilled labor, and business groups were busy drumming it up throughout Europe, selling Colorado as a new "Switzerland" and Minnesota as the place where "the hand of labour" was needed to "bring forth the rich treasures" of a new economy. The appeals were sent in a dozen languages and handled in some places by local middlemen and agents who, as Matthew Frye Jacobson explains in his excellent history *Barbarian Virtues*, "steered their compatriots toward specific work in specific regions of the United States — Chinese or Japanese laborers toward the Western railroads, Hungarians toward the Pennsylvania mines, Mexicans toward the Texas smelter industry, Greeks toward the Western copper mines, Italians toward the city-building projects of the Eastern Seaboard and the Midwest."

The result was a tremendous wave of immigration, landing 26 million here in the fifty years between 1870 and 1920. For America, this was a new kind of immigrant, fashioned for a new kind of society, an industrial society, and the shift made traditionalists uneasy in the way that Thomas Jefferson had once been uneasy about mixing up the American population with the wrong types. John R. Commons, an economist of the time, was vocal in his concern that "races wholly incompetent as pioneers and independent proprietors" were now finding a place for themselves here, threatening the "democratic theories" of the founders with the "inroads of alien stock."

Cartoons like the one above, from an 1896 issue of Frank Leslie's Illustrated, *were indicative of the fear that the arrivals of different peoples struck among old-line Americans. It was titled "Unrestricted Immigration and Its Results — A Possible Curiosity of the Twentieth Century, the Last Yankee."*

In 1870, over half of American workers toiled on the farm — closer to, if not exactly an emblem of, Jefferson's vision of a nation of yeoman farmers. By the first decade of the twentieth century, two thirds of workers were in factories doing what amounted to little more than machine-tending, what Commons described as "semi-intelligent work" and Henry Ford described as the kind of job that "the most stupid man could learn in two days." Soon, this social transformation began to emerge as the unintended consequence of a new, mechanized, factory-driven age: for it turned out that the price of becoming the world's most potent industrial power was that America would exchange its idealist political message for an economic message and replace what sociologist Edward A. Ross described at the time as the "Old Immigration" of "home seekers" with a New Immigration of "job seekers."

The worries fueled two principal developments: schools, churches, and synagogues of the late nineteenth century organized "Americanization" courses to teach the new immigrants fundamental American ideas. If they had not exactly been inspired to come here by them, went the thinking, then perhaps they could learn to appreciate them now that they were here. But the wave of new immigrants also inspired a "nativist" movement, dedicated to protecting America for people of Anglo-Saxon stock.

This was not the first expression of such sentiment. In the 1850s, the Order of the Star Spangled Banner, a secret society based in New York City, had inspired the development of the Know-Nothing party, which inveighed against the arrival of Irish Catholics and with them "popish" allegiances. In this they were expressing the view of some Protestants who had fled Europe to get away from friction they encountered with Catholic populations there. Now they feared that with Catholics arriving here in large numbers, their old troubles would be rejoined. The name "Know Nothing" was a holdover from the group's once secret origins, when they plotted to undermine the political power of Catholics and told their members to say, if challenged about their activities, that they

In Queens, New York: Fashioning miniature "lady liberties"

Twenty-four years after he first saw the Statue of Liberty, arriving here as a Romanian immigrant, Ovidiu Colea, above, now oversees the production of thousands of replicas of Lady Liberty in his Queens factory. Though the full statue was not dedicated until the end of 1886 (ten years late), portions of the French-built work, left, began to arrive on Bedloe's Island in the spring of 1885. The statue is now known as a symbol of freedom the world over. In 1986, Manfred Anson incorporated it into a Hanukkah lamp, opposite page, to commemorate the Statue of Liberty's one hundredth birthday — and his own appreciation for America as a haven from Nazi Germany.

The first time Ovidiu Colea tried to come to America, it was 1958, he was eighteen, and he only got as far as a cornfield on the banks of the Danube River. For his troubles, he was sent to a Romanian labor camp for five years. But it didn't quell his desire to come here — a hunger nourished by the Voice of America on the radio in a darkened back bedroom of his Bucharest house and by his father's own whispered dreams of someday seeing the United States. "He told me stories about the Statue of Liberty," recalls Colea, "ones that helped me to remember what she stands for." And so, when the Romanian government opened its doors briefly in 1978, Colea scooped up one of the rare exit visas and left, for good.

In many respects Ovidiu Colea's story is similar to that of many millions of immigrants who came before him; the Romanian refugee, fleeing a harsh Communist dictatorship, went on to become an American citizen and a successful entrepreneur, to see one of his sons go to business school and another join the U.S. Marine Corps. But Colea is different than most in that he lives with the very dream that brought him here, operating a business that makes souvenir replicas of the Statue of Liberty. "Sometimes people born here don't realize how lucky they are," says Colea, now sixty-two. "I don't think there is anything more important than being an American."

Colea arrived at the Liberty statue replica business almost by a fluke. In 1984, he received a form letter from Lee Iacocca, the Chrysler CEO who was leading the effort to restore the Statue for its one hundredth birthday. "He was asking for a contribution of $25," recalls Colea, who was about to send in his check when his wife, Adriana, also from Romania, suggested another kind of donation. "She said, 'Why not make a statue instead?'" Colea had been trained as a ceramic sculptor in Romania and his first job in America was casting and finishing small reproductions of well-known sculptures for Alva Museum Replicas in New York. He earned three dollars an hour there and, like many immigrants in New York City, Colea drove a taxi at night ("the toughest job I've ever had," he says) to supplement his meager income. By 1982 he had saved enough to go into business with an immigrant partner and managed to land a $5 million contract casting athletes on telephones for AT&T, an Olympic sponsor. Part of the reason for Colea's success was the use he made of polyester resin which, when combined with marble dust, he found, yielded more realistic reproductions.

When Colea contacted the Statue of Liberty–Ellis Island Foundation with his wife's suggestion that a replica be sold as a fund-raising incentive, it sparked their interest. Soon, Colea and a sculptor, himself a refugee from Communist China, were climbing around the scaffolding on the monument, measuring and taking pictures. Though there remains some debate about whom French sculptor Auguste Bartholdi used as a model for the original lady liberty — several years ago a rumor on the Internet spread that he had used an African-American, but most histories suggest that he used his mother — Colea realized the difficulty of overcoming one's ethnic biases when he saw that the face of his Chinese sculptor's first model had a distinctly Asian cast to its features. Yet such is the power of this international icon of freedom that whoever looks at it projects his or her own story onto the dream of freedom.

The first year of the contract with the foundation, Colea sold nearly 600,000 of the statues at various venues. His agreement was that he would pay a royalty to the Statue of Liberty–Ellis Island Foundation from each sale. Instead of the $25 donation that "Lee Iacocca" had requested of him, Colea and his statues eventually contributed $250,000 to the cause. Today, Colea's statues are still the best-selling replicas at the Liberty Island gift shop and his Colbar Art company, housed in a Queens factory building and employing thirty-five people — mostly immigrants — ships several hundred thousand of the reproductions from its Liberty Collection around the world every year. It is no secret, he points out, that labor costs are cheaper in other parts of the world, but Colea says that it is important, in his mind, to give something back to the country that afforded him such wonderful opportunities. Furthermore, he says, it makes "little sense" to make "statues of liberty" in a country where there is no liberty.

It seems incredible that a man born in Bucharest would own a business headquartered in Queens that sells symbols of liberty conceived near Versailles. Even more so, perhaps, that the idea of a monument to "the principles of liberty" was hatched in the shadow of the palace built by France's most famous monarch, Louis XIV, when Edouard Laboulaye, a prominent French historian and republican, first proposed, in 1865, a statue to commemorate the centennial of America's independence from Great Britain. Laboulaye and an informal group of his friends — who decided that they would offer the statue as a gift from the French people to the American people if the Americans would raise funds for a pedestal — dispatched Bartholdi, one of France's most respected sculptors, to scout for locations and enlist support for the idea. Bartholdi found the spot as he sailed into New York Harbor in 1871.

Bartholdi would propose a statue of a classical goddess, fully robed, with tablets of freedom cradled in her crooked left arm and a torch of liberty held high in the other. The tablets would be etched with the date July 4, 1776, to leave no doubt that the law of liberty was America's Declaration of Independence. Her crown would be a nimbus, a halo worn by the Greek sun god Helios, with seven jutting rays, the longest eleven and a half feet, signifying the world's seven continents and seven seas, and at her feet would be the broken links from the chain of servitude that she was leading the world away from. Laboulaye and Bartholdi called their American maiden "Liberty Enlightening the World." Unfortunately, American skepticism (many thought it too grand and expensive a project for a democracy) slowed attempts to raise money for the statue's base and the 1876 centennial came and went. Not until newspaperman Joseph Pulitzer (himself a Hungarian immigrant) decided to get behind the project did the tide turn. Offering to print the name of each donor in his paper, *The World*, no matter how small the contribution, Pulitzer raised almost as much in five months as had been contributed in the previous seven years (and swelled his paper's circulation by fifty thousand in the process). A full 120,000 contributed through Pulitzer alone. Finally, on October 28, 1886, ten years behind schedule, President Grover Cleveland dedicated the fifteen-story statue (thirty, including the pedestal and base).

Though Edouard Laboulaye would die before seeing his dream fulfilled, his monument surely achieved the "far-reaching moral effect" that he hoped for. Over the years, the Statue's image has been plastered onto postcards and T-shirts, shaped into cookie jars and incorporated into menorah candles, a beacon to the world, one of the most famous of all symbols in human history. Between 1892 and 1924 more than 12 million immigrants sailed by

Liberty's outstretched arm. One third that many people now visit the monument each year, many of whom climb the 354 steps to the statue's crown.

One of the most ambitious replica ideas was hatched by a Kansas City businessman in the 1950s who had a Chicago foundry create some two hundred reproductions, each over eight feet tall and weighing 290 pounds, which were sold for $350 to Boy Scout troops all over the country. Today those mini-liberties can be seen in thirty-nine different states, in towns from Colorado Springs to Atlanta, Austin to Des Moines. Iris November, a retired librarian from Cleveland, whose mother escaped the pogroms of Odessa, started the Statue of Liberty Collector's Club 1991, after, she says, she "got this incredible tug." November now has some one thousand items in her collection, two hundred members in her club, and says, "I live with the Statue of Liberty." Indeed, she was in Tiananmen Square just three weeks before the 1989 "revolution" and recalls how excited the Chinese students were to wear the little Statue of Liberty pins she passed out to them. In the end, one of the most enduring images of that brief and bloody period in Chinese history was the raising of a thirty-seven-foot-high Goddess of Liberty and Democracy, modeled after the Statue of Liberty, to stand facing the giant portrait of Mao Zedong hanging at the entrance of the Forbidden City. "We have made this statue," a woman spoke into a loudspeaker on a May morning in 1989, "as a memorial to democracy . . ."

That same beacon of liberty inspired Ovidiu Colea when he was living behind an "iron curtain" but growing up with "this idea of freedom in mind." Yet when he finally set his eyes on the statue, peering out of an airplane approaching John F. Kennedy Airport, it didn't quite register. "You dream all your life about it and then when you see it, you just don't believe it," he says. "Then you look again." The second time he saw it.

> **"It seems unquestionable that the unfittest class of immigrants that have ever come to our shores is increasing yearly in numbers. We may and should be willing to permit our native stock to be annihilated by a superior people; but it is inconceivable that we should knowingly promote, by conscious act, an intermarrying and intermingling of peoples, which will indefinitely lower the standard of American or any other manhood."**
>
> — Robert Hunter
> sociologist, 1904

"know nothing." But as they started to gain a national following, and even seemed to be strong enough to hold sway over the 1856 presidential elections, the Know-Nothings incurred the wrath of Abraham Lincoln and other mainstream Americans. "As a nation, we began by declaring that '*all men are created equal*,'" Lincoln wrote his friend Joshua Speed in 1855. "We now practically read it 'all men are created equal, *except negroes*.' When the Know-Nothings get control, it will read 'all men are created equal except negroes, *and foreigners and Catholics*.' When it comes to this I should prefer emigrating to some country where they make no pretense of loving liberty — to Russia, for instance, where despotism can be taken pure, and without the base alloy of hypocracy [*sic*]."

The Know-Nothings, who later renamed themselves the American Party, had disappeared by 1860, but the tendency toward defining an American according to ethnic boundaries came back in force after the Civil War in reaction to the immigration boom encouraged by America's industrial fervor. It grew out of the same conflict that had confused Thomas Jefferson in the republic's earliest years and which now visited the public at large. On the one hand, there remained a dewy-eyed nostalgia for the immigrant experience, and for that natural right of a man to choose his nation as freely as he chose his spouse. Indeed, the same Philadelphia centennial exhibition that unveiled the Corliss engine also showed the first peek at the Statue of Liberty in the form of the arm, hand, and torch (the rest of it was still being forged in France). The work of the statue's sculptor, Frédéric-Auguste Bartholdi, was not immediately intended as a statement about immigration. Bartholdi and his colleague, Edouard-René Lefebvre de Laboulaye, impressed by American democracy and the abolition of slavery, had hoped to spur reform in Napoleonic France by showing admiration for American liberties. It was the Emma Lazarus poem, added to the base in 1903, which spoke directly to that image of America as an asylum for the oppressed and poor of the world: Lady Liberty as the "Mother of Exiles," giving the back of her hand to "ancient lands" and "storied pomp" while holding wide the "golden door" for the "huddled masses."

But even within the poem of Emma Lazarus there was language — "the wretched refuse," "the homeless, tempest-tost" — that showed concern about the growth of an illiterate class, made up of people neither interested in America nor entirely sure that they wanted to stay here, often sending the money they made here home to Italy or Spain or Ireland or Russia, sometimes sporting a radical unionist tendency and in general, as even the social reformer Jacob Riis wrote, spreading "moral contagion" and crime in "nurseries of pauperism."

A new theory of Americanness emerged in reaction to this, one which found an incompatibility between the ideas of Jefferson and certain peoples of the world. A New England organization, which called itself the Immigration Restriction League, asked, rhetorically, if Americans preferred a nation populated by those of British, German, and Scandinavian stock — "historically free, energetic," and "progressive" — or by Slavic, Latin, and Jewish races, whom they regarded as "historically downtrodden, atavistic, and stagnant." Some of the supporters of such ideas were laborers, who feared that the new immigrants would take away their jobs, but others came from the intellectual class, enamored of biological theories that promoted Nordic superiority.

By the early years of the twentieth century, nativists, while representing a sizable constituency, were still somewhat to the sidelines of American life, with assimilationists like Theodore Roosevelt and other politicians holding the middle ground. Roosevelt joined those who wanted to keep out "idiots" (by which he meant the insane and the mentally retarded), prostitutes, and anarchists. It was, after all, an anarchist with a very foreign-sounding name, Leon Coglosz, who had assassinated William McKinley and made Roosevelt president. Still Roosevelt insisted that foreigners merely needed to embrace America to become one of us. To make his point, Roosevelt railed against "hyphenated Americans" but applauded those who accepted the image of America as the "melting pot."

"Americanization" classes, like the one above in New York City featuring people of twenty-nine nationalities, were a frequent turn-of-the-century response to immigration. Once politicians woke up to the votes that could be won by courting new immigrants, all manner of assistance was offered to arriving immigrants in exchange for loyalty to the political machine.

Throughout the 1910s, this melting pot notion of "Americanization" gained favor. After all, the number of immigrants had reached a critical mass. By now, fully one third of the American population had either been born abroad or had at least one parent born abroad. These immigrant families were here to stay and their sense of belonging, if nurtured, would only grow. At its best moments, American democracy did that to people. In the way that it let newcomers participate in civic life, it joined them to the community so that in the end, they loosened the hold of their native country and embraced the one that they now were helping to make. That was Tocqueville's observation when he came here back in 1831. He called this a "reflective" or "rational" patriotism in that it was built on thought and experience, not some command emanating from the soil or from the lips of a monarch. But since it was a sincere patriotism born of "free inquiry and private judgement" (to borrow from Jefferson's phrase about the free practice of religion), it took time to evolve. And indeed, in the succeeding decades of the twentieth century, that is precisely what happened to this great wave of immigrants or, more precisely, to their children and grandchildren: as they became more and more a part of American society they became American patriots of the first order, embracing the stories of Ellis Island and their own humble beginnings here with the same kind of fervor that attached America's early generations to their ideal.

But before that could happen the nation endured more confrontation over immigration. With the arrival in 1914 of the First World War, many nativists grew fearful that the bloodthirstiness of Old Europe, with its ethnic squabbles and ancient hatreds, would be brought to America in the form of immigrant loyalties. To some degree, it was. In Chicago, which had a large German-American population, there were rallies in support of the German kaiser and some mobilization among German reservists who had been stranded in the United States when war broke out.

Then, early one July morning in 1916 a tremendous explosion rocked Black Tom Island in the Hudson River, just off the coast of Jersey City. The island, which got its name from the "swarthy" complexion of the fishermen who lived there, was a munitions depot, though at the time America was neutral in the war that occupied Europe. The explosion killed several people and sent flames shooting over New York Harbor and debris over Manhattan and Ellis islands. Shrapnel was lodged in the Statue of Liberty. Firemen spent weeks fighting the blaze that eventually consumed Black Tom and caused, at final count, $40 million of damage. Afterward, suspicions arose that this was the work of German saboteurs and years later it was proven to have been exactly that, executed with the help of a Slovakian immigrant who came to America in 1899 to work at one of those many factory jobs, in his case at Jersey City's Tidewater Oil Plant near Black Tom. Before the strikes against the World Trade Center towers, the destruction of Black Tom Island was the most violent attack on New York City and its environs by a hostile force.

EXTRA THE JERSEY JOURNAL EXTR

SUNDAY EVENING, JULY 30, 1916

BIG MUNITIONS EXPLOSION AT BLACK TOM; 50 BELIEVED DEAD; 21 HURT, IN CITY HOSPITAL; DAMAGE $75,000,00

Fire At National Docks Set Off Big Shells and Shrapnel and Then Came Two Terrific Explosions of Dynamite Which Rocked the Country For 25 Miles Around; Showers of Glass From Wrecked Windows In Homes, Churches, Stores and Public Buildings Littered the Streets Here, New York, Brooklyn, Staten Island and Points Even More Distant; Not One of Dead Recovered, So Far; One Man Blown Nearly To Liberty Island Survives and Swims Ashore; Damage Many Times Greater Than Last Big Explosion At Communipaw.

CITY HALL HARD HIT.

The news of the explosion at Black Tom Island, above, near the Statue of Liberty, struck fear into Americans. Like it or not, they would have to join the fighting in Europe. But later, immigrants were blamed by many for maintaining loyalties that forced America into the war.

A year later, in 1917, America went to war in Europe. Before it was over, 2 million Americans would go to war in Europe, the continent of the ancestors. At home people reacted with one of the fiercest waves of anti-immigrant feeling in the nation's history and Congress advanced the first attempt since the Alien and Sedition Acts to clamp down on free speech. The Espionage Act of 1917 and the Sedition Act of 1918 created an opening to prosecute pacifists, socialists, and other left-wing organizations, many of which had large immigrant followings. The resentment toward immigrants was visited first upon German-Americans; then, in the 1920s, when the bitterness over the futility of the First World War set in, the anger came roaring down upon Catholics, Jews, and other non–Anglo-Saxon newcomers as if to punish them for getting Americans involved in the first place. The war had not been fought as President Woodrow Wilson had so idealistically hoped, for the good of democracy, but for the good of some tired old tyrannies that were ready to collapse anyway. This time, nativist emotions were turned into legislation. The Johnson-Reed Act of 1924 imposed quotas to preserve America as an essentially Anglo-Saxon nation. For the next forty years, as a result of those quotas, immigration slowed to a trickle. In the 1930s, at the height of the Great Depression, there were years when more people left America than came to live here.

Tom Draschil, above, conducts his afternoon drive–time radio show at KTKK. "I love the Mexican people," he says. "But if we give the illegal aliens amnesty they will jump past all those people who've been standing in line for years and years to get here. Is that the right thing to do?"

VI

The studios of KTKK, or K-TALK, a conservative talk radio station, are twenty-six miles south of downtown Salt Lake City. There, in a strip mall, in between "Dr. Ramsey, pediatrics" and "Great Clips," a hair salon, beyond a reception area adorned with a reproduction of Arnold Friberg's 1976 painting showing George Washington at Valley Forge kneeling on one knee and deep in prayer, Tom Draschil, Jim Kirkwood, and Gayle Ruzicka spend hours talking about how ill-served the country was by Bill and Hillary Clinton, about the "radical homosexual agenda" and the liberal media, about welfare cheats and, of course, immigration. This is hardly the big time. The talkers work in a tiny twelve-foot by nine-foot studio, screen their own calls, and once in a while, if there's a big Utah wind blowing, the station goes off the air until someone goes outside and climbs atop the roof to reconnect the satellite dish. But KTKK has a devoted, if small, following and it has become a favorite place for people to vent their frustrations with the Latino invasion.

Each KTKK talker has a pet point of view. For Kirkwood (Scottish and Jewish, though his Jewish mother converted to Mormonism), it is the way that illegal aliens "bring other problems with them," like crime, bad health, and dependency. For Draschil (who is regularly teased about having a name that rhymes with Tom Daschle, the Democratic leader in the U.S. Senate), it is the "globalists like George Bush" and the United Nations, which want, he says, "to get rid of national borders." For Ruzicka (a Mormon of English and German ancestry, married to a Czech Jew who also converted to Mormonism), it is the tolerance for "lawbreakers," plain and simple, and the precedent that it sets. Imagine, she says, that we give amnesty to people whose first act is to break our laws. Do we expect them to become good, respectful citizens after that? Ruzicka heads up the Utah chapter of the Eagle Forum, the organization founded by the social conservative leader Phyllis Schlafly, who made a name for herself opposing the Equal Rights Amendment.

"The jobs that the illegal people are taking," says State Representative David Ure, moving hay, above, on his dairy farm, "are jobs that the white American workers won't even touch. And if they want to prove me wrong, they can come here. I have 250 head of cows to milk every night. I'll be glad to pay them and see how long they last."

It would be too easy to caricature the KTKK crowd as a tamer version of the conservative chatter one finds all over the AM radio dial these days, those high energy commentators who bark about the "illegal invaders" and make up for their lack of pedigree with the volume of their voice and the occasional outrageousness of their claims. The K-TALK jocks try to shake the tree once in a while with some nativist bombast, but their take on the Latino issue also has some nuance. Kirkwood acknowledges, for instance, the importance of the illegal alien to the Utah economy. "Without the Mexican worker," he says, "our economy is legs in the air, dead." He bemoans the fact that Americans will not do these jobs at these low wages. "What have we done with our children," he asks, "that they are afraid to work?" He finds a middle ground on the issue attractive. Why not, he says, go the route some have suggested and invite the Mexican here as a guest worker, employed on a contract that expires and then requires his return to Mexico? Otherwise, what will happen when the economy dips and there are no jobs for these people? They will become wards of the state, he says, bringing more of the crime and "other problems" that Kirkwood already complains about.

Still, the clearest sign that even KTKK has ambivalence on immigration comes not from one of its talk jocks, but from the station's owner, Richard Perry. When Perry (Scottish background, going back to the

American Revolution, and a Mormon) bought KTKK eight years ago he hoped that it could serve as a mouthpiece for the conservative views he wanted to reinforce for the people of Utah. At the same time, he also purchased the license on another frequency, which two years ago he turned into KBJA to fulfill what he recognized was an overlooked market niche: the growing Hispanic audience which KBJA now appeals to with a talk, sports, and music format. Perry suspects that he has more listeners on KBJA than on KTKK (so do the advertisers, who have made KBJA more profitable), and he sees nothing inconsistent in the partnership of the two stations. In fact, Perry even found a Hispanic-American to run KBJA who shared his conservative views. The only subject they differ on, of course, is immigration.

Immigration does make for strange bedfellows. Here in conservative Utah, two Republicans, Senator Orrin Hatch (English, Swiss, and Irish, with ancestors going back to seventeenth-century Massachusetts) and Congressman Christopher Cannon (English, with Mormon roots going back to the beginning of the church in the 1840s), have become national advocates for the rights of illegal aliens, pushing for an "amnesty" for those already here much like the one that was declared in the Reagan Administration in 1986. In the Utah Statehouse, Republican David Ure, another conservative, has found himself at odds with the local party establishment by advancing legislation to allow illegal aliens to have driver's licenses and, under certain circumstances, go to state colleges and universities paying the reduced rates of in-state residents.

The driver's licence bill, which passed in 1999, created all kinds of confusion. The illegal alien worried that if he got one, the motor vehicles bureau would share information about him with the INS and he would be deported. But the general public was also mystified. How was it, many asked, that someone could at once be illegal and yet legally drive? Ure defended the idea with a practical argument. Utah, he said, did not create the illegal immigration problem. It does not determine immigration policy. That's the responsibility of the federal government. Yet since the INS doesn't, except in extreme circumstances, enforce immigration, Utah is left to live with it. "We're stuck with the problem," he says, "and my opinion is let's make a bad situation better. I do not believe it's right to keep a race of people down in the trenches."

Ure, who is a fourth-generation dairy farmer and cattle rancher, also believes that education, even the education of illegal aliens, lifts everyone because it leads to people earning more money and more earnings mean more tax revenues. Finally, he insists that there is an essential place for the poor unskilled Mexican laborer in the American economy and, at least as far as agriculture goes, rejects the idea advanced nation-

Riding through the Dakotas: Holding forth on the Bill of Rights

As the daughter of a man who helped force North Dakota to cease posting the Ten Commandments in the public schools, Jennifer Ring, left, finds herself on familiar ground fighting Fargo's prominent public display. Her weapon is the same one her father used: the 211-year-old Bill of Rights, right. James Madison, opposite page, who was known as the "Father of the Constitution," was at first a reluctant proponent of the Bill of Rights; but once persuaded, he led the fight to ratify the bill.

Jennifer Ring and her 1991 Geo Metro, pockmarked by hailstones from a recent storm and on its third engine, were halfway through the eight-hour drive between Fargo, North Dakota, and Fort Randall, South Dakota, when static forced her to shout into her cell phone, "Let me get on the other side of this hill." As the sole area representative for the American Civil Liberties Union (ACLU), the forty-two-year-old Ring is the unofficial guardian of the civil rights of a million and a half people spread over some 150,000 square miles of Midwestern scrub, farm, and ranch land in the two states. Her cell phone and her car are an extension of her tiny office in Fargo; on the passenger seat is her purse, laptop computer, worn Fargo phonebook, and bag of gas station food (she prefers string cheese, she says, because "it bears a resemblance to nutrition"), and, in the rear, several other city directories, a suitcase, a box of documents, ACLU brochures, and, this being the Dakotas, winter coats, a snow shovel, and survival gear. But what "keeps me safe," Ring says solemnly, "is the Bill of Rights. It's like a warm blanket."

On this spring Sunday Ring is headed for a town on the Nebraska border, where the ACLU had sued the school district for practices it said kept Native-Americans off the school board and where, she had just been told, police with drug-sniffing dogs had recently marched unannounced through several schools that had high percentages of Native-American student populations. "I want to find out if they singled these kids out," says Ring as the little car arrives at the hill's summit. "Because if they did, it's a no-no."

Given the stature today of the Bill of Rights, which is comprised of the first ten amendments to the Constitution (including free speech, a free press, the right to keep and bear arms, and the right to freely practice religion), it is hard to believe that the founders entered into fierce argument over whether to have such a bill. James Madison was initially opposed to the idea. In fact, at the 1787 Constitutional Convention in Philadelphia, most of the forty-two delegates from twelve states — Rhode Island refused to send anyone — believed that the Constitution, which they conceived as a blueprint for "limited" government, was sufficient to protect individual rights. The document itself, Alexander Hamilton wrote, "is, in every rational sense and to every useful purpose, a Bill of Rights." They also believed that if they started listing rights, they would give the government "implied powers" over rights not enumerated. Finally, Madison believed, no enumeration could overcome the will of the majority. "Experience proves," he would write Jefferson, "the inefficacy of a bill of rights on those occasions when its control is most needed. Repeated violations of these parchment barriers have been committed by overbearing majorities in every State."

That would have been the end of it except for the necessity of a road show — eleven states had to ratify the Constitution — and a wholly different attitude beyond the Philadelphia conclave. An anonymous letter writer summed up the mood, declaring the omission "an insult on the understanding of the people." From Paris, where he was America's new minister to France, Thomas Jefferson complained in a letter to Madison that, "a bill of rights is what the people are entitled to against every government on earth." Indeed, without a bill of rights, support for the new federal government was perilously weak, with key states like Massachusetts, New York, and Virginia only reluctantly ratifying the Constitution and North Carolina and Rhode Island still withholding ratification, still outside the union. "The Constitution was on very shaky ground," says University of Kentucky historian and Madison biographer Lance Banning. "Technically speaking, it was in effect. But whether it actually worked was another question."

Jefferson was worried about the health of the new nation. But by writing to Madison, he was complaining to the one person who could do something about it. Madison was the preeminent legislative strategist of his day and his opposition to a bill of rights was as significant as his support for one would be. An unlikely leader, Madison was a small man — barely five foot, seven inches tall and 140 pounds — who was sickly throughout most of his youth and painfully shy in social situations. But, as the eldest son of a wealthy Virginia planter, he had cultivated his intellect as revolutionary fires were being lit — studying Greek and Latin at a boarding school while Patrick Henry was railing against the hated Stamp Act in 1865 and immersing himself in the works of David Hume and John Locke at the College of New Jersey (later known as Princeton) as Bostonians were dumping crates of British tea into their harbor in 1773. By 1776, at age twenty-five, Madison was ready to join the revolutionary brotherhood, becoming a member of the Virginia Constitutional Convention. Four years later, he was the youngest member of the Continental Congress. By the time of the national Constitutional Convention in 1787, Madison, still not forty, had distinguished himself as an expert legislator who would become known as the "Father of the Constitution," having drafted most of its essential elements.

Whether it was the influence of Jefferson or Madison's own reverence for popular will, on June 8, 1789, while the Constitution still roiled public opinion (and North Carolina and Rhode Island still refused ratification), the young congressman from Virginia executed one of the most spectacular about-faces in American political history. Keeping his beloved Constitution intact, he proposed to Congress a set of amendments that guaranteed individual rights. The changes that he offered included an ingenious way around a key worry: the bill simply included an amendment that said flat out, "the enumeration in the Constitution of certain rights shall not be construed to deny or disparage others retained by the people." In one masterful stroke, Madison won a Constitution and a Bill of Rights, securing, in the process, the essential popular approval for both.

Ironically, perhaps, Madison's initial fears about a bill of rights being just a "parchment barrier" to popular will proved true. Throughout most of the nineteenth century the bill was rarely employed by the courts. It was understood, correctly, that it only protected people from the abuse of the federal government (not the states) and that the federal government had very little to do with people's lives in a way that would have put individual liberties at risk. Indeed, not until the Espionage Act in 1917 and its "sedition" amendments the following year did citizens wake up to the fact that the Bill of Rights offered them genuine protection. When the American Civil Liberties Union was founded in 1920, the Supreme Court had yet to strike down a law or stop a government action on First Amendment grounds. But the next forty years were a watershed. "Americans were looking internationally and seeing dictatorships on the right and the left and saying this is bad," says historian Samuel Walker. "America is different and America is better. What makes us different? It's our bill of rights and the respect for individual rights."

Today, Jennifer Ring carries on the founders' work while cruising I-29 at 70 miles per hour. Like a Constitutional country doctor, she travels the Dakotas handing out her ACLU business cards, giving speeches about search

and seizure, counseling Native-Americans about how to ensure voting prerogatives, helping gays and lesbians get equal rights, and agnostics and atheists their freedom from state-sponsored religious activity. Though not a lawyer, Ring is a former state legislator. Her love for the subject comes easy. "I grew up in the ACLU," she says, recalling a federal district court case in 1980 in which her father, Benjamin, a philosophy professor at the local college, took on a North Dakota law that required the posting of the Ten Commandments in public schools and won. Twenty-two years later Jennifer Ring is helping orchestrate another Ten Commandments case, this one concerning a six-foot-high slab of granite with the Ten Commandments etched on its surface that sits on a public green in downtown Fargo. "It's a classic violation of the First Amendment prohibition against making a 'law respecting an establishment of religion,'" asserts Ring.

Though the phones in Jennifer Ring's office and car go nonstop, delivering complaints about violations of rights, she sees that as a healthy thing, a sign that Madison's amendments have become, as he once offered they might, "maxims of free government." "The Bill of Rights is one thing that most Americans get," she says. "They know what it means. You can say any damn fool thing you want . . . The police can't come in your home and roust you out of bed . . . You can be any religion you want." But it's her job to make sure the rights are enforced. In that town on the Nebraska border, Ring spent two days meeting with dozens of parents and school officials to find out if there was cause for concern that the rights of Native-Americans had been violated by the drug searches. There was — and she turned it over to lawyers for evaluation and alerted the ACLU's national office. She then climbed back in her Geo and drove the long highway home, enjoying not just the wide-open spaces, but the political liberties that make the vista even broader.

ally by Pat Buchanan and locally by some of the hosts of KTKK that employers simply need to pay more for these jobs so that they would become attractive to the average American worker. American society, he says, is built on a belief in cheap food. It is central to our notion of abundance, and to keep that food cheap, American dairy farmers cannot afford to pay higher wages. We would be drummed out of business, says Ure.

"I'm a liberal in some people's minds," says Ure (English and Scottish, and a Mormon), shaking his head in disbelief, "and I've taken a lot of beatings in the newspaper and on the radio. But let's be blunt and honest about this. These people are here to stay and they are just like my forefathers or your forefathers. They came here to make a better life."

VII

- What are the colors of our flag?
- How many stars are there in our flag?
- Can the Constitution be changed?
- What are the duties of the Supreme Court?
- Who wrote "The Star-Spangled Banner"?
- Why did the Pilgrims come to America?
- Name three rights of freedom guaranteed by the Bill of Rights.

Civics Questions offered as a study guide for the Immigration and Naturalization citizenship exam

The Frank E. Moss Federal Courthouse sits on South Main Street in the heart of Salt Lake City. It was named for the Democratic politician who served Utah in the U.S. Senate from 1959 to 1977 and who is still, at age ninety, a practicing attorney here in town. The building itself goes back much further than that, to the early years of the twentieth century when it doubled as the main Salt Lake City post office. The Moss building has the Greek-columned majesty one used to associate with federal structures and banks — architecture conceived to command the respect of those who enter and put at ease the worries of those who value what is held there, be it mail, money, or the scales of justice.

In the 1930s, at the height of the Great Depression, the building was renovated to include Room 246, its largest courtroom and the room where, once a month, about a hundred people arrive to take one of the biggest steps in their lives. They raise their hands and complete the oath to officially become citizens of the United States.

They have followed a lengthy procedure. First they must fill out form N-400 and sit for an interview, but both are meant to confirm the essentials for naturalization as they have stood (with some back and forth) since the eighteenth century: five years or more of legal residence and a "good moral character," an "attachment to the principles of the U.S. Constitution," and — representing the abiding influence of Jefferson's antimonarchical passions — the forswearing of allegiance to any "prince, potentate, state or sovereignty." The demand for a "proficiency in English" was, interestingly, only added in 1906, in the middle of America's nativist push; the standardization of the oath only completed in 1929.

Some of the questions written to determine a candidate's eligibility have almost outlived their usefulness. "Between March 23, 1933, and

May 8, 1945," reads one, "did you work for or associate in any way with the Nazi government of Germany?" Others are as old a judgment of character as man himself. "Have you ever been a habitual drunkard? Have you ever been a prostitute?" and, in what Mormons, with their exaggerated reputation as practicing polygamists, must worry has been inserted especially for them, "have you ever been married to more than one person at a time?" (The church actually banned the practice back in 1890.) But one question, particularly in the days after September 11, 2001, rings with a special resonance. "Have you ever been a member of or in any way associated with a terrorist organization?"

Once a naturalization candidate has passed the interview, he or she can in special circumstances be sworn in on-site at the INS district office processing the application. But most sense the unique quality of this moment and insist upon the public oath-taking anyway, where they will be joined with others making the same leap, an invariably eclectic and emotional crowd.

On a Thursday at the end of May 2002, the ninety-seven men and women gathered in Room 246, waiting eagerly for their ceremony to begin, included representatives of twenty-nine countries of origin (thirty, if you included the Chinese-occupied state of Tibet). Some people had come here fleeing oppression, some had been in search of opportunity, and some had been recruited by businesses for their special talents. But all had crossed an intellectual or emotional threshold to put themselves here, where they were ready to relinquish their roots and formalize their impulse to start anew. With the friends and family of the candidates in attendance as well, the mood in the room was giddy with excitement, like in the minutes before a wedding, which, for most, is what a naturalization ceremony is. Here is the one place where the American anxiety about immigration disappears in a wellspring of good feeling.

Naiyana Buckner was there. Born in Bangkok, she had already become a Mormon before moving to Salt Lake City in 1973 to be nearer the church and study business. Since then she had graduated from Brigham Young University, married an American, and is raising her two children — Glen, seventeen, and Matthew, eleven — in Utah without their knowing a word of Thai. Still, it took her twenty-eight years to make this decision. "I was proud to be Thai," she says. "That's who I was." She flirted with the idea of becoming an American citizen over and over again until the terrorist attacks of September 11 convinced her to start the process. She says she stood watching the image on television of the World Trade Center towers collapsing and listened to story after story of the loss and the grief, and as she did she felt a tremendous sense that she, too, had been attacked, that these were her people who died, and

Number of people who became naturalized American citizens

1990: 270,101

1999: 839,944

Number of Mexican nationals who became naturalized American citizens

1990: 17,564

1999: 193,709

that this, this America, was her home. "I said to myself, I am ready, and started filing papers almost immediately."

Shirin Assadi was there. Born in Baghdad, Iraq, in 1969, she came here on February 27, 1996, a date she recites with pride in her exactitude. Assadi's husband is a Kurd and in Iraq, which has brutalized its Kurdish minority, they were concerned for his safety. In 1994, the couple crossed the border into Turkey and eventually applied for refugee status at the American Embassy in Ankara. A refugee organization assigned them to Salt Lake City. "I didn't have a clue where that was," says Assadi. She laid out a map on the floor of their apartment in Ankara and tried to find Utah. Her first job once she got here was at Ambassador Pizza, tossing dough and slathering out tomato sauce. She had never eaten a pizza before and yet within weeks she was serving pies like a seasoned New Yorker. From there she went on to be an assistant manager at a grocery store and then to work in customer service at a local jewelry manufacturer.

Shirin Assadi, foreground, and the ninety-six other naturalization candidates raise their right hands and prepare to recite the oath of citizenship. "I wanted to be part of this country," says Assadi, who was born in Iraq, "and I wanted it so bad."

Suleman Maqsud was there. Born in Lahore, Pakistan, Maqsud came here to follow the path of his uncle, Hamid Bashir, who had arrived in Salt Lake City in 1977 as an itinerant rug weaver and now runs his own carpet business right across the street from the courthouse. When Maqsud arrived in 1997 he went first to attend the University of Utah. Having earned his degree, he moved to Atlanta two months ago to take a job as a financial analyst but came back here to Salt Lake City for his swearing in because this is "where it all began."

Mirsad Avdagic, who started in Bosnia-Herzegovina, was there. So was Judit Pungor, who was born in Budapest, Hungary, and Irina Efros who began life in Kirovgrad in the old Soviet Union. "In Stalin's time we had a constitution," says Efros, "but it never worked. It wasn't organic. It wasn't like . . . "—she pauses before using the possessive — "ours." But this ceremony also included Guillermo Ambriz, who came here from Mexico as a migrant worker in 1980 and became legal with the Reagan administration's amnesty in 1986. Ambriz, who is now a carpenter and concrete finisher, arrived at the event fresh from his job, his hair wet from a shower, his white shirt carefully pressed. It also included Irma Alvarez and Miguel Cruz, Jorge Arechiga and Guadalupe Cortes. There were, altogether, twenty-six Mexicans and fifteen other Hispanics, and looking at the group one simply had to conclude that there was no way to distinguish the smiles of those who crawled belly down across the southern border to get here from those who split with some piece of political oppression in another part of the world.

At precisely 2:12 P.M., Judge David Sam entered the courtroom to begin the ceremony. As always, he basked in the moment. Two Girl Scouts from Salt Lake City Troop 538 presented the color guard and all rose to recite the Pledge of Allegiance, the familiar phrases carrying here the lilt and turn of dozens of foreign accents. A student, Wesley Johnson, sang the national anthem and when he finished, the room broke out in applause. Johnson smiled at them as if he had not quite expected such an ovation. On the other hand, he has rarely sung the anthem for a room full of people hungry for citizenship. A representative from the Daughters of the American Revolution (DAR) spoke to the group about the proper etiquette to follow with the American flag. But few seemed to listen to her. They were eager to get on with their reason for being here. Then, while what seemed like thousands of bulbs flashed from the cameras of relatives, the ninety-seven candidates stood as Naturalization Clerk Marc Mathis (German ancestry dating to the 1850s when his great-great-grandfather came to New Orleans and was forced to fight for the Confederate army) led the group in the oath of citizenship.

With everyone seated, Judge Sam took the next moment to tell his story. "I'm the son of immigrant parents from a peasant village in Romania," he began. He has clearly told this story scores of times, but he relished the chance once again to show the high places simple lives can lead to here in the United States. The Judge's father had arrived in Gary, Indiana, in 1914, one of those Eastern European immigrants who was drawn by the factory jobs here. His name was changed for him, perhaps at Ellis Island (the judge never got the story down before his father died), but from then forward Andre Sirb was known as Andrew Sam and he even gave his son the same name so that now, offered the judge with a smile, "I bear the great name of America, Sam, like Uncle Sam." Judge Sam spoke Romanian at home until the age of four, when his mother died, but he forgot most of the old language as he grew and prospered here. "This first generation, this influx of new blood, that's the strength of America," he had said earlier in his chambers. "Sometimes it fades by the third or the fourth, but that first generation . . . " Then, this being a nation of individuals, the judge invited each new citizen to step forward and say something. One by one they did, with the pride of knowing that their search for America had been realized. "I am Praneel Prakash Singh and I am from Fiji . . . " "My name is Naiyana Buckner and I am from Thailand . . . " and "I am Jesus Sanchez and I am from Mexico. I am happy to be a citizen . . . "

"What then is the American, this new man? . . . I could point out to you a family whose grandfather was an Englishman, whose wife was Dutch, whose son married a French woman, and whose present four sons have now four wives of different nations . . . Here individuals of all nations are melted into a new race of men whose labors and posterity will one day cause great changes in the world."

— J. HECTOR ST. JOHN DE CRÈVECOEUR
Letters from an American Farmer, 1782

Riverhead, New York

The senior prom is a ritual of American life that seems as old as the republic but dates only to the early twentieth century. It began as the democratic response to the debutante ball. By the beginning of the twenty-first century several million American teens were spending a couple billion dollars a year dressing up in "adult" clothes and having parties featuring drinks ("mocktails"), catered dinners, and when the lights were turned low, a special person to dance with. So it was for Janet Sosnicki (far left), a senior at Copiague High School on Long Island, and Rachele Pellegrino, a sophomore at Riverhead High, as they giddily prepared for a dinner dance at Island Hills Golf and Country Club in tony Sayville, Long Island. But this was very much a twenty-first-century prom, one that took democratization to a new level. "We loved each other," says Janet, who recalls the night as one of the happiest of her life. "Being able to go to your prom with your girlfriend, being that I am a girl. That was very exciting." Gay rights, which came to the foreground of American discussion in the 1970s, is the kind of issue in which two classic American impulses — the desire to leave private behavior private and the desire to forge a political and moral consensus — clash. The Gay Prom organized by Long Island Gay and Lesbian Youth attracted 200 people, and along with all the traditional decorations, it included mannequin displays showing same-sex couples getting married and gays as soldiers and Boy Scout leaders. There was even a replica of the Stonewall Inn, the Greenwich Village bar that police stormed in 1969 in what is considered the beginning of the gay rights movement. Thirty-some years later, Vermont became the first state in America to recognize gay civil unions. But this issue inspires emotions on both sides. Soon "Take Back Vermont" signs began to appear on lawns in the Green Mountain State and other states passed "defense-of-marriage" laws declaring such gay unions null and void.

Ridgefield, Connecticut

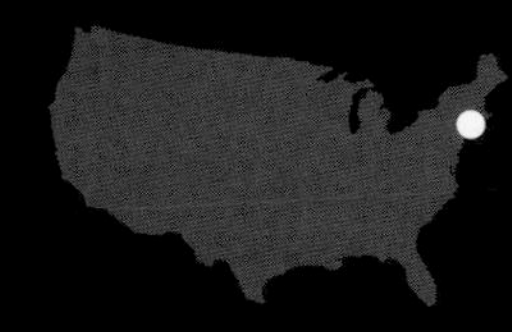

Traveling through America in 1831, Alexis de Tocqueville noticed that people here took the idea of citizen self-government seriously. They resisted — were even suspicious of — the concept of professionalism. Today, if there is one place to still witness that volunteer commitment it is the local school board. As early as 1647 the Massachusetts Bay Colony passed a law requiring towns to establish and maintain their own schools; and in 1789 Boston, led by Revolutionary warhorse Samuel Adams, created a public committee to run the city's schools, an arrangement replicated throughout the new republic. Part of the concern was the protection of democracy, that need to maintain access to the centers of learning lest, as Tocqueville explained, forces of tyranny block access to knowledge as a way of holding on to power. Yet while state and federal bureaucracies have grown, American public schools have remained, with the exception of a few big cities, under local (and volunteer) control. At least twice a month, the nine members of the Ridgefield, Connecticut, public school board, led by chairwoman Linda Bunyan (standing), meet over matters affecting their 5,000 students in eight different schools run on a budget of $47 million. "The decisions made by a school board deeply affect the lives of families and children," says Bunyan, a forty-seven-year-old former theology professor and mother of three who moved here from Yonkers, New York. "Since school expenditures are normally the largest part of a town budget, and the greatest burden on taxpayers, we are on the hot seat." Nationally, almost 50 million children are educated in public schools run by 15,000 individual boards that, in turn, are comprised of 95,000 average citizens like Bunyan, who is unpaid, and estimates that she spends fifteen to twenty hours a week on her school board duties. Here she listens to a public discussion on a proposal to increase second grade class size to twenty-six students. She stands, she says, both to help keep order and "to show respect to the people who have come to talk to us." But parents, and other taxpayers, don't always return the favor. Bunyan admits that she can't go shopping — or golfing — without being confronted by someone wanting her ear.

MINUTE MAID
MINUTE MAID

Old Mission Peninsula, Michigan

From the time he was a boy, the only life that Mexican-born Leo Ocanas knew was the dawn-to-dusk drudgery of a migrant farmworker. Together with his widowed mother, brother, and three sisters, Ocanas (standing, near left) followed the crops across America — picking cotton in Texas and Mississippi, digging potatoes in Idaho, picking apples in Michigan and tomatoes in Florida and Georgia. By the time he was eleven, Ocanas knew what he wanted out of life: his own thriving fruit farm. It took him more than twenty years to scrape together the down payment, working as a farm laborer during the day and driving a truck at night, sleeping in the cab between loads. "If I made $100 a week, I tried to save $50," he says. "It sounds like nothing, but to me it was a lot." In 1978, the year before he became an American citizen, Ocanas put down $29,000 on twenty-two acres of Michigan farmland. He paid the remainder of the $100,000 price in yearly installments. That was not the end of Ocanas's striving, but now, at least, he was in business for himself. Married to Carmen (in red sweater), and with two kids, Ocanas hired himself out spraying, pruning, and harvesting for other farmers in order to earn money to buy equipment. And always he saved in order to buy more land. Today his four farms on Michigan's Old Mission Peninsula comprise 200 acres (and he manages another 200 for other farmers in the area). Ocanas grows more than 2 million pounds of apples and cherries each year. The former migrant, shown here at a cookout for his twelve-person crew, is considered one of the most successful farmers in this part of the state. It's a hard life. Farm prices have been low for a couple of years, and Ocanas is increasingly concerned about cheap apples imported from Eastern Europe and even China. Still, Ocanas cannot imagine life any other way. He recalls that his mother once told him, shortly after he bought his first farm, "Son, the way you are going, your dream will come true." And it has, says Ocanas. "So far, it has."

Acknowledgments

After our last book on the twentieth century we both wanted to work on an "America project." We have been supported by many people in that effort, for which we are very grateful. Robert Miller, Hyperion's president, Ellen Archer, publisher, Will Schwalbe, editor in chief, and Leigh Haber, executive editor, all guided this endeavor with great skill. We were also impressed by the enthusiasm and professionalism of Hyperion's Michael Burkin, Jane Comins, Phil Rose, Deirdre Smerillo, David Lott, Navorn Johnson, Lisa Stokes, Linda Prather, Jill Sansone, Katie Long, and Cassie Mayer. We are grateful to Laura Starrett and Claire McKean for their sensitive copyediting. Thank you, Marly Rusoff, for your energy, imagination, and continuing faith in us. On the television side, at ABC we have benefited from the great interest and enthusiasm of Bob Iger, chief operating officer of the Walt Disney Company, and Alex Wallau, president, ABC Television Network. At ABC News, David Westin and Paul Friedman saw right at the beginning that exploring the American character was a wonderful news story. As always we rely a great deal on Tom Yellin, the executive producer of Peter Jennings Reporting. He also served as executive producer for "In Search of America." We truly value his intellect. Craig Leake, Mark Obenhaus, and Marty Smith, as well as Elise Pearlstein, Abby Schwarzwalder, Jordan Kronick, and Gretchen Crary, have been invaluable to the work of the book. Our thanks as well to Joe Armstrong, Cathie Levine, and Lauren Lipani of ABC for their work. In addition to our tireless book staff, listed at the front of this volume, we also thank Harvey B. Loomis, Peter Lerangis, Jay Weinstein, Doris G. Kinney, Ellen Bakalian, Sean Kelliher, Trevor J. Julien, Christopher Schmidt, and Melissa Stanton. Historians Richard Sylla, Joyce Appleby, Deane Root, Donna Demetri Friedman, David Arnold, Alfred Tauber, Herrick Chapman, Gabor Boritt, Eugenie Scott, Kenneth Miller, Michael Shermer, H. W. Brands, Wesley Wildman, Scott Hartwig, Raymond Mohl, James Lane, Joseph Ellis, David Nasaw, Richard Brookhiser, John Patrick Diggins, and Lance Banning were all generous with their time and invaluable in their insights. For their work on photo research we thank Karolyn Kallinikos, Parul Agrawal, and Sophia Power Dev. Our agent, Esther Newberg, was a dedicated ally. And our lawyers, Michael Rudell, Neil Rosini, and Rip Beyman of Franklin, Weinrib, Rudell, and Vassallo were invaluable, each of them. We are grateful for the work of Christopher Brewster and Jay Waks of Kaye Scholer LLP. We thank Tina Brewster, as always, for her counsel. We were introduced to each other almost eight years ago now, and for that we are grateful to George Colt and Bill Abrams. Kayce Freed, Peter's wife, and Sylvia Steinert, Todd's wife, put up with a lot. We thank them for their patience and faith. Peter's children, Elizabeth and Christopher Jennings, are living the American experience to the fullest. They are a great sounding board for their father. Jack Brewster and his new brother Ben, who wasn't born when this project began, will be very happy when their father is no longer quite such a slave to the deadline. For all of our children we wish that you, in your own ways, as members of the next generation of Americans, add to, build upon, enhance, and expand the founders' vision.

An *In Search of America* Reading List

Even before it became a republic, America was a place of libraries. Each of the founders owned a distinctive collection of books that he prized. The first circulating library in America was founded by Benjamin Franklin. John Adams's personal library, which occupies a separate cottage at his estate in Quincy, Massachusetts (and can be toured by visitors there), is an impressive array. In 1771, Thomas Jefferson's neighbor, Robert Skipwith, asked him for a list of books to form a suitable library for a Virginia gentleman. Skipwith seems to have been more interested in being seen as erudite than actually engaging the reading. He wanted his books finely bound and gold-embossed. But he also wanted to spend no more than thirty pounds. Jefferson's letter back to him, a gem, offers a list all right, filled with Pope and Chaucer, Dryden and Locke, Hume and Swift and Addison (whose play *Cato* enters our discussion in Chapter 5, "The Stage"). All of it was plainly bound and yet, at 107 pounds, much more of an investment than Skipwith had intended. Finally, Jefferson asks him, "whence the necessity of this collection?" He then urges him to come instead to Monticello and enjoy Jefferson's own extensive library where "we should talk over the lessons of the day, or lose them in music, chess, or the merriments of our family companions." Jefferson later sold the six thousand volumes in his collection to the Library of Congress for $24,000. Herewith, we offer our own modest list of one hundred books, assembled by our historian adviser, Fred Siegel, as a kind of literary journey through America, from the inception of the republic to present day.

The Autobiography of Benjamin Franklin by Benjamin Franklin
Letters from an American Farmer by J. Hector St. John de Crèvecoeur
Common Sense by Tom Paine
Notes on the State of Virginia by Thomas Jefferson
The Federalist Papers by Alexander Hamilton; James Madison; John Jay
The Legend of Sleepy Hollow by Washington Irving
Democracy in America by Alexis de Tocqueville
The Deerslayer by James Fenimore Cooper
The American Democrat by James Fenimore Cooper
The Scarlet Letter by Nathaniel Hawthorne
Moby Dick by Herman Melville
Israel Potter by Herman Melville
Essays by Emerson by Ralph Waldo Emerson
Song of Myself by Walt Whitman
Walden by Henry Thoreau
The California and Oregon Trail by Francis Parkman
Uncle Tom's Cabin by Harriet Beecher Stowe
The Red Badge of Courage by Stephen Crane
Patriotic Gore by Edmund Wilson
Little Women by Louisa May Alcott
Life and Times of Frederick Douglass by Frederick Douglass
Huckleberry Finn by Mark Twain
A Connecticut Yankee in King Arthur's Court by Mark Twain
Up from Slavery by Booker T. Washington
The Common Law by Oliver Wendell Holmes, Jr.
The American Commonwealth by James Bryce
Progress and Poverty by Henry George
The House of Mirth by Edith Wharton
A Hazard of New Fortunes by William Dean Howells
The Theory of the Leisure Class by Thorstein B. Veblen
The Education of Henry Adams by Henry Brooks Adams
The Financier by Theodore Dreiser
Looking Backward by Edward Bellamy
The Will to Believe by William James
O Pioneers! by Willa Cather
Rough Riders by Theodore Roosevelt
The Souls of Black Folk by W. E. B. DuBois
A Century of Dishonor by Helen Hunt Jackson
The Public and Its Problems by John Dewey
The Shame of the Cities by Lincoln Steffens

The Jungle by Upton Sinclair
Twenty Years at Hull House by Jane Addams
The Phantom Public by Walter Lippmann
The Rise of David Levinsky by Abraham Cahan
American Ideals by Theodore Roosevelt
The Magnificent Ambersons by Booth Tarkington
The Curse of Bigness by Louis D. Brandeis
The Promise of American Life by Herbert Croly
Trans-National America by Randolph S. Bourne
Dynamite by Louis Adamic
A Carnival of Buncombe by Henry Louis Mencken
Winesburg, Ohio by Sherwood Anderson
The Great Gatsby by F. Scott Fitzgerald
Intruder in the Dust by William Faulkner
The Mind of the South by Wilbur Cash
Southern Politics in State and Nation by V. O. Key
U.S.A. (trilogy) by John Dos Passos
The Grapes of Wrath by John Steinbeck
Our Town by Thornton Wilder
Ideas Are Weapons by Max Lerner
Their Eyes Were Watching God by Zora Neal Hurston
The Ox-Bow Incident by Walter Van Tilburg Clark
The Folklore of Capitalism by Thurman W. Arnold
Across the Wide Missouri by Bernard DeVoto
The Course of Empire by Bernard DeVoto
The Managerial Revolution by James Burnham
Point of No Return by John P. Marquand
The Crucible by Arthur Miller
A Preface to Morals by Walter Lippmann
The Liberal Tradition in America by Louis Hartz
All the King's Men by Robert Penn Warren
The Last Hurrah by Edwin O'Connor
Long Day's Journey into Night by Eugene O'Neill
The Lincoln Nobody Knows by Richard N. Current
Senator Joe McCarthy by Richard Rovere
Witness by Whittaker Chambers
On the Road by Jack Kerouac
Invisible Man by Ralph Ellison
Black Boy by Richard Wright
The Lonely Crowd by David Riesman
The American Political Tradition by Richard Hofstadter
The Affluent Society by John Kenneth Galbraith
The Best and the Brightest by David Halberstam
The Other America by Michael Harrington
Tom Watson: Agrarian Rebel by C. Vann Woodward
Beyond the Melting Pot by Daniel Patrick Moynihan and Nathan Glazer
The Future of American Politics by Samuel Lubell
Silent Spring by Rachel Carson
The Feminine Mystique by Betty Friedan
The Greening of America by Charles A. Reich
Mr. Sammler's Planet by Saul Bellow
Capitalism and Freedom by Milton Friedman
The Right Stuff by Tom Wolfe
Losing Ground by Charles Murray
The Culture of Narcissism by Christopher Lasch
The Closing of the American Mind by Allan Bloom
The Lost Soul of American Politics by John Patrick Diggins
The Bonfire of the Vanities by Tom Wolfe
Primary Colors by Joe Klein
Hunger of Memory by Richard Rodriguez

The Library Company, which Benjamin Franklin founded, was the first subscription library in America. Above, the library's 1790 building. A replica of the building now stands at its original site, but the library itself remains in business at a different location.

Source Notes

Throughout the writing of this book, when researching the ideas and lives of the founding fathers, we relied upon the original source material as published in the excellent Library of America editions of the writings, speeches, and letters of Thomas Jefferson, Benjamin Franklin, Alexander Hamilton, George Washington, and James Madison. We also relied upon the University of North Carolina Press edition of *The Adams-Jefferson Letters*. There are many editions and translations of Alexis de Tocqueville's *Democracy in America*. We used the recent and wonderful University of Chicago Press edition, which features a translation and introduction by Harvey C. Mansfield and Delba Winthrop. We were also aided by several books on Tocqueville's work, principally Henry Steele Commager's classic, *Commager on Tocqueville*, and Michael Ledeen's terrific *Tocqueville on American Character*. Several recent works on the founders were immensely valuable throughout, especially Joseph J. Ellis's *Founding Brothers: The Revolutionary Generation*; *American Sphinx: The Character of Thomas Jefferson*; and *Passionate Sage: The Character and Legacy of John Adams*. We were helped, too, by a reading of David McCullough's *John Adams*, H. W. Brands's *The First American: The Life and Times of Benjamin Franklin*, Lance Banning's *The Sacred Fire of Liberty: James Madison and the Founding of the Federal Republic,* Richard Brookhiser's *Alexander Hamilton, American* and his *Founding Father: Rediscovering George Washington.*

God's Country

The chapter on Aiken, South Carolina, and our discussion of religion, secularism, and evolution was greatly helped by readings of a number of sources, including *Finding Darwin's God* by Kenneth R. Miller, *Rocks of Ages: Science and Religion in the Fullness of Life* by Stephen Jay Gould, *How We Believe* by Michael Shermer, and *The American Mind* by Henry Steele Commager. The chapter was also aided by the reading of two classics of American thought by Richard Hofstadter, *Anti-intellectualism in American Life* and *Social Darwinism in American Thought*. *Under God* by Garry Wills, a good book about religion and politics in America, was essential to this section and to our retelling of the story of the *Scopes* trial, as was Edward J. Larson's Pulitzer Prize winning *Summer for the Gods*, and Daniel J. Kevles's *New York Review of Books* essay based in part on that book. The summary of 1920s history in America was greatly helped by Geoffrey Perrett's *America in the Twenties,* and Warren I. Susman's *Culture as History*, an original study of culture and society in the twentieth century. We derived much of our research on the history of Aiken and the Savannah River Site from David Cole's pictorial history of Aiken, *The Many Faces of Aiken*, and from a special series of articles on the fiftieth anniversary of the Savannah River Site in the *Aiken Standard*. Historian Merrill Peterson's December 1994 article, "Jefferson and Religious Freedom," in the *Atlantic Monthly* was a valuable source and essential to our understanding of Thomas Jefferson's views on the separation of church and state. We frequently turned to two great books by historian Joseph Ellis, *American Sphinx*, a biography of Jefferson, and *Founding Brothers*, about the relationships between the founding fathers. H. W. Brands's study of Benjamin Franklin, *The First American,* gave us Franklin's point of view. Our discussion of eugenics and its implications comes largely from a chapter on the subject in William H. Tucker's *The Science and Politics of Racial Research* and from *Abraham Lincoln's DNA and Other Adventures in Genetics*, a fascinating look into the ethics of genetics research by Philip R. Reilly.

For the short sidebar essays appearing in this chapter we relied on a number of terrific sources, including *Tom Paine and Revolutionary America* by Eric Foner; the introduction to the *Thomas Paine Reader*, edited by Michael Foot and Isaac Kramnick; Paul Semonin's *American Monster*, on the mastodon; Francis Fitzgerald's *America Revisited: History Schoolbooks in the Twentieth Century*; a June 11, 1998, *New York Review of Books* article by Alexander Stille called "The Betrayal of History" about politically correct textbooks; and, finally, *Edison: A Life of Invention* by Paul Israel and *Thomas Alva Edison: An American Myth* by Wyn Wachhorst on the cultural impact of Thomas Edison in America.

The Colossus

A number of excellent histories helped bring to life the story of growth of the federal government. On the famous debates between federalists and anti-federalists, we turned to Joseph Ellis's *Founding Brothers*, which was also a critical source on the famous "dinner" at Thomas Jefferson's home, in which a compromise was reached. On Thomas Jefferson's and James Madison's views more specifically, we relied on Ellis's study of Jefferson, *American Sphinx,* and Lance Banning's *Sacred Fire of Liberty*. In addition, Richard Brookhiser's *Alexander Hamilton, American,* a succinct and readable biography; *America Afire: Jefferson, Adams and the Revolutionary Election of 1800* by Bernard A. Weisberger; and Garry Wills's *A Necessary Evil* were frequent references. John Steele Gordon's *Hamilton's Blessing* and Gordon's May 1996 article in *American Heritage*, "American Taxation," were important for our understanding of Hamilton's views and on the rise of America as a global economic power. *The Greedy Hand* by *Wall Street Journal* columnist Amity Shlaes was our main source on the origins of "withholding," and we also read *Federal Taxation in America* by W. Elliot Brownlee to understand the evolution of the income tax system, and *For Good and Evil* by Charles Adams to understand early anti-tax revolts. Our study of Abraham Lincoln was helped by readings of *Lincoln in American Memory* by Lincoln scholar Merrill D. Peterson; *Lincoln* by David Herbert Donald; *Abraham Lincoln and the Second American Revolution* by James M. McPherson; and Garry Wills's Pulitzer Prize–winning *Lincoln at Gettysburg*. The story of Lincoln and Alexander Stephens draws largely from an essay by Allen G. Guelzo in *The Lincoln Enigma*, edited by the outstanding Gettysburg historian Gabor Boritt. The story of the peaceful surrender of the Confederate troops is derived largely from Jay Winik's *April 1865*, a retelling of the final days of the Civil War.

The main sources for the sidebars in this chapter are "At Large and At Small," an essay by Anne Fadiman in *The American Scholar*, Winter 2002; "Seasons of the Flag," by Stuart Lutz in *American Heritage*, February/March 2002; and *The American Flag, 1777–1924* by Scot M. Guenter and *Desecrating the American Flag: Key Documents of the Controversy from the Civil War to 1995* edited by Robert Justin Goldstein. Also valuable were James MacGregor Burns's *The Workshop of Democracy*; *The Civil War* by Geoffrey Ward, Ric Burns, and Ken Burns; *American Violence* by Richard Hofstadter and Michael Wallace; *A Necessary Evil* by Garry Wills; *Lincoln at Gettysburg: The Words That Remade America* by Garry Wills; *Founding Father: Rediscovering George Washington* by Richard Brookhiser; and *Washington: The Indispensable Man* by James Thomas Flexner (1969).

Headquarters

Our story of the history of business begins in the present, in the ongoing globalization of American business practices. We drew on several sources, with differing points of view on the impact of globalization in the United States and the world: *Lexus and the Olive Tree* by Thomas L. Friedman, *Jihad vs McWorld* by Benjamin Barber, and *Golden Arches East*, a series of essays, edited by James L. Watson. Our discussion of the history of business in America draws on readings of the chapter "The Businessman as an American Institution" in *Americans: The National Experience* by Daniel J. Boorstin; *200 Years of American Business* by Thomas C. Cochran; *A History of American Business* by Keith L. Bryant, Jr., and Henry C. Dethloff; and *The Capitalist Philosophers: The Geniuses of Modern Business — Their Lives, Times and Ideas* by Andrea Gabor. Our understanding of how the writings of Adam Smith influenced the founding fathers comes from a reading of John Steele Gordon's "Land of the Free Trade," *American Heritage,* July/August 1993. For the story of the development of our more consumer-oriented society, we turned to four books: *The Mirror Makers*, Stephen Fox's classic study of the advertising industry; *Fables of Abundance: A Cultural History of Advertising in America* by Jackson Lears; *Advertising the American Dream* by Roland Marchand; and *America in the Twenties* by Geoffrey Perrett, an enjoyable cultural history of the twenties. *Ford: The Man and the Machine* by Robert Lacey was important to our understanding of Henry Ford, and we turned to Alfred P. Sloan's own autobiography, *My Years with General Motors*, to understand the corporate maverick. Bob Stoddard's pictorial history, *Pepsi: 100 Years*, was our principal source on the history of PepsiCo and Frito-Lay.

The sidebar story of the origin of Monopoly draws from another wonderful John Steele Gordon piece in *American Heritage*, this one entitled "The Monopoly Nobody Doesn't Like," appearing in the September 2000 issue. H. W. Brands's biography of Benjamin Franklin, *The First American*, was helpful to our essay on Franklin, and for our essay on Jefferson's views on meritocracy and the history of the SAT, we drew heavily from Nicholas Lemann's history of the SAT, *The Big Test*, and Willard Sterne Randall's biography of Thomas Jefferson, *Thomas Jefferson: A Life*. For our story on prison businesses, we examined Gustave de Beaumont and Alexis de Tocqueville's *On the Penitentiary System in the United States and Its Application in France*.

Streets

Our understanding of the story of the early history of Gary, Indiana, comes from a reading of several books on the city, among them *City of the Century*, James B. Lane's definitive history of the industrial city from its founding to the early years of Richard Hatcher's mayoralty, and *Steel City: Urban and Ethnic Patterns in Gary, Indiana 1906-1950* by Raymond Mohl and Neil Betten. The story and assessment of Richard Hatcher's mayoralty come from readings of *Black Power Gary Style* by Alex Poinsett. Marshall Frady's 1969 *Harper's* magazine piece "Gary, Indiana" gave an interesting perspective in the middle of the Hatcher years. *Racial Politics and Urban Planning 1980–1989* by Robert Caitlin and James Lane's analysis of Hatcher's mayoralty in *African American Mayors*, edited by David Colburn and Jeffrey S. Adler, were also helpful. Fred Siegel's *The Future Once Happened Here* was terrific in its assessment of the failures of liberal social policy in the cities. Our understanding of the founding fathers and the legacy of slavery comes largely from several biographies and critical histories of the period, including *John Adams* by David McCullough; *American Sphinx* and *Founding Brothers* by Joseph Ellis; *The Wolf by the Ears: Thomas Jefferson and Slavery* by John Chester Miller; *From Slavery to Freedom,* a classic study of the black experience in America by John Hope Franklin; Merrill Peterson's several books on Jefferson; and Conor Cruise O'Brien's studies as well. Our description of the 1972 National Black Political Convention in Gary draws from "Coming Together in Gary," by Erwin A. Jaffe, appearing in *The Nation* on April 3, 1972. And our understanding of the debate between W. E. B. DuBois and Booker T. Washington comes from readings of the works of John Hope Franklin; of *Before the Mayflower: A History of Black America* by Lerone Bennett, Jr.; and from Alan Brinkley's excellent review of the second volume of David Levering Lewis's trilogy on DuBois, which appeared in *The New Republic* on January 1, 2001.

Borderland by John R. Stilgoe and *Crabgrass Frontier* by Kenneth L. Jackson were helpful sources for our essay on the perfect front lawn, and the idea for the sidebar on civic journalism comes from a reading of *Breaking the News* by journalist James Fallows.

The Stage

We were aided by many wonderful cultural histories of America and the Broadway stage, among them *Going Out: The Rise and Fall of Public Amusements* by David Nasaw; *Broadway Babies Say Goodnight: Musicals Then and Now* by Mark Steyn; *The Poets of Tin Pan Alley: A History of America's Great Lyricists* by Philip Furia; and *Enchanted Evenings: The Broadway Musical from Show Boat to Sondheim* by Geoffrey Block. We were also aided by readings of *Getting to Know Him: A Biography of Oscar Hammerstein II* by Hugh Fordin and *George M. Cohan: The Man Who Owned Broadway* by John McCabe. John Steele Gordon's excellent article in the February/March 1993 issue of *American Heritage*, "Oklahoma!," was a helpful summary of that musical's importance, and Norman Corwin's essay, "Entertainment and the Mass Media" in the book *Making America: The Society and Culture of the United States* by Luther S. Luedtke was the source for much of the early history of entertainment in America, as was *Thomas Jefferson, Musician* from the wonderful Monticello Monograph Series.

Among the many entertaining sources we turned to for the sidebars in this chapter were *Doo-Dah! Stephen Foster and the Rise of American Popular Culture* by Ken Emerson; Deane L. Root's excellent summary of Foster's work and impact in *New Grove Dictionary of American Music;* and on the uniquely American language, Bill Bryson's *The Mother Tongue: English and How It Got That Way* and *Made in America: An Informal History of the English Language in the United States.*

Homeland

We are deeply in debt to two wonderful books we used for much of the historical research on this chapter. Matthew Frye Jacobson's *Barbarian Virtues: The United States Encounters Foreign Peoples at Home and Abroad, 1876–1917* is a volume that should be in the library of every American interested in immigration. We reserve the same praise for Arthur Mann's classic *The One and the Many: Reflections on the American Identity*. Our discussion was also developed from readings of *Strangers in the Land: Patterns of American Nativism 1860–1925* by John Higham; *The Reckless Decade: America in the 1890s* by H. W. Brands; Merrill Peterson's *Thomas Jefferson and the New Nation; What Kind of Nation: Thomas Jefferson, John Marshall, and the Epic Struggle to Create a United States* by James F. Simon; *American Sphinx* by Joseph Ellis; and *Passionate Sage* by Joseph Ellis. Our discussion of the modern trends in immigration borrows from James Goldsborough's excellent article in the September/October 2000 issue of *Foreign Affairs*, "Out-of-Control Immigration," and from a reading of *The Clash of Civilizations and the Remaking of World Order* by Samuel P. Huntington and *The Unmaking of Americans: How Multiculturalism Has Undermined America's Assimilation Ethic* by John J. Miller.

The sidebars for this chapter were helped by readings of *Origins of the Bill of Rights* by Leonard Levy; *The Sacred Fire of Liberty: James Madison and the Founding of the Federal Republic* by Lance Banning; *From Parchment to Power: How James Madison Used the Bill of Rights to Save the Constitution* by Robert A. Goldwin; and *In Defense of American Liberties: A History of the ACLU* by Samuel Walker. Our essay on the Dust Bowl was enhanced by a re-reading of the American classic *Grapes of Wrath* by John Steinbeck and the fascinating history *American Exodus: The Dust Bowl Migration and Okie Culture in California* by James N. Gregory. On intermarriage we turned to, once again, Arthur Mann's *The One and the Many* and *Love and Tradition: Marriage Between Jews and Christians* by Egon Mayer; *Protestant, Catholic, Jew: An Essay in American Religious Sociology* by Will Herberg; and *A New Religious America* by Diana L. Eck. *The Statue of Liberty Encyclopedia* by Barry Moreno provided marvelous historic details for our essay on the Statue of Liberty.

Credits

We would like to thank the hundreds of photographers who sent their pictures for consideration in the photo essay section. It was amazing to hear from so many people and we are grateful to everyone for contributing. We would also like to thank the chapter photographers Tony O'Brien, David Scull, Judy Walgren, Karen Ducey, and Jay Dickman, for their talent, creativity, and enthusiasm toward the project. Others who deserve a big thanks are Kim Tsoi at Spectrum Photo Lab, Ida Astute, and Paul Shorr.

Pictures

Cover Photos:
from front flap, right to left:
Culver Pictures; Library of Congress; David Scull; Culver Pictures; Veronnica Kimm; David Scull; Jay Dickman; Judy Walgren; Tony O'Brien; Library of Congress; © 1992 Raven Maps & Images; James Edward Bates/*The Sun Herald,* Biloxi, Mississippi; © 1992 Raven Maps & Images; Judy Walgren; Collection of Madeline Kripke; David Scull; Oldsmobile History Center, Lansing, Michigan; Jon Lowenstein/CITY2000; Mount Vernon Ladies' Association; John Huffer

Front pages: i: James Edward Bates/*The Sun Herald*, Biloxi, Mississippi **ii–iii:** Judy Walgren **vi–vii:** Bridget Besaw Gorman/Aurora

Introduction: viii–ix: Jason Fulford **xi:** Jim Attwood; Private Collection/Bridgeman Art Library/Christie's Images **xii:** University of Wisconsin-Madison Archives x252982 **xiii:** Chateau de Versailles, France/Lauros-Giraudon-Bridgeman Art Library **xvii:** Book Cover from *A Study in Contemporary Culture* by Helen Lynd and Robert S. Lynd ©1929 by Harcourt, Inc. 1957 by Robert S. Lynd, reproduced by permission of the publisher; John Huffer **xviii:** Richard Greene Collection, Archives and Special Collections, Ball State University

Essay Photos: xx–xxi: Veronnica Kimm **xxii–xxiii:** Sage Sohier **xxiv–xxv:** Ken Schles

Chapter 1: page 1: ©Cary Wolinsky 2002 **2:** ©1992 Raven Maps & Images **4, 5, 8, 12, 20, 21, 23, 25, 29, 38, 41:** Assigned chapter photography by Tony O'Brien **7:** Wes Childer/Courtesy of the University of South Carolina, Aiken **10:** (center) Maryland Historical Society, Baltimore, MD (right) Sheryl D. Sinkow **15:** (right) Bill Foley **16:** Getty Images; Bill Foley **17:** Getty Images **18:** Mary Ann Lundquist; Culver Pictures **22:** Savannah River Site Photographic Services **26:** Getty Images; Friends of the Governor's Mansion, Austin **27:** Book Cover from *The Story of America Beginnings to 1877* by John Garraty, © 1992 by Harcourt Inc. reprinted by permission of the publisher **31:** U.S. Department of the Interior, National Park Service, Edison National Historic Site; Nancy Jo Johnson **32:** Getty Images **34:** Associated Press **35:** Getty Images **36:** Francis Alexander's *Ralph Wheelock's Farm* Gift of Edgar William and Bernice Chrysler Garbisch, Photograph © 2001 Board of Trustees, National Gallery of Art, Washington; Eric Grant **37:** Infigen

Essay Photos: 42–43: Reuben Cox **44–45:** Mark Hertzberg/*Racine Wisconsin Journal Times* **46–47:** Sarah Leen

Chapter 2: page 48: ©1992 Raven Maps & Images **51, 55, 57, 59, 60, 64, 68, 70, 72, 73, 77, 79, 81, 87, 89:** Assigned chapter photography by David Scull **50:** Susana Raab **53:** Collection of Kit Hinrichs; Dvideography.com **54:** Underwood & Underwood/Corbis **61:** G. Jill Evans ©2001 Oklahoma City National Memorial Trust; Steve Liss/TimePix **62:** Mary Elizabeth Hull **65–66:** (all) Courtesy of Mount Vernon Ladies' Association **67:** Library of Congress **74:** National Park Service; Adams County Historical Society, Gettysburg, PA **75:** Justin Lane/*The New York Times* **83:** © Thomas Haley/Sipa Press; Brown Brothers, Sterling, PA **85:** Office of Congressman DeMint **88:** National Portrait Gallery, Smithsonian Institution, and Jefferson Foundation; gift of the Regents of the Smithsonian Institution and the Enid and Crosby Kemper Foundation

Essay Photos: 90–91: Lauren Ronick **92–93:** Serge J-F. Levy/Matrix **94–95:** Les Stone/Matrix

Chapter 3: page 96: ©1992 Raven Maps & Images **98, 99, 101, 109, 110, 111, 112, 117, 118, 132, 133, 135:** Assigned chapter photography by Judy Walgren **102:** Judy Walgren; Library Company of Philadelphia **103:** The Metropolitan Museum of Art, Bequest of Michael Friedsam, 1931. Photograph ©1981 The Metropolitan Museum of Art **107:** Library of Congress; Peter Howard **108:** ©Genevieve Naylor/Corbis **114:** Snack Food Association **115:** ©Thomas Haley/Sipa Press; Culver Pictures **116:** Walter P. Reuther Library, Wayne State University **120:** Oldsmobile History Center, Lansing, MI; Clay Mollman **121:** Oldsmobile History Center, Lansing, MI **124:** Jeanine Taghon-Oleszczuk; The Forbes Magazine Collection, NY ©All rights reserved **125:** Monopoly® & ©2002 Hasbro, Inc. Used with permission **126:** From the Collections of Henry Ford Museum & Greenfield Village **127:** Culver Pictures **129:** Dennis Marsico; ©Bettmann/Corbis **130:** Getty Images

Essay Photos: 136–137: Jon Lowenstein/CITY2000 **138–139:** W. P. Fleming **140–141:** Nina Berman/Aurora

Chapter 4: page 142: ©1992 Raven Maps & Images **145, 148, 149, 151, 155, 163, 172, 173, 175, 183:** Assigned chapter photography by Karen Ducey **144:** Ted S. Warren/Associated Press **146:** (both)The Scotts Company **147:** The Brooklyn Historical Society **153:** *Marion Chronicle Tribune*; Alan Petersime **154:** Courtesy *New York Post* **159:** Union Run Baptist Church; Monticello/Thomas Jefferson Foundation, Inc.; Monticello/Getting Word Project **160:** Monticello/W. Mogielnicki **164:** Calumet Regional Archives, Indiana University Northwest **165:** Schomburg Center **166:** Declan Haun/TimePix **168:** Maggie Steber/Corbis Saba; Courtesy, Georgia Department of Archives and History **169:** Richard Fowlkes/*Atlanta Journal-Constitution* **170:** Robert A. Sengstacke **176:** Getty Images **177:** Getty Images **179:** (all) Michael Sexton

Essay Photos: 184–185: Bob Sacha **186–187:** Peggy Peattie/*San Diego Union Tribune* **188–189:** Brian E. Harkin

Chapter 5: page 190: ©1992 Raven Maps & Images **192, 193, 199, 203, 204, 205, 216, 219, 220, 228, 229:** Assigned photography by Jay Dickman **195:** University of Michigan's Making of America *http://moa.umdl.umich.edu/;* Madeline Kripke Archives; Collection of Madeline Kripke **197:** Triton Gallery **201:** Jennifer Keyser **202:** Library of Congress **208:** Matthew Warren; Heritage Plantation of Sandwich, MA **209:** ©Bettmann/Corbis **211:** (left) Eleanor DeSantis/*Lake City Reporter* **211**(right)–**212:** Foster Hall Collection, Center for American Music, University of Pittsburgh Library System **213:** ©Bettmann/Corbis **214:** Culver Pictures **217:** Susan Stone; Mary Long **218:** Getty Images **222:** Culver Pictures **223:** T.B. Harms Company, NY/Museum of the City of New York **224:** Culver Pictures

Essay Photos: 230–231: Justine Kurland **232–233:** Andreas Gursky, courtesy Matthew Marks Gallery **234–235:** Hillery S. Garrison/AP-Wide World Photos

Chapter 6: page 236: ©1992 Raven Maps & Images **238, 239, 241, 246, 248, 251, 258, 260, 261, 269, 270, 276:** Assigned photography by Judy Walgren **243:** Collection of Earl Shelton; Monica Almeida/*The New York Times* **244:** ©Dorothea Lange Collection, Oakland Museum of California, Gift of Paul S. Taylor **249:** TimePix; Peter Meyer **250:** Culver Pictures **253:** Library of Congress **255:** Getty Images **256:** (both) Courtesy of the Richard L.D. & Marjorie J. Morse Department of Special Collections, Hale Library, Kansas State University; Hannah Bennett **257:** The Schlesinger Library, Radcliffe Institute, Harvard University **263:** Corbis **264:** National Park Service: Statue of Liberty National Monument; Lisa Patrick **265:** Manfred Anson courtesy of Iris November **267:** Brown Brothers, Sterling, PA **272:** Darren Gibbins; Courtesy of National Archives **273:** Library of Congress

Essay Photos: 278–279: Mark Peterson/Corbis Saba **280–281:** Christine Osinski **282–283:** J. Carl Ganter/MediaVia
287: American Philosophical Society Library, Print Collection

Concluding Essay Photo: Harry Zernike

Endpapers:
Front: Original map courtesy of Geography and Map Division of Library of Congress
Back: Data courtesy Marc Imhoff of NASA GSFC and Christopher Elvidge of NOAA NGDC. Image by Craig Mayhew and Robert Simmon, NASA GSFC.
http://earthobservatory.nasa.gov/study/lights

While every effort has been made to trace the copyright holders of photographs and illustrations reproduced in this book, the publishers will be pleased to rectify any omissions or inaccuracies in the next printing.

Lyrics

Chapter Five
Ol' Man River
Words and Music by Jerome Kern and Oscar Hammerstein II
©Copyright 1927 Universal – Polygram International Music Publishing, Inc.
(ASCAP)
International Copyright Secured. All Rights Reserved. Used by Permission.

HAIR (Selections) by James Rado, Gerome Ragni, Galt MacDermot
©1966, 1967, 1968, 1970 (Copyrights renewed) James Rado, Gerome Ragni, Galt MacDermot, Nat Shapiro, and EMI U Catalog Inc. All Rights Reserved. Used by Permission.
Warner Bros. Publications U.S. Inc., Miami, FL 33014

"America" by Leonard Bernstein and Stephen Sondheim
© 1957 Amberson Holdings LLC & Stephen Sondheim. Copyright Renewed. Leonard Bernstein Music Publishing Company LLC, Publisher.

"Boys and Girls Like You and Me," "Oklahoma," and "Oh, What a Beautiful Mornin'" by Richard Rodgers and Oscar Hammerstein II
Copyright © 1943 by Williamson Music. Copyright Renewed. International Copyright Secured. All Rights Reserved. Used by Permission.

"You've Got to Be Carefully Taught" by Richard Rodgers and Oscar Hammerstein II
Copyright © 1949 by Richard Rodgers and Oscar Hammerstein II
Copyright Renewed
Williamson Music owner of publication and allied rights throughout the World. International Copyright Secured. All Rights Reserved. Reprinted by Permission.

Index

Page numbers in *italics* refer to photo captions and picture essays.

C

G

H

Monument Valley, Utah

"The space doesn't stop," Andrew DiRosa remembers thinking of the grand vistas he witnessed through the front windshield on his first visit to the American Southwest. "Everything I knew was tossed out the window." An Italian living in Toronto with his wife, Tania, and expecting their first child, DiRosa had agreed to meet their good friend Harry Zernike, a New York photographer, for a week's vacation. The three flew to Albuquerque, New Mexico, and drove northwest to the four corners, where Colorado, New Mexico, Arizona, and Utah meet. As a child, DiRosa had lived in the Swiss Alps, but not even that experience of natural grandeur prepared him for the vastness of the West, for the red-rock buttes and lofty mesas that dwarf the human form here. The image of the West first became known to Americans through the work of painters in the middle of the nineteenth century, whose renderings of exotic landscapes and otherworldly openness were greeted the way that photographs of the surface of the moon and, later, Mars have been in recent times. "In Europe, wherever you stand, you can throw a rock and hit another person," says DiRosa. "When we arrived here, I was breathless when I saw a road that went straight for thirty miles. There was nothing — just desert, sagebrush, and mesas." Zernike shot this

When Thomas Jefferson dispatched Meriwether Lewis and William Clark west on their voyage of discovery in 1804, he made sure that the party would have "light articles for barter and presents among the Indians," but also "instruments for ascertaining, by celestial observations, the geography of the country." Today not only can we look upward to the stars, we can look down from space at a complete image of the America that Jefferson helped to found. Using sophisticated satellite technology that detects lights on the earth's surface, researchers at NASA's Goddard Flight Center have created the simple map of twenty-first-century America seen here. The NASA scientists have dubbed their picture "visible Earth," but it may be most striking for what you don't see. Even after two centuries of development and industrial growth, when the population rose from a few million to over a quarter billion, America is only about 3 percent urbanized, still a place of wide open spaces and wide open imaginations.